The Law at Work

The Law at Work

A practical guide to key issues in employment law

First published in 2003 by
Spiro Press
17–19 Rochester Row
London SW1P 1LA
Telephone +44 (0)870 400 1000

© Spiro Press, 2003

ISBN 1 904298 982

British Library Cataloguing-in-Publication Data.
A catalogue record for this book is available from the British Library.

This book is intended to be a guide and, whilst we have endeavoured to be as helpful as possible, Spiro Press and the authors cannot accept liability for any losses resulting. Readers are advised to seek professional help to deal with particular issues arising from the law stated herein.

Typeset by: Wyvern 21 Ltd, Bristol
Printed in Great Britain by: The Cromwell Press
Cover image by: PhotoDisc
Cover design by: Cachet Creatives

About the Contributors

The Editor

Malcolm Sargeant is a Reader in Employment Law at Middlesex University Business School, where he is a member of the Centre for Research in Industrial and Commercial Law. He is joint author of *Essentials of Employment Law* (CIPD) and author of *Employment Law* (Longman).

The Authors

Joanna Blackburn is a partner in the Employment Group of the London law firm, Mishcon de Reya. She advises a wide range of companies on all aspects of employment law, and has a particular expertise in City related work and the media. She is a regular contributor to *Personnel Today* and *Employers' Law*.

Stephen Cavalier is Head of the Employment Rights Unit at Thompsons Solicitors. He is the Chair of the Industrial Law Society and a member of the Institute of Employment Rights and ETUC Legal Experts Network, as well as an expert witness to European Parliament on revisions to the Acquired Rights Directive. He has acted for trade unions in many major cases including the first UK reference to the European Court on the Working Time Directive.

Caroline Humphries qualified as a solicitor in 1989. After extensive experience advising clients on all aspects of employment law, Caroline now works as the Professional Support Lawyer in the employment team at CMS Cameron McKenna.

David Lewis is Professor of Employment Law and Head of the Centre for Research in Industrial and Commercial Law at Middlesex University. He is the editor of and main contributor to *Whistleblowing at Work* (Athlone Press) and is joint author of *Essentials of Employment Law* (CIPD). He is an ACAS arbitrator and a member of the editorial board of the *Industrial Law Journal*.

Susan Mayne is a senior assistant at CMS Cameron McKenna where she has worked since 1991. Susan has made numerous contributions to a wide variety of legal periodicals and has contributed a number of chapters to Tolley's *Employment Law* loose-leaf and Tolley's *Employment and Personnel Procedures* loose-leaf. She is also joint editor of *Employment Law in Europe*, published by Butterworths.

Lawrence Milner is a lawyer at Clifford Chance LLP specialising in data protection, privacy and other e-business issues. He has extensive experience of advising on international data protection compliance projects and employee related data protection issues.

Erica Neustadt qualified as a solicitor in 1990. She has worked both as a litigator and an employment lawyer, latterly as a professional support lawyer in a major city firm. She has lectured for several years at the College of Law and recently completed an LLM in Employment Law at Middlesex University Business School.

Helen Sargeant is an Assistant Solicitor in the employment team at CMS Cameron McKenna. She specialises in all aspects of employment law, with a particular interest in discrimination law.

Bob Simpson is a Reader in Law at the London School of Economics who specialises in labour law. In addition to the law on pay his interests include the effects of the law on trade union recognition and industrial conflict.

Contents

Abbreviations

AAL	Additional adoption leave
ACAS	Advisory, Conciliation and Arbitration Service
AML	Additional maternity leave
ARD	Acquired Rights Directive
BPD	European Burden of Proof Directive 1997
CA	Court of Appeal
CAC	Central Arbitration Committee
CML	Compulsory maternity leave
CRE	Council for Racial Equality
DDA	Disability Discrimination Act 1995
DRC	Disability Rights Commission
DRCA	Disability Rights Commission Act 1999
DTI	Department of Trade and Industry
EAT	Employment Appeal Tribunal
EC	European Community
ECHR	European Convention on Human Rights
ECJ	European Court of Justice
EEA	European Economic Area
EFTA	European Free Trade Association
EOC	Equal Opportunities Commission
EPA	Equal Pay Act 1970
ERA	Employment Rights Act 1996
ETD	Equal Treatment Directive 1975
EU	European Union
EWC	European Works Council
FTC	Fixed-term contract
FTD	Fixed-term Work Directive 1999
GMB	General Municipal Boilermakers and Allied Trades Union; following a further merger it became GMB with effect from 1 March 1989
GOQ	Genuine Occupational Qualification
HRA	Human Rights Act 1998
HSWA	Health and Safety at Work Act 1974
ICR	Industrial Cases Reports
IRLR	Industrial Relations Law Reports
LEA	Local educational authority
LGPS	Local Government Pension Scheme
LPC	Low Pay Commission
MPL Regulations	Maternity and Parental Leave etc Regulations 1999
NACAB	National Association of Citizens Advice Bureaux
NIC	National insurance contributions

NMW	National minimum wage
NMWA	National Minimum Wage Act 1998
OAL	Ordinary adoption leave
OML	Ordinary maternity leave
PCAW	Public Concern at Work
PFI	Private Finance Initiative
PIDA	Public Interest Disclosure Act 1998
PRP	Pay reference period
PT Regulations	Part-time Workers (Prevention of Less Favourable Treatment) Regulations 2000
PTWD	Part-time Work Directive 1997
RIPA	Regulation of Investigatory Powers Act 2000
RRA	Race Relations Act 1976
SAP	Statutory adoption pay
SDA	Sex Discrimination Act 1975
SMP	Statutory maternity pay
SNB	Special negotiating body
SPP	Statutory paternity pay
SRSC Regulations	Safety Representatives and Safety Committee Regulations 1977
Task Force	Disability Rights Task Force
TGWU	Transport and General Workers Union
TICE Regulations	Transnational Information and Consultation of Employees Regulations 1999
TUC	Trades Union Congress
TULRCA	Trade Union and Labour Relations (Consolidation) Act 1992
TUPE	Transfer of Undertakings (Protection of Employment) Regulations 1981

List of cases

Abbey Life Assurance Co Ltd v Tansell (2000) IRLR 410
Arboshe v East London Bus & Coach Co Ltd (1998) Unreported
Abrams v Performing Rights Society (1995) ICR 1028
ACAS v Taylor EAT 788/97
Adams & others v Lancashire County Council (1997) IRLR 436
ADI (UK) Ltd v Willer (2001) IRLR 542
Allen v Amalgamated Construction Co Ltd (2000) IRLR 119
Angus Jowett & Co v NUTGW (1985) IRLR 326
Armitage, Marsden and HM Prison Service v Johnson (1997) IRLR 162
Aziz v Trinity Street Taxis Ltd (1988) ICR 534 (1988) IRLR 204
Bakers' Union v Clarks of Hove Ltd (1978) IRLR 366
Balgobin and Francis v London Borough of Tower Hamlets (1987) ICR 829
    (1987) IRLR 401
Banks v Chief Adjudication Officer (2001) ICR 877
Baynton v Saurus General Engineers Ltd (1999) IRLR 604
BBC v Kelly Phillips (1998) IRLR 16
Beloff v Pressdram Ltd (1973) 1 All ER 241, 250
Bernadone v Pall Mall (2000) IRLR 487
Berriman v Delabole Slate (1985) IRLR 305
Berwick Salmon Fisheries Co Ltd v Rutherford (1991) IRLR 203
Bilka-Kaufhaus v Weber van Hartz (1987) ICR 110
Bladon v ALM Medical Services Ltd Case 2405845/99
Booth & others v United States of America (1999) IRLR 16 EAT
Botzen v Rotterdamsche Droogdok Maatschappij BV (1985) ECR 519
Boughton v National Tyre Ltd Case 1500080/00
Bridges v Sita (GB) Ltd (1999) Unreported
Briggs v North Eastern Education and Library Board (1990) IRLR 181
British Gas Services Ltd v McCaull (2001) IRLR 60
British Nursing Association v Inland Revenue (National Minimum Wage
    Compliance Team) (2001) IRLR 659
British Sugar plc v Kirker (1998) IRLR 624
British Telecommunications plc v Roberts and Longstaffe (1996) ICR 625
British Telecommunications v Ticehurst (1992) ICR 383
Brookes v Borough Care Services (1998) IRLR 636
Brown v Rentokil Ltd (1998) IRLR 445
BSG Property Services Ltd v Tuck (1996) IRLR 134
Buchanan Smith v Schleicher & Co (1996) IRLR 547
Burston v Superior Creative Services Ltd FT Case 72892/95
Burton v De Vere Hotels (1996) IRLR 596
Callagan v Glasgow City Council (2001) IRLR 724

Introduction

MALCOLM SARGEANT

The purpose of employment law has been described as the regulation of the employment relationship, both at an individual level, between employer and worker, and at a collective level, between employer and workers' representatives. Whilst this is true, there is perhaps a further question to be asked when considering the current approach to employment legislation.

This question relates to the purpose for which the employment relationship is being regulated. A wide range of legislation is considered in this book, much of it introduced or amended in the last 10 years. The common theme is clearly not some egalitarian notion that the weak ought to be protected from the strong (although that might be a useful by-product on occasions), or an ideological view that there should be a shift in the balance of power between an employing class and a working class. There are obviously different views about the extent to which there ought to be regulation and these views may be influenced by contrasting opinions of the need to strengthen workers' rights on the one hand, and the need not to impose additional burdens on business on the other hand.

The current justification for action however, both at a European Union level and at the UK Government level, does not appear concerned with arguments about workers' rights or employers' rights. The approach now appears to be that certain improvements in workers' rights are also in the interests of employers. Thus, at an EU level, the European Commission can argue that improved protection of temporary agency workers is necessary to improve the status of such work, which in turn will improve the availability of temporary agency workers. This will then be to the benefit of employers who have an increasing need for a flexible workforce to cope with the demands of the new economy.[1]

At the national level, this approach is illustrated by a DTI discussion paper on "the role of employee involvement in the modern economy".[2] This discussion paper was part of the consultation process on implementing the EU Directive on Information and Consultation (see Chapter 9). In Chapter 1 of the paper there is a justification for such information and consultation:

> Modern, high performance workplaces have a variety of features. A common characteristic is high levels of employee involvement and regard. They build on the simple insight that individuals are more likely to give of their best if they feel valued and are given the opportunity to contribute their ideas; and that people who are well-prepared for change can help to introduce it and thereby help to secure employment within the business.

There is no attempt to justify greater information to and consultation with employees on the basis that it might be right in itself. The justification is that it is good for the business. Employees who are involved will contribute more and employees who are prepared for change, because they are kept informed and consulted, will help employers to introduce that change. All this may be true, but it is interesting here because it helps justify intervention in the regulation of the employment relationship. There is a marrying up of the interests of employees and employers which is perhaps different from the arguments of previous generations.

The influence of the EU

To an extent this approach is a reflection of the views of the European Commission in proposing various measures to extend protection to, and extend the rights of, workers. The influences of the EU on UK employment legislation is significant and it is arguable that there would be a lot less employment protection in the United Kingdom, if it had not been for the intervention of the EU. This is illustrated by the opposition of the UK Governments to, for example, the measures contained in the Aquired Rights Directive,[3] the Working Time Directive[4] and the Information and Consultation Directive.[5] Although it is not possible to say with certainty, it is doubtful whether any of these measures would now be part of national law had it not been because of the necessity to transpose an EU Directive.

This influence is set to continue in the future, with the need to implement the Equal Treatment in Employment Directive.[6] Article 1 of this Directive states:

> The purpose of this Directive is to lay down a general framework for combating discrimination on the grounds of religion or belief, disability, age or sexual orientation as regards employment and occupation, with a view to putting into effect in the Member States the principle of equal treatment.

The management of change

The management of change, and the consequent joining up of the interests of employers and workers, is an important issue for the European Community. The development of the internal market and now the introduction of the single currency have resulted in significant structural change, and are likely to continue to do so. In the Commission's view, the creation of an internal European market is likely to lead to a more unified European market, rather than a series of fragmented national ones. This, in turn, will continue to result in increasing numbers of mergers and acquisitions as enterprises restructure.

In its Green Paper on Partnership at Work[7] the European Commission discussed the changing nature of the workplace and work habits. It stated that:

> The new organisation of work will challenge industrial relations. The old organisation is characterised by specialisation of tasks and skills and the separation of design from the production phase. Industrial relations will . . .

be built on a basis of co-operation and common interest. Therefore, new forms of industrial relations have to be developed, including, for example, greater participation by employees, since efficient production requires enhanced levels of both trust and commitment in firms.

Thus there is a particular perception of a new order of work, which requires a new approach to industrial relations. This new order results from the change of structures resulting from the ending of static and specialised forms of mass production. These changes are, according to the Commission, driven by an increasingly skilled workforce, more discerning markets and a continually developing technology. The result is the need for the "flexible firm" which undergoes a continuous process of change and development and for whom the skills of the workforce and its ability to change and develop are crucial to success. The Green Paper states the need for enhancing levels of trust in order to help create this new form of work organisation, hence the need for an industrial relations system which will include employees in the process much more.

The contents

Not all the subjects covered in this book are the result of European intervention. In some cases the United Kingdom has been far in advance of any measures introduced by the EU. This is especially true in the fields of race discrimination and disability discrimination. The Goverment has introduced measures which do not fit into the neat formula put forward above. Important measures such as those on whistleblowing and the national minimum wage may have different justifications, and the development of a grand theory to cover them all is perhaps left to a more theoretical and all-encompassing book than this one.

This book has brought together a group of employment lawyers who are a mixture of practitioners and academics. The first purpose has been to explain the law and then critically to consider it. No attempt has been made to limit the style of individual authors. The authors have written in a style that suits them and this variety adds to the attractiveness of a book which brings together so many different people in its creation.

The subjects covered were chosen because of their current relevance and interest. Employment law is developing at a great pace, so future editions may cover different topics, but the intention is to be relevant and useful.

Thanks

I would like to extend my thanks to all the authors who have contributed chapters to this book. Rarely can an editor have found a group of people so willing to produce quality work within the time constraints set them. All have contributed to a book which, I am sure, will be helpful to those who are concerned with the practical aspects of the law, in relation to employment, at their workplace.

Notes

1 See Proposal for a Directive on the working conditions for temporary agency workers COM (2002) 149
2 High Performance Workplaces DTI July 2002
3 Directive 77/187/EEC
4 Directive 93/104/EC
5 Directive 2002/14/EC
6 Council Directive 2000/78/EC establishing a general framework for equal treatment in employment and occupation
7 Partnership for a New Organisation of Work; Green Paper, European Commission 1997

1

Part-time and fixed-term workers

SUSAN MAYNE

Susan Mayne is a senior assistant at CMS Cameron McKenna.

Introduction

Traditionally, statutory employment protection has been aimed at those in the conventional working relationship – that of full time employment. However, in recent years there has been a huge growth in non standard and "flexible" types of work and the status of many of these types of worker has been uncertain. Legislation has attempted to go some way to extending protection in certain respects to many of these atypical workers but the boundaries remain, to a certain degree, unclear.

Flexible working can be a multiplicity of different styles of working ranging from a moderate variation in hours or starting and finishing times of work to more radical forms of working such as zero-hours or annualised hours contracts. In this chapter we will look at two of the most common forms of flexible (atypical) working, namely part-time and fixed-term employment.

In order to consider the position of fixed and part-time workers it is first important to clarify their status and the legislation that might apply to them.

While increasing numbers of atypical workers are male, the vast majority of these workers are female, many trying to balance home demands with those of their working lives. To this extent, it is important to consider the anti-discrimination legislation which will afford protection to many of these workers (see Chapter 4 for a consideration of the law on discrimination). The main acts protecting employees against discrimination (the Sex Discrimination Act 1975 "SDA", the Race Relations Act 1976 "RRA"; the Equal Pay Act 1970 "EPA" and the Disability Discrimination Act 1995 "DDA") consider discrimination in relation to employment (see the definitions in section 82(1) SDA; Section 78(1) RRA; section 1(6)(a) EPA and section 68(1) DDA and below for consideration of employee/worker). It is also necessary to consider whether the worker is an employee, self-employed or a "worker" within the wider definition afforded by legislation for the purpose of attaining important employment protection rights.

Employee or self-employed?

The security of employment afforded to those who work still depends largely on the worker's status – the greatest statutory protection being afforded to those who are, in the strict legal definition, employees. Many self-employed persons are excluded from this body of protection while others (within the various statutory definitions of "worker") have more limited rights.

The traditional tests which allocate these rights among the various categories of employee, worker and self-employed can at times be uncertain. Importantly, these categorisations may not reflect the changing face of working practices in the UK with the growth of atypical forms of employment such as casual or seasonal workers, fixed or part-time workers, those on annualised or zero-hours contracts, homeworkers, teleworkers, freelancers and so on.

The difficulty in defining exactly who is an employee, a worker or self-employed has led to a considerable body of case law. It is of course to some degree unavoidable that there will be some uncertainty as the boundaries become increasingly blurred.

Difficulties also arise from the application of different tests by different bodies to assess employment status. For example, a person who is classified as self-employed under the employment law tests may be classified as an employee under tax and social security law. Such a person would have their income deducted at source and be unable to set off work expenses against earnings and have deductions for both employer and employee Class 1 NICs. He would also have none of the statutory protections afforded to those who enjoy employee status.

The following is an overview of the tests applied to assess employee status for the purposes of employment law only.

Employee status

An employee enjoys the greatest statutory protection. The most important rights assigned only to employees are set out in the Employment Rights Act 1996 (ERA). Section 230(1) ERA defines an employee as "an individual who has entered into or works under (or where the employment has ceased, worked under) a contract of employment". A contract of employment is "a contract of service or apprenticeship, whether express or implied, and (if it is express) whether oral or in writing" (Section 230(2) ERA).

It should however be noted that other legislation containing other rights only afforded to employees defines an employee slightly differently (see for example the definitions of employee in Regulation 2(1) of the Transfer of Undertakings (Protection of Employment) Regulations 1981 SI 1981/1794; Section 295 Trade Union and Labour Relations (Consolidation) Act 1992; Regulation 21 Part-time Workers (Prevention etc) Regulations1999; Regulation 2(1) Maternity and Parental Leave etc Regulations 1999 SI 1999/3312; Section 82 Sex Discrimination Act 1975; Section 78 Race Relations Act 1976; Section 68(1)

Disability Discrimination Act 1995; Social Security Contributions and Benefits Act 1992).

The courts and tribunals have developed a rather complex set of tests to assess when a person is an employee, a worker or self-employed. In *Ready Mixed Concrete v Minister for Pensions*,[1] McKenna J held:

A contract of service exists if these three conditions are fulfilled:

(1) The servant agrees that, in consideration of a wage or other remuneration, he will provide his own work and skill in the performance of some service for his master.

(2) He agrees, expressly or impliedly, that in the performance of that service he will be subject to the other's control in a sufficient degree to make that other his master.

(3) The other provisions of the contract are consistent with its being a contract for service

Case law sets out the criteria for assessment and can, in essence, be reduced to four main tests:

(i)   the control test
(ii) the integration test
(iii) the economic reality test
(iv) the multiple test (including mutuality of obligation).

Recent tribunal decisions (*Motorola v Davidson*[2] and *Montgomery v Johnson Underwood Ltd*)[3] highlighted the minimum requirements needed to establish an employment relationship – mutuality of obligation and control.

These will all be looked at briefly in turn.

Control test

The control test is the most traditional and is still regarded as an important part of the employment relationship. In *Lane v Shire Roofing Co (Oxford) Ltd*,[4] the Court of Appeal suggested that this test was

who lays down what is to be done, the way in which it is to be done, the mean by which it is to be done, and the time when it is done.

The essence of the test is whether the person works under the orders of another who controls not only what he must do but how and when he does it.

In *Motorola Ltd v Davidson*, Mr Davidson worked full time from 1996 until 1998 for Motorola pursuant to terms and conditions of Melville Craig Group (MCG), an employment agency. When Motorola dismissed Mr Davidson they argued that he could not claim unfair dismissal against them as they had not exercised sufficient control over him. The EAT noted that

Mr Davidson received instructions from Motorola's staff, wore a company uniform, was obliged to book holidays and raise a grievance with Motorola. Further, Motorola itself had suspended Mr Davidson and after a disciplinary hearing, dismissed him. Significantly, the EAT said that the control exercised by an employer over an employee did not need to be exercised directly between the parties. Whilst MCG could remove Mr Davidson from the service of Motorola the fact that MCG had some control over Mr Davidson which was similar to the control of Motorola did not mean that Motorola did not have sufficient control over Mr Davidson to satisfy the "control" test.

Integration test

The essence of the integration test is that under a contract of service or employment, "a man is employed as part of the business and his work is done as an integral part of the business; whereas under a contract for services his work, although done for the business, is not integrated into it but is only accessory to it" (see *Stevenson, Jordan & Harrison v Mac Donald & Evans*).[5] It has also been suggested that "the greater the skill required for an employee's work, the less significant is control in determining whether the employee is under a contract of service" (*Beloff v Pressdram Ltd*).[6]

So, factors to be considered would include, for example, whether any disciplinary or grievance procedure applies to the individual and whether he or she benefits from any occupational benefits.

Economic reality test

This test involves looking to see where the financial risk lies and whether and how far the worker has an opportunity of profiting from sound management in the performance of his task.[7]

In other words, there is an element of economic dependence – whether the worker is in business on his or her own account or works for another who takes the risk of loss or profit. The employment status results from "the extent to which the individual is dependent or independent of a particular paymaster for the financial exploitation of his talent" (*Hall v Lorimer*).[8]

Those persons who are autonomous in the way they carry out their work may still be seen to be employees if they are financially dependent on their employer (for example, casual workers).

Following *Market Investigations Ltd v Minister of Social Security*[9] relevant factors include:
(i)   whether the individual provides his or her own equipment
(ii)   whether he or she hires his or her own helpers
(iii) what degree of financial risk he or she takes
(iv)   what degree of responsibility he or she has for investment and management

(v)   whether and how far he or she has an opportunity of profiting from sound management in the performance of his or her task

(vi)   whether he or she is entitled to sick pay or holiday pay

(vii) the method of payment.

Multiple test

This flexible approach has been adopted by the courts to try and attain an overview of the whole working relationship.

Early on, MacKenna J in *Ready Mixed Concrete* conceived the multiple test and posed the three following questions:

(i)   Did the worker provide his or her own work and skill in return for remuneration?

(ii)   Was there a sufficient degree of control for the relationship to be one of servant and master?

(iii) Were the other factors consistent with a contract of service?

However, the "checklist" approach has since been disapproved of and emphasis has been placed on the importance of taking a step back from the detail and looking at the overview from a distance. Not all details are of equal weight or importance in a given situation. In a contract of service the "mutuality of obligation" test can be summarised as an obligation on the employer to provide work and a corresponding obligation on the employee to accept and perform it.

> In *O'Kelly v Trusthouse Forte plc*[10] the applicants, regular but casual wine waiters, "entered into their relationship with the company in the expectation that they would be provided with any work which was currently available". The waiters' names were kept on a list and they were given some preference above others when applying for jobs as they came up. The tribunal said that this "was a purely commercial transaction for the supply and purchase of services for specific events, because there was no obligation for the company to provide work and no obligation for the applicants to offer their services."

In the Court of Appeal Sir John Donaldson approved the tribunal's approach that a tribunal must consider all aspects of the relationship, no single factor being in itself decisive and each of which may vary in weight and direction, and having given such balance to the factors as seems appropriate, to determine whether the person was carrying on business on his own account.

The application of the mutuality of obligations test is of importance to atypical workers since many of these will not have a regular or stable pattern of employment even though they are not in business on their own account. They cannot take advantage of the various benefits of being self-employed yet may not otherwise appear to be in a stable employment relationship thereby enjoying the protections of statute.

As a number of factors are increasingly being taken into account by the courts in deciding employment status, there has been considerable uncertainty. For example, of relevance to employment status are the intentions of the parties, financial considerations (for example, the provision of sick pay, holiday, pension and the incidence of tax and NICs), whether the person can delegate duties, carry out work for others or employ/dismiss other employees and so on. In *O'Kelly v Trusthouse Forte plc* the tribunal identified factors which were consistent with employee status, those which were "not inconsistent" with employee status and those which were inconsistent with employee status.

The weight a particular tribunal may place on any one – or any set of – factors may vary and the tribunal has to consider all the circumstances on mixed law and fact. A tribunal decision will be difficult to challenge. Further, it will not be possible for the parties to agree on employment status between themselves – a court or tribunal will look at all the facts in any given set of circumstances and disregard any labels. More importantly, if the court believes the parties have colluded in adopting a particular working arrangement in order to avoid tax/NICs, the contract may be void on the grounds of illegality with the consequence that the worker will not qualify for any statutory employment protection rights.

Worker status

Statute has extended protection in certain respects to a wider category of "worker" after this concept was first introduced by European legislation (see Article 39 of the Treaty of Rome). The definition of worker varies according to the legislation from which the protection derives.

Under the ERA 1996 Section 230(3) a worker is defined as

> an individual who has entered into or works under (or where the employment has ceased worked under) – (a) a contract of employment or (b) any other contract, whether express or implied and (if it is express) whether oral or in writing, whereby the individual undertakes to do or perform personally any work or services for another party to the contract whose status is not by virtue of the contract that of a client or customer of any profession or business carried on by the individual.

Similar definitions are contained in the Trade Union and Labour Relations (Consolidation) Act 1992, National Minimum Wage Act 1998 s 54(3) and the Working Time Regulations 1998 SI 1998/1833 Regulation 2(1). See also Regulation 1(2) of the Part-time Workers (Prevention of Less Favourable Treatment) Regulations 2000 SI 2000/1551 (the "PT Regulations") and ERA 1996 Sections 43A-43l (dealing with whistleblowing).

So, there must some type of contract (whether written or oral) to supply personal services (that is, the person must not be able to delegate his or her services) to another who is not a client or customer of any profession or business carried on by an individual. The latter limb of this definition (business carried on by an individual) was considered in *Watkins & others v BMI Healthcare Ltd t/a Clementine Churchill Hospital.*[11]

A "worker" includes an "employee" but, importantly, also some independent contractors who personally contract to supply their services to the employer. Many atypical workers will fall into this category. For example, the PT Regulations (which implement the Part-time Work Directive) apply to "workers" although the FT Regulations (which mirror the PT Regulations in many respects) apply only to employees.

The definition of worker is intended to exclude, however, those who are in business on their own account, that is, the genuinely self-employed. The DTI Guidance on "worker" (for the Working Time Regulations) states that in general a worker will be someone to whom an employer has a duty to provide work, who controls when and how it is done, supplies the tools and other equipment and pays tax and national insurance contributions. However, these are indicators rather than exhaustive or exclusive criteria. The majority of agency workers and freelancers are likely to be workers.

A key question is the degree of economic dependence between the employer and the individual. However, the dividing line between an employee and a worker is bound to be rather uncertain. Many working arrangements are particularly difficult to assess such as zero- and annualised hours contracts, casual (or "seasonal") workers and home or tele-workers.

Continuity of employment

In order to qualify for many employment rights (such as protection against unfair dismissal and an entitlement to a statutory redundancy payment, ordinary and enhanced maternity rights and written reasons for dismissal), an individual must not only show an employment relationship but must also have a continuous period of employment. The length of this period varies according to the right.

Atypical workers are more likely than those in traditional employment relationships to be affected by the rules on continuity. For example a fixed-term worker would be more likely not to accrue sufficient service to benefit from some of these protections.

ERA 1996 Sections 210-219 set out the key rules governing continuity of service for the purpose of accruing sufficient service for statutory employment protection rights. Many key rights depend on having sufficient service – or the amount due to the employee is calculated according to length of service (for example statutory redundancy payment and basic award for unfair dismissal).

Historically, part-time workers were expected to accrue longer service than full timers on the premise that they were not actually working as much as their full time colleagues. Part-timers working between 8 and 16 hours a week would have to work five years as opposed to two years for those working at least 16 hours a week in order to accrue sufficient service. This position was reversed with the impact of anti-discrimination legislation (see *R v Secretary of State for Employment, ex parte Equal Opportunities Commission*[12] which ruled that UK legislation was in breach of Article 119 [now Article 141] of the EC Treaty) and now, for the purposes of calculating continuity of service, part-timers are treated no differently than those who work full time. It should be noted that the rules on continuity in ERA apply to employees only, not workers.

Computing periods of employment

Section 211 ERA provides that an employee's period of continuous employment begins with the day on which the employee starts work and ends with the day by reference to which the length of his period of continuous employment is to be ascertained for the purposes of the particular employment right.

An employee's employment is presumed to be continuous unless the contrary is shown.[13] A week runs from Sunday to Saturday.[14] A gap has to include a week running from a Sunday to a Saturday to break continuity.

Any gap of more than a week which does not count in computing the length of a period of continuous employment breaks continuity of employment[15] (subject to Sections 215 to 217 ERA). If, after such a gap, the employee recommences work for the old employer, he will have to start building up continuity again.

Section 212 deals with weeks counting in computing periods of employment. Section 212(3) specifically deals with weeks during which there is no employment. This area has given rise to a considerable body of case law. Section 212(3) contains special provisions which allow breaks in employment to be treated as continuous with periods of work.

Absence which does not break continuous periods of work are weeks during the whole or part of which an employee is:

(i)   incapable of work due to sickness or injury (up to 26 weeks)
(ii)   absent from work due to a temporary cessation of work
(iii) absent from work in circumstances such that, by custom or arrangement, he is regarded as continuing in the employment of his employer for any purpose, or
(iv)   absent from work wholly or partly because of pregnancy or childbirth.

We will deal below with the two types of breaks in employment which apply mainly to atypical workers, namely temporary cessations and absences due to custom and arrangement.

Temporary cessation

The provisions dealing with temporary cessation and custom and arrangements are of particular significance for atypical workers. fixed-term contract workers (such as teachers) will have gaps in their employment but could be long serving and fully integrated members of staff. Indeed such employees may have worked on a regular basis for many years, only latterly entering into a series of fixed-term contracts. The provisions in Section 212 (3) above go some way to assuring protection for such employees although there will undoubtedly be many who fall outside the ambit of the provisions.

In *Ford v Warwickshire County Council*[16] (a case concerning a teacher who was employed under a succession of fixed-term contracts for 8 years) the House of Lords held that temporary meant lasting only for a relatively short period of time and that it must be asked whether the gap between the two periods of employment was short in relation to their combined duration. Whether cessation is temporary is a matter of fact to be determined by a tribunal. The House of Lords thought that temporary meant "transient, ie lasting only for a short period of time".

In *Flack v Kodak Ltd*[17] the Court of Appeal said that when considering an irregular pattern of intermittent employment all the circumstances of the case must be looked at. "Temporary" should be considered not as "very short" but relatively. It is necessary to look at all the relevant circumstances with hindsight. However it is sometimes appropriate to apply a strict mathematical approach after considering all the facts (*Sillars v Charrington Fuels Ltd*[18]). In Sillars, the tribunal compared the periods when the employee was absent with the periods when he was working – this approach was upheld on appeal. In *Berwick Salmon Fisheries Co Ltd v Rutherford*[19] (a case concerning seasonal work during the salmon netting season) it was held that where a greater time was spent out of employment than in the period of employment it cannot be regarded as absence on account of a temporary cessation of work.

Arrangement or custom

This provision only has effect where there is no contract of employment in place during the period of absence (if the contract expressly provides for the absence continuity is preserved by virtue of Section 212(1)). If a contract subsists (for example where an employee works one week on one week off by agreement) he or she will in any event accrue continuity of employment during the weeks not worked. To meet the requirement of "arrangement" the employee has to demonstrate that there is some kind of arrangement or understanding with the employer to return and carry on more work, for example, a waitress who is asked to return in the next season and has all her details kept, her uniform retained and her P45).

A custom will apply where, for example, within a certain industry a particular practice becomes accepted as the norm.

An employer who deliberately dismisses an employee prior to that employee attaining sufficient continuity of service for various statutory employment protection rights will not be caught by the "custom and arrangement" provisions even though it is clear that the purpose in dismissing the employee and then re-employing him or her a few weeks later was to avoid the effect of the continuity provisions (see *Booth & others v United States of America*).[20]

However, successive contracts, for example where the employee is employed under a series of fixed-term contracts will be treated as continuous employment provided that there has been no break of more than one week between the contracts which breaks continuity. A gap may still not prevent employment from being treated as continuous if that gap is a temporary cessation of work (see above).

Table of Rights

Employment right	Qualifying period
Assertion of a statutory right (ERA 1996, Section 108(3)(G))	No qualifying period
Employment right	**Qualifying period**
Disability discrimination	No qualifying period
Equal pay	No qualifying period
Guarantee payments/payments during medical suspension in the qualifying period is one month ending with the day before the period for which guarantee payment is claimed. (ERA 1996, Section 29 (1) and Section 65(1))	
Health and safety related reason (ERA 1996, Section 108(3)(C))	No qualifying period
Maternity related reason (ERA 1996, Section 108(3)(B))	No qualifying period
Minimum period of notice	1 month (ERA 1996, Section 86(1) and Section 87(1)
Race Discrimination Act	No qualifying period
Right to paid annual leave	13 week qualifying period for the right to paid annual leave under Regulation 13(7), Working Time Regulations 1998
Sex Discrimination Act	No qualifying period

Statutory redundancy payment	2 years (ERA 1996, Section 155)
Unfair dismissal	1 year (ERA 1996, Section 108(1) and 92(3)
Union related reason (TULRCA 1996)	No qualifying period
Was the reason connected with the performance by an employee who is a pension scheme trustee or his functions as such a trustee (ERA 1996, Section 108(3)(E))	No qualifying period
Was the reason connected with the refusal of Sunday work by a shop worker or betting worker (ERA 1996, Section 108(3)(D))	No qualifying period
Employment right	**Qualifying period**
Was the reason relating to working time (ERA, 1996 Section 108(3) (DD))	No qualifying period
Was the reason connected with the assertion of rights under the National Minimum Wage Act 1998	No qualifying period
Was the reason connected with the making of a protected disclosure under ERA 1996	No qualifying period
Was the reason connected with the assertion of rights under the Part-Time Workers (Prevention of Less Favourable Treatment) Regulations 2000	No qualifying period
Was the reason connected with trade union recognition or bargaining arrangements (TULRCA 1992)	No qualifying period
Whistleblowing	No qualifying period

Discrimination

A full consideration of the anti-discrimination legislation is set out in Chapter 3. This part simply looks briefly at the area of discrimination which is most likely to affect atypical workers such as fixed and part-time workers who are predominantly women.

Sex discrimination:
The Sex Discrimination Act 1975(SDA) prohibits three main types of sex-based discrimination:

    (i)   indirect sex discrimination
    (ii) indirect marital discrimination
    (iii) direct discrimination.

Article 2 of the Equal Treatment Directive 75/207 (ETD) provides "There shall be no discrimination whatsoever on grounds of sex either directly or indirectly by reference in particular to marital or family status". Article (1) sets out the principle of equal treatment in the employment context "as regards access to employment including promotion and to vocational training and as regards working conditions..." The Burden of Proof Directive provides that

> Indirect discrimination shall exist where an apparently neutral provision, criterion or practice disadvantages a substantially higher proportion of the members of one sex unless that provision, criterion or practice is appropriate and necessary and can be justified by objective factors unrelated to sex.

Directives are binding upon Member States as to the result to be achieved by the Directive but the means of reaching that end is down to the individual Member States. A private individual cannot invoke a Directive against a private employer.

Under domestic legislation indirect discrimination on the grounds of sex results from the imposition of a requirement or condition which, although universally applied, has a disproportionate impact on one sex in practice (Section 1(2)(b) SDA).

An individual wishing to challenge the requirement must show that he or she cannot comply with the requirement herself and that it is to his or her detriment that he or she cannot do so. If the employer is able to show that the requirement or condition is justifiable objectively, that is, irrespective of the sex of the individual concerned, the employee's claim will fail. Each case must be analysed on its own merits in the light of the ERA and the case law including decided cases of the ECJ. Employment tribunals must take into account the requirement in Article 2 of the ETD that "there shall be no discrimination whatsoever on grounds of sex either directly or indirectly by reference to marital or family status" and also the way in which the ECJ has interpreted indirect discrimination.

It may also be possible for a woman to claim that her employer is guilty of direct discrimination on the ground of sex if she can show that her employer has treated or would treat a similar request for flexible working more favourably if it had been made by a man (or vice versa) (*British Telecommunications plc v Roberts and Longstaffe*).[21]

It should be noted that Section 6(1) SDA also renders discrimination unlawful at the recruitment or selection stage.

In order to make a claim of discrimination the employee must show that the employer has committed an act of discrimination prohibited under the SDA. Under Section 6(2)(b) SDA it is unlawful for an employer to discriminate against a woman by dismissing her or submitting her to "any other detriment". Dismissal includes constructive dismissal and it is possible that an employer's refusal to allow an employee to work part-time or to job share (if the refusal is unlawful) or to become an indefinite term worker not a fixed-term worker, may be a breach of the employer's contractual duty of trust and confidence such that an employee who is forced to resign in this situation may be able to say that she has been constructively dismissed. Submitting a woman to a detriment means no more than putting her under a disadvantage (*Jeremiah v Ministry of Defence*).[22] In *Home Office v Holmes*[23] the EAT said that an employee who continues to work full time but under stress and protest may well be able to establish that she has been subjected to a detriment.

Fixed-term workers

Background

The growth of workers on fixed-term contracts in the EC has increased greatly in recent years and it is estimated from the Labour Force Survey (Spring 2000) that the number of people working on fixed-term contracts in the UK is between 1.1 and 1.3 million with the number rising by approximately 100,000 or 7% between 1994 and 2000. The public sector makes more use than the private sector of this type of contract and long fixed-term contracts (over two years) are less common in the private sector. Generally, more women than men are likely to be employed on a FTC (approximately 55% of fixed-term employees are women) although the DTI believes there is no evidence to suggest that discrimination against fixed-term employees disproportionately affects either sex in benefits.

A fixed-term contract is one where employment commences on a certain date and ends on another certain date (see *BBC v Kelly Phillips*)[24] even if it can be terminated earlier on notice by either party (*Dixon v BBC*).[25] A contract for the performance of a specific job or purpose is not a fixed-term contract (*Ryan v Shipboard Maintenance Ltd*).[26] An employee working under a fixed-term contract will accrue continuity of employment for the purposes of ERA in the usual way and a succession of fixed-term contracts without a break of one week or more may be aggregated to calculate the length of employment (see Continuity of employment above).

The European Community (EC) Directive on fixed-term Work (Council Directive 1999/70/EC of 28 June 1999, the "FT Directive") was agreed in 1999 and aimed to prevent fixed-term employees from being less favourably treated than similar permanent employees by

(i) improving the quality of fixed-term work by establishing the principle of non-discrimination; and

(ii) establishing a framework to prevent abuse arising from the use of successive fixed-term contracts.

The FT Directive states:

in respect of employment conditions, fixed-term workers shall not be treated in a less favourable manner than comparable permanent workers solely because they have a fixed-term contract or relationship, unless justified on objective grounds.

The FT Directive specifically required the UK to

(i) prevent employers from giving their fixed-term employees less favourable terms and conditions of employment than comparable permanent employees unless this can be objectively justified;

(ii) take some measures to prevent abuse of fixed-term contracts arising from successive renewals;

(iii) require employers to inform their fixed-term employees of vacancies in their organisation on the same basis as permanent employees.

The definition of "fixed-term worker" in the FT Directive is a person having an employment contract or relationship entered into directly between an employer and a worker where the end of the employment contract or relationship is determined by objective conditions such as reaching a specific date, completing a specific task, or the occurrence of a specific event.

Concern has been expressed that there has been widespread abuse of FTCs (although this has been less of a concern in the UK than in other European countries where FTCs are less common). So far as the principle of non abuse is concerned, most other EU countries already have systems in place which prevent employers from continually renewing a fixed-term employee instead of offering him a permanent post. The FT Directive provides several options for putting a limit on the number of renewals.

The FT Directive obliged the UK government to introduce legislation to prevent discrimination against employees on FTCs and accordingly the Fixed-term Employee (Prevention of Less Favourable Treatment) Regulations 2002 (the FT Regulations) were introduced after public consultation which ended on 15 April 2002. The consultation proved to be difficult with broadly opposing stances taken by the TUC and the CBI.

It has been estimated by the DTI that in the UK 25,000 to 53,000 employees will benefit from the changes in domestic legislation in (non-pay) benefits by £19–40 million. Employees would benefit by the changes in pay and pensions by a further £51–124 million. Estimates also state that improved access to training would benefit fixed-term employees by £33–76 million and could have benefits to business of £26–180 million per year from increased productivity.

However, there are also significant estimated compliance costs – the cost to employers of legislation compelling them to comply with non-discrimination in non-pay benefits is estimated at £24–51 million and legislation to cover pay and pensions will be an extra £52–127 million. Increased access to training for fixed-term employees could cost £33–76 million. There will also be additional costs such as introducing measures to prevent abuses and administration costs.

Fixed-term employees – general

As mentioned above, a fixed-term contract is one where the start and end dates (and therefore the duration of the contract) are certain. A contract will not be for a fixed-term if there is simply a minimum length to the contract or if it is for a specific purpose or if it is terminable in the event of a future contingency (*Wiltshire CC v NATFHE*).[27] It may still be a fixed-term contract if there is a notice provision (*Dixon v BBC*).

As will be seen below when the FT Regulations are considered in greater depth, the regulations will apply to a wider category, that is, to employment contracts whose end is determined by objective conditions (contracts ending once a specified date is reached, a specified task is completed or a specified event happens). The Government cites examples of an employment contract for a research project of specific duration, a contract for an employee to complete a specific task such as setting up an IT system or a contract of employment ending when the permanent job holder returns from absence such as maternity leave.

Notice
Section 86(4) ERA contains a protective provision where an employee who has been continuously employed for three months or more on a contract for a fixed period of one month or less is to be treated as if he or she were employed for an indefinite period and entitled to notice in accordance with Section 86(1) ERA. This is to prevent unscrupulous employers from avoiding the minimum statutory notice provisions (four weeks being the initial qualifying period for statutory notice).

Continuous employment
An employee under a fixed-term contract accrues continuous service for statutory employment protection rights in the same way as other permanent employees. Indeed successive fixed-term contracts without breaks will be viewed as unbroken continuous service and so most statutory rights can be acquired in this way. Continuity of service for such rights is dealt with above.

Waiver of rights

The expiry – and non-renewal – of a fixed-term contract will constitute a dismissal according to Section 95(1)(b) of the ERA 1996. Previously Section 197(1) ERA allowed the exclusion of the right to complain of unfair dismissal when that contract expired provided the contract was for a fixed period of one year or more and the employee had expressly agreed in writing to the exclusion. This has now been repealed by the Employment Relations Act 1999. However, an employee employed under a FTC for two years or more was still able to agree in writing to waive his right to a redundancy payment on expiry and non renewal of the FTC (Section 197(3)). Such a waiver lapsed automatically at the end of the fixed-term.

The Government's consultation paper on the then draft FT Regulations welcomed views on the proposal that employees on fixed-term contracts should no longer be able to waive their rights to statutory payments that would apply after two years service. The argument for retaining the waiver was that a redundancy payment is there to compensate an employee for the unexpected loss of a job through market forces and this is generally not the case for fixed-term employees who expect their employment to end at the end of the fixed-term.

The FT Regulations include provisions for the repeal of this waiver – the effect of this Regulation will apply to contracts signed, extended or renewed after the Regulations have come into force, that is, after 1 October 2002.

Indirect sex discrimination

Case law outside the ambit of the FT Regulations has gone some way to protecting employees on fixed-term contracts. In *Whiffen v Milham Ford Girls School*[28] the Court of Appeal held that a selection process for redundancy was unjustified because of a requirement that fixed-term employees, irrespective of service, could not avoid redundancy. It was found, for the purposes of establishing indirect sex discrimination, that the requirement to be on a permanent contract to avoid redundancy was such that a smaller proportion of women could comply with it than men. It was clearly to the employee's detriment and could not be objectively justified.

> In *Tele Danmark A/S v Handels-og Kontorfunktionaerernes Forbund I Danmark (HG)*[29] the employee was recruited to work for a fixed-term of 6 months and failed to tell her employer she was pregnant at the time of recruitment. She told the employer shortly after and was dismissed. The ECJ made clear that the prohibition against dismissal of a female worker on account of pregnancy applies even where the employee is a fixed-term worker and even though she had failed to tell the employer of her pregnancy at the time of recruitment. So, there is a clear warning for employers who recruit a replacement to cover for an employee on maternity leave – such a replacement must be given the same rights and protections as an employee on an indefinite term contract.

In *Melgar v Ayuntamiento de los Barrios*[30] the employee was employed on a number of fixed-term contracts. When she advised her employer she was pregnant her contract was not renewed. The ECJ held that the prohibition against dismissal of a pregnant worker in Article 10 applies equally to fixed-term and indefinite term contracts.

The Fixed-term Employees Regulations

The FT Regulations 2002 cover all employees (although the FT Directive contains a wider definition of worker) – the self-employed will not be covered. Other legislation is being considered to cover other types of workers who are not caught within the definition (such as temporary workers supplied by an agency). An "agency worker" is defined as any person who is supplied by an employment business to do work for another person under a contract or other arrangement made between the employment business and the other person. An "employment business" is defined as the business (whether or not carried on with a view to profit) of supplying persons in the employment of the person carrying on the business, to act for, and under the control of, other persons in any capacity. The TUC were particularly concerned at the exclusion of agency workers but this question is now being considered as part of the framework for agreement on agency workers at EU level. The FT Regulations also do not have effect in relation to fixed-term employees employed under contracts of apprenticeship, students on work placements or the armed forces.

The FT Regulations should be read in conjunction with the Compliance Guidance which clarifies the regulations and gives practical examples with regards to implementation. It also includes a list of frequently asked questions.

The decision not to extend the application of the FT Regulations to workers has also been controversial. The government has committed itself to reviewing the question of employment status and rights, so this position may change.

Definitions

A fixed-term contract means a contract of employment
(a) which is made for a specific term which is fixed in advance, or
(b) which terminates automatically on the completion of a particular task or upon the occurrence or non occurrence of any other specific event other than
  (1) the attainment by the employee of any normal and bona fide retiring age in the establishment for an employee holding the position held by him, or
  (2) a breach of the terms of the contract of employment arising from conduct of the employee that, in the absence of the provision for automatic termination upon the breach and any provision in the contract to the contrary, would entitle the employer to dismiss him summarily.

Examples of fixed-term employees:

(i)   employees doing so called "seasonal" or "casual" work who have contracts for a short period or task that end when the period expires or the task is completed (such as employees at children's summer camps, agricultural workers and shop assistants over the Christmas period)
(ii) employees on fixed-term contracts concluded specifically for maternity
(iii) parental or paternity leave or sick leave
(iv) employees hired to cover peaks in demand and whose contracts expire when demand returns to normal levels
(v)   employees whose contracts will expire when a specific task is complete (such as running a training course).

An employee means an individual who has entered into or works under or, where the employment has ceased, worked under a contract of employment being a contract of service (or apprenticeship) whether express or implied and whether oral or in writing. The Regulations also apply to some crown servants, House of Lords and House of Commons staff and police officers.

For the purposes of the FT Regulations a permanent employee is defined as an employee who is not employed under a fixed-term contract.

Finally, there is the important definition of the "pro rata principle" which means that where a comparable permanent employee receives or is entitled to pay or any other benefit, a fixed-term employee is to receive or be entitled to such proportion of that pay or other benefit as is reasonable in the circumstances bearing in mind the length of his or her contract of employment and the basis on which the pay or other benefit is offered. For example, there are some benefits which may be offered on an annual basis or over a specified period of time such as season tickets, season ticket loans or health insurance. Where a fixed-term employee is not expected to work for the entire period for which a benefit is offered, it may be appropriate to offer it in proportions to the duration of the contract.

Principle of comparable employee

The FT Regulations compare treatment of a fixed-term employee and a permanent employee. There is no right for a fixed-term employee to compare himself or herself with another fixed-term employee or for a permanent worker not to be less favourably treated than a similar fixed-term employee. For the purposes of the regulations, an employee is a comparable employee in relation to a fixed-term employee if, at the time the alleged "less favourable" treatment takes place, both employees are employed by the same employer and are engaged in the same or broadly similar work (having regard to their qualification, skills and experience). The phrase "same or broadly similar work" is the same definition as "like work" in the EPA 1970 but goes wider to encompass the regard to be had to a similar level of qualification skills and experience.

The comparable employee must also be based or work at the same establishment as the fixed-term employee or, where there is no such employee at that establishment, be based or work at a different establishment. A fixed-term employee cannot compare conditions with someone at an associated employer's establishment. It is not possible to use a hypothetical comparator as can be done under the SDA. This means that a fixed-term worker will have no remedy if there is no actual comparator who falls within the narrow definition. Concern has been expressed that it will be difficult to find such a comparator, as fixed-term employees are often asked to perform a more limited range of duties than permanent employees.

Principle of non-discrimination
The principle of non-discrimination is set out in Regulation 3 which adopts a similar approach to the Part-time Workers (Prevention of Less Favourable Treatment) Regulations 2000 (the "PT Regulations") (see below).

Regulation 3(1)(a) provides that a fixed-term employee shall not be treated less favourably than a comparable permanent employee in respect of the terms of his contract – these include, for example, company cars, mobile telephones and other "perks" or benefits and terms covering sick and holiday entitlement. For example, permanent employees may be given free membership of a workplace gym which fixed-term employees do not get. Regulation 4(2) specifies that this also covers protection against discrimination in respect of any qualifying period for benefits, the opportunity to receive training and opportunities to secure permanent employment with the employer. Originally, the Government thought that the Directive did not apply to pay and pensions and so the original draft of the FT Regulations did not cover these. However, following consultation during which the TUC pointed out that of 200 unionised workplaces they surveyed half paid temporary staff less than permanent staff. Clause 45 of the Employment Bill enabled the government to extend the regulations to pay and pensions.

Regulation 3(1)(b) provides that a fixed-term employee shall not be treated less favourably than a comparable permanent employee by being subjected to any other detriment by any act, or failure to act, of the employer. This is aimed at combating all types of discrimination against fixed-term employees and is far-reaching. It will cover, for example, an employee who is not afforded training given to other permanent employees or who is passed over for promotion and, specifically, the opportunity to secure a permanent position.

The wording of less favourable treatment in the FT Regulations is similar to that in the PT Regulations (see below) and S1(1)(a) SDA. On the basis of case law, if the fact that the claimant was part-time or a fixed-term worker was an important factor in the employer's decision to apply less favourable treatment, the requirements of the legislation will be met. It need not be the only reason for the treatment.

In determining whether a fixed-term employee has been treated less favourably than a comparable permanent employee the pro rata principle (defined above) must be applied unless it is inappropriate to do so.

Defence
There is an employer's defence – the protection against less favourable treatment only applies if the ground on which the less favourable treatment is meted out is that the employee is fixed-term and the treatment is not justified on objective grounds. Less favourable treatment may be justified on objective grounds if it can be shown that the less favourable treatment

(i)   is to achieve a legitimate objective (for example, a genuine business objective)
(ii) is necessary to achieve that objective, and
(iii) is an appropriate way to achieve that objective.

The consultation paper suggests this would be decided on a case-by-case basis – for example, the offering of a season ticket loan to permanent employees only which might be justified as it is repaid over a long period. Employees will need to consider whether it is possible to offer fixed-term workers certain benefits such as annual subscription and insurance policies on a pro rata basis. Further, Regulation 4 states that the treatment will be objectively justified if the terms of the fixed-term employee's contract are as a whole no less favourable than a comparable permanent employee's terms. However, it will be difficult to work out how to quantify various benefits. Employers will need to balance a less favourable condition against a more favourable one provided they ensure that a fixed-term employee's overall employment package is not less favourable than that of a comparable permanent employee's.

Informing of vacancies
Regulation 3(5) provides that in order for an employee to be able to exercise the right to the opportunity to secure permanent employment (Regulation 3(2)(c)) the employee must be informed by his or her employer of "available vacancies in the establishment". This requirement is only satisfied if the vacancy is contained in an advertisement which the employee has a reasonable chance of reading in the course of his or her employment or the employee is given reasonable notification of the vacancy in some other way, such as on a notice board or on the Intranet. The wording of the section is arguably far too wide since it does not actually limit the right to be informed of suitable vacancies.

Right to written statement
Regulation 5 gives the fixed-term employee the right (but not an obligation) to request from his or her employer a written statement giving the reasons for the less favourable treatment. The employer must respond to this request within 21 days. If the employer fails to respond or provides an evasive or equivocal response, an employment tribunal may draw any inferences which it considers just and equitable to draw. There is a similar provision in the PT Regulations. During consultation the Government said "providing written statements of reasons for less favourable treatment should in principle help to prevent unnecessary litigation."

Protection against dismissal

The fixed-term employee is also protected in Regulation 6 against being unfairly dismissed in certain circumstances, namely, that he or she has

(i)   brought proceedings against the employer under the FT Regulations
(ii)   requested a written statement of the reasons for less favourable treatment
(iii)   given evidence in connection with such proceedings
(iv)   otherwise done anything under the FT Regulations in relation to the employer or any other person
(v)   alleged that the employer infringed the FT Regulations
(vi)   refused to forego a right conferred by the FT Regulations
(vii) or that the employer believes or suspects that the employee has done or intends to do any of these things. In such a case, the employee shall be regarded as having been unfairly dismissed.

Regulation 6 mirrors the wording in the PT Regulations and is like other recent discrimination legislation in that victimisation by the employer against an employee who has exercised his rights under the regulations will be automatically unfair dismissal and automatic detrimental treatment. The provisions of Regulation 8 can be varied by a collective agreement or a workforce agreement.

The Fixed-term Regulations have also made changes to some statutory employment rights which previously treated some or all fixed-term employees less favourably than permanent employees.

Where a contract of employment terminates automatically on the completion of a particular task or the occurrence of non occurrence of a particular event, the termination will be classified in law as a dismissal. This means employees on "task contracts" now have a number of statutory rights on the same basis as employees working under permanent contracts including the right not to be unfairly dismissed, the right to a written statement of reasons for dismissal, and the right to a statutory redundancy payment.

Claim to employment tribunal
An employee can present a claim to an employment tribunal in respect of any infringement of his or her rights under Regulation 3 (less favourable treatment) within three months, beginning with the date of the less favourable treatment or detriment (or the last of a series of acts) or, in the case of an infringement of Regulation 3(5) with the date (or last date) on which other individuals were informed of the vacancy. A complaint which is beyond the time limit may be considered if it just and equitable to do so.

It is for the employer to identify the ground for less favourable treatment or detriment when facing a claim under Regulation 3 or 6(2). A tribunal has power to make a declaration, order compensation to be paid to the employee and recommend that the employer take action within a specified time to obviate or reduce the adverse effect on the employee of any matter to which the complaint relates.

Compensation shall be such as the tribunal considers just and equitable having regard to the infringement and loss attributable to the infringement. There is no element of compensation for injury to feelings. The wording on this section mirrors that in the PT Regulations (below).

Successive fixed-term contracts

Regulation 8 deals with the iniquity of successive fixed-term contracts used by unscrupulous employers who try to avoid statutory obligations as highlighted in *Booth & others v USA*.[31] The Directive gave Member States three options, namely to limit the number of renewals to limit the total duration of successive fixed-term contracts or to allow renewal only where objectively justified. The UK has attempted to encompass all three options.

Regulation 8 provides that where an employee is employed under a contract purporting to be a fixed-term contract and the contract has previously been renewed (or the employee was employed by the same employer on a fixed-term contract) or on a series of successive fixed-term contracts for a period of four years or more, the provision which restricts the duration of the contract shall be ineffective and it shall be an indefinite term contract with statutory minimum notice applying. The key points to note are that the employee must have been continuously employed for a period of four years or more and that there is a defence of objective justification for continued engagement on a fixed-term basis. For example, professional sports people and actors may agree that the nature of the profession requires a fixed-term contract and that the nature of the job should be regarded as an objective reason for renewals. Any period of continuous employment before the Regulations come into force is disregarded. There is also no limit on the length of the first fixed-term contract – the Regulations are aimed at successive contracts.

If an employer attempts to circumvent this Regulation by employing a person on a series of fixed-term contracts with short breaks to break continuity, it is arguable that such behaviour would constitute a detriment.

If an employee, who considers his or her employment to be of indefinite duration by virtue of this provision, requests in writing a written statement from the employer confirming this, the employer must provide within 21 days such a statement, or a statement giving reasons why the employer thinks this should not be an indefinite term contract.

Section 10 of the FT Regulations provides that the parties to a contract cannot contract out of the effect of these Regulations except where this forms part of a conciliated settlement or valid compromise agreement.

Part-time employees

Background

Labour Force statistics for June – August 2001 (around the time the PT Regulations were introduced) showed that there were around seven million part-time workers in the UK – this is about a quarter of the total workforce and the numbers are likely to increase significantly. There is a pool of labour consisting largely of women returning to work or balancing caring responsibilities. There is also the flexibility offered to part-timers to help employers even out the peaks and troughs of periodic or seasonal demand.

Sex discrimination legislation (outlined above and in more detail in Chapter 4) has gone some way to affording protection to part-time workers particularly by way of legislation against indirect sex discrimination and, to a lesser extent, legislation on equal pay. However, the inherent difficulties in bringing such a complaint and establishing all the necessary factors can be burdensome for an employee who has been unfairly treated. Consequently, the EC Part-time Work Directive[32] ("PTWD") was adopted in 1997 to protect part-time workers. The framework agreement implemented by the PTWD applies to part-time workers who have an employment contract or employment relationship as defined by the law, collective agreement or practice in force in each Member State.

A part-time worker is one whose normal hours of work, calculated on a weekly basis or over a reference period of up to one year, are less than the normal hours of work of a comparable full time worker (that is, somebody employed in the same establishment, with the same type of employment contract or relationship and doing the same or similar work).

The framework agreement has two main provisions: the principle of "non-discrimination" (Clause 4) and "opportunities for part-time work" (Clause 5). Clause 5 requires Member States and the social partners to identify and review legal and administrative obstacles to part-time working and, where appropriate, eliminate them.

Sex discrimination and part-time working

Request for flexible work
A common scenario is the wish for women with childcaring responsibilities to work on a flexible basis, most usually part-time. By insisting that a woman continues to work full time on her return from maternity leave an employer may be imposing a requirement or condition despite the fact that there is no change to the woman's contractual terms. The EAT has accepted that full time working could be a requirement or condition, despite the fact that there is no change to the woman's contractual terms. The EAT has accepted that full time working could be a requirement or condition: "words like 'requirement' and 'condition' are plain, clear words of wide import fully capable of including any obligation of service whether for full or part-time and we see no basis for giving

them a restrictive interpretation in the light of the policy underlying the Act [SDA]."

Right to return part-time
Under the ERA a woman has the right to return to the same job that she did before her leave and on broadly the same terms and conditions. There is presently no statutory right to return to work on a part-time basis but under the SDA any condition imposed by an employer which can only be complied with by a considerably smaller proportion of women than men will constitute indirect discrimination on the ground of sex. Case law has established that the need to work full time falls into that category of condition and that any woman returning to work after maternity leave will have a prima facie case of unlawful indirect discrimination against the employer if her request to return part-time has been refused.

Objective justification
However, employers may raise the defence of justification, that is, that it will be lawful to refuse the woman to return part-time if the employer can show a good business reason for the refusal.

The employer must be able to show that the case in question has considered on its merits and that all relevant factors have been taken into consideration such as:

(i)   whether the job can be done effectively on a part-time basis
(ii) if the job cannot be done part-time is it possible to cover the hours when the employee will not be present, for example, by a job share?
(iii) how many hours the employee wishes to work
(iv) for how long the employee wishes the part-time arrangement to be in place
(v)   how many other people already work part-time.

Employers should consider different options to achieve the balance between their needs and those of the employees; there is an obligation to consider balance between the discriminatory effect of the requirement and the reasonable needs of the employer.

In *Clymo v Wandsworth London Borough Council*[33] the EAT decided that there are some jobs such as managing director which require full time attendance and in such a case it cannot be said that the employer has imposed a distinct "requirement or condition" to work full time. However the decision in *Clymo* was rejected in *Briggs v North Eastern Education and Library Board*[34] (Northern Ireland Court of Appeal) and since disappeared. This court decided that even if a job by its nature involves full time attendance an employer is still imposing a "requirement" to work full time.

Under EC law, provided the employee is able to show that the practice or policy complained of has a disproportionate impact on one sex, it is not necessary to establish a requirement or condition. In *Enderby v Frenchay Health Authority and Secretary of State for Health*[35] the ECJ stated that an employer's pay practice may need to be objectively justified if it has a disproportionate adverse impact on women. The EAT seems now to have accepted the ECJ's ruling in Enderby (see *Falkirk Council v Whyte*).[36] If the employee manages to show that all the elements of indirect discrimination are present, the employer may still defeat the employee's claim if it can show that it is justified in requiring the woman to continue working full time. It is up to the employer to prove this to the satisfaction of the employment tribunal.

The test for justifiability was set out in the ECJ in the judgement in *Bilka-Kaufhaus v Weber van Hartz*,[37] an equal pay case. The test was confirmed by the ECJ in connection with other aspects of discrimination in employment in the case of *Gerster v Freistaat Bayern*.[38] The ECJ stated that a practice which has a disproportionate and adverse impact on one sex is justifiable if it corresponds to a real need on the part of the employer, is appropriate with a view to achieving the object in question and is necessary to that end. The same test is set out in the Burden of Proof Directive (see above). The employer must satisfy the principle of proportionality, that is, the greater the adverse impact on employees of an employer's practice, the more substantial the justification for the practice must be. The Court of Appeal endorsed this approach in *Hampson v Department of Education and Science*[39] stating that there must be an objective balance between the discriminatory effect of the condition and the reasonable needs of the employer. Justifiability must be individually determined on the basis of evidence produced by the employer. It is not sufficient to say that a particular practice is prevalent in a particular industry and it must therefore be justifiable.

Statistical analysis
When an employee is trying to establish a claim for indirect discrimination, the employee may not have to use reams of detailed statistical analysis to show that the practice or requirement imposed by the employer has or is likely to have a disproportionate impact. Tribunals may be prepared to accept, without detailed statistical analysis, that women are disproportionately affected by a requirement to work full time because they recognise that a majority of those with primary childcare responsibility are women. However, if a tribunal wishes to undertake a detailed statistical analysis, it will first define the relevant pool of people for the purpose of assessing the impact of the requirement on each sex. The tribunal might also examine the impact on working people as a whole.

The latter approach may be more appropriate in most cases, as many women who cannot comply with a requirement to work full time may have been prevented by the requirement from applying to join the employer's workforce or been forced to resign, so that a pool consisting of the employer's existing workforce (or part of it) is likely to contain a misleadingly high number of women able to work full time. The pool applicable in any case is a question of fact for the tribunal and the tribunal's decision concerning the applicable pool cannot usually be challenged on appeal. Once the tribunal has decided which pool is relevant it will decide whether the proportion of women able to comply with a requirement to work full time is "considerably smaller" than the proportion of men able to work full time. There has been no attempt to determine what percentage figure may be regarded as being "considerably smaller" and the disparity of impact may not therefore be very large at first sight but it may still be regarded as being "considerably smaller".

Detriment

If the employer's requirement that the employee works full time is shown to have a disproportionate impact on women, the next step is to determine whether the requirement is a detriment for the employee. The employee only has to show that it is not possible for her to comply with the requirement to work full time, not that it is physically impossible for her to do so. If the employee returns to work full time but simultaneously requests a change to part-time, the fact of her working full time is not necessarily a bar to her being able to show that she cannot comply with the requirement to work full time. If the employee is working full time "under both difficulty and protest" this may be enough to show that the employee could not in practice comply with the requirement to work full time. However, if an employee has access to childcare of a suitable standard that is affordable and convenient, the employee may have difficulty in showing that she cannot work on a full time basis.

Bringing a claim

An employee wishing to bring a claim in relation to an employer's refusal to allow her to work part-time or to job share must lodge her claim within three months of the date on which the act of discrimination occurred under Section 76(1) SDA. In *Cast v Croydon College*[40] the Court of Appeal overturned the decision of the EAT that time began to run for Mrs Cast from the date on which her employer first refused to allow her to work part-time, this date being before Mrs Cast when on maternity leave. The Court of Appeal held that the employer's series of refusals amounted to a continuing act of discrimination and that therefore time did not begin to run for Mrs Cast until the date of the final refusal. This therefore means that a woman wishing to negotiate with her employer and explore the possibility of returning to work part-time may do so without lodging a claim until this becomes absolutely necessary.

The tribunal may, where indirect discrimination is found, award compensation even though the indirect discrimination was unintentional. The aim of compensation is to compensate the applicant, not to punish the employer. Compensation payments are largely made up of payment for loss of earnings which can be substantial as tribunals are also entitled to take into account the fact that the woman may find it more difficult to obtain alternative employment if she has a young child or children.

Marital discrimination
A married woman who is refused the possibility of working part-time on her return from maternity leave may also be able to claim indirect marital discrimination under Section 3(1)(b) SDA in addition to indirect sex discrimination. This will be possible if the employee is able to show that married women are less likely to be able to work on a full time basis than unmarried women because of the greater likelihood that they have childcare responsibilities.

Male sex discrimination
It is unlikely that a man would be able to use the indirect sex discrimination claim to combat an employer's refusal to allow him to alter his working arrangements in order to allow him to play a greater part in caring for his child, because he will be unable to establish that the requirement to work full time has a disproportionate impact on his sex. He may however be able to prove marital discrimination if he is able to obtain statistics showing that a considerably smaller proportion of married men than single men are able to comply with a requirement to work full time. A man may also be able to claim direct discrimination if he is able to show that a woman in the same or not materially different circumstances to his who asked to work on a part-time basis or job share would be allowed to do so because his employer could not justify requiring a woman to work full time. The employer in such circumstances must treat the man no less favourably than a woman (Section 11A and Section 53 SDA).

Equal pay
The Equal Pay Act 1970 (EPA) applies to discrimination between men and women in pay or conditions where they are doing comparable work. The Equal Pay Directive[41] provides that the principle of equal pay means "for the same work or for work to which equal value has been attributed, the elimination of all discrimination on grounds of sex with regard to all aspects and conditions of remuneration".

Together, the EPA and SDA attempt to eliminate discrimination in employment between the sexes and are mutually exclusive. The SDA deals with non contractual issues such as access to benefits, promotion, less favourable treatment and dismissal. The EPA deals with all contractual terms (not just pay). It protects both men and women and allows comparison between employees of the same or associated employer.

The EPA applies equally to direct and indirect discrimination. Whilst intentional indirect discrimination is always unlawful, unintentional indirect discrimination may not be unlawful if it justified. There is no clear distinction between direct and indirect discrimination as there is under the SDA.

An employer may have a defence if he can show that the difference between the term in the woman's contract and that in the man's contract is genuinely due to a material factor which is not the difference of sex.

Since women generally find it more difficult to work full time than men, the difference between full time and part-time working is not of itself a material difference other than sex. The employer will have to show that there are objectively justified grounds for paying full time workers a higher hourly rate than part-time workers (see *Jenkins v Kingsgate (Clothing Productions) Limited (No 2)*[42] and *Bilka-Kaufhaus GmbH v Weber von Hartz* (1987) ICR 110).

The ECJ has emphasised that it is not sufficient for the employer to say that part-timers are less committed or are not as integrated as full time workers (see *Rinner-Kuhn v FWW Spezial-Gebaudereinigung GmbH & Co KG*).[43]

The Part-time Workers (Prevention of Less Favourable Treatment) Regulations 2000[44]

The Directive (PTWD)
The PT Regulations were introduced to implement the terms of the PTWD which sought to give part-time workers the same basic rights and opportunities as their full time colleagues. The PTWD recognises the need for the flexible organisation of working time and encourages employers and unions to work together to remove obstacles to part-time working. At the time the PTWD was introduced it was estimated that approximately 90% of all part-time workers in the UK would be covered by it. The framework agreement noted that part-time work has had an important impact on employment law in recent years and stated that it was the intention to consider the need for similar agreements relating to other forms of flexible work.

The framework agreement recognised the diversity of situations in Member States and that part-time working is an employment feature in certain sectors and activities and so set out the general principles and minimum requirements relating to part-time work. The intention of the Social Partners was to establish a general framework for the elimination of discrimination against part-time workers and to assist the development of opportunities for part-time working on a basis acceptable to both employer and employee.

In clause 4 of the "general considerations" the need for measures to promote both employment and equal opportunities for men and women was emphasised with a call for measures aimed at

> increasing the employment intensiveness of growth, in particular by more flexible organisation of work in a way which fulfils both the wishes of employees and the requirements of competition.

Clause 5 deals with opportunities for part-time work and provides that Member States after consultation with the Social Partners should identify and review obstacles of a legal or administrative nature which may limit opportunities for part-time work and where appropriate eliminate them.

As far as possible employers should give consideration to:
(i)   requests by workers to transfer from full time to part-time work or to

(ii) increase their working time should the opportunity arise
(iii) requests by workers to transfer from part-time to full time work or to increase their working time should the opportunity arise
(iv) the provision of timely information on the availability of part-time and full time positions in the establishment in order to facilitate transfers from full time to part-time or vice versa
(v)   measures to facilitate access to part-time work at all levels of the enterprise, including skilled and managerial positions, and where appropriate, to facilitate access by part-time workers to vocational training to enhance career opportunities and occupational mobility
(vi) the provision of appropriate information to existing bodies representing workers about part-time working in the enterprise.

The PT Regulations
The Government has implemented the PTWD in the UK by way of regulations and guidance to take account of the specific nature of the British labour market. On introduction of the proposals, Stephen Byers, Secretary of State for Trade and Industry, stated

> this revised package safeguards the position of part-timers whilst avoiding unnecessary burdens on business... Full time workers who start working part-time will now be able to compare their new terms and conditions with their previous package... However, the regulations will be introduced with a light touch by ensuring that comparisons can only be made between part-time and full time workers with the same type of contract.

The benefit for many part-timers (80% of whom are women) is that they will generally no longer have to go down the indirect sex discrimination route when claiming they have suffered less favourable treatment. The PT Regulations protect all part-timers not simply women. The new measures are expected to encourage more people to work flexibly as their circumstances change, for example students, carers and those nearing retirement.

Scope of the Regulations and definitions
The PT Regulations apply to a wider category of worker, not just employees. For the purpose of the Regulations, an employee is an individual who has entered into or works under or, where the employment has ceased, worked under a contract of employment.

A worker is defined as an individual who has entered into or works under or, where the employment has ceased, worked under

(a) a contract of employment; or
(b) any other contract, whether express or implied and (if it is express) whether oral or in writing, whereby the individual undertakes to do or perform personally any work or services for another party to the contract

whose status is not by virtue of the contract that of a client or customer of any profession or business undertaking carried on by the individual.

The "pro rata principle" is defined as where a comparable full time worker receives or is entitled to receive pay or any other benefit, a part-time worker is to receive or is entitled to receive not less than the proportion of that pay or other benefit that the number of his weekly hours bears to the number of weekly hours of the comparable full time worker.

The PT Regulations also provide a definition of full time and part-time workers as follows:

(i) A worker is a full time worker if he is paid wholly or in part by reference to the time he works and, having regard to the custom and practice of the employer in relation to workers employed by the worker's employer under the same type of contract, is identifiable as a full time worker (Regulation 2(1)).

(ii) A worker is a part-time worker if he is paid wholly or in part by reference to the time he works and, having regard to the custom and practice of the employer in relation to workers employed by the worker's employer under the same type of contract, is not identifiable as a full time worker (Regulation 2(2)).

As the PT Regulations apply to both employees and workers, the wording of the Regulations can sometimes be difficult as new rights are given to workers which may not be relevant to employees who have protections from other areas of employment legislation. It should also be noted that the Regulations do not confer on workers a right to work part-time.

Regulation 2(3) sets out a list of workers who should be regarded as being employed under different types of contracts for the purposes of determining who are comparable full and part-time workers.

Protection for part-time workers:

Regulation 2(4) defines the comparable employee which is one of the key concepts of the Regulations. This provides that a full time worker is comparable with a part-time worker if, at the time the alleged less favourable treatment to the part-time worker takes place:

(i) both workers are employed by the same employer under the same type of contract and engaged in the same or broadly similar work having regard, where relevant, to whether they have a similar level of qualification, skills and experience, and

(ii) the full time worker works or is based at the same establishment as the part-time worker or, where there is no full time worker working or based at that establishment who satisfies the requirements above, works or is based at a different establishment and satisfies those requirements.

Comparable treatment
It should be noted that the Regulations have been amended so that the previous requirement that a part-time fixed-term worker must be compared with a full time fixed-term worker, rather than a full time permanent contract worker, was removed. This is because the distinction might have encouraged less favourable treatment of fixed-term workers and thus be contrary to the FT Directive.

Whilst there is always the right to make a comparison under Regulation 2(4) Regulation 3 provides that such a worker can also compare his or her treatment with the way in which the worker was treated when he or she worked full time. Likewise, Regulation 4 applies to a worker who previously worked full time before an absence of not more than twelve months who returns to work for his employer for less hours than he previously did – such an employee can compare his treatment after his return with his treatment before his absence.

Non-discrimination principle
Regulation 5 contains the central right not to be discriminated against on the ground of working fewer hours. A part-time worker is entitled not to be treated less favourably by his employer than a comparable full time worker as regards the terms of his contract or by being subjected to any other detriment by any act, or deliberate failure to act, of his employer. This right only applies if the less favourable treatment is because the worker is part-time and if it cannot be justified on objective grounds. In determining whether a part-time worker has been treated less favourably than a comparable full time worker, the pro rata principle (see above) shall be applied unless it is inappropriate to do so.

Written statement of less favourable treatment
A worker can request in writing from his or her employer a written statement giving particulars of any alleged less favourable treatment (Regulation 6). A written response should be furnished by the employer within 21 days. Such a statement is admissible as evidence in any proceedings under the Regulations and a tribunal can draw any inference which it is just and equitable to draw from any deliberate failure to provide a response or if the response appears evasive or equivocal.

Unfair dismissal/detriment
Regulation 7 of the PT Regulations sets out protections for part-time workers who have been unfairly dismissed or subjected to a detriment.

It will be automatically unfair to dismiss an employee for the purposes of Part X ERA and unlawful to subject a worker to a detriment if the reason for that treatment is
(a) that the worker has
(i) brought proceedings against the employer under these Regulations

(ii) requested from his employer a written statement of reasons of less favourable treatment

(iii) given evidence or information in connection with such proceedings brought by any worker

(iv) otherwise done anything under the PT Regulations in relation to the employer or any other person

(v) alleged that the employer had infringed the PT Regulations

(vi) refused (or proposed to refuse) to forego a right conferred on him by the PT Regulations, or

(b) that the employer believes or suspects that the worker has done or intends to do any of the things above.

There will be no protection for a worker who makes a claim under grounds (a)(v) or (b) above if the allegation made by the worker is false and not made in good faith.

Complaints to Employment Tribunal

Complaints about breaches of any of the rights should be made to a tribunal in the usual way. A complaint shall not be considered unless it is presented before the expiry of three months beginning with the date of the less favourable treatment or detriment to which the complaint relates (or the last act of a series of acts). A complaint which is out of time may be considered if it is just and equitable to do so. Rules for working out the date for the less favourable treatment or detriment are set out in regulation 8 (4).

Where a worker presents a claim it is for the employer to identify the ground for the less favourable treatment or detriment.

If an employment tribunal finds that a complaint presented to it is well founded it can make a declaration as to the rights of the complainant and the employer; order the employer to pay compensation to the complainant and/ or recommend that the employer take reasonable action to obviate or reduce the adverse effect on the complainant of any matter to which the complaint relates. If compensation is awarded, it shall be of such amount as the tribunal considers just and equitable in all the circumstances having regard to the infringement and any loss (including expenses incurred by the complainant and loss of any benefit which he or she might reasonably be expected to have but for the infringement). Compensation will not include any element for injury to feelings. The tribunal shall also be entitled to take account of any contributory conduct of the complainant and can reduce the award to such proportion as it considers just and equitable.

Compliance and Best Practice Guidance

The Compliance Guidance and Best Practice Guidance complement the notes accompanying the PT Regulations. They provide further information on complying with the law and offer examples of how to adopt best practice in relation to part-time working. It is intended that the guidance will form part of an ongoing programme of information.

> The Compliance Guidance sets out a number of examples of issues that need to be addressed to comply with the PT Regulations. The following are examples:
>
> (i)   In reorganising workloads, part-time workers should not be treated less favourably than full time workers unless this can be objectively justified.
>
> (ii)   Previous or current part-time status should not of itself constitute a barrier to promotion to a post, whether the post is full time or part-time.
>
> (iii) Part-time workers should receive the same hourly rate as comparable full time workers.
>
> (iv)   Part-time workers should receive the same hourly rate of overtime pay as comparable full time workers once they have worked more than the normal full time hours.
>
> (v)   Part-time workers should be able to participate in profit sharing or share option schemes available for full time staff unless there are objective grounds for excluding them.
>
> (vi)   The benefits part-time workers receive under these schemes should be pro rata to those received by comparable full time workers.
>
> (vii) Part-time workers should not be treated less favourably than full time workers in terms of
>   (a) calculating the rate of sick pay or maternity pay
>   (b) the length of service required to qualify for payment
>   (c) the length of time the payment is received.
>
> (viii) Employers should not discriminate between full time and part-time workers over access to pension schemes unless different treatment is justified on objective grounds.
>
> (ix)   Employers should not exclude part-time staff from training simply because they work part-time.
>
> (x)   The criteria used to select jobs for redundancy should be objectively justified and part-timers must not be treated less favourably than comparable full time workers.
>
> (xi)   Benefits such as subsidised mortgages and staff discounts should be applied to part-time workers unless an exception is justified on objective grounds.
>
> (xii) Where a benefit, such as health insurance, cannot be applied pro rata, this is not of itself an objective justification for denying it to part-time workers. The less favourable treatment of part-time workers will still need to be justified on objective grounds. These might include the disproportionate cost to the organisation of providing such a benefit or the imperative to meet a real need of the organisation.
>
> (xiii) The holiday entitlement of part-time staff should be pro rata to that of full time workers.

(xiv) Contractual maternity leave and parental leave should be available to part-time workers as well as full time workers.

(xv) Career break schemes should be available to part-time workers as well as full time workers unless objectively justifiable on grounds other than part-time status.

Best Practice in employment:

The Best Practice Guidance sets out the Government's recommendations on a number of issues which it urges employers to deal with as a matter of best practice. These include:

(i) At all levels of the organisation including skilled and managerial posts employers should seek to maximise the range of posts designated as suitable for part-time working or job sharing.

(ii) Employers should seriously consider requests for job sharing and larger organisations should keep a database of those interested in entering job sharing arrangements.

(iii) Employers should look seriously at requests to change to part-time working and where possible explore with their workers how this change could be accommodated.

(iv) Employers should consider establishing a procedure for discussing with workers whether they wish to change from full time to part-time employment for any reason.

(v) Employers should periodically review how individuals are provided with information on the availability of part-time and full time positions.

(vi) Organisations should consider how to make it easier for workers to vary their hours, including transferring between part-time and full time work, to the benefit of both workers and employers.

(vii) Larger firms with staff bodies for representation should be kept informed about certain aspects of the organisation's use of part-time workers.

(viii) The provision of training should be arranged so as to ensure that it is as conveniently located and timed for part-time staff as for full-time staff unless this is not possible.

(ix) Other measures to support the career development of the part-time worker should be considered including, for example, paying part-time workers for the extra hours they attend outside their normal working hours, offering an equivalent course from an alternative provider at a convenient time and place and offering other training or training methods.

Best Practice for part-time work:

The Best Practice Guidance also specifically addresses the handling of an employee's request to work part-time. Some of the factors to be taken into account may include:

(i)   Does someone need to be present in this post during all hours of work?

(ii)   Can the post be filled as a job share?

(iii)   Is there a suitable candidate for a job share? Could one be recruited?

(iv)   Can all the necessary work be done in the hours requested?

(v)   Is there another job of similar level which the worker could do part-time?

(vi)   Is the change for a known period?

(vii)   How much would it cost to recruit and train a replacement if the worker left?

(viii)   What benefits would the organisation get from this arrangement? For example, more commitment, keep a valued member of staff, a better skilled worker if time is used for training or education, lower wage bill, keep staff cover for peak periods?

(ix)   Effect on the morale and commitment of other staff.

Best Practice for full-time work:

When considering a request to increase hours or work full time some of the factors to be taken into account may include:

(i)   Is there sufficient work for those hours?

(ii)   Could the extra hours be used to reorganise a number of jobs more efficiently?

(iii)   Can the organisation afford the increase in pay?

(iv)   Will the increase save money on recruitment?

Other measures to facilitate part-time working are addressed – in larger organisations it may be appropriate to consider:

(i)   Would it be cost effective to provide childcare facilities onsite?

(ii)   Could a contribution towards childcare costs be offered?

(iii)   Both large and small organisations might consider whether it would be appropriate to consider introducing flexible forms of working, such as term-time working, lunch-time working, flexi-time, homeworking, a parental leave scheme and reduced hours working.

Request for flexible working: the future

In June 2001 a taskforce was asked to consider how to meet parents' desire for more flexible work patterns in a way that is compatible with business efficiency – "About Time: Flexible Working". On 20 November 2001 the DTI set out new proposals to encourage the discussion of flexible working arrangements – see "Government Response to the Recommendations from the Work and Parents Taskforce". The Government made clear that it intended to introduce legislation that would place a duty on employers to consider seriously requests for flexible working from the parents of young children. Accordingly, the government has published the first draft of the Flexible Working (Procedural Requirements) Regulations 2002 (the "FW Regulations"), made under the Employment Act 2002 (intended to come into force on 6 April 2002). The duty to consider will apply in respect of parents of children under the age of six where the parents are employees and have worked for the same employer for at least six months. For parents of disabled children the limit will be the age of 18.

Such parents will be able to request changes to their working patterns without fear of dismissal or other detriment. The employer will be under an obligation to consider such requests seriously, following basic minimum procedural standards. Where requests are not accepted, there is provision for an appeal stage, and ultimately, recourse to an external dispute resolution stage which could be an employment tribunal.

The DTI accept that legislation must provide employers with clear business reasons justifying the rejection of a request. A written explanation should be given and where employers do not give such an explanation, employment tribunals will have the power to require them to do so.

Business reasons should include:
(i)   burden of additional costs to the business
(ii)   inability to meet customer demand
(iii)   inability to organise work within available staffing
(iv)   detrimental impact on quality
(v)   detrimental impact on performance
(vi)   inability to find extra staff; and
(vii)   other means that the employer will need to specify.

The DTI also cautiously accepted the recommendation that parents be given two weeks to appeal in writing against the decision setting out reasons for the appeal. The appeal should be heard at a meeting which can be part of an existing procedure, for example, grievance. The employer should respond within two weeks of the meeting. The right to require flexible working hours is set out in the Employment Act 2002 but fleshed out by the FW Regulations.

The procedural steps must include the establishment by employers of a clear business case if rejecting the request and the explanation of it to the parent making the request:

(i)   Parents should make requests in writing setting out the working pattern they want and how it could be made to work.

(ii) Employers should consider the business case for accepting or rejecting the request.

(iii) There should be a meeting within four weeks to consider the request. Parents should, if they wish, be able to bring someone with them. The meeting should be an opportunity for discussing the request, the issues it raises for the business and any compromises required.

The employer should write to the parent within two weeks either

(a)   accepting the request, setting out any action on which the agreement is dependent and establishing a start date (suggested by the DTI to be at least two months to allow new arrangements to be set up); or

(b)   confirming the compromise offered in the meeting and setting a date for the response; or

(c)   rejecting the request and giving a short explanation of the business reasons for doing so; and

(d)   setting out the appeals procedure.

The draft Flexible Working (Eligibility, Complaints and Remedies) Regulations 2003 further provide a penalty if the employer fails to hold a meeting with the employee (or fails to notify the employee of his/her decision) of up to eight weeks' pay (statutory cap applying).

The Government intends to provide for a year's waiting period between a parent's unsuccessful request and a second one.

If an employer does not respond to the request or does not hold a meeting to consider it or refuses to allow the parent to be accompanied by someone, the parent should complain through the employer's grievance procedure. Under the Employment Act 2002, all employees will have a contractual right to a grievance procedure.

Notes

[1] (1968) 2QB 497
[2] *Motorola Ltd v (1) Davidson (2) Melville Craig Group Ltd* (2001) IRLR 4
[3] (2001) IRLR 269
[4] (1995) IRLR 493
[5] (1952) 1 TLR101
[6] (1973) 1 All ER 241
[7] *Lane v Shire Roofing Co. (Oxford) Ltd* (1995) IRLR 493, 496
[8] (1994) IRLR 171,174
[9] (1969) 2 QBD
[10] (1983) IRLR 369
[11] ET Case 6004508/99
[12] (1994) ICR 317
[13] ERA section 210 (5)

14 ERA section 235
15 ERA 210(4)
16 (1983) ICR 273
17 (1986) ICR 775
18 (1989) IRLR 152
19 (1991) IRLR 203
20 (1999) IRLR 16
21 (1996) IRLR 601
22 (1980) ICR 13
23 (1984) ICR 678
24 (1998) IRLR 16
25 (1979) ICR 281
26 (1980) IRLR 16
27 (1980) ICR 455
28 (2001) IRLR 468
29 (2001) IRLR 853
30 C-439/99 (2001) IRLR 848
31 (1999) IRLR 16
32 Directive 97/81
33 (1989) IRLR 241
34 (1990) IRLR 181
35 C 127/92 (1993) IRLR 591
36 (1997) IRLR 560
37 (1987) ICR 110
38 (1997) IRLR 699
39 (1988) ICR 278
40 (1998) IRLR 318
41 75/117/EEC
42 (1981) ICR 715
43 C171/88 (1989) IRLR 493
44 SI 2000/1551

2

Maternity and parental rights

ERICA NEUSTADT

Erica Neustadt has extensive experience as an employment law practitioner and an academic.

Introduction

This chapter looks at the law relating to maternity and parental leave. It explains the statutory rules and highlights changes in prospect. The legislation that will be considered primarily is the Employment Rights Act 1996 (ERA) and the Maternity and Parental Leave etc Regulations 1999 (MPL Regulations).[1]

The MPL Regulations came into force on 15 December 1999, and were amended by The Maternity and Parental Leave (Amendment) Regulations 2001, which came into force on 10 January 2002.[2]

As far as possible, this chapter is organised chronologically. Rights during pregnancy are addressed first, followed by maternity leave and rights during the post-birth period. Rights and obligations attaching to the return to work will then be examined. Miscellaneous issues such as health and safety and other employment rights, which may interact with maternity rights will be covered, followed by parental leave.

Finally, changes resulting from the Employment Act 2002 will be reviewed.

Remedies will be considered in association with the rights they protect. Where the remedies for breaches of maternity leave and parental leave rights are the same they will be dealt with together in the section on parental leave.

Maternity provisions

The law regulating maternity leave and benefits has, in the past, been very complicated, and often difficult to interpret and calculate. To a great extent, recent legislation has simplified this area. The Employment Act will make further changes, but, as far as maternity provisions are concerned, these are likely to centre on such things as length of leave and statutory pay levels, rather than the core rights.

European law, and, in particular, cases decided by the European Court of Justice have also influenced, and, in some cases, enhanced rights in this jurisdiction.

Maternity rights and obligations contained in the ERA and the MPL Regulations apply to employees only.

Time off for antenatal care

A woman has the right to paid time off work for the purpose of having antenatal care. There is no qualification period for this right which is contained in ERA Sections 55 and 56. A woman who is pregnant may take time off during working hours to attend antenatal appointments. This includes sufficient time to travel to and from work to the appointment together with the time necessary to attend the appointment itself. The right is to time off during normal working hours. An employer may not rearrange the employee's working hours to minimise the time that she is absent, nor may it require her to make up the time.

A woman may attend her first appointment without providing any proof to her employer of either her pregnancy or the appointment. After that, if her employer requests a certificate from her doctor, midwife or health visitor confirming the pregnancy, or proof that such an appointment has been made, she will lose her right to time off if she fails to provide such evidence.

ERA Section 56 sets out the entitlement to be paid for such time off. By Section 56(1), the employee should be paid at the appropriate hourly rate during her absence. (Note that this is subject to Section 56 (5), which provides that this does not override a woman's rights in relation to contractual remuneration). Again, this right is dependent upon a woman providing the same evidence as above that she is pregnant and that she has an antenatal appointment.

Section 56 provides detailed methods for calculating the amount a woman should be paid for her time off to attend antenatal appointments, although it may be simpler, where possible, and not to the employee's detriment, to agree to pay her the salary she would normally receive, as though she had not taken time off.

By ERA Section 57, an employee may complain to an employment tribunal that her employer has *unreasonably* refused to permit her to take time off, or having allowed time off, has failed to pay her for her absence. The complaint must be made during a three-month period triggered by the date of the antenatal appointment for which these rights were denied.

The remedies are hardly preventative. A tribunal may

(i) make a declaration that the employee's rights have been infringed
(ii) order appropriate payment where the employer has failed to pay the employee for time off, or
(iii) order the employer to pay the employee the amount to which she would have been entitled had her time off not been refused.

In the third scenario, where an employee has been denied time off, the employee has presumably worked instead and been paid wages during this period. It is unclear whether such wages are sufficient compensation or whether an additional payment will be ordered.

Childbirth

This is defined in MPL Regulation 2 as the birth of a living child, or the birth of a child whether living or dead, after 24 weeks of pregnancy. A stillbirth before the 24th week therefore will not amount to childbirth and the mother will not fall within the ambit of the maternity leave provisions. Her absence will be treated, legally, as sickness absence.

Maternity leave

There are three types of maternity leave: ordinary, compulsory and additional.

Ordinary Maternity Leave (OML)
The right to OML is contained in ERA Section 71:

> An employee may, provided that she satisfies any conditions which may be prescribed, be absent from work at any time during an ordinary maternity leave period.

There is no qualification period for OML – a woman is entitled to it, subject to satisfying conditions, from the moment she is employed.

The conditions for qualification are set out in MPL Regulation 4. These are that, at least 21 days before the date upon which she would like her OML to start (from April 2003 no later than the end of the 15th week before her expected week of childbirth), a woman must inform her employer of 3 things; that she is pregnant, the week during which she expects to have the baby and the date she wants her OML to start. If for any reason it is not "reasonably practicable" to give the prescribed notice, a woman should give notice as soon as possible. This information may be given orally unless the employer requires it in writing. If requested to do so by her employer, a woman must also provide a certificate from a doctor or midwife which sets out the expected week of childbirth.

By ERA Section 71(3), the period of OML is 18 weeks (26 weeks from April 2003), and a woman may choose when her OML is to start, with the limitation that she may not start her leave before the 11th week before the expected week of confinement.[3]

A woman's OML will begin on the earliest of three dates:[4]
(i)   the date on which she has told her employer that she wants it to start, or
(ii) if the beginning of the 6th week (4th week from April 2003) before the expected week of birth has passed, the first day upon which she is absent from work, wholly or partly because of pregnancy, or
(iii) the day her child is born.

Thus, if a woman has an antenatal appointment which requires a day off work, or is ill for a reason related to her pregnancy, this may trigger her OML. Presumably an employer may agree with the employee, if it suits both parties, to waive this provision. If OML is triggered automatically, the employee must still take action to preserve her right to it.

Where she is absent after the beginning of the sixth week, she should notify the employer as soon as reasonably practicable that her absence is pregnancy-related. If OML is triggered by the birth itself, an employee must notify her employer as soon as reasonably practicable that she has given birth. All notification should be in writing if requested by the employer.

During OML, an employee is entitled, except for remuneration, to the benefit of term and conditions of employment, which would have applied had she not been absent (ERA Section 71 (4)(a)). Note that "terms and conditions" are drawn very widely. ERA Section 71 (5) makes it clear that they include matters connected with the employee's employment whether or not they arise under the contract of employment. An employer should therefore be extremely hesitant about withholding any elements during OML that a woman receives whilst at work.

What does the suspension of the employee's right to remuneration mean in practical terms?

"Remuneration" is defined in several different places; for the purposes of ERA Section 71, the relevant definition is contained at MPL Regulation 9, where it is specified that remuneration includes only wages and salary. This is a narrow definition. Thus, the benefit of a company car, private health insurance and any bonus payment that cannot be defined as wages and salary should be paid to the employee as though she was at work throughout this period. Annual holiday should continue to accrue and salary reviews should ignore her absence.

In *Gillespie v Northern Health and Social Services Board (1996)*[5] the applicants argued that any reduction in pay and benefits during maternity leave amounted to direct sex discrimination contrary to Article 119 (now 141) of the EC Treaty, the Equal Pay Directive or the Equal Treatment Directive, irrespective of the comparable treatment of men. They also claimed discrimination on the basis that they received no benefit from a back-dated pay increase, awarded during the time they were on maternity leave.

The European Court of Justice held that

women taking maternity leave are in a special position, which requires them to be afforded special protection, but which is not comparable with that of a man or a woman actually at work.

Although [maternity pay] constitutes "pay" within Article [141] . . . and the Equal Pay Directive, ...neither Article [141] or the [Equal Pay] Directive required that women should continue to receive full pay during maternity leave.

A woman on maternity leave must receive a pay rise awarded before or during maternity leave... even if backdated.

This decision concerned a period before the implementation of the Pregnant Workers Directive, and at this time, the court held that it was for the national legislature to set the amount of the benefit, with the proviso that such amount should not be

so low as to undermine the purpose of maternity leave, namely the protection of women before and after giving birth.

It has subsequently been held[6] that the Pregnant Workers Directive determines that such pay must be adequate.

A woman is bound, during the period of OML, to honour any obligations arising out of her terms and conditions of employment, which are not inconsistent with her temporary absence from work.[7]

Following OML, a woman is entitled to return to her previous job. This right is, to an extent, qualified by ERA Section 71(7): she is in fact entitled to return to a job carrying the same seniority, pension rights and

similar rights as they would have been if she had not been absent (subject to paragraph 5 of schedule 5 to the Social Security Act 1989 (equal treatment under pension schemes: maternity)), and ... on terms and conditions not less favourable than those which would have applied if she had not been absent.

This last emphasises a woman's right to benefit from an enhancement of terms and conditions occurring during absence on OML.

A woman is automatically entitled to return to work at the end of her OML and there are no requirements for notifying her employer. If the employer refuses to continue to employ the woman, this will amount to unfair dismissal under MPL Regulation 20.

By MPL Regulation 11, where a woman wishes to return earlier than at the end of 18 weeks, she must give her employer at least 21 days' notice of her intention to do so (28 days' notice from April 2003). If she attempts to return to work without having given this notice, her employer is entitled not to accept her return: it may be postponed for 21 days (effectively providing the employer with the requisite 21 days' notice) (28 days' notice from April 2003). If an employee's return has been postponed in this way, but she returns to work nevertheless, MPL Regulation 11 releases the employer from any obligation to pay her.

Compulsory Maternity Leave (CML)

CML applies to everyone qualifying for OML. It falls within the period of OML. Women are obliged to take maternity leave for two weeks following the birth of a child.

By ERA Section 72 and MPL Regulation 8, an employer must not allow a woman to work for the two weeks starting with the day of her child's birth.

Any employer allowing a woman to work during this period will be guilty of an offence and liable on conviction to a fine not exceeding level 2 on the standard scale.

Additional Maternity Leave (AML)

The right to AML is contained in ERA Section 73 and MPL Regulation 5.

When is additional maternity leave granted?

A woman is entitled to AML if
(i)   she is entitled to OML, and
(ii)   she has, at the beginning of the eleventh week (fourteenth week from April 2003) before the expected week of childbirth, accrued at least a year's (26 weeks from April 2003) continuous employment with her employer.

Calculating continuous employment is done in accordance with ERA Sections 210 to 218. A period of continuous employment is typically calculated from the date that an employee starts work. To establish the first day of employment or the period of continuous employment is not always as simple as it sounds; not all employment counts towards the continuous period. For instance, if the employee started working for the employer on a temporary contract, and then accepts a permanent contract, the time spent working under the first, temporary contract is unlikely to count towards continuous employment under the subsequent contract.

So what employment counts? Any week during the whole or part of which the employee's relationship with the employer is governed by a contract of employment counts. This is so even where the employee is sick, absent because of a temporary cessation of work, or absent in circumstances where, by arrangement or custom, she is regarded as continuing to be employed by her employer.[8]

The recent case of *Curr v Marks and Spencer plc*[9] is of interest here. Ms Curr's continuous employment with Marks and Spencer began in 1973. She became pregnant in 1989 and took maternity leave. Whilst on leave, she decided to take advantage of her employer's child break scheme, which allowed for a prolonged absence from work, and the ability to return at a management level. To take part in the scheme, an employee had to resign, (which Ms Curr did in November 1990), and, during each year of the break, work a minimum of 2 weeks full-time, or the equivalent time part-time. All employee benefits stopped during the break. In 1995, after four years on the scheme, Ms Curr returned to her employment. She was made redundant in 1999. Her redundancy package was calculated on the basis of 5 years' employment. (In other words, on the basis of her employment following, but not before or including, her participation in the child break scheme). She complained to a tribunal of unlawful deduction of wages.

The tribunal had to decide when Ms Curr's continuity of employment began. The key issue was whether taking part in the child break scheme had broken continuity. On appeal, it was held that the scheme was an arrangement that fell within ERA Section 212 (3) and that the contacts between the parties whilst Ms Curr was on the scheme clearly continued the relationship between the parties (even though the relationship did not amount to a contract of employment). As a result, Ms Curr had continuity of employment from 1973.

The Court of Appeal has subsequently overturned this decision, on the basis that Ms Curr's resignation broke continuity of employment.

Where an employee is entitled to AML, this additional period may continue until the end of the 29th week beginning with the week of childbirth (26 weeks from the end of OML, from April 2003).[10] The exception to this is where the employee is dismissed whilst absent on OML or AML, before she would otherwise have returned to work. In this case, the period of maternity leave ends at the time of the dismissal. In other words, if a woman is dismissed whilst on maternity leave, termination of her contract of employment terminates her leave, and the fact that she is on maternity leave cannot prevent such termination.

AML starts when OML ends. So, currently, if a woman starts her OML at the earliest possible time, (11 weeks before the expected week of childbirth), and her child arrives on time, she will have seven weeks of OML left following the birth, and her AML will only start after that. In this case she would only be entitled to 22 weeks' AML as her total entitlement to maternity leave is for 29 weeks following the birth.

Contractual rights during any period of AML are far more limited than those during OML. By ERA Section 73 and MPL Regulation 17, a woman is only entitled to the benefit of the employer's implied term of trust and confidence, plus the basic contractual terms, such as notice of termination, compensation for redundancy, and disciplinary or grievance procedures.

During the AML period, a woman continues to be bound by the implied obligation of good faith and any contractual terms relating to notice of termination of contract, confidential information, acceptance of gifts or other benefits or her participation in any other business.

MPL Regulation 18 stipulates that a woman returning from AML is entitled to the job that she was employed to do before her absence. If it is not reasonably practicable for her employer to give her the same job, she may be given another job that is both suitable and appropriate for her to do. She is entitled to terms and conditions of remuneration which are "not less favourable" than she would have had if she had not been absent since she went on OML. Generally, her terms and conditions of employment must not be less favourable than they would have been had she not taken AML.

She is entitled to the seniority, pension rights and "similar rights" that she would have had if the period of her employment before taking AML were continuous with her employment following her return to work.[11] This suggests that such rights are suspended, but not lost, during AML. Further, an employer who believes that it is not reasonably practicable for the woman to return to the same job must be exceptionally careful to ensure that the terms of any new post match up to those of her previous position.

When returning to work without taking her full entitlement to AML, an employee must give her employer not less than 21 days' notice of her intention to return (28 days from April 2003). Where an employee fails to give notice of early return, then as with OML, an employer can postpone her return for 21 days (28 days from April 2003), and need not pay her if she returns during this period.[12]

Where an employee wants to return at the end of AML, the position is somewhat different. In accordance with MPL Regulation 4, she will already have given her employer notice of her pregnancy, the week that her child is expected and provided any supporting documentation requested by the employer.

Beyond this, the onus is on the employer to make the first move regarding notice of intention to return. Where a woman qualifies for AML, pursuant to MPL Regulation 12, her employer may request her, not earlier than 21 days before the end of her OML, to provide written notification of the date the child was born and whether she intends to return to work following AML. The employee must respond within 21 days of receiving this request. If she does not do so, she loses her rights under MPL Regulations 19 and 20 to protection from detriment and the right to claim unfair dismissal (see below). The employer's request must be written and must include a statement explaining how the employee can calculate the date that her AML will end. It must also warn her that she will lose her statutory protection if she fails to respond within the 21-day time limit. Note that the Maternity and Parental Leave Amendment Regulations 2002 remove MPL Regulation 12.

Termination of the contract of employment during maternity leave

Termination in three ways will be considered: resignation by the employee, redundancy or dismissal.

Resignation

If an employee decides not to return after maternity leave, she should resign in accordance with the terms of her contract of employment. Her right to statutory maternity pay is not affected by her resignation.

Where she has a contractual right to enhanced maternity pay, any conditions attached to her non-return, such as repayment of any amount above statutory levels, may be enforced. For example, an employer may have a policy of paying additional sums during maternity leave, on condition that the employee returns to work, or continues employment, at the end of the leave period for a specified time, such as a year. Where the employee resigns and therefore fails to comply with any such conditions, the policy may allow for the additional sums to be repaid. The statutory element is, of course, not repayable.

Where a woman simply does not turn up at the time that she should return, it may be that she is resigning in response to a perceived breach of contract by her employer. This should be investigated to minimise the employer's exposure to a possible claim for constructive dismissal.

Redundancy

Provided that a woman is genuinely redundant, there is no obligation on the employer to continue her employment contract just because she is pregnant or on maternity leave. To this extent, there is no positive discrimination. On the other hand, where an employer has a genuine need to make redundancies, and chooses a woman for redundancy because she is either pregnant or on maternity leave, this will be automatically unfair. The selection criteria for redundancy must ignore such issues.

MPL Regulation 10 deals with the situation where an employee becomes redundant during her OML or AML. In this case, if there is a suitable available vacancy, her employer has a duty to offer it to her, prior to termination of her existing contract. A failure to do so will render the dismissal automatically unfair. There is no qualification period for a claim of unfair dismissal in these circumstances. Her employer should look widely to establish if there is such a vacancy: it could be with the original employer, an associated employer or a successor.

An employer's ignorance of the existence of such a vacancy is no defence. Such a vacancy will be appropriate where the work to be done is both suitable in relation to the employee and appropriate for her to do in the circumstances.

Further, the job's provisions regarding the capacity in which and place that she is to be employed, and regarding any other terms and conditions of her new employment, should not be substantially less favourable to her than if she had continued to be employed under her previous contract.

Unfair dismissal

A woman who is dismissed for a reason connected with either her pregnancy, having given birth, taken maternity leave, or as a consequence of her suspension from work on maternity grounds,[13] (for example, having been selected for redundancy on any of these bases), will be regarded as having been automatically unfairly dismissed. In *Clayton v Vigers*,[14] no causal connection between the reason for dismissal and the pregnancy was necessary.

Very small employers are exempt from this liability. Where the employer's workforce, together with that of any associated employer, is less than 5 before the end of the woman's AML or dismissal, and it is not reasonably practicable for the employer to allow the woman to return to a suitable and appropriate job, this is an exception to the automatic unfairness rule.[15]

Further, it may be that it is not reasonably practicable for an employer to offer the returning employee a job that is both suitable and appropriate, but an associated employer is able to do so. In this case, if the woman accepts or unreasonably refuses this offer, this will not be an automatically unfair dismissal.[16]

Sex discrimination

Employees who are dismissed for reasons connected with pregnancy, birth, maternity leave or suspension, (see below) may also have a claim under the sex discrimination legislation.

The more likely claim in these circumstances is that of direct discrimination. This is less favourable treatment of a person on the ground of his or her sex. Direct discrimination has been considered in the leading cases in this area, starting with *Webb v EMO Air Cargo (UK) Ltd.*[17] This line of cases makes it clear that pregnancy is a special case and that there is no need for a male comparator to demonstrate direct discrimination.

Indirect discrimination occurs where an employer applies a requirement or condition to a person or group of one sex that it would apply equally to a person or group of the opposite sex, but the effect on one sex, compared with the effect on the other, is disproportionate and detrimental.

Note that changes to the burden of proof and the definition of indirect discrimination have been made by the Burden of Proof Directive.[18] This was implemented as law in this jurisdiction on 12 October 2001, by the Sex Discrimination (Indirect Discrimination and Burden of Proof) Regulations 2001.[19]

These Regulations amend the Sex Discrimination Act 1975. Now, indirect discrimination may be found where an apparently neutral provision, criterion or practice disadvantages a substantially higher proportion of the members of one sex than the other. This is subject to the defence that such a provision, criterion or practice is appropriate and necessary and can be justified by objective factors unrelated to sex. This removes the need for an employee to prove any requirement or condition imposed. All the employee needs to show is a discriminatory practice. Indirect discrimination is more likely to be relevant to issues concerning women as primary carers for children, such as requests for part-time work, or having to work shift systems.[20]

Women may be able to claim sex discrimination on a further ground; the Sex Discrimination Act 1975 outlaws discrimination on the ground of marital status. It remains true that the majority of women with children are married and therefore to discriminate against a woman for reasons related to her pregnancy might also be sex discrimination on the basis of marital status. Here, the comparison would be that of married, with unmarried women.

Protection from detriment, automatically unfair dismissal & complaint to an employment tribunal

ERA Section 99 and the MPL Regulations 19 and 20 deal with both protection of a woman's rights whilst pregnant or on maternity leave, and protection of the rights of an employee taking parental leave. These issues are therefore considered together below.

Statutory maternity pay (SMP)

SMP is payable for 18 weeks to all qualifying employees (26 weeks after April 2003). It is not dependent on the employee returning to work. The statutory source of this right is the Maternity Allowance and Statutory Maternity Pay Regulations 1994.[21]

SMP is subject to tax and National Insurance contributions, and is generally paid through the employer's payroll. Employers must keep records of such payments, and can reclaim the majority of, or, if a small employer, all, SMP paid.

Failure by the employer to keep records is a criminal offence.

To qualify for SMP, a woman must
(i)   be an employee
(ii)   be pregnant at the start of the 11th week before the baby is due, or have had the baby by then
(iii)   have worked for the employer for at least 26 weeks ending with the qualifying week, which is the 15th week before the expected week of childbirth
(iv)   had normal weekly earnings at a rate not less than the lower earnings limit for National Insurance contributions
(v)   have stopped working, (that is, an employee may not receive SMP at the same time as receiving her normal salary)
(vi)   be over 16
(vii)   give at least 21 days' notice of intention to take maternity leave
(viii) produce medical evidence of the expected week of childbirth.

Failure to comply with any of these conditions will disqualify a woman from receiving SMP.

Maternity allowance

This is paid to women who do not qualify for SMP but who have worked and paid national insurance contributions for at least 26 weeks during the 66 weeks before the expected week of childbirth. It is payable for a maximum period of 18 weeks (26 weeks from April 2003). The earliest date upon which the 18-week period may start is the beginning of the 11th week before the expected week of childbirth.

Pregnancy-related illness

The dismissal of any woman during her pregnancy for absence from work caused by pregnancy-related illness is direct discrimination. There is no need for a comparison with the treatment of any other employee to establish this.

In *Brown v Rentokil Ltd*,[22] Ms Brown was absent over a long period due to a variety of pregnancy-related illnesses. In accordance with its rule that employees who exceeded 26 weeks' continuous sick leave would be dismissed, her employer terminated her employment.

The ECJ held

> Dismissal of a woman at any time during her pregnancy for absences...caused by an illness resulting from that pregnancy is direct discrimination on the grounds of sex contrary to the EC Equal Treatment Directive.

The ECJ further found that since a dismissal on the ground of pregnancy is unique to women, pregnant workers who are unfit for work cannot be compared with male workers who are ill.

A woman who is unable to return at the end of her maternity leave is no longer treated as a special case, but as any other sick employee. This was established in *Hertz*[23] and confirmed in *Brown v Rentokil Ltd*.

> Absence after maternity leave may be taken into account under the same conditions as a man's absence through incapacity for work of the same duration.

Request to return on a part-time contract

The Part-time Workers (Prevention of Less Favourable Treatment) Regulations[24] do not provide a statutory right to employees to change from a full-time to a part-time contract. However, the employer is obliged to take such a request seriously. If an employer unreasonably refuses to consider a request to go part-time, it risks a claim of indirect sex discrimination, following *British Telecommunications plc v Roberts and Longstaffe*.[25]

To avoid liability, the employer must be able to show good objective reasons why the job must be carried out by a full-time worker. The courts require a balance to be struck between the discriminatory impact of such a requirement and the employer's reasonable commercial needs. The employer will have to show that there is a requirement for a full-time worker, not merely that it is preferable or convenient.

Suspension from work on maternity grounds

The ERA contains a general provision covering the situation where an employer suspends an employee on medical grounds. Such an employee is entitled to be paid by the employer during such suspension for a maximum of 26 weeks,[26] provided that he or she has at least one month's continuous employment ending with the day before that on which the period of suspension began.

Where an employee is suspended on grounds of maternity, this means where, because of any relevant requirement or relevant recommendation, she is suspended from work by her employer because she is pregnant, has recently given birth or is breastfeeding a child.[27] "Relevant requirement" means a requirement imposed by or under a specified provision of a statute or statutory instrument, and "relevant recommendation" means a recommendation in a specified provision of a code of practice issued or approved under Section 16 of the Health and Safety at Work etc Act 1974 (HSWA).

HSWA Section 16 provides for the Health and Safety Commission, with the approval of the Secretary of State, to approve codes of practice for the purpose of giving practical guidance on how to carry out various duties specified in HSWA Sections 2 to 7. Where such a code is approved, breach of such a code, whilst not giving rise to civil or criminal liability, may be used as evidence in criminal proceedings. "Specified provision" means a provision for the time being specified in an order made by the Secretary of State.

An employee is suspended from work on maternity grounds only if, and for so long as, her contract of employment continues with her employer, but she is not given any work to do, or does not do the work that she normally did, before being suspended.

Where an employer is able to offer suitable alternative work to the employee, and this is a viable alternative to suspending her, the employee has the right to be offered this work before being suspended on maternity grounds.[28] For such work to qualify as suitable, it must be both suitable to her and appropriate for her to do in the circumstances. Further, if the terms and conditions of her doing this work are different from her contractual terms and conditions for carrying out her usual work, these substitute terms must not be substantially less favourable. It does not appear from the ERA that the employee is obliged to accept an offer of suitable alternative work. However, her right to remuneration, which is preserved if she is suspended, will be lost if she unreasonably refuses.[29]

The amount of remuneration payable to the employee is a week's pay (calculated in accordance with ERA Sections 220 to 225) for every week of suspension. Where suspension is only for part of a week, remuneration will be pro-rated. The statutory right to remuneration does not affect an employee's right to contractual remuneration. Paid contractual remuneration goes towards discharging an employer's liability to pay statutory remuneration, and any payment of statutory remuneration goes towards discharging an employer's liability to pay contractual remuneration.[30]

An employee may complain to an employment tribunal that the employer has failed to pay the appropriate amount of remuneration during suspension from work. Such a complaint must be presented to the tribunal within three months of any day on which a complaint arose. The tribunal has the usual discretion to extend this time limit where it is satisfied that it was not reasonably practicable for the complaint to be presented within the three months.[31] Presumably, an employee could also make a complaint of unauthorised deductions under ERA Section 13.

Health and safety

Employers are under a duty to carry out suitable and sufficient risk assessments of the risks to the health and safety of its employees (and others) of the workplace under Regulation 3 (1) of the Management of Health and Safety at Work Regulations (1999).[32]

As part of this, Regulation 16 obliges employers to consider what risks might be posed to new or expectant mothers, because of their condition, or to the baby, by any processes, working conditions, or physical, biological or chemical agents.

Parental leave

Part III of the MPL Regulations implements the directive on the framework agreement on parental leave, as concluded by the social partners and adopted by the Council of the European Union.

In the majority of Member States, the concept of parental leave was nothing new, but long established at national level. Therefore, the European legislation did not present a culture shock, and in fact drew on the schemes already in place around the Union. This was not the case in the UK. Parental leave is unprecedented and met with resistance from both the state and employers' representatives. Probably as a result of this lack of cultural familiarity, the parental leave directive was implemented in a minimalist way in this jurisdiction.

References to the MPL Regulations will, unless otherwise stated, include changes made by the Maternity and Parental Leave (Amendment) Regulations 2001, ("the amendments").[33]

The MPL Regulations provide a default position for employees who have no contractual provision for, or less favourable rights to, parental leave under their employment contracts, or are not covered by collective or workforce agreements[34] incorporated into their contracts. Thus, the MPL Regulations provide a "bottom line" for such rights.[35]

There is no provision in the legislation for payment for parental leave.

The MPL Regulations only apply to employees[36] (someone entering into or working under a contract of employment), and not workers. Qualification is earned by having one year's continuous employment, together with "parental responsibility" for a child.

Parental leave accrues per parent, per child. So a married couple with two children will each be entitled to 13 weeks' leave per child over the first five years of each child's life. Therefore, in total, that family will be entitled to 52 weeks' leave. A family consisting of a single parent with two children will be entitled to a total of 26 weeks' leave. Parental leave is not transferable from one parent to another.

Where a child's mother and father are married to each other at the time of the child's birth, they will each have parental responsibility for that child. Where they are not married, the child's mother will have sole parental responsibility, unless the father acquires such responsibility. He may do so by successfully seeking a court order or by reaching a "parental responsibility agreement" with the mother.[37] In general, only a child's mother and father may have parental responsibility. No other adult, for example, a grandparent, appears to be able to have parental responsibility.[38]

Initially the right to parental leave was only available to employees with parental responsibility for children born or adopted on or after 15 December 1999. This limitation was challenged by the TUC by way of judicial review[39] and the MPL Regulations have now been amended so that the right to parental leave is available to all those with parental responsibility for children who were under five years old on 15 December 1999. This affects parents of children born or adopted between 15 December 1994 and 14 December 1999, who now have until 31 March 2005 to take their leave.

Entitlement

Leave must normally be taken before the child's fifth birthday.[40] An employee with responsibility for a child is entitled to 13 weeks' leave over this period,[41] up to a maximum of four weeks per child, per year.[42]

Where a child is entitled to a disability living allowance, the entitlement is for 18 weeks' parental leave. This may be taken until the child's eighteenth birthday. It applies to parents of children born on or after 15 December 1994.

A year is the period of 12 months beginning with the date that the employee first became entitled to parental leave for the child in question.

Where a person changes job and begins to work under a new contract of employment, he or she will not be entitled to parental leave until a year's continuous employment has accrued. In this case, a year will be measured from the date the employee most recently became entitled to take parental leave in respect of that child.[43]

An exception to this is made by the amendments. Parents of children born or adopted between 15 December 1994 and 14 December 1999 may rely on a period of at least one year's continuous service with a previous employer in order to qualify for parental leave.[44] Parents wishing to take advantage of this amendment must give their current employer notice of the relevant period of notice, and, if reasonably required, evidence.[45] This amendment covers parents who controversially did not qualify for parental leave when the MPL Regulations were first introduced, and who risk being excluded under the amendments, because they have changed jobs and have not accrued enough continuous employment in their new post.

A week's leave

Where an employee's contract provides that he or she works a standard period per week, a week's leave is equal to that period. Where working hours vary from week to week, or over a longer period, or where the contract requires work during some weeks, but not during others, a week's leave for the purpose of the MPL Regulations is calculated by totalling all the periods over the course of a year that an employee is normally required to work, and dividing this total by 52.

Unless the contract spells out very specifically the irregular working pattern that an employee in this situation has, or an employee has been working for a sufficient time in this way, so that the calculation may be done by reference to past periods of work, there is room for uncertainty in carrying out this calculation. Where records have been kept for payroll purposes, these may help.

The MPL Regulations suggest that an employee may take parental leave of periods of less than one week, and that he or she will complete a week's leave when the aggregate of the time taken equals the period of one week.[46] However, this is misleading and at odds with the MPL Regulations Schedule 2 which states the true position. Schedule 2 requires that parental leave may only be taken in minimum units of one week, unless the child in respect of whom leave is being taken is entitled to a disability living allowance.[47] Where a child does receive a disability living allowance, this leave can be taken flexibly in blocks of a day or more, up to four weeks in total each year. The timing of the leave has to be agreed with the employer and notice has to be given.[48]

This lack of flexibility for the majority undermines the effectiveness of parental leave. It is frequently unnecessary and unaffordable for parents of children who are not in receipt of a disability living allowance to take a whole week as parental leave. This provision is also unhelpful to children, as a parent is likely to take no parental leave rather than lose a whole week's pay. Businesses too will have to manage without a member of staff for a whole week rather than just as long as is necessary. This may well be an area where employers and employees may reach agreement about how parental leave will work, and agree that the minimum unit of leave may be a day or half a day.

"Qualifying" children

The right to parental leave may be exercised in respect of a child younger than five, or, where a child is entitled to a disability living allowance, before he or she reaches 18. Where the child is adopted, leave may be taken before the fifth anniversary of the date of the placement for adoption, or the child's eighteenth birthday, whichever is the earlier.[49]

An employer may require such evidence to be produced by the employee as is reasonably required

(i)   to demonstrate the employee's current or expected responsibility for the child for which the employee wishes to take parental leave

(ii)   to show the child's date of birth, or date of placement for adoption, and

(iii) where leave is required in respect of a child entitled to disability living allowance

(iv) to show the child's entitlement to that allowance.

An employee may not exercise an entitlement to parental leave unless he or she has complied with such a request.[50]

Notice

The employee must also give the employer notice of the proposed period of parental leave. Generally, the notice required will specify the dates upon which the period of leave is to begin and end, and must be given to the employer at least 21 days before the day that leave is to start.

The exceptions to this are as follows:

(i)   Where the employee is the father of an unborn child, and the period of leave is to be triggered by the child's birth, the employee's notice should specify the expected week of childbirth and the duration of the period of leave. It should be given at least 21 days before the beginning of the expected week of childbirth.

(ii)   To clarify, notice should not be given 21 days before the due date of birth itself, but before the Sunday at the beginning of the week during which it is expected that the birth will occur.

(iii) Where leave is to be taken following the placement of a child with the employee for adoption, and the leave is to start on the date of the placement, the notice should specify the week in which the placement is expected to happen, the duration of the leave and, as above, be given to the employer at least 21 days before the beginning of that week. If that is not reasonably practicable, notice should be given as soon as is reasonably practicable.[51]

Postponement of leave[52]

Unless leave is requested in anticipation of the birth or adoption of a child, the employer may refuse to allow leave to be taken at the requested time if it considers that such leave would unduly disrupt its business. The employer may only refuse a request for leave if it agrees to permit the employee to take a substitute period of leave. This substitute period should be for the same length of leave, and should be scheduled to begin on a date no later than six months after the date that the refused leave would have started.

The employer must give the employee written notice of postponement within seven days of the employee's notice. This means that where an employee gives notice to the employer more than 21 days before the start date of the requested leave, the employer is still obliged to reply within the seven-day period. It should not count 21 days back from the start date of the requested leave and base the seven-day period on that calculation. The employer's notice should state the reasons for the postponement and specify the dates of the substitute period of leave that the employer agrees the employee may take.

On a strict reading of the legislation, it would seem that the employer may decide unilaterally when, within the following six months, the employee should take the leave. Whilst there is a duty to consult with the employee regarding substitute leave, there is no requirement for agreement between the parties, nor any duty on the employer to act reasonably. (Although see enforcement, below). If an employer does decide on a substitute period which the employee does not want, is the employee obliged to take leave then? Although in effect it would seem not, as this might be viewed as detriment (see below) particularly in view of the non-payment of parental leave, the fact that there is a need only for consultation and not agreement obfuscates the answer.

Where the postponement of parental leave is near the end of an employee's entitlement, for example, when the child reaches five, an employee will not lose the leave that has been postponed, but may take it after the child's fifth birthday.[53]

The status of the contract of employment during parental leave

The status of the contract whilst an employee is on parental leave is the same as during AML. Thus, the contract continues to subsist, but rights do not accrue, during the period of parental leave. Also, an employee on parental leave is entitled to the benefit of the employer's obligation of trust and confidence and any contractual terms relating to notice of termination of contract, compensation for redundancy and disciplinary or grievance procedures.

Similarly, the employee is bound by his or her implied obligation of good faith to the employer, and any terms and conditions of employment relating to notice of termination of contract, the disclosure of confidential information, acceptance of gifts or other benefits and participation in any other business.[54]

Right to return[55]

The basic position is that an employee who has taken parental leave of four weeks or less has the right to return from leave to the job that he or she was doing before taking leave.

Where an employee takes parental leave for a period greater than 4 weeks, (presumably by taking two years' entitlement, back to back), he or she is entitled to return to the same job unless it is not reasonably practicable. In this case, the employee is entitled to return to another job which is both suitable and appropriate to him or her in the circumstances.

If an employee takes parental leave immediately following AML, she is entitled to return to the same job, unless it would not have been reasonably practicable to return to that job at the end of AML *and* it is not reasonably practicable for the employer to permit her to return to that job following parental leave.

This must beg the question of what rights a woman has, and what duties the employer owes, where the same job would have been available had the employee returned to work straight after AML, but, during the period of parental leave following on from AML, it became impracticable for her to return to it. There is no explanation why a woman who seeks to prolong her maternity leave by taking parental leave compromises a degree of protection by doing so.

An employee has the right to return with the same seniority, pension rights and similar rights that he or she would have had if his or her employment prior to taking parental leave were continuous with his or her employment following the return to work.

> An employee also has the right to return on terms and conditions regarding remuneration not less favourable than those which would have been applicable to him or her
> (i)   if returning from parental leave, at the commencement of the period of parental leave
> (ii)   if returning from parental leave leave taken immediately after AML, at the beginning of OML.

Bearing in mind that, during a woman's OML, she is entitled to benefit from any pay rises as though she had not been absent, it is strange that if she takes parental leave after AML, her rights regarding remuneration appear to be suspended for the entirety of the period for which she is on leave. This again is inconsistent, but can only point to a diminution of the rights of a woman who follows her AML with parental leave. It may also be open to challenge.

Force majeure

Under ERA Section 57A, an employee has a right to take a reasonable amount of "emergency leave" to take necessary action in response to a range of domestic demands. These include providing assistance when a dependant falls ill, dies, or their care arrangements are disrupted, at school or otherwise.

> An employee's "dependant" may include, in addition to immediate family members
> (i)   a person who lives in the same household as the employee, otherwise than.. his employee, tenant, lodger or boarder
> (ii)   any person who reasonably relies on the employee
>   – for assistance…when the person falls ill or is injured or assaulted, or
>   – to make arrangements for the provision of care in the event of illness or injury

(iii) any person who reasonably relies on the employee to make arrangements for the provision of care.

Thus, the word "dependant" is framed widely. It may include cohabitees of either sex, who are not traditionally given rights by legislation. The dependency relationship is clearly a less stringent relationship to show than that of "parental responsibility" in the MPL Regulations. Thus, it is clear that a grandparent could reasonably take emergency leave.

The categories of incident qualifying for emergency leave are set out apparently as an exhaustive list.[56]

In order to qualify for this right to emergency leave, the employee must explain the reason for absence to the employer. Here, the notice provisions are realistic, as the employee is obliged to inform the employer as soon as reasonably practicable. In other words, the employee may deal with the emergency first, as long as he or she informs the employer what is happening as soon as possible. Where an employee cannot explain the reason for absence to the employer until after his or her return to work, he or she should tell the employer how long the absence is expected to last.

Leave taken by an employee under this provision must be reasonable. There is no provision for it to be paid. There is no qualification period. Typically, employers have long provided such a right informally, and do not generally suspend pay. These are again minimum standards and cannot be ousted by less favourable provisions in a collective or workplace agreement.

Protection from detriment

Employees are protected from detriment by reference to ERA Section 47C for either taking or seeking to take maternity or parental leave under the MPL Regulations or time off under ERA Section 57A. The entitlement is not to be subjected to any detriment by any act or deliberate failure to act by the employer for any of the listed reasons.[56A]

These are, that the employee

(i) is pregnant
(ii) has given birth
(iii) has been suspended from work, or is the subject of a recommendation to suspend, on the grounds of maternity
(iv) has taken or tried to take OML, AML, parental leave or time off for dependants under Section 57A
(v) has declined to sign a workforce agreement for the purposes of the MPL Regulations or
(vi) being an employee representative or a candidate in such an election, performed or proposed to perform such functions or activities.

This provision makes the protection offered to a woman who takes or tries to take OML very wide. It covers acts or deliberate failure to act if, during OML, the employee

> avails herself of the benefit of any of the terms and conditions of her employment that are preserved by ERA Section 71....

That is, any terms and conditions of her contract, plus any matters connected with her employment, whether or not they arise under her contract. As ever, the exception to this is any terms and conditions about remuneration.

Protection against detriment relating to giving birth applies only to acts (or failures to act) which happen during OML or AML. Where an act continues over a period of time, the date of that act (for the purposes of calculating time) is the last date of that period. The date of any failure to act is treated as being the date of the decision not to act. This may be problematic; sometimes the decision will be a passive rather than a conscious one, which will be difficult to date. However, some further help is given; unless there is evidence establishing the contrary, an employer shall have been taken to decide not to act

(i) when it does an act inconsistent with doing the failed act, or
(ii) when it does nothing inconsistent, when the period expires within which the employer might reasonably have been expected to do the failed act if it were to be done.

The right to complain to an employment tribunal is contained in three places; ERA Section 48 allows for complaint of detriment in contravention of Section 47C. Section 57B allows complaint of the employer's refusal to allow leave under Section 57A. Section 80 allows complaint of unreasonable postponement or prevention of parental leave.

An employee should make complaint of detriment pursuant to Section 47C within three months starting with the date of the act or failure to act complained about. Where the complaint refers to a series or acts or failures, time starts to run from the last of the series. A tribunal has discretion to extend this period where it is satisfied that it was not reasonably practicable for the employee to have presented the complaint within the time limit.

Having made a complaint, the onus is on the employer to show the ground on which any act, or failure to act, was carried out. Complaint of unreasonable refusal to allow leave pursuant to Section 57B must be made within three months of the date the refusal occurred, subject to the tribunal's discretion to extend as above. There is no transfer of any onus to the employer.

Under Section 80, an employee may complain to an employment tribunal that his or her employer has unreasonably postponed a requested period of parental leave, or has prevented or attempted to prevent the employee from taking parental leave. The complaint must be presented within three months of the date, or last date of the matters complained of, subject again to the tribunal's discretion to extend. There is no transfer of any onus to the employer.

It is arguable, since Section 47C covers an employer's failure to act, but Sections 57B and 80 do not, that these latter sections do not cover an employer's negative action. There are also interpretative difficulties with Section 80.

Schedule 2 (6)(b) to the MPL Regulations allows an employer to postpone parental leave where

> the employer considers that the operation of his business would be unduly disrupted if the employee took leave during the period identified ...

Section 80, as noted, provides that

> an employee may present a complaint to an employment tribunal that his employer ... has unreasonably postponed a period of parental leave requested by the employee ...

It is not obvious how to reconcile these two provisions. This is because Schedule 2(6) allows the employer to make a subjective evaluation of the potential effect of the employee's leave on business needs; there is no obligation to make such an evaluation, or a decision to postpone leave reasonably. However, the remedy at Section 80 is for *unreasonable* postponement.

Under Section 80, it is for the employee to show unreasonableness by the employer. The employer is also provided with the strong defence that in its assessment, its business would have been unduly disrupted. It remains to be seen if an employment tribunal would be prepared to substitute the employer's subjective assessment with its own objective one.

Remedies[57]

Where an employment tribunal finds a complaint of detriment well founded, there are various remedies it can offer. First, it shall make a declaration of its finding of detrimental treatment. Second, it may also award such compensation to the employee as is just and equitable, taking into account

(i) any expenses reasonably incurred by the employee because of the act or failure complained about, and

(ii) loss of any benefit resulting from the act or failure that the employee might reasonably be expected to have received had the act or failure not occurred.

A tribunal may consider whether the employee caused or contributed to his or her own loss. Where it finds this is so, it must reduce any compensation by a proportion which justly reflects the degree to which the employee is to blame. The employee is, in any event, under a common law duty to mitigate his or her loss where possible. Nevertheless, this duty is specifically set out in relation to detrimental treatment. Failure to mitigate is likely to result in a parallel reduction in any award of compensation.

Sections 57B and 80 also provide the remedy of a declaration that the complaint is well founded, together with a power to award just and equitable compensation. Whilst the duty to mitigate is not spelt out, the common law duty must apply.

The main financial loss suffered by an employee whose parental leave has been postponed is likely to be childcare costs. However, the employee will be paid for working during this period, whereas had parental leave not been postponed, but taken, it would have been unpaid. When a tribunal is assessing an employee's loss, it may be open to the employer to argue that any loss suffered by the employee from the refusal of parental leave was fully mitigated by the income earned by the employee during the relevant period.

In light of this, it appears that the remedies provided are weak.

Future developments affecting parents

The Employment Act 2002 will introduce changes throughout the area of employment law. Broadly the changes to maternity, paternity, parental and adoption leave provisions will affect those whose expected week of childbirth, adoption or return from parental leave takes place on or after 6 April 2003.[58]

With regard to maternity and parental leave, the government hopes that the Employment Act will

> deliver a balanced package of support for working parents, at the same time as reducing red tape for employers by simplifying rules governing maternity, paternity and adoption leave and pay, and make it easier to settle disputes in the workplace.

> It marks a significant step towards the government's election manifesto commitment to "help parents devote more time to their children early in life"...[59]

In these areas, the Employment Act amends current legislation, specifically, the ERA and the Social Security Contributions and Benefits Act 1992.

Clauses relating to the pay and administration of statutory paternity and adoption pay will be free standing.[60] Whilst most of the detail will be set out in Regulations, the "headline" changes will be as follows.

Maternity leave

OML is increased from 18 weeks to 26 weeks. This right is, of course, available to all employees, regardless of length of service. Women with 26 weeks' continuous employment by the fifteenth week before the expected week of childbirth will be entitled to 26 weeks' AML to follow on immediately from OML. Overall, therefore, their maternity leave will increase from a maximum of 40 weeks to 52 weeks.

In the fifteenth week before the expected week of childbirth, a woman will have to tell her employer of her pregnancy and from when she intends to take leave. There will be no obligation to provide this information in writing. An employer will be obliged to reply, within 28 days of being told of the pregnancy and intention to take maternity leave. This reply should set out the woman's rights, including her expected return date and that it will be her responsibility to tell the employer if she wants to change her return date.

If a woman does want to change her return date, for example, because she wishes to return early, she will have to give a minimum of 28 days' notice, (previously 21 days).

Flat rate SMP goes up to £100 per week. Higher rate SMP remains at 90% of average weekly earnings. Qualification for SMP remains the same. That is, a woman will have to be continuously employed for at least 26 weeks up to and including the qualifying week (that is, the fifteenth week before the expected week of childbirth) and should receive average earnings not less than the lower earnings limit for National Insurance contributions.

Finally, maternity leave will only be triggered by pregnancy-related illness following the beginning of the fourth week before the expected week of childbirth.

Paternity leave

An unprecedented legislative change is the introduction of paid paternity leave. Whilst such leave is already offered by many employers, either on an ad hoc basis or as part of their employment policy, this will be the first time that there is a statutory right to such leave.

Employees with 26 weeks' continuous service ending with the fifteenth week before the expected week of childbirth (or the week when a match with a child to be adopted is made) will have the right to two weeks' paternity leave. This qualification period is at odds with a woman's right to OML, for which there is no qualification period. It remains to be seen whether this will be challenged under sex discrimination legislation, or whether the principle in *Gillespie v Northern Ireland and Social Services Board*,[61] that pregnant women are in a unique position and not comparable to men, will be upheld.

Regulations are likely to provide for leave to be taken in one block, unless the employer agrees otherwise.

Paternity leave relating to the birth of a child

The purpose of the leave must be to support the other parent and/or to care for the child. The entitlement includes the situation where a child is stillborn after 24 weeks of pregnancy.

The earliest that leave may be taken is from the date of birth. It must be taken within 56 days of the birth.

Regulations will clarify the relationship that the employee wishing to take paternity leave will have to have with both the child and the mother, in order to qualify for the right. Regulations may also cover the evidence to be produced of such a relationship; this is likely to be self-certification of entitlement to leave.

Notice of intention to take paternity leave should be given 15 weeks before the expected week of the birth, or as soon as reasonably practicable. If there is any change to when paternity leave is required and, for example, the parents decide that it would be more useful to take it later, rather than immediately after the birth, the employee must give 28 days' notice of this change.

Paternity leave relating to the adoption of a child
Adoption leave (see below) will only be available to one spouse where a couple adopt a child. Paternity leave will be available to the other spouse.

Such an employee is entitled to two weeks' paid paternity leave. Leave may be taken from the date of placement for adoption, and must be taken within 56 days of placement. Notice of intention to take leave should be give to the employer 28 days before the child is placed for adoption, or as soon as reasonably practicable.

An employee taking paternity leave will be entitled to the benefit of the terms and conditions of employment as would have applied had he not been absent. He will also be bound by obligations arising under those terms and conditions. "Terms and conditions" are again widely drafted to include matters connected with an employee's employment, whether or not they arise under his contract of employment. Terms and conditions regarding remuneration are excluded.

There will be a mechanism to protect fathers against detriment and dismissal for exercising their right to paid paternity leave.

Statutory paternity pay (SPP)

This right will be financed by the state, and administered in a similar way to SMP. Employers will be able to recover most or all of the SPP paid out. SPP will be paid at the rate of flat rate SMP, (that is, from April 2003 it will be £100 per week), or 90% of average weekly earnings, if less. SPP will generally be payable for paternity leave taken within 56 days of the date that a child is born or placed for adoption.

To qualify, a man will have to
(i)   satisfy prescribed conditions regarding his relationship with the child and the mother
(ii) have been employed for a continuous period of at least 26 weeks ending
      – with the relevant week, and
      – have normal weekly earnings for the eight weeks ending with the relevant week of not less than the lower earnings limit.
The relevant week is the week immediately preceding the fourteenth week

before the expected week of the child's birth – which is the fifteenth, or qualifying week.

Employers should

    (i)   keep appropriate records for inspection by the Inland Revenue. They should make periodic returns to the Inland Revenue

   (ii)   give their employees information about entitlement.

Adoption leave

This is a further right to be introduced by the Employment Act.

Leave will be available to employees where a child is matched or placed for adoption on or after 6 April 2003. It will be available to both individuals and married couples who adopt.

There are two types of adoption leave; ordinary (OAL) and additional (AAL).

The OAL period is 26 weeks. AAL is for an additional 26 weeks. This is in line with maternity leave provisions. Where a couple adopts a child, adoption leave will be available to one spouse and paternity leave available to the other. In order to qualify for adoption leave, an employee must have 26 weeks' continuous employment prior to the date that the child is matched.

Leave is only available where a child is under 18 and newly placed for adoption. So foster parents who decide to adopt a foster child will not be eligible, nor will parents adopting within a family (that is, "step-family" adoptions).

Employers have the right to request proof of adoption. This may be provided in the form of certification from an approved adoption agency.

Adoption leave will operate slightly differently if the adoption takes place abroad rather than in the UK. Regulations will provide for these various situations.

Statutory adoption pay (SAP)

    A person will be entitled to SAP where he or she

      (i)   is a person with whom a child is, or is expected to be, placed for adoption

     (ii)   under the law of any part of the UK

    (iii)   has been continuously employed for at least 26 weeks before being

    (iv)   matched with a child for the purposes of adoption

     (v)   has ceased working for the employer

    (vi)   has normal weekly earnings for the 8 weeks before being matched that

    (vii)   are not less than the lower earnings limit, and

  (viii) has elected to receive SAP (as opposed to SPP, or where his or her spouse has elected to receive SAP).

Entitlement is also dependent upon giving notice, to the person liable to pay SAP, of the date the employee expects payment to begin, at least 28 days before that date. If this is not reasonably practicable, then notice must be given as soon as is reasonably practicable. It appears that SAP is payable at the flat rate throughout the period of leave.

The rights and duties of parents on adoption leave are the same as those on paternity leave. These rights are in addition to parental leave rights and parental leave may be taken back-to-back with both.

Parents of young children

The Employment Act will introduce a duty on employers to give serious consideration to requests for flexible working from employees with six months' continuous employment who are parents of young children. Employees with a child who is younger than six years old, or, where the child receives a disability living allowance, younger than 18 years old, will be entitled to ask their employer for a change to their contractual hours. The purpose of the change must be to care for a child.

The employee will have to make such a request in writing, and state his or her relationship with the child, the purpose of the request and that it is made under the statutory provisions. The request should set out the changes envisaged and the date from which such changes should become effective. The employee should set out the effects that he or she anticipates the changes may have upon the employer's business and how those effects may be dealt with.

"Serious consideration" by the employer requires the following,

(i)   holding a meeting with the employee within 28 days of the request, to discuss it
(ii) giving a decision within 14 days of the decision, and explaining any refusal.

An employee has the right to be accompanied to the meeting, and the right of appeal against any refusal.

The employer may only refuse the request for sound business reasons. These might include a material costs burden, problems in consequential reorganisation of workloads, a detrimental effect on either the ability to meet customer demands, quality or performance. If the request is refused, and any appeal unsuccessful, the employee may not make another request within the following 12 months.

Where an employer fails to respond to a request, to follow the correct procedure or refuses the request on incorrect grounds, an employee will be able to complain to an employment tribunal. A tribunal will be able to order compensation and reconsideration of the request. Employees will also be protected against detriment or dismissal for making such a request.

Notes

1 SI 1999/3312
2 SI 2001/4010. See also the Maternity Paternal Leave (Amendment) Regulations 2002 (SI 2002/2789); where applicable, the amendments are mentioned in brackets
3 MPL Regulation 4(2)(b)
4 MPL Regulation 6
5 (1996) IRLR 214
6 *Boyle and others v EOC*, Case C-411/96 (1998) ECR I-6401
7 ERA s 71 (4)
8 ERA s 212
9 Employment Appeal Tribunal 1284/00, before the Court of Appeal, case number EATRF/2002/0702/A2
10 MPL Regulation 7 (4)
11 MPL Regulation 18 (5)(b) states that this is subject to the requirements of paragraph 5 of Schedule 5 to the Social Security Act 1989 (equal treatment under pension schemes: maternity)
12 MPL Regulation 11
13 ERA s 66 (2)
14 (1990) IRLR 177
15 MPL Regulation 20
16 MPL Regulation 20
17 (1994) IRLR 482
18 (1997/80 EEC)
19 SI 2001/2660
20 *London Underground v Edwards* (1998) IRLR 364 CA
21 SI 1994/1230
22 (1998) IRLR 445
23 Case 179/88 *Handels-OG Kontorfunktionaerernes Forbund I Danmark v Dansk Arbejdsgiverforening* (1991) IRLR 31
24 SI 2000/1551
25 (1996) ICR 625
26 ERA Section 64
27 ERA Section 66
28 ERA Section 67
29 ERA Section 68
30 ERA Section 69
31 ERA Section 70
32 SI 1999/3242
33 SI 2001/4010. See also the Maternity and Parental Leave (Amendment) Regulations 2002 (SI 2002/2789)
34 As defined in the Trade Union and Labour Relations Act 1992 Section 178, and MPL Regulations Schedule 1
35 MPL Regulation 16
36 MPL Regulation 2
37 Children Act 1989 Sections 2 and 4
38 Subject to obtaining a court order

[39] *R v Secretary of State for Trade and Industry ex parte Trades Union Congress* (2000) IRLR 565 HC
[40] MPL Regulation 15
[41] MPL Regulation 14(1)
[42] MPL Regulations Schedule 2 paragraph 8
[43] MPL Regulations Schedule 2 paragraph 9
[44] MPL Regulations 13 (1A)
[45] MPL Regulations Schedule 2 paragraph 2A
[46] MPL Regulation 14(4)
[47] Schedule 2 paragraph 7, which renders Regulation 14(4) otiose, except with respect to parents of disabled children
[48] DTI press release 25 April 2001
[49] MPL Regulation 15
[50] MPL Regulations schedule 2 paragraphs 1 and 2
[51] MPL Regulations schedule 2 paragraph 3, 4 and 5
[52] MPL Regulations schedule 2 paragraph 6
[53] MPL Regulation 15
[54] MPL Regulation 17
[55] MPL Regulation 18. Note that the Maternity and Parental Leave (Amendment) Regulations 2002 redrafts Regulation 18 and inserts Regulation 18A
[56] ERA Section 57A (1)
[56A] From April 2003, the listed reasons will also include failure of the employer properly to notify the employee of the date upon which maternity leave would end
[57] ERA Section 49
[58] The Maternity and Parental Leave (Amendments) Regulations 2002 (SI2002/2789)
[59] DTI website
[60] The Paternity and Addoption Leave Regulations 2002 (SI2002/2788) and the Statutory Paternity Pay and Statutory Adoption Pay (Weekly Rates) Regulations 2003 (SI2002/2828), both in force from 8 December 2002
[61] Case C-342–93 (1996) ECR I-475

3

Sex and race discrimination

CAROLINE HUMPHRIES AND HELEN SARGEANT

Caroline Humphries is the Professional Support Lawyer in the employment team at CMS Cameron McKenna.

Helen Sargeant is an Assistant Solicitor in the employment team at CMS Cameron McKenna.

Introduction

The law on discrimination is becomingly increasingly sophisticated as lifestyles and working patterns change and the relationship between employers and workers becomes more complex. At present English law prohibits discrimination based on the grounds of sex,[1] race,[2] marital status[3] and disability.[4] There is currently no legislation outlawing age discrimination.[5] However, what appears as discrimination on the basis of age may be discrimination on the grounds of sex, race or disability.[6] Positive discrimination in favour of certain sexual or racial groups[7] is generally unlawful.

This chapter concentrates on sex and race discrimination, which are the most common forms of discrimination. There is a separate chapter covering disability discrimination (see Chapter 4).

The key legislation dealing with sex discrimination is the Sex Discrimination Act 1975 (SDA). This prohibits discrimination on the basis of the person's sex and/or marital status. What is meant by the word "sex" has been the subject of judicial debate recently and this is explored further in this chapter when transsexuals and sexual orientation are considered. At present the meaning of the term "sex" is confined to meaning "gender". This means that there is a narrow interpretation and if the discrimination is not directly related to the person's gender then there will be no protection against sex discrimination under the SDA. Most of the cases under the SDA deal with sex discrimination rather than marital status discrimination. In fact cases about marital status discrimination are now rare. This suggests that there has been a considerable change in attitude since the legislation was passed in 1975 and married women are no longer widely discriminated against. However this protection is not entirely unnecessary and was tested again in the recent case of *Chief Constable of Bedfordshire Constabulary v Graham*.[8]

In *Chief Constable of Bedfordshire Constabulary v Graham* the EAT held that there was marital discrimination when the Chief Constable rescinded the appointment of a female inspector to the division commanded by her husband, a chief superintendent, on the basis of a possible conflict of interest. The fact that the two people were married had directly affected the decision not to appoint the woman. As they were married they could not be competent and compellable witnesses against each other in any criminal proceedings and this may have been necessary. For a marital discrimination case to succeed the applicant must establish that the discrimination is by reason of the fact that the person is married and not by reason of the particular person the individual married.

The key legislation dealing with race discrimination is the Race Relations Act 1976 (RRA). Race discrimination covers discrimination on the grounds of race, colour, nationality (including citizenship) or ethnic or national origins. The most controversial element of this definition is what constitutes "ethnic origins" and this has caused substantial difficulty. The 1983 House of Lords case of *Mandla v Dowell Lee*[9] is arguably the most significant case.

In this case "ethnic" was widely construed in a broad cultural and historical sense and a shared history and cultural tradition were deemed to be essential characteristics of an ethnic group. Other (non-essential) characteristics could include a common language, a common literature, a common religion and a sense of being an oppressed or minority group within a larger community. It is interesting to note that there are some unexpected consequences of this definition. It will come as no surprise that Romany gypsies[10] are regarded as an ethnic group. However, Jewish people are both an ethnic and a religious group and so care has to be taken in determining whether the purported discrimination is on ethnic or religious grounds.[11] If the discrimination is on religious grounds then there is no special protection under the RRA (although note the future developments section of this chapter which discusses the new European Directives giving protection on religious grounds). For many the most unusual consequence is that Muslims are not expressly covered by the RRA (see *Nyazi v Rymans*).[12] As the only common denominator of a Muslim is a religious one, and as religious beliefs are not yet protected, a Muslim person cannot claim protection from discrimination purely by reason of being Muslim. The terrorist events in September 2001 triggered a degree of anti-Muslim feeling in the UK and many people were very surprised (and angered) that there was no specific protection against discrimination for Muslims. Where Muslims seem to be protected by the RRA, it is in fact their ethnic origins (such as their originating from the Indian subcontinent) rather than their religious beliefs which provide the protection.[13]

In both sex and race discrimination the legislation also protects complainants who suffer victimisation on unlawful grounds.[14]

The sex and race discrimination legislation is very similar as both the SDA and RRA were enacted in the mid-1970s and the intention was to provide similar protection in sex and race discrimination cases. However, there are some differences, many of which are subtle, and it is vital to refer to the correct legislation when considering discrimination issues.

Scope of both the SDA and RRA

Both the SDA and the RRA have a wide scope. They cover not only the employment field but also other fields, such as education. They also cover discrimination in the provision of goods, facilities and services. This chapter only covers discrimination in the employment field.

Both the SDA and RRA impose obligations upon employers and potential employers. The legislation protects both employees and workers. Workers are defined as those working under a contract personally to execute any work or labour.[15] This would cover independent contractors. Workers employed by an agency to work for a client are also specifically protected.[16] The legislation ensures that such workers are able to claim redress in the event of discrimination perpetrated by the client organisation for which they actually work even though they may be employed by a different person (for example, an agency). Client organisations are prevented from discriminating in the terms on which the individual is allowed to do the work by not allowing him or her to do it or continue to do so, in the way in which he or she is afforded access to benefits, facilities or services or by subjecting him to any other detriment. This provision (Section 9 in the SDA and Section 7 in the RRA) is a good example of a subtle difference in the provisions of the two Acts. The RRA specifically excludes certain contract workers ordinarily resident outside Great Britain but no similar provision appears in the SDA.

Although both the SDA and RRA cover the armed forces,[17] employment on some ships and aircraft as well as police,[18] prison[19] and firefighting services, special provisions may apply. For example, police officers are treated as being employed either by the chief constable for their authority or by the authority itself. The appropriate respondent depends on which is claimed to have treated the police officer less favourably.

It is possible, and indeed common, for discrimination claims to be made in addition to other claims, such as unfair dismissal. However, unlike unfair dismissal claims or claims for redundancy payments, discrimination claims are not subject to any length of service requirements before such a claim can be made. Rights against employers apply whatever the length of employment (if any) and whatever hours are or have been worked. This means that discrimination claims are often the only claims that can be made by an applicant.

In addition, discrimination claims are not subject to any statutory maximum compensation limit. Compensation for unfair dismissal claims is limited to a basic award of £7,500 and a compensatory award of £52,600 (in 2002). However discrimination claims are potentially unlimited and an employment tribunal can make awards not just to compensate the person for the financial loss suffered by the discrimination but it can also make an award to compensate the individual for "injury to feelings". This means that discrimination claims can be expensive and awards can be unpredictable, depending upon the evidence given at the employment tribunal hearing and the views of the panel hearing the complaint.

Territorial jurisdiction for both the SDA and RRA

The legislation applies in relation to employment at an establishment in Great Britain (that is, England, Scotland and Wales). Unless the employee works "wholly outside" Great Britain, this requirement will be met.[20]

It is interesting to note that the wording in the SDA and the RRA differs from the wording in the Employment Rights Act 1996 ('ERA') which sets out the jurisdiction for unfair dismissal cases. ERA states that unfair dismissal cannot apply to employment "where under the employee's contract of employment he ordinarily works outside Great Britain". The Court of Appeal in the case of *Carver v Saudi Arabian Airlines*[21] concluded that Parliament had deliberately distinguished between the place where under the contract of employment the employee "ordinarily works", the test under the ERA, and the place where at the time of the alleged discrimination a person wholly or mainly worked, the test for jurisdiction under the SDA. It concluded that although the two usually will be the same, that need not be the case and so, in practice, this is another example of when a discrimination claim may be possible when other employment claims cannot be made.

Agencies

The Equal Opportunities Commission (EOC)[22] promotes equal opportunities and may provide assistance to complainants in sex discrimination cases. The Commission for Racial Equality[23] promotes racial equality and may provide assistance to complainants in race discrimination cases. The websites for these organisations are well developed and provide useful guidance for both employers and individuals (see Useful websites).

Direct and indirect discrimination

Discrimination on the grounds of race, sex or marital status may be direct or indirect. Although neither of these terms is expressly defined in the legislation, they are well established and have specific meanings. They describe the primary and secondary types of discrimination which are covered in both the SDA and RRA. The language of the SDA is unusual as it assumes that the "victim" will be feminine and that the "discriminator" will be masculine. This seems to be an anachronism reflecting the time when the legislation was made and, of course, the SDA protects both men and women. In fact, one of the key cases under the SDA involved a man. This is the case of *James v Eastleigh Borough Council*.[24] Although not specifically an employment case it is a good example of direct sex discrimination.

Direct sex discrimination

Direct discrimination occurs where the employer treats the complainant less favourably than another employee (the comparator) on the basis of gender, marriage or because an individual has undergone, intends to undergo or is undergoing gender reassignment. For the purposes of sex discrimination, the comparator is a person of the opposite sex, either male or female. For the purposes of marital discrimination, the comparator is an unmarried person of the same sex.[25]

In the *James* case Mr and Mrs James were both aged 62. In the days when the state retirement age differed and the old age pension was granted to women at aged 60 but to men at aged 65, Mr and Mrs James decided to go for a swim. When they reached the ticket desk of their local public pool they discovered that OAP's could swim for free. This meant that Mrs James, as an OAP, was able to swim for free whereas her husband, Mr James, who was exactly the same age, had to pay. This is an obvious case of direct discrimination and when Mr James challenged this the House of Lords agreed that the different entry charges were discriminatory.

Section 6 SDA provides that

(1) It is unlawful for a person, in relation to employment by him at an establishment in Great Britain, to discriminate against a woman:

 (i) in the arrangements he makes for the purposes of determining who should be offered that employment, or
 (ii) in the terms on which he offers her that employment, or
 (iii) by refusing or deliberately omitting to offer her that employment.

It is also

(2) …unlawful for a person, in the case of a woman employed by him at an establishment in Great Britain, to discriminate against her:

 (i) in the way he affords her access to opportunities for promotion, transfer or training, or to any other benefits, facilities or services, or by refusing or deliberately omitting to afford her access to them, or
 (ii) by dismissing her or subjecting her to any other detriment.

Motive or intention of the employer is irrelevant when determining whether there has been discrimination, although it must be shown that the complainant's treatment was caused by his or her sex or marital status.

An employer has to make a choice on redundancy between dismissing a man or a woman, both of whom are married with children. He decides to dismiss the woman, on the basis of an assumption that her husband is likely to be the family's main source of income. Although he may have had no conscious desire to discriminate against the woman on the basis of her sex, his assumption has directly caused her to suffer less favourable treatment on unlawful grounds.

Comparing treatment
The complainant must find an appropriate person with whom to compare the employer's treatment of him or her.[26] If a complainant can identify an individual (a colleague or another job applicant) who has been treated more favourably than the complainant because of his or her gender, marital status, or because of some racial reason, then the complainant will have a very persuasive case. The relevant circumstances of the complainant and the comparator must be the same or not materially different.

However, there is no absolute requirement that the complainant identifies a living individual and in some cases a hypothetical comparator may be adopted. A woman can therefore claim that she has been treated less favourably than a man would have been in the same circumstances.

Genuine occupational qualifications in sex discrimination cases
Positive action taken in order to redress an imbalance is generally unlawful although there are a number of limited statutory exceptions to the prohibition on direct discrimination. However as these are exceptions to the basic principles these tend to be construed narrowly and great care should be taken when positive action is taken. Indeed the case of *ACAS v Taylor*[27] is a salutary one. Here the EAT concluded that a policy which gave women an advantage in promotion exercises was unlawful discrimination even though the purpose was to help women who were underrepresented at the next grade.

There are, in addition, certain "genuine occupational qualifications" (GOQs) under the SDA. Note that this is a defence to any claim of less favourable treatment and it cannot be relied upon if the discrimination is because of the person's marital status. The GOQ's are listed in the legislation and will apply in only limited circumstances. For example, being a man (or conversely a woman) is a GOQ only where the essential nature of the job calls for a man/woman for reasons of physiology (excluding physical strength or stamina) or in theatrical performances for reasons of authenticity. It can also be one where the job needs to be done by a man (or woman) to preserve decency or privacy or the nature or location of the work make it impracticable for the worker to live elsewhere than in the premises provided for the employer and there are no separate sleeping or sanitary facilities and it is not reasonable to expect the employer to provide those facilities. As modern standards and living arrangements change and domestic circumstances become ever more flexible, these GOQ's will be increasingly challenged. It should be noted that there is no exclusion of men from midwifery (since 1984).

Unless an employer can justify direct discrimination by one of the recognised statutory exceptions, it cannot be justified in any other way.

Proving direct discrimination in sex discrimination cases

The Sex Discrimination (Indirect Discrimination and Burden of Proof) Regulations 2001[28] came into force on 12 October 2001. These implement the European Directive on the burden of proof. The Directive is intended to deal with claims of equal pay and equal treatment, so it covers provisions in relation to the SDA, the Equal Pay Act and maternity and pregnancy rights.

These regulations, however, only amend the SDA 1975 and make changes *only* to sex discrimination cases in the employment field. The regulations do not apply to sex discrimination cases outside the employment field. Significantly they do not apply to any cases (including employment cases) of race discrimination, so unless the RRA is also amended there will continue to be differences in the wording of these Acts.

The regulations change the burden of proof in employment tribunal proceedings. The burden of proof shifts from the complainant to the respondent if the complainant can prove facts from which the tribunal could conclude, in the absence of an adequate explanation, that discrimination has occurred. This means that once a complainant has made a prima facie case of discrimination, the burden is now on the employer to disprove that discrimination. This change has caused some controversy, with some commentators arguing that this breaches the principle that a defendant is presumed innocent unless proved guilty. However, the SDA already requires an employer objectively to justify a practice or procedure which would otherwise amount to indirect sexual discrimination and so, in our view there is little change in this respect from the traditional position under case law. In particular the guidance in the Court of Appeal case of *King v The Great Britain China Centre*[29] has been followed for some. However, the regulations do make the change express, and put this in a mandatory form, so that tribunals no longer have the ability to draw inferences from established facts. Employers must take extra care that they can give a clear non-discriminatory reason whenever men and women are treated differently.

Direct race discrimination

As in sex discrimination cases, direct discrimination in race discrimination cases occurs where the employer treats the complainant less favourably than another employee (the comparator). For the purposes of the RRA, the comparator is someone from another racial group: less favourable treatment must be based on "racial grounds". Less favourable treatment can include words, actions and the failure to provide opportunities.

Section 4 (1) RRA provides that

It is unlawful for a person, in relation to employment by him at an establishment in Great Britain, to discriminate against another

(a)   in the arrangements he makes for the purpose of determining who should be offered that employment; or

(b)   in the terms on which he offers him that employment; or

(c)   by refusing or deliberately omitting to offer him that employment.

Section 4 (2) RRA provides that

It is unlawful for a person, in the case of a person employed by him at an establishment in Great Britain, to discriminate against that employee:

(a)   in the terms of employment which he affords him; or

(b)   in the way he affords him access to opportunities for promotion, transfer or training, or to any other benefits, facilities or services, or by refusing or deliberately omitting to afford him access to them; or

(c)   by dismissing him, or subjecting him to any other detriment.

Motive or intention of the employer is irrelevant when determining whether there has been discrimination, although it must be shown that the complainant's treatment was caused by race. The test is an objective one. If the person would not have received the less favourable treatment "but for" his race, the treatment is on grounds of race. It is no defence to state that the employer discriminated against an employee for good commercial reasons or because of customer preference or simply to save money. In addition it is not necessary for the racial grounds to be the only cause of the discrimination. Provided the racial grounds are a substantial cause of the treatment it will be discrimination.

Genuine occupational qualifications in race discrimination cases
In the same way as there can be a defence to discrimination under the SDA, there can be a defence to discrimination under the RRA because of the exception for genuine occupational qualifications. However, GOQ's are much narrower under the RRA than they are under the SDA. These exceptions only apply to arrangements made for recruitment, failure to recruit, and access to promotion and transfer. They do not apply to the terms on which a job is offered or provided or to other benefits, facilities or services provided.

Being of a particular race is only a genuine occupational qualification in the following circumstances:

(i)   The job involves participation in a dramatic performance or other entertainment in a capacity for which a person of that racial group is required for reasons of authenticity.

(ii)   The job involves participation as an artist's or photographic model in the production of a work of art, etc. for which a person of that racial group is required for reasons of authenticity.

(iii)   The job involves working in a place where food and drink is provided to members of the public in a particular setting for which in that job a person of that racial group is required for reasons of authenticity (for example, it would be lawful to employ a Chinese waiter in a Chinese restaurant, although it would not be lawful to require a Chinese waiter in a take away establishment).

(iv)   The holder of the job provides individuals from a particular racial group with personal services promoting their welfare and those services can be most effectively provided by a person of that racial group.

It should be noted that if the employer already has sufficient employees of the racial group required with capacity to perform the tasks required then an employer cannot use the GOQ defence if he discriminates when seeking a new employee.

Proving direct discrimination in race discrimination cases
The burden of proof still rests on the complainant to show that he or she has suffered less favourable treatment on the specified grounds in race discrimination cases (and there has been no change to the RRA along the lines of the Sex Discrimination (Indirect Discrimination and Burden of Proof) Regulations 2001). However as direct discrimination can be proved by inference, a tribunal or court will look to the absence of any other, legitimate explanation for the different treatment in question and may draw an inference of unlawful discrimination.

Statistical evidence may also be used by a complainant to draw attention to imbalances in the workforce which may then persuade the tribunal to draw an inference of unlawful discrimination.

Indirect sex discrimination

Indirect discrimination in sex discrimination cases occurs where an employer applies a provision, criteria or practice to all employees which has a disproportionate impact on members of one sex or married persons and cannot be justified. A simple example is where an employer requires all it's employees to be at least six foot tall. Although this is not directly discriminatory the effect is discriminatory. This is because a much higher proportion of men would be able to comply with this requirement than women. Unless the employer could justify this requirement there would be indirect sex discrimination.

Section 1(2)(b) of the SDA provides that a person discriminates against a woman where he applies to her a provision, criteria or practice which he applies or would apply equally to a man but

   (i)   which is such that it would be to the detriment of a considerably larger proportion of women than of men; and

   (ii)   which he cannot show to be justifiable irrespective of the sex of the person to whom it is applied; and

   (iii)   which is to her detriment.

Four elements to consider in cases of indirect sex discrimination:

   (i)   provision, criteria or practice
   (ii)   disproportionate impact
   (iii)   detriment suffered
   (iv)   absence of justification.

Provision, criteria or practice

The Sex Discrimination (Indirect Discrimination and Burden of Proof) Regulations 2001 see a relaxation of the historical test for indirect sex discrimination although arguably this has already been effected by case law in the UK. Instead of having to establish the strict application of a condition or requirement a claimant now only has to demonstrate that there has been a *"provision, criteria or practice"* and that provision, criteria or practice has disadvantaged a substantially higher proportion of the members of one sex than another. This means that non-contractual policies (for example of working long fixed hours) can now be challenged and employers may need to make cultural changes to avoid non-contractual practices or corporate attitudes that are discriminatory.

Another change is that a woman no longer has to show that the relevant (discriminatory) provision, criteria or practice is to her detriment "because she cannot comply with it". A woman simply needs to show that the provision, criteria or practice is to her detriment. This means that some claims which historically have been unsuccessful (because the tribunal has concluded that the woman can in fact comply with the requirement) will now succeed. For example, in the past some tribunals have concluded that although a requirement to work full time may be to a mother's detriment the fact that the particular mother is well paid and can afford the necessary childcare means that, in practice, she can comply with it. Now all a woman need show is that the requirement (now provision, criteria or practice) is detrimental to her family commitments.

Disproportionate impact

Once a person has established that a provision, criteria or practice has been applied the next step is to show that the proportion of one sex that can comply is considerably smaller than the proportion of the other sex. To show this, the appropriate pool for comparison needs to be identified. The absolute numbers involved are not important; it is the proportions which are key. The relevant circumstances of those in the pool for comparison must be the same or not materially different. Unless the correct pool can be identified the claim is likely to fail. As identifying the correct pool is a matter for judgement (and the selection of the pool is a question of fact for the employment tribunal) this is a tricky area. Where different pools are available, best practice is to prepare evidence from all the relevant pools. This may involve elaborate statistics, questionnaires or publicly available information.

Once the pool has been identified the proportions are compared. The test is not whether it is physically possible to comply with the provision, but whether this would be consistent with typical customs and behaviour. Therefore, in the key case of *Price v The Civil Service Commission*[30] an age requirement of between 17 and 28 years was deemed to be discriminatory. Although there were roughly the same number of men and women in these groups significantly less women than men could comply with it as a substantial number of women in this age range were busy with child commitments.

What is meant by "considerably larger" (and indeed the converse "considerably smaller") has also caused some difficulty in interpretation. These terms are not legally defined and are deemed to be "common words in ordinary usage". The ultimate decision is a matter of fact for the tribunal. Guidance suggests that the smaller the pool the more likely differences will be deemed to be considerable, whereas the larger the pool the more likely it is that a tribunal will want to rely on a larger difference.

Detriment

The complainant must suffer a detriment. Although the Courts originally adopted a narrow view, concluding that detriment had to be something unpleasant or burdensome arising in the course of employment, most recent cases have adopted a broader approach.[31] The current approach suggests that subjecting an employee to a detriment means no more than putting the employee at a disadvantage.

Justification

The SDA allows the defence of justification. Justification is when the employer has a satisfactory reason for imposing the provision, criteria or practice on his workers.

In order to prove justification, the employer must show not only that the requirement is justifiable irrespective of sex, but also that the means chosen correspond to a real need and are appropriate and necessary to that end. This will be a question of fact for the tribunal. A tribunal will look at a number of factors. Firstly, it is likely to check that the objective for which the provision, criteria or practice has been introduced is clear and whether this objective could be reached in other, non discriminatory ways. If such an alternative is available then the tribunal will consider the costs of implementing that alternative in comparison with current costs and indeed the number of people adversely affected by the provision, etc. and the extent of the detriment. Although defences of justification are not uncommon, tribunals are aware of the purposive nature of the legislation and other European directives so this defence is usually thoroughly tested before being accepted.

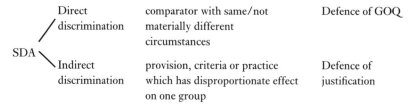

Indirect race discrimination

Indirect discrimination in race discrimination cases occurs where an employer applies a requirement or condition to all employees, which has a disproportionate impact on members of one racial group. Note that this is a slightly different, more restrictive, test than that used in sex discrimination cases.

Section 1(1)(b) of the RRA states that a person discriminates against another if

he applies to that other a requirement or condition which he applies or would apply equally to persons not of the same racial group as that other but

(i)   which is such that the proportion of persons of the same racial group as that other who can comply with it is considerably smaller than the proportion of persons not of that racial group who can comply with it; and

(ii) which he cannot show to be justifiable irrespective of the colour, race, nationality or ethnic or national origins of the person to who it is applied; and

(iii) which is to the detriment of that other because he cannot comply with it.

Four elements to consider in cases of indirect race discrimination:

(i)   requirement or condition
(ii) adverse impact
(iii) detriment suffered
(iv) absence of justification.

Requirement or condition
To establish indirect discrimination a complainant must establish that a

requirement or condition was imposed which he/she was obliged to comply with. It is not enough to show that a particular factor weighed particularly heavily against the complainant.

In *Perera v Civil Service Commission* (2),[32] the complainant alleged that a factor taken into account by his prospective employer, use of the English language, had disadvantaged him because of his race. The Court of Appeal refused to accept that this was a complete bar to his appointment. There was no single "requirement or condition" which had to be met, and Mr Perera's claim of indirect discrimination therefore failed.

Disproportionate impact

The complainant must show that although the requirement or condition is applied equally to the complainant and the comparator, proportionately fewer members of the complainant's group are able to comply with that requirement or condition than those of the comparator group who can comply.

If the requirement or condition is not applied equally to members of all racial groups, there cannot be indirect discrimination (although there may be direct discrimination). Identification of the comparator group is often extremely difficult in indirect race discrimination cases.

The complainant must next show that a considerably smaller proportion of the relevant group can comply with the requirement as compared to the comparator group. The question of what constitutes a "considerably smaller" proportion is a question of fact for a tribunal to decide.

Detriment

The complainant must suffer a detriment because he or she cannot comply with the relevant requirement or condition. The issue is whether the complainant can comply with the requirement or condition in practice or that it is consistent with the customs and cultural traditions of the racial group to comply with the requirement. It is not whether the complainant could physically or theoretically do so. Thus in the *Mandla* case although the 5 Sikh boys were physically able to take off their turbans during the school day, the court held that they were not able to comply with the requirement as to do so would have meant ignoring their own culture and customs.

Justification

The RRA also allows the defence of justification.

In order to prove justification, the employer must show not only that the requirement is justifiable irrespective of race, but also that the means chosen correspond to a real need and are appropriate and necessary to that end. This will be a question of fact for the tribunal. Justification may be based on the particular circumstances of the employer or on broader social policy reasons.[33]

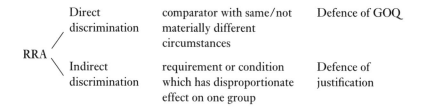

Direct discrimination	comparator with same/not materially different circumstances	Defence of GOQ
Indirect discrimination	requirement or condition which has disproportionate effect on one group	Defence of justification

Victimisation

The SDA and RRA protect those who complain of unlawful discrimination. An employer victimises a person if he treats that person less favourably than he treats or would treat other persons, and does so because the person victimised[34] has carried out one of the "protected acts" listed in the legislation.

Protected acts include:

(i)   bringing proceedings against the employer; for discrimination or under the Equal Pay Act

(ii) giving evidence or information in connection with any such proceedings

(iii) otherwise doing anything under or by reference to the discrimination legislation in relation to the employer or any other person

(iv) alleging that the employer or any other person has committed an act which would amount to a contravention of the discrimination legislation.

The House of Lords has recently examined the test linking less favourable treatment to the protected act. It has held[35] that the correct test of whether less favourable treatment is "by reason" of the protected act is not to look for causation but to examine the real reason for the treatment complained of. In this case the House of Lords concluded that the refusal to give a reference was not because the complainant had brought a claim of race discrimination but because the employer believed that to do so would prejudice the proceedings at the employment tribunal.

If a person brings a claim of victimisation the employer has a defence if the employee's allegations of discrimination are both false and not made in good faith.

A former employer may be liable for victimisation in connection with discrimination proceedings previously brought against him by an individual.[36]

Harassment

Sexual harassment

Although the term sexual harassment has not (yet) been legally defined in UK legislation, harassment by an employer or a fellow employee may constitute unlawful direct discrimination and there is a substantial body of case law on sexual harassment. This concludes that the harassment must comply with the normal tests for sex discrimination. In other words an employee must have been less favourably treated on the ground of sex or marital status than a person of the opposite sex or marital status.[37]

The test is a subjective one. The intentions of the harasser are not relevant to the determination of whether a detriment has been suffered. It is the complainant who determines what he or she finds offensive. A single incident of sexual harassment may constitute an act of discrimination.

In April 2002 the European Commission announced that a joint text had been adopted amending the original 1976 Directive on Sex Discrimination. This must be implemented by 2005. Although this does not change the law in the UK very much, it is likely to have a significant impact on some EU countries, such as Portugal and Greece, which have not developed this area of the law.

The new law is important in some key respects. This is the first time that the law on sexual harassment is defined in legislation, so that UK employers and Courts no longer have to rely on case law and judicial interpretation to deal with the basic principles. Much of the new law simply consolidates established UK practice, for example, it confirms that sexual harassment constitutes discrimination and that there is no upper limit on compensation. However, for the first time the term sexual harassment is given a legal definition that is applicable across the EU.

> Sexual harassment is defined as a situation where any form of unwanted verbal, non-verbal or physical conduct of a sexual nature occurs with the purpose or effect of violating the dignity of a person, in particular when creating an intimidating, hostile, degrading, humiliating or offensive environment.

Although it has long been advisable for employers to have specific policies on equal opportunities and sexual harassment, it seems that employers may now need to be even more proactive in their approach. The new law requires employers to take preventive measures against all forms of discrimination, especially sexual harassment, as well as introducing what are referred to as "enterprise level equality plans" which are to be made available to workers.

It is clear that the prevention of sexual harassment is now high on the agenda. Employers should make every effort to review their policies, procedures and practices to ensure that they are not the first company to make unwanted salacious headlines when the new laws are implemented here.

Racial harassment

Racial harassment by an employer or a fellow employee may constitute unlawful direct discrimination. Again the same tests for race discrimination apply and an employee must have been less favourably treated on the ground of race than a person of a different racial group.[38] The intentions of the harasser are not relevant to the determination of whether a detriment has been suffered. It is the complainant who determines what he or she finds offensive. A single incident of racial harassment may constitute an act of discrimination.

Criminal liability in harassment situations

The provisions of the Criminal Justice and Public Order Act 1994, which make intentional harassment a criminal offence, should also be noted.[39]

An offence under this provision is punishable by fine or imprisonment (which may be greater where the offence was racially aggravated). A person who pursues a course of conduct which amounts to harassment or which he knows or ought to know amounts to harassment of another commits an offence under the Protection from Harassment Act 1997 (which is again punishable by fine or imprisonment). The victim of such conduct is also entitled to seek an injunction to stop the harassment and/or pursue a civil claim for damages against the perpetrator.

Vicarious liability

An employer may be vicariously liable for an act of discrimination carried out by an employee. It is possible for a complainant to bring a claim for discrimination against both the employee who carried out the discriminatory act and against his or her employer.

The common law situation is that an employer may become vicariously liable for the acts of his employee or agent if the acts take place "in the course of his employment". *Lister & others v Helsey Hall Ltd*[40] has confirmed that in determining whether an employee's wrongful act has been committed in the course of their employment, the correct approach is to concentrate on the relative closeness of the connection between the nature of the employment and the employee's wrongdoing.

> *Lister* concerned a boarding school which was sued for damages by boys who were sexually abused by the school warden. Applying the "close connection" test, the House of Lords found that the employee's position as warden and the close contact with the boys which that work involved created a sufficiently close connection between the acts of abuse and the work which he had been employed to do so as to make it fair and just to hold the employers vicariously liable. An employer can therefore be vicariously liable for the actions of his employee even if they are unauthorised actions, provided they are so closely connected with acts which he has authorised that they may be regarded as modes although improper modes of doing them. The test is whether the acts were so closely connected with the employment ("inextricably interwoven" with it) that it would be fair and just to hold the employer liable.

In a similar case, J suffered physical and verbal racial abuse committed by his colleagues at his place of work. The Court of Appeal held that the employer was liable for the acts in question, and referred to the purpose of the legislation as being to deter harassment in the work place through "a widening of the net of responsibility beyond the guilty employees themselves".[41]

An employer may escape vicarious liability if he can show that he took such steps as were reasonably practicable[42] to prevent the employee from carrying out that particular act, or from carrying out acts of that description in the course of his or her employment.

The burden is on the employer to make out the defence. An equal opportunities policy alone will not be sufficient. An appropriate policy must be understood, implemented and observed by all employees. A complaints procedure must be available to employees.

An employer may also be primarily liable for discrimination against a fellow employee, for example by failing to address a complaint of discrimination properly and seriously.

It is also unlawful for an employer to instruct another person to discriminate[43] or to induce or attempt to induce a person to carry out a discriminatory act.[44] If the person asked refuses to carry out the discriminatory act and suffers a detriment, as a result he or she will be able to claim that of discrimination. The interesting point here is that it is not necessary for the person making the claim to be the person whose race leads to the less favourable treatment. This is another example of where the wording of the RRA and SDA differ slightly. The SDA prohibits discrimination "on the grounds of (her) sex" whereas the RRA prohibits discrimination on "racial grounds". This means that under the SDA only the person who is actively discriminated against can make a claim. However under the RRA the only point the complainant has to prove is that there was discrimination and it was on racial grounds.

> J, who is white, worked for a car hire agency. On her first day she was told by her employer not to hire out cars to black people. She refused to obey the instruction and was dismissed. Her employer has discriminated against her on racial grounds.[45]

Subjected to discrimination by a third party in the course of employment

Burton v De Vere Hotels[46] deals with the situation where the actual abuser or harasser is a third party and not a servant or agent of the employer for whose actions the employer would not normally be vicariously liable. The case concerned an insult caused to two black casual waitresses at a Round Table dinner by the guest speaker, Bernard Manning. The EAT held that an employer subjects an employee to the detriment of racial harassment if he causes or permits harassment serious enough to amount to a detriment to occur in circumstances in which he can control whether it happens or not. A person "subjects" another to something if he causes or allows that thing to happen in circumstances where he can control whether it happens or not. The question of whether the employer could foresee the events does not however determine whether the events were under the employer's control.

In order to show that the employer "subjected" the employee to the detriment of racial abuse or harassment, the tribunal should ask itself, in its capacity as an industrial jury, whether the event in question was something which was sufficiently under the control of the employer that he could, by the application of good employment practice, have prevented the harassment or reduced the extent of it.

Discrimination outside the course of employment

Acts that are wholly outside the sphere of employment will not be covered by the SDA or RRA. The SDA or RRA will not therefore afford an individual protection from abuse or harassment on the street or in the home which is unrelated to his or her employment.

An employer will not be liable for the acts of an employee merely because his or her employment presented him or her with the opportunity to commit the wrongful act, or because the act was committed during the period of that particular employment.[47] It should be noted however that an employer will not always escape liability because the act was done outside working hours or outside working premises.

> In *Sidhu v Aerospace Composite Technology Ltd*[48] the applicant was attacked by an employee out of working hours at a racetrack during a social event organised by their common employer. The Court of Appeal held that the employment tribunal had been entitled to find that such behaviour did not fall within the "course of employment" in circumstances where the majority of those attending the event were friends and family rather than employees.

Personal liability for employees

The RRA and SDA expressly state that an employee can be personally liable for knowingly aiding the doing of an act by his or her employer.[49] The employee must however know that the employer is treating, is about to treat, or is contemplating treating someone "less favourably" on the basis of their race or gender.[50]

> *LM Read v Tiverton District Council*[51] confirmed that an individual employee can be separately liable for acts of unlawful discrimination which he or she

commits. Mrs Read suspected discrimination and a preliminary issue was raised as to whether proceedings could be taken against the Council's solicitor personally as well as the Council. The tribunal found that the individual discriminator could be sued as well as the employer, implying that the employee remained personally liable. In any event, it was open to Mrs Read to allege that the Council's solicitor had aided any discrimination by the Council.

Vicarious liability and the police

As explained above the RRA made employers vicariously liable for acts of race discrimination committed by their employees in certain circumstances, subject to a defence that the employer took such steps as were reasonably practicable to prevent the employee discriminating. However, police officers were defined as officeholders and not employees. This meant that they were exempt from various obligations under the RRA and one of these was that they could not be made vicariously liable. The practical effect of this was that chief officers of police could not be held responsible for acts of discrimination by police officers. Indeed discrimination by police officers could largely go unchecked as there was no effective sanction against them.

The Race Relations (Amendment) Act 2000 ("the Amendment Act") which came into force in April 2001 changes this and provides for chief officers of police to be vicariously liable in relevant circumstances. The chief officer of police can now be vicariously liable for acts of race discrimination by constables under his direction or control. The consequence of this is that there are now effective sanctions against police officers. In practice it should be noted however that just as the RRA provides a defence for vicarious liability, this Amendment Act also includes one and where a police authority has implemented a proper procedure and policy on discrimination issues it may be able to successfully defend specific claims. This will mean in practice that it is now unlawful for a police officer to discriminate on racial grounds in carrying out any policing functions such as stop and search, arresting and detaining suspects, assisting victims and controlling demonstrations.

Race Relations (Amendment) Act 2000

The RRA makes it unlawful to discriminate on racial grounds in relation to employment, training and education, housing, the provision of goods, facilities and services and certain other specified activities only. The Commission for Racial Equality ("the CRE") in its Third Review of the RRA proposed that the RRA should be extended to all public services.

The Government passed the Amendment Act as part of its response to the Stephen Lawrence inquiry[52] which identified institutionalised racism in the police force and therefore the need to eradicate race discrimination in all public authorities.

The Amendment Act extends the RRA to make it unlawful for any public authority to discriminate on racial grounds in carrying out any of its functions. It applies for the first time to the regulatory or enforcement powers of the police, customs and excise, prison service, local authorities and licensing bodies.

The Amendment Act creates

(i)   a general duty on public authorities to not do any discriminatory act when carrying out its function
(ii) a general duty on specific public authorities to work towards the elimination of discrimination and promoting equality of opportunity and good relations
(iii) specific duties on certain public authorities. (These had to be actioned by 31 May 2002)
(iv) CRE Code of Practice which is a statutory code approved by Parliament
(v)   enforcement procedures.

General duty

The Amendment Act makes it unlawful for a public authority to carry out any act that constitutes discrimination.[53] The definition of public authority is very wide and is defined as any person whose function is that of a public nature.

There is also a general statutory duty on specified authorities. The specified authorities are listed in Schedule 1A of the Amendment Act which consists of five pages of specific organisations. It includes the main central and local government bodies, the police, educational bodies and housing bodies. However the Secretary of State has the power to amend, by order, the list of bodies in that schedule. It requires public authorities to adopt a proactive approach in the promotion of race equality.

A public authority with a contract or arrangement with a private company or voluntary organisation is responsible for the duty to promote race equality within that company or organisation. The consequence of this is that although private organisations are not expressly covered by the Amendment Act many will be affected by it as their policies, procedures and practices relating to racial equality will be scrutinised by public authorities where the private organisation has a contract or arrangement. This means public authorities have a very wide duty which may be difficult to comply with and regulate. However, at a minimum a public authority must consider whether the existing arrangements can meet the general duty and any specific duties.

Codes of practice

The CRE has published

a statutory code of practice ("the Code") for authorities in England and Wales[54]

The Code gives practical guidance on the general and specific duties on how to reduce racial discrimination, encourage good race relations and promote equal opportunities and. The Code's appendices set out whether and how the authority is affected by these duties. A breach of the Code (or further codes) will not be actionable as such but can be used in evidence where relevant to the proceedings. (A draft code for Scotland has been prepared separately, and specific duties have been imposed by order of Scottish Ministers. The specific duties came into effect on March 2002 and public authorities needed to have their timetable and plans for meeting the specific duties in place by 30 November 2002)

good practice guides for public authorities, schools and further and higher education institutions

The guides do not have any legal standing but provide practical guidance

(a)   for public authorities

(b)   for schools, and for further and higher education institutions. These two guides are aimed mainly at governing bodies but will provide practical guidance for all users of the system.

a guide to ethnic monitoring for public authorities

This guide explains the main principles of ethnic monitoring and how to put it into practice. It explains in more detail the specific duty in relation to employment for public authorities.

The code and guides were published in order to allow for a period of consultation and representation as provided in the Amendment Act.[55]

Specific duties

There are specific duties[56] placed upon certain public authorities to help them meet their general duty which is to promote race equality. These are to publish a race equality scheme, specific employment duties and specific duties for educational institutions.

Race Equality Scheme

Certain public authorities[57] must prepare and publish a Race Equality Scheme. This had to be done before 31 May 2002. The scheme should set out the "functions" or "policies" that are relevant to meeting the general duty, and the arrangements that will help to meet the duty in policy and service delivery. This needs to be reviewed at least every three years.

Public authorities will have to:

(i)   assess whether functions and policies or proposed policies are relevant to race equality

(ii)   assess and consult on the likely impact of the proposed policies on the promotion of race equality

(iii)   monitor their policies to see how they affect race equality

(iv)   publish the results of consultations and assessment

(v)   ensure that the public have access to information and services which it provides

(vi)   train their staff in connection with the duties.

The Code gives practical guidance to implementation. It states that the scheme provides for a set of minimum standards necessary to meet the general duty. Many public authorities will already have systems in place to meet the statutory requirements. However, by publishing a Race Equality Scheme, the public authority is accountable for its actions.

Employment procedures

Most public authorities that must publish a Race Equality Scheme also have specific employment duties. The arrangements for meeting the employment duty must be included in the above scheme. Schools, further education and higher education institutions have their own responsibilities as set out below. The arrangements needed to be in place before 31 May 2002.

These duties include:[58]

(i)   the collection of ethnic monitoring data by reference to racial groups:

    – on the numbers of staff in post, applicants for employment, training and promotion, from each such group;

    – where there are 150 or more full-time staff, the numbers of staff from each such group who receive training, the number who benefit or suffer detriment as a result of its performance assessment procedures, those involved in grievance procedures, those who are the subject of disciplinary procedures, those who cease employment with that person;

(ii)   an obligation to publish the results annually.

The specific duties on employment are meant to provide a framework for measuring the progress of equality of opportunity in public sector employment which could result in targeting certain areas to lead to a more representative public sector. The Code sets out further reasoning and practical guidance for implementing the policy.

Educational institutions

Educational institutions[59] must not only meet the requirements of the general duty, but also have had specific duties in place before 31 May 2002 to:[60]

(i) prepare a race equality policy
(ii) put in place arrangements for:
- assessing the impact of its policies on pupils, staff, parents of different racial groups, and in particular the impact on attainment levels of such pupils;
- monitoring, with reference to their impact on such pupils, staff and parents, the operation of such policies, including, in particular, their impact on the attainment levels of such pupils.

The responsibility for monitoring lies with the local education authorities (LEAs), with assistance from the schools in their area. Further and higher education institutions have other specific duties. The Code sets out the aims of the specific duties and provides detailed guidance on how institutions can achieve their specific duties.

A recent study, highlighted in *The Observer* in June 2002[61] revealed that there is a clear bias against non-white candidates, in particular at the older universities. The authors of the study, funded by the Nuffield Foundation claim their finding show a disturbing pattern of entry into higher education, which has far-reaching social implications. Higher education has some way to go in eradicating race discrimination and it remains to be seen whether the new laws will have a significant impact on its elimination from higher education institutions.

Positive action

The Code recommends that a public authority could consider using positive action[62] where monitoring reveals underrepresentation in targeting job training and recruitment. Positive action does not allow discrimination when deciding who will be offered a job. The Code does not expand on the use of positive action.

The existing provisions of the RRA allow for limited positive action to:

(i) afford access to facilities and services to meet the special needs of a particular ethnic group in respect of education, training or welfare
(ii) encourage members of a particular racial group to apply for particular work where they are under-represented
(iii) provide training for existing employees from a particular racial group in respect of work where their group is under-represented.

Enforcement of the duty[63]

The general duty upon public authorities is enforceable through judicial review.

The specific duties imposed by the Secretary of State are enforceable by the CRE as follows.

Step 1   The CRE issues a compliance notice if an authority has failed or is failing to comply with a specific duty. The notice will state that the public authority must meet its duties and has 28 days to inform the CRE. It might state the public authority must volunteer written information in order to verify the duty has been complied with.

Step 2   The authority must inform the CRE within 28 days of the steps being taken to comply with the duty or steps it will make to do so. The burden is on the public authority to comply with the duty.

Step 3   The CRE can apply for a court order if after three months from when the compliance notice was served the CRE considers that the public authority has still not met one of its specific duties. This will require the public authority to comply with a requirement of a compliance notice.

If the compliance notice required the public authority to provide information and it did not do so within the given time, or the CRE believes that the public authority does not provide the information, the CRE can apply to the county court in England, or sheriff court in Scotland for an order stating that the public authority must provide the relevant information.

Step 4   The county court or sheriff court may grant the order in the terms that the CRE applied for, or in more limited terms.

Step 5   Non-compliance with the order – if the court makes an order and the public authority does not obey, the public authority may be found in contempt of court.

Gender re-assignment and sexual orientation

The rights of a person who intends to undergo, is undergoing, or has undergone gender reassignment, are protected under the Sex Discrimination (Gender Reassignment) Regulations 1999. This makes less favourable treatment of such persons unlawful. There are a number of additional "genuine occupational qualification" defences and supplementary defences to a claim of discrimination on such grounds.

However, the courts have taken a much narrower approach in relation to discrimination against men and women on the grounds of sexual orientation. In *Smith v Gardner Merchant Limited*[64] Mr Smith suffered harassment from a female colleague on the grounds of his homosexuality. The Court said that to be successful, Mr Smith would have to show that he was treated less favourably as a homosexual man than a homosexual woman (that is, not because of his sexual orientation which is not at present covered by the SDA).

> In *Grant v South West Trains*,[65] Ms Grant, a lesbian, worked for South West Trains. Company policy allowed concessionary travel permits to spouses and common law partners of employees, but not to same-sex partners. The European Court of Justice ruled that Ms Grant had not been discriminated against on the grounds of her sex; a male employee with a male partner would not be entitled to a concessionary travel pass for his partner either. The fact of her sexual orientation was not protectable under EC or domestic law. The Court of Appeal in the case of *Pearce v The Governing Body of Mayfield Secondary School*[66] and the Scottish Court of Session in the case of *Secretary of State for Defence v MacDonald* [67] have confirmed that sexual orientation is not covered by the SDA and that the meaning of "sex" is simply "gender".

> In the case of *Smith & Grady v UK*,[68] the applicants, both homosexual army service personnel, successfully brought claims before the European Court of Human Rights under the European Convention on Human Rights (ECHR). Ms Smith and Mr Grady had been dismissed for being homosexual, in accordance with army procedure. This was held to be a breach of Articles 8 (right to a private life) and 13 (right to an effective remedy) of the ECHR.

Part-time workers

For many years part-time workers had no specific protection under the law. However as most part-timers are women it became standard practice for part-time working women to rely on the protection afforded under the sex discrimination legislation (see Chapter 1). This is because many employers treated their part-time workers less favourably than their full time employees. For example many employers paid part-timers proportionately less than their full time employees or did not give them the same benefits. Women were able to successfully argue that such a policy although not directly discriminatory against women did, in fact, have a disproportionate impact on women as most part-timers were women and the policy could not be justified. However the sex discrimination legislation was little help to male part-timers and could not always be relied upon.

In response to the Part-time Work Directive the UK implemented the Part-time Workers (Prevention of Less Favourable Treatment) Regulations 2000 (the "Regulations"). These came into force on 1 July 2000. This means that part-time workers now have independent free-standing rights and no longer have to resort to the sex discrimination legislation for protection.

The Regulations apply to workers as well as to employees, and therefore only the genuinely self-employed will be excluded. The Regulations provide that a part-time worker must be treated no less favourably than a full-time worker, unless the treatment can be objectively justified.

The Regulations also provide that women who return to work part-time after maternity leave are entitled to pro rata terms and conditions as compared to their former full-time package.

Examples of less favourable treatment could include paying a part-time worker a lower hourly rate than a full-time worker, or excluding a part-time worker from benefits, such as training or company sick pay, or treating part-timers differently on redundancy. The rights of part-time workers are dealt with in greater detail in Chapter 1.

Enforcement and remedies in discrimination cases

Employment tribunals have jurisdiction to hear complaints of discrimination on the grounds of sex, race, marital status and disability.[69] There were 25,940 claims of sex discrimination in the period 2000-2001 according to the Employment Tribunal Service Annual report 2000-2001. This marks a huge rise in claims as there were only 7,801 claims in 1999-2000. There were 4,238 claims of race discrimination in 2000-2001 contrasting with 4,015 claims in 1999-2000.

An application must be made within three months of the act complained of, although where an act of discrimination is continuing (for example where the discriminatory act takes the form of some policy, rule or practice) or where there is a series of discriminatory acts, a tribunal may permit a claim to be made within three months of the most recent act of discrimination.

An employee may claim that failure to resolve a grievance or disciplinary procedure to his or her satisfaction constitutes a fresh act of discrimination, thus extending the period of time available to the employee for making a tribunal complaint.[70]

An employee may issue proceedings both against the employer (either as the primary discriminator or on the basis of vicarious liability for the actions of other employees) and/or against individual employees alleged to have carried out discriminatory acts. An employee may serve a questionnaire[71] upon his or her employer or any other respondent to a claim of discrimination within three months of the act of discrimination, or if proceedings have already been issued before a tribunal. It must be served within 21 days of the presentation of that complaint. Standard forms of questionnaires are available for use by complainants.

Although an employer is not obliged to answer a questionnaire, a failure to do so without reasonable excuse, or the fact that evasive or unhelpful answers are given, may lead the tribunal to draw an adverse inference from that failure.

A tribunal, on finding that there has been an act of discrimination, may order one or any of the following:

(i)   a declaration of the rights of the parties

(ii) a recommendation that the employer should take certain steps, for example to introduce an equal opportunities policy and appropriate training

(iii) payment of compensation by the employer.

Declaration

A declaration can be made in both SDA and RRA cases. It is an order declaring the rights of the parties in relation to the matter at issue. Although a declaration may have some psychological assistance, it is of limited value. However a declaration that something (a particular policy for example) is unlawful can often prevent further discrimination. It is sometimes used in subsequent proceedings if the employer was originally able to argue that indirect race discrimination was unintentional but nevertheless carried on that discrimination once he knew it was unlawful.

Recommendations

Recommendations are not often made. This is because there are a number of limitations to them and substantial case law indicating the types of recommendations which are not, in fact, enforceable! Recommendations must be specific to the complainant and must relate to the specific act or acts complained of. Therefore general recommendations on wider practices are not possible. Typical recommendations include recommendations in relation to training and career development opportunities, recommendations on the content of references and recommendations that apologies should be made. Compensation (if none already awarded) or additional compensation may be payable if an employer fails to comply with a recommendation.

Compensation

Financial compensation is by far the most common remedy. Compensation will be awarded to compensate the complainant for losses already suffered (that is, loss of earnings to the date of the tribunal hearing), losses which are likely to be suffered (such as loss of future earnings, including loss of value of benefits associated with the complainant's employment) and for injury to feelings.

The way in which compensation is calculated for injury to feelings is perhaps the most difficult area. The principles for assessing such awards are set out in the case of *Armitage, Marsden and HM Prison Service v Johnson*.[72] This makes it clear that awards for injury to feelings are compensatory and that although they should compensate fully they should not punish the discriminator. Awards are at the tribunal's discretion, but in exercising that discretion tribunals should remind themselves of the value in every day life of the sums they have in mind. This may be done by reference to purchasing power or by reference to earnings. Awards should bear some general similarity to the range of awards in personal injury cases. Finally awards should be restrained, but not too low. Tribunals should at all times bear in mind the need for public respect for the level of awards made.[73]

The evidence of the complainant as to the particular injury suffered to his or her feelings is important. In rare cases, a tribunal may award aggravated damages. These will be available only where the employer's conduct was particularly high-handed or oppressive.[74]

If an employer is able to show in a case of indirect race discrimination that the discrimination was unintentional, no compensation will be awarded. This is in contrast to unintended indirect discrimination on the grounds of sex or marital status, where the tribunal may still award compensation where it has given a declaration or made a recommendation and considers it just and equitable to make an award of compensation as well.[75]

Where compensation is awarded for discrimination, the amount is not limited by legislation. In October 2000 Michael Bourgeois settled his race discrimination claim against Saga Petroleum (UK) limited for £1.8 million. In this case Mr Bourgeois successfully argued that he would not have been dismissed if he had been Norwegian. Although Mr Bourgeois was on a high income (basic salary of over £100,000 plus approximately £60,000 in annual benefits) the amount of the award largely reflected the fact that he had been dismissed at aged 55 and he was unlikely to get another job.

Despite cases like this with headline grabbing figures, in practice most sex and race discrimination awards made in the employment tribunal are not as high as the headlines would suggest. According to the Employment Tribunal Service Annual Report 2000-2001, the maximum award in sex discrimination cases was £139,896. The median award for sex discrimination cases was £5,499. The average award was £11,024. According to the same report the maximum award for race discrimination cases was £201,260. The median award for race discrimination cases was £8,012. The average award was £15,484.

These figures show that despite the hype, successful discrimination claims do not always result in very high awards. However there does seem to be a substantial increase. According to the Employment Tribunal Service Annual Report 1999-2000, the median award for all sex discrimination cases was £2,180 and the median award for race discrimination claims was £2,378. It should be noted that interest may be awarded on compensation awards.

Set against the trend of increasingly high awards, employers should be aware that of the 4,390 sex discrimination cases disposed of in 2000-2001 only 322 were successful at the employment tribunal. 1,634 were ACAS conciliated settlements, 1,614 were withdrawn and the remainder were either dismissed at the hearing or disposed of otherwise. There were 3,334 race discrimination cases disposed of in 2000-2001. Only 204 of these were successful; 1,006 were ACAS conciliated settlements; 1,136 were withdrawn and the remainder were either dismissed at the hearing or disposed of otherwise. These figures do not, of course, show how many cases were settled without ACAS or how much was paid in compensation in those cases.

Future developments

Anti-discrimination was included as a principle of the European Union by way of Article 13 of the Treaty of Amsterdam in 1997, which was an amendment to the Treaty of Rome. Article 13 states:

> Without prejudice to the other provisions of this Treaty and within the limits of the powers conferred by it upon the Community, the Council, acting unanimously on a proposal from the Commission and after consulting the European Parliament, may take appropriate action to combat discrimination based on sex, racial or ethnic origin, religion or belief, disability, age or sexual orientation.

The European Commission has acted on Article 13 and proposed two directives which have since been adopted which provide for minimum standards of legal protection against discrimination, as well as an Action Programme to assist Member States. The Action Programme runs from 2001 to 2006 and allocates 100 million euros to fund practical action by Member States. It is administered by the European Commission. The directives require EU countries to amend their anti-discrimination laws and procedures to comply with the directives.

The two directives are Council Directive 2000/78/EC (the "Employment Directive"), and Council Directive 2000/43/EC (the "Race Directive"), together referred to as the "Directives".

Implementation

The Race Directive must be implemented by the UK Government by 19 July 2003. The sexual orientation and religious discrimination parts of the Employment Directive must be implemented by 2 December 2003. The age discrimination part must be implemented by 2006.

The UK Government published a consultation document (the "Consultation Document") in December 2001 entitled, "Towards Equality and Diversity, Implementing the Employment and Race Directives" which contains the Government's proposals for compliance with the directives. This involves amending the existing legislation on race and introducing entirely new legislation to outlaw discrimination on grounds of age, sexual orientation and religion, in employment and training.

The Government intends to introduce regulations in respect of race, sexual orientation and religious discrimination in 2003. Responses to the consultation on age discrimination will lead to more detailed proposals and further consultation in 2003.

The Directive covers the following areas:
(i) conditions for access to employment, self-employment and occupation, including selection criteria and recruitment conditions

(ii)   employment and working conditions
(iii) vocational guidance and training
(iv) membership of and involvement in employers or workers organis-
      ations or professional bodies.

However, the Race Directive goes further than the Employment Directive. It also
covers social protection, including social security and healthcare, social advantages
(that is, economic and cultural benefits such as concessionary travel schemes,
housing benefit), education and access to and supply of goods and services which
are available to the public, including housing.

Both Directives apply to both the public and private sectors, regardless of the
size of the organisation.

Direct and indirect discrimination

The Directives prohibit direct and indirect discrimination on the grounds of racial
or ethnic origin, sexual orientation, religion or belief, disability or age. The
definition of direct discrimination is very similar to that in the RRA. The
Government has proposed in its Consultation Document to make no change to
the RRA regarding the definition. The definition for indirect discrimination is
broader than current legislation and is defined as an

> apparently neutral provision, criteria or practice would put persons having a
> particular religion or belief ... a particular age, or a particular sexual
> orientation at a particular disadvantage compared with other persons.[76]

The Government intends to adopt this definition in the new sexual orientation,
religion and age legislation. It proposes two options for the RRA. The first is to
replace the current RRA definition with that contained in the Directives. This
will bring it more in line with the amended SDA definition, although "apparently
neutral" seems to relax the definition even more. The second is to make only
minor changes to the RRA definition.

Justification: genuine occupational requirement

The Directives provide for exceptions where differences in treatment based on a
characteristic related to a particular racial or ethnic origin, sexual orientation,
religion or belief, or age will be allowed. These include where the

> genuine and determining occupational requirement, provided that the
> objective is legitimate and the requirement is proportionate.[77]

The Government proposed not to include a list of specific occupational
requirements as part of any new legislation on sexual orientation, religion or belief,
and age, but instead include a provision of general application, allowing employers
to recruit staff on the basis of a "genuine occupational requirement", and then

for the courts and tribunals to decide. It does propose to issue guidance listing examples. At present the RRA provides for specific circumstances whereby it can be objectively justified by means of a genuine occupational qualification for someone of a particular racial group to carry out a job. The Government intends to amend the RRA to ensure that it is consistent with the other discrimination legislation, and simply provide that membership of a particular racial or ethnic group could be a genuine occupational requirement where it is essentially a defining feature of a job.

Other justifications

The Employment Directive also includes a provision to enable churches and other religious or belief organisations to retain their particular ethos.[78] The Employment Directive does not provide any definition of "religion or belief" and the Government has also decided not to define it (although it states that it should not be a political belief), but to leave to the Courts to decide. Therefore a religious organisation may be able to demonstrate that it is a genuine requirement that all or senior staff should belong to the religion concerned. The Government proposes to include this in the new legislation, but does not propose to define which organisations are covered by this. The Government intends then to issue guidance to assist religious or belief organisations.

Further justifications are provided where discriminatory measures are to be laid down by national law in circumstances of national security, protection of health, and prevention of criminal offences.

Harassment

Both the Directives now specifically set out and define harassment as a form of direct discrimination. The definitions in the Directives state that it is

> unwanted conduct…which violates a person's dignity and creates a hostile, degrading, humiliating or offensive environment.[79]

In the Government's Consultation Document, it stated that this definition cannot be adopted for the RRA, as harassment in race relations cases has been defined more widely, and it does not want to reduce the protection this provides. Case law states that an individual does not have to show the existence of a hostile working environment in order to bring a claim. The Government proposes either to restrict the Directives' definition to all new discrimination legislation, or to expand this definition and adopt the provision provided currently by the RRA to all discrimination legislation.

Bodies for the promotion of equal treatment

The Race Directive requires Member States[80] to designate a body to promote race equality, and to assist individuals to pursue complaints. The CRE already exists. There is no corresponding requirement in the Employment Directive. However, the Government is considering moving the existing bodies into a single Equality Commission.

Positive action

Both Directives allow (yet do not require) Member States to maintain or adopt specific measures to prevent or compensate for disadvantages linked to:

(i) racial or ethnic origin
(ii) religion or belief, sexual orientation as regards employment and occupation.[81]

The Government proposes that the new legislation will allow for similar positive action as that provided in the RRA. The RRA currently provides for employers to encourage job applications from particular underrepresented racial or ethnic groups, and to offer training programmes to develop the potential of particular ethnic or racial groups that are in the workforce.

However, this does not fall as far as providing for positive discrimination. The Consultation Document provides an example of positive discrimination (page 31, Consultation Document) where a company only recruits new staff who are of a particular racial or ethnic group because they are underrepresented in the workforce.

Enforcement

The Directives provide for Member States to have procedures in place for a person who considers himself or herself wronged even after the relationship in which the discrimination is alleged has ended, to have access to judicial and/or administrative procedures, including conciliation procedures.[82] Member states shall also provide for organisations such as trade unions or special interest groups to bring cases on applicants' behalf. The Government states that the current court system already meets the requirements of the Directive, but will be extended to cover complaints of discrimination on grounds of sexual orientation, religion and age. The Government also proposes to amend the RRA to allow individuals to seek redress in certain situations after the relationship has ended, and the Government provides an example whereby an employer refuses to provide a reference for a former employee who has brought a discrimination claim based on either Directive.

Remedies

Where discrimination contrary to either Directive is proved to have taken place in any case, the complainant must be given a remedy, including compensation where appropriate, which is "effective, proportionate and dissuasive".[83] The Government, in its Consultation Document, considers that the current system provides for adequate remedies, and therefore they recommend to extend the remedies to that where discrimination is proved for sexual orientation, age, religion and belief.

Third country nationals

Both Directives cover any person who is in a member state when the act of discrimination occurs. However, discrimination based on nationality is outside its scope and cannot be used to challenge conditions that a member state applies to the entry or residence of third-country nationals, and any treatment they receive as part of their legal status.

Burden of proof

The Directives contain provisions about the burden of proof.[84] When persons establish facts from which it may be presumed that there has been direct or indirect discrimination, it shall be for the respondent to prove that there has been no breach of the principle of equal treatment.

The approach is in line with the Burden of Proof Directive[85] which only applies to sex discrimination, which the Government has recently implemented into the SDA by the Sex Discrimination (Indirect Discrimination and Burden of Proof) Regulations 2001. The Government proposes to include similar provisions in the RRA and in the new legislation on sexual orientation, religion and belief, and age.

Protection against victimisation

The Directives state that Member States shall provide for protection against victimisation by the employer as a result of complaining about discrimination or undertaking any legal proceedings.[86] The Government has stated that there are already specific provisions in the RRA, but proposes to include similar provisions in the new legislation on sexual orientation, religion and belief, and age.

Conclusion

The UK has had thorough and extensive discrimination legislation since the 1970s. The new Directives will not require huge changes to the current legislation. However, the Government will need to introduce new legislation on age, religion and belief, and sexual orientation.

Notes

1 Sex Discrimination Act 1975 (see Section 6)
2 Race Relations Act 1976 (see Section 4)
3 Sex Discrimination Act 1975 (see Section 3)
4 Disability Discrimination Act 1995 (see Section 4)
5 Although the Code of Practice "Age Diversity in Employment" sets out best practice, it has no legal force
6 See *Bullock v Alice Ottley School* (1992) IRLR 564 and *Perera v Civil Service Commission and another* (No 2) (1982) ICR 350
7 Sections 35–38 RRA give a limited right to discriminate positively but the provisions do not apply in recruitment or in relation to the treatment of employees
8 (2002) IRLR 239
9 (1983) IRLR 209
10 *CRE v Dutton* (1989) IRLR 8, CA
11 *Seide v Gillette Industries Ltd* (1980) IRLR 427, EAT
12 (1988) EAT 6/88
13 *JH Walker Ltd v Hussain* (1996) IRLR 11, EAT
14 (Section 4 SDA and Section 2 RRA)
15 See Section 230(3) ERA 1996
16 (See Section 9 SDA and Section 7 RRA)
17 (Section 85 SDA and Section 75 RRA)
18 (Section 17 SDA and Section 76 RRA)
19 (Section 18 SDA)
20 See Section 10 SDA and Section 8 RRA
21 (1999) IRLR 370
22 www.eoc.org.uk
23 www.cre.gov.uk
24 (1990) ICR 554
25 It is lawful to discriminate against unmarried persons
26 *Webb v EMO Air Cargo Ltd* (1995) IRLR 645; Section 5(3) SDA
27 EAT 788/97
28 SI 2001/2660
29 (1991) IRLR 513
30 (1978) ICR 27
31 For examples see (1) *Briggs v North Eastern Education and Library Board* (1990) IRLR 181 NI, CA, (2) *Burston v Superior Creative Services Ltd* (FT case 72892/95) and (3) *United Distillers v Gordon* (EAT 12/97)
32 (1983) IRLR 166
33 *R v Secretary of State for Employment ex parte EOC* (1994) IRLR 176
34 Section 2 RRA; http://www-homeoffice.gov.uk/race act/racerel/htm; Section 4 SDA; see *Aziz v Trinity Street Taxis Ltd* (1988) ICR 534
35 *Chief Constable of West Yorkshire Police v Khan* (2001) IRLR 830
36 *Coote v Granada Hospitality Limited* (1998) IRLR 656; victimisation where employer refused to give a reference to a former employee who had brought sex discrimination proceedings against it
37 *Porcelli v Strathclyde Regional Council* (1986) ICR 564
38 Ibid

[39] The offence is inserted at Section 4A (1) and (5) Public Order Act 1986 http://www.hmso.gov.uk/acts/acts1996/1996059.htm

[40] (2001) IRLR 472

[41] *Jones v Tower Boot Co Ltd* (1997) IRLR 168

[42] *Balgobin and Francis v London Borough of Tower Hamlets* (1987) ICR 829

[43] Section 30 RRA http://www.homeoffice.gov.uk/raceact/racerel1.htm; Section 39 SDA

[44] Section 31 RRA http://www.homeoffice.gov.uk/raceact/racerel1.htm; Section 40 SDA

[45] *Weathersfield Ltd v Sargent* (1998) *The Times*, 31 December

[46] (1996) IRLR 596

[47] *Irving and Irving v Post Office* (1987) IRLR 289

[48] (2000) IRLR 602

[49] Section 33(2) RRA and s 42(2) SDA

[50] *Hallam v Avery* (2000) ICR 583, CA (upheld (2001) UKHL 15)

[51] (1977) IRLR 202

[52] Report of an inquiry by Sir William McPherson, TSO, CM, 4261–1

[53] Section 19B The Amendment Act

[54] The Race Relations Act 1976 (General Statutory Duty: Code of Practice) Order 2002 came into force on 30 May 2002

[55] The Amendment Act S.71(d)

[56] Race Relations Act (Statutory Duties) Order 2001

[57] Listed in Schedule 1 to the Race Relations Act 1976 (Statutory Duties) Order 2001

[58] Sections 5(1), (2) and (3) of the above Order

[59] as specified in Part I and II of Schedule 2 of the above Order

[60] Sections 3(1), (2) and (3) of the above Order

[61] Racial bias at UK's elite universities, Tracey McVeigh, education editor June 23, 2002

[62] It is permitted by the RRA

[63] Section 71D of the Amendment Act

[64] (1998) IRLR 510

[65] (1998) IRLR 206

[66] (2001) IRLR 669

[67] (2001) IRLR 748

[68] (1999) IRLR 734

[69] For guidelines in disability cases, see *Goodwin v Patent Office* (1999) IRLR 4

[70] *Cast v Croydon College* (1998) IRLR 318

[71] The Sex Discrimination (Questions and Replies) Order 1975, the Race Relations (Questions and Replies) Order 977 and the Disability Discrimination (Questions and Replies) Order 1996 http://www.legislation.hmso.gov.uk/si/si1996/Uksi_19962793_en_1.htm

[72] (1997) IRLR 162

[73] *ARG Armitage, Marsden and HM Prison Service v Johnson* (1997) IRLR 162

[74] Ibid

[75] Sex Discrimination and Equal Pay (Miscellaneous Amendments) Regulations 1996 SI 1996/438 http://www.legislation.hmso.gov.uk/si/si1996/Uksi_19960438_en_1.htm

[76] Section 2 (b) of the Directive

[77] Article 4 of the Directives

[78] Article 4 (2) of the Employment Directive

[79] Article 2 (3) of the Directives
[80] Article 13 of the Race Directive
[81] Article 5 of the Race Directive, and Article 7 of the Employment Directive
[82] Article 7 of the Race Directive and Article 9 of the Employment Directive
[83] Article 15 of the Race Directive and Article 17 of the Employment Directive
[84] Article 8 of the Race Directive, and Article 10 of the Employment Directive
[85] 97/80/EC
[86] Article 9 of the Race Directive and Article 11 of the Employment Directive

4

Disability discrimination

JOANNA BLACKBURN

Joanna Blackburn is a partner in the Employment Group of the London law firm, Mishcon de Reya.

Introduction

The Disability Discrimination Act was passed in 1995 and the employment provisions came into force on 2 December 1996. In many respects, the provisions of the DDA are unique in employment law. Caution should be exercised in placing too much reliance on existing decisions and concepts in the other discrimination acts.

> Contrary to what might be reasonably assumed, the exercise of interpretation [of the DDA] is not facilitated by familiarity with the pre-existing legislation prohibiting discrimination in the field of employment (and elsewhere) on the grounds of sex [Sex Discrimination Act 1975] and race [Race Relations Act 1976]. Indeed, it may be positively misleading to approach the 1995 Act with assumptions and concepts familiar from experience of the workings of the 1975 Act and the 1976 Act.[1]

The DDA differs from the SDA and RRA in that it provides a defence for direct discrimination. It also imposes a duty on employers to consider whether they can make "reasonable adjustments" to facilitate the employment of disabled people. Also important to remember is that whilst the SDA derives from European Law,[2] the DDA is not the result of European legislation. Europe has looked at the issue of disability before. In 1986, the European Commission adopted the Recommendation on the Employment of Disabled People.[3] Falling short of a Directive (which would have led to primary legislation in EU Member States), the Recommendation set out a general intention to consider future action in eliminating disability discrimination. This was followed up by reference to the rights of disabled people in the EC Charter of Fundamental Social Rights of Workers[4] and the Social Chapter.[5]

However, on 27 November 2000, the Directive Establishing a General Framework for Equal Treatment in Employment and Occupation[6] was passed.

The Directive covers discrimination on the grounds of racial or ethnic origin, religion or belief, disability, age or sexual orientation. In short, it is comprehensive discrimination legislation. The provisions relating to disability must be in force by no later than 2 December 2003.

Other European discrimination law may also have an impact on the DDA. The Burden of Proof Directive (BPD) was implemented in the UK on 20 July 2001 and came into force on 12 October 2001. Currently, the BPD deals only with sex discrimination (because there is no EU-driven legislation in respect of other forms of discrimination).

The BPD provides that where there is an adverse impact on one sex it is for the employer to prove that provision, criterion or practice is appropriate and necessary and can be justified by objective factors unrelated to sex (see Chapter 3). In other words, once an employee has raised a prima facie case of unequal treatment, the burden of proof moves from employee to employer to demonstrate that the unequal treatment can be objectively justified. For example, once an employee can show on statistical evidence that there are significantly fewer women at a level to which she sought promotion, it will be for the employer to demonstrate that the denial of the promotion was objectively justified.

Although this directive only applies to sex discrimination, it is likely that pressure will mount for it to apply equally to race and disability discrimination. Naturally, at such time as the General Framework for Equal Treatment in Employment and Occupations Directive comes into force in the form of domestic legislation, the BPD is likely to be expanded to include all forms of prohibited discrimination.

In disability discrimination the effect of the BPD would be significant. Disabled people are twice as likely as non-disabled people to be unemployed and have no formal qualifications.[7] As such, it will be easier to show, on a statistical basis, that most employers are employing proportionally less disabled people as are represented in the available work force. If the employer is then obliged to bear the burden of proving that the reason for this is non-discriminatory, even before considering the other obligations placed on employers by the DDA, the employer's task in defending DDA claims becomes more difficult.

The various elements of the legislation

The DDA cannot be read alone. It was introduced with the Disability Discrimination (Employment) Regulations,[8] the Code of Practice for The Elimination of Discrimination in the Field of Employment against Disabled Persons or Persons who have had a Disability[9] (Code) and Guidance on Matters to be Taken into Account in Determining Questions Relating to the Definition of Disability[10] (Guidance). Each of these documents, but particularly the Code and the Guidance, is essential in interpreting and implementing the obligations of the DDA. Employers making decisions in relation to disability issues must make reference to them. Failure to do so may render decisions made inadvertently discriminatory. Whilst this has been stressed on many occasions in the tribunals and the EAT, it was emphasised in *Goodwin v The Patent Office*.[11] In reaching its decision, the EAT made several points about how the DDA should be interpreted and the assistance given in interpretation by the Code and Guidance.

First, the EAT stressed the inquisitorial and interventionist roles of the tribunal in making its decisions. In dealing with social legislation such as the DDA, tribunals are obliged to take a purposive approach to construction. In other words, whilst regard must be given to the natural meaning of the words in the DDA, tribunals must also look, insofar as it is consistent, at the stated or presumed intention of Parliament. In doing this tribunals are given explicit assistance in two forms,[12] namely the Guidance and the Code:

> The EAT repeats what it has said on previous occasions…reference should always [the EAT's emphasis] be made, explicitly, to any relevant provision of the Guidance or Code which has been taken into account in arriving at its decision.[13]

The reason for this emphasis is because these documents set out in clear and direct language (and with many very helpful examples) the objectives of the legislation.

This is not something for consideration only by the tribunals and the EAT. The Guidance and the Code provide invaluable assistance to any person seeking to address issues of disability in employment situations. Not only will adherence to the Guidance and Code lead to less likelihood of unlawful discrimination arising and cases being brought, they also set out a list of practical considerations that will enable employers to adopt best practice and encourage equal opportunities.

Particularly helpful is the general guidance to avoid discrimination at the beginning of the Code. The key practical piece of advice is to talk to disabled employees in order to discuss with them the effects of the disability or what may be done to help. A huge proportion of disputes could probably be avoided if this advice is implemented in a sensible and sensitive way. A review of many of the decisions under the DDA reveals case after case where decisions are taken about an employee without any consultation or discussion. Much of what the Code has to say is simple common sense and will only reinforce much of the thinking about employment practices generally.

The Disability Rights Commission

The DRC was established by the Disability Rights Commission Act 1999 (DRCA). It came into being in April 2000. Similar to the Equal Opportunities Commission and the Commission for Racial Equality, it has wide ranging powers and responsibilities.

The Disability Rights Commission:

(i)   Its objective is to work towards the elimination of discrimination against disabled persons and to promote equal opportunities.

(ii) It can take such steps as it considers appropriate with a view to encouraging good practice in the treatment of disabled people, including keeping the working of the DDA and DRCA under review.

(iii) It has powers to make recommendations to the government on issues under its remit.

(iv) It can conduct formal investigations and where it discovers that an unlawful act has been committed it can issue non-discrimination notices.

(v)   It can provide assistance in relation to proceedings.

At the head of the DRC are between 10 and 15 commissioners. All are appointed by the Secretary of State and must provide adequate representation of disabled people. A person who is not disabled (and has not been disabled) can only be appointed as a commissioner if the appointment of that person will not lead to half or less of the commissioners being disabled people (or people who have had a disability). Initially commissioners will serve for between two and five years, but can be reappointed thereafter.

Disability and the disabled person

Section 1(1) of the DDA sets out the definition of who will constitute a disabled person. It states that a person has a disability if he or she "has a physical or mental impairment which has a substantial and long term adverse impact on his or her ability to carry out normal day-to-day activities". A person will only qualify as disabled for the purposes of the DDA if he or she satisfies each element of the definition. However, appraising whether a person will satisfy each element of the definition requires more than consideration of the usual meanings of the language used in the definitions. Some terms have been given statutory meanings, whilst others are clarified by Regulation (for example, the Disability Discrimination (Meaning of Disability) Regulations 1996 SI 1996/1455 Regulation 3 (1)), the Code and the Guidance.

The onus is on the individual to prove that he or she is disabled. However, the EAT has emphasised that it is important for tribunals to put aside their preconceptions as to what is a disabled person. As they pointed out in *Vicary v British Telecommunications plc*,[14] "a relatively small proportion of the disabled community are what one might describe as visibly disabled, that is, people in wheelchairs and carrying white sticks or other aids". Stereotypical images of what constitutes a disability will not suffice in determining whether a person is disabled for the purposes of the DDA. Given that the Tribunal is obliged to put aside its preconceptions in determining who is disabled, employers must do likewise if they are to avoid successful DDA claims.

Physical and/or Mental Impairment

The disabled person must show that he or she has a physical or mental impairment. A mental impairment will only be covered if it is a clinically well recognised illness.[15] To be clinically well recognised, it must be recognised by a respected body of medical opinion. The World Health Organisation's International Classification of Diseases may provide clarification as to whether a mental illness is clinically well recognised.[16]

Conditions expressly not covered by the DDA:

(i)   Addiction to or dependency on alcohol, nicotine or any other substance (save where the substance is medically prescribed).

(ii)   Seasonal allergic rhinitis (for example, hayfever), save where it aggravates the effect of another condition.

(iii)   Tendency to set fires.

(iv)   Tendency to steal.

(v)   Tendency to physically or sexually abuse other people.

(vi)   Exhibitionism.

(vii)   Voyeurism.

(viii) Self inflicted disfigurements, such as tattoos or piercings.

Table 1 shows the tribunals' approach to determining whether particular conditions can constitute physical or mental impairments. Where there is any doubt as to whether a particular condition constitutes a physical or mental impairment, medical advice should be sought. However, that medical advice will not always be interpreted by the Tribunals in a consistent manner.

> In *Rugamer v Sony Music Entertainment UK Limited* and *McNicol v Balfour Beatty Rail Maintenance Limited*,[17] the applicants both suffered from a condition known as psychological "overlay", where they claimed to be suffering from physical impairments but no source could be found for the physical complaints. Instead, the alleged physical impairments were believed to be a manifestation of the applicants' mental state. The applicants had not sought to argue that they suffered from a mental impairment and had not adduced medical evidence in this regard. In any event, the tribunal found that psychological "overlay" was not a clinically well recognised disease and thus, however the applicants had sought to put their cases, they would not have been disabled. This approach was upheld by the EAT.

However, a separately constituted EAT found that the physical manifestations of a mental disorder could constitute a physical impairment, even where there was no organic reason for the physical impairment. In *College of Ripon and York St John v Hobbs*,[18] the applicant was suffering from slow, progressive muscle weakening and wasting. Whilst accepting that the applicant's condition was caused by her mental state rather than a physical illness, the Tribunal (and later the EAT) were prepared to conclude that the applicant had a physical impairment. The EAT were aware of the decision in *Rugamer* and *McNicol* at the time that they reached their decision in *Hobbs*. *Rugamer* and *McNicol* are to be heard by the Court of Appeal and this should assist in obtaining clarification on this issue.

As regards mental impairments, the EAT have determined that there are four possible routes for an applicant to follow in showing the existence of a mental impairment:[19]

(i)   The illness can be specifically mentioned in the WHO International Classification of Diseases.

(ii)   The illness can be mentioned in a publication that is like the WHO International Classification of Diseases, which is likely to be some other form of classification widely accepted by the medical profession.

(iii)   The illness is accepted as a mental impairment by a respected body of medical opinion.

(iv)   Medical opinion agrees that a condition is a mental impairment although it is not a mental illness. In practice, it is hard to envisage circumstances where this could apply.

The EAT further recommended that in considering mental impairment cases, tribunals are mindful of the following:

(i)   It is for the applicant to prove that he or she is suffering from a mental impairment.

(ii)   Tribunals are not expected to have more than a lay understanding of psychiatric conditions.

(iii)   Tribunals will often need to draw on expert evidence.

(iv)   The demeanour of the applicant in the Tribunal hearing should not usually be of relevance to the determination of the issue of whether he or she is suffering from a mental impairment.

(v)   In appropriate cases (and particularly where an applicant is unrepresented), the Tribunal can adjourn a case to enable medical evidence to be obtained.

Substantial adverse effect

The meaning of "substantial" has been clarified by the Guidance. It is defined as being more than "minor" or "trivial", rather than the usual definition of large or considerable. It is a difference that is greater than those differences that would normally exist amongst people.[20]

The Guidance sets out a number of considerations to be taken into account in determining whether a person is suffering from a substantial adverse effect:

Table 1

The tribunal's attitude to physical and mental impairments

Impairment **can** be disability	Case
Paranoid Schizophrenia	*Goodwin v Patents Office*
Serious stress and depression	*Kapadia v London Borough of Lambeth*
Chronic Fatigue Syndrome	*HJ Heinz Co Ltd v Kenrick* ME *London Borough of Hillingdon v Morgan*
Depression	*Greenwood v British Airways*
Back pain	*Laws Hospital NHS Trust v Rush*
Diabetes	*Arboshe v East London Bus and Coach Co Ltd* Epilepsy *Jewell v Stoke Mandeville Hospital NHS Trust*
Repetitive Strain Injury	*Grigg v HM Land Registry*

(i) The time that it takes for a person to carry out an activity may be relevant. It should be compared with the amount of time it might take a person to carry out the same activity without the impairment.

(ii) Another factor to consider is the way in which a person with an impairment carries out a normal day-to-day activity, compared with the way the person might carry out the day-to-day activity if he or she did not have the impairment.

In *Vicary v British Telecommunications plc*, the EAT considered a decision by the Tribunal that Mrs Vicary's impairment did not have a substantial effect on her ability to carry out day-to-day activities. Mrs Vicary had an upper arm condition that rendered her unable, amongst other things, to carry baskets of washing, do heavy shopping or carry a handbag. The tribunal held that Mrs Vicary could carry her washing in smaller quantities, use a shopping trolley and unload her shopping in small quantities and use a shoulder bag as opposed to a handbag. On appeal, the EAT held that the tribunal had taken the wrong approach to determining whether her impairment had a substantial adverse effect. It should have considered the fact that the adjustments that Mrs Vicary had to make in order to cope with her impairment were indicative of it having a substantial effect.

(iii) The cumulative effect of the impairment may also need to be considered. The impairment needs to have a substantial effect on the person's ability to carry out normal day-to-day activities. What is meant by normal day-to-day activities is considered below. However, where there is not a substantial effect on any particular day-to-day activity, but when the effects of the impairment on the person's ability to carry out a number of day-to-day activities is considered, the cumulative effect of the impairment may still be substantial.

The Guidance gives an example of someone with mild cerebral palsy. The person may suffer a number of effects on their ability to carry out day-to-day activities, such as fatigue, which may hinder walking, poor visual perception and poor co-ordination and balance. Taken alone, none of these things may amount to a substantial adverse effect, but taken together, they may amount to a substantial adverse effect.

It may also be necessary to consider the cumulative effect of two unrelated impairments. A person may have a minor impairment which affects physical co-ordination and a minor but permanent leg injury which affects mobility. Taken together, the effects may be substantial.[21]

(iv) Consideration needs to be given to the extent to which a person can be expected to modify their behaviour. If a person can modify his or her behaviour to alleviate the effect of the impairment, it may mean that the impairment does not have a substantial effect on the person. However, if the coping technique breaks down in certain situations, for example when the person is under stress, then this factor will need to be weighed up when considering whether the impairment has a substantial effect. Similarly, if a person is advised by a medical practitioner to take certain steps to alleviate the effect of the impairment, this treatment may be disregarded in assessing whether the effect of the impairment is substantial.

This issue was examined by the EAT in *Kapadia v London Borough of Lambeth*.[22] Mr Kapadia was an accountant with London Borough of Lambeth. He was suffering from anxiety, stress, tension and depression. As a result, he was sent for counselling, receiving about 20 treatments over a two year period. Eventually, and having had increasingly large amounts of time off work, he was retired on medical grounds. When he complained to the tribunal, it held that Mr Kapadia was not disabled as his depression only had a trivial effect on his normal day-to-day activities. On appeal, it was argued that the tribunal had erred in not considering what the effects of Mr Kapadia's illness would have been had he not had counselling. He asserted that without that medical help, he would have had a complete breakdown. As such, he should still be treated as disabled and not penalised for having taken steps to help himself.

The EAT agreed with Mr Kapadia. Where an impairment is treated, the effects of that treatment need to be discounted in considering whether the effect of the impairment is substantial. Counselling amounted to treatment – the fact that Mr Kapadia could be treated without resorting to medication or in-patient treatment was not an indication that he had not received medical treatment. Accordingly, he was disabled.

(v)   Environmental effects on the impairment may also need to be considered. Some impairments will be worsened by external effects such as temperature, light conditions and time of day. Others may be affected by other factors influencing the person, such as tiredness or stress.

For some disabled people, the extent to which an effect is "substantial" will vary depending on the time at which it is assessed.

In *Greenwood v British Airways plc*,[23] the EAT held that the tribunal should have looked at the effects of the impairment that Mr Greenwood suffered up to the tribunal date, even though this was some nine months after the date on which British Airways discriminated against Mr Greenwood. Mr Greenwood had been absent from work for periods between October 1993 and February 1997 due to a depressive illness. In June 1997, he was denied promotion on the grounds that he was unreliable due to his previous sickness. His illness recurred and he was absent from August 1997 for an indefinite period. The tribunal held that although he had a mental impairment, at the time that he was denied promotion, he was not suffering from a substantial long-term impairment because his illness had ceased and was not likely to recur. The EAT held that the tribunal's decision was fatally flawed because it had failed to take into account the adverse effects that had led Mr Greenwood to be absent from August 1997 in determining the substantial, long-term adverse effect. Had the tribunal directed itself properly, it would have concluded that Mr Greenwood's illness had a substantial and long-term effect on him.

Where an applicant asserts that he or she is still suffering from the same substantial adverse effect of the disability at the time of the hearing as suffered at the time of the alleged discrimination, the tribunal is entitled to consider how an applicant conducts himself or herself in the tribunal. However, the tribunal will also need to take into account the effect the tribunal environment may have and the additional stress that this may place on the applicant.[24] The tribunal must also not substitute its impression of the applicant where there is undisputed medical evidence that the applicant is disabled.[25]

Where the effects of the illness are periodic, it may well mean that the effects of an illness are not substantial.

In *Foster v Hampshire Fire and Rescue Service*,[26] Mrs Foster had been employed for 25 years, until her dismissal for incapacity on 19 February

1997. Mrs Foster suffered from asthma and migraine and had taken a considerable amount of time off due to ill health in the previous three years. Mrs Foster had asthma attacks about two or three times a year and migraine attacks about eight or nine times a year. When she had a migraine, she had to lie down in a darkened room. The tribunal decided that the combined effect of the two conditions was not enough to have a substantial effect on Mrs Foster. The attacks were only periodic and were short lived. For this reason, Mrs Foster's complaint of discrimination failed.

However, if a person has an illness which is likely to become worse and have a substantial adverse effect on the person, the effects may be deemed to be substantial even before the full effects are seen. This type of progressive condition, such as HIV, multiple sclerosis and some forms of cancer, will be brought within the ambit of the DDA provided that it has "some" effect on the person at the time of the discrimination and is likely to have a substantial adverse effect in due course. The effect does not need to be continuous or substantial at the time of the discriminatory act.[27] However, an assumption should not be made that a person with, for example, multiple sclerosis will always be disabled after diagnosis. In *Mowat-Brown v University of Surrey*[28] the EAT held that the applicant was not disabled despite the fact that he had multiple sclerosis. The medical evidence did not indicate that it was likely that his impairment would have a substantial adverse effect in due course.

Where a person has a severe disfigurement (other than a tattoo or piercings), it will be assumed that the disfigurement has a substantial effect on the person's ability to perform day-to-day activities. The person does not need to prove such an effect. Disfigurements might include scarring (including scarring as a result of removal of a tattoo), skin diseases, birthmarks or limb and postural deformation. What may be of relevance is whether the disfigurement is apparent in normal circumstances. For example, scarring to the face or hands may be treated differently to scarring on the back.

Past disabilities

A person whose name appeared on the Disabled Persons Register, which existed prior to the DDA coming into force, on both 12 January 1995 and 2 December 1995 was automatically designated as having a disability until 2 December 1998. Now, such persons will either continue to be assessed as disabled or will be classified as having had a past disability. If a person is discriminated against on the basis of a past disability, he or she can still bring a claim under the DDA.

Long-term effect

The DDA states that the long-term effect of an impairment is one that:
(i)   has lasted at least 12 months

(ii)   is likely to last 12 months

(iii)   is likely to last for the rest of the person's life.

Where the person is asserting that they had a disability in the past, the impairment must have lasted for 12 months. The effect of the impairment may change throughout the 12-month period. Where a condition is progressive, the effect may worsen during the period – it is not necessary for the condition to have had a substantial adverse effect on the person throughout the period.

Similarly, some conditions may be of a type where remissions may occur. Again, as long as the underlying impairment continues for a total of 12 months and it is more than likely that the effects of the impairment will recur, the effect will be deemed to be long-term. In these circumstances, it will be necessary to consider the effects of medical treatment. If it is likely that the impairment will be cured within 12 months and not require further treatment, it may indicate that the impairment is not long-term. However, if the medical treatment merely delays or prevents a recurrence of the impairment and removal of treatment will probably cause a recurrence of the impairment, it will have to be discounted in assessing the length of time the impairment is likely to last.

Conditions with sporadic effects can still have a long-term effect on the individual, even though the person may not be suffering substantial adverse effects on a daily basis. For example, a person with epilepsy may be treated as disabled even if he or she only has periodic episodes.

Day-to-day activities

As the EAT pointed out in *Goodwin v the Patents Office*, the meaning of "day-to-day activities" is the most difficult aspect of the definition of "disability" to judge; easily recognised, but defined with difficulty.[29]

Again, the Guidance seeks to illuminate the interpretation of day-to-day activities. It states that it is not intended to include activities that are only normal for a specific group of people. As such, work of any particular form is not included in the definition, because work is different for different people. Nor are particular skills that some people may possess a relevant consideration in determining a day-to-day activity. The fact that a person cannot play the piano is not an issue, even if the person alleging a disability is a professional musician.[30] Instead account should be taken of how far an activity is normal for most people and carried out by most people on a daily or frequent and fairly regular basis.[31]

The EAT considered what type of activity might amount to a normal day-to-day activity in *Vicary v British Telecommunications plc*. In this case, the tribunal had determined that DIY, filing nails, tonging hair, ironing, shaking quilts, grooming animals, polishing furniture, knitting, sewing and cutting with scissors were not normal day-to-day activities. The EAT rejected this conclusion, pointing out that all those activities were ones performed by people on a frequent and fairly regular basis. As a matter of common sense, these activities were normal every day activities.

The definition of day-to-day activities:

Specifically, the DDA states that an impairment is only to be treated as affecting the person's ability to carry out normal day-to-day activities if it affects one of the following:

(i)   mobility
(ii)   manual dexterity
(iii)   physical coordination
(iv)   continence
(v)   ability to lift, carry or otherwise move everyday objects
(vi)   speech, hearing or eyesight
(vii)   memory or ability to concentrate, learn or understand
(viii) perception of the risk of physical danger.[32]

In some cases, a person will be able to perform an activity, but only at some cost to themselves, either due to the fact that the performance of the activity causes pain or fatigue. The fact that a person can perform the activity in these circumstances does not mean that the person is to be treated as able to perform the activity. The pain or fatigue must be taken into account and it may mean that the person should be treated as having an impairment that affects their ability to perform the activity at all. However, it is a question of degree for the tribunal.

> In *Cooper v Jaguar Cars Limited*[33] the tribunal held that the fact that the applicant could walk for two miles although he experienced some pain and discomfort in doing so was not an indication that he was unable to perform day-to-day activities. On appeal, the EAT refused to interfere with the tribunal's opinion. The tribunal had indicated that their decision was marginal, and in the absence of an apparent point of law, their determination would stand.

The fact that a person is able to continue to perform their job to all or some degree will not be determinative of whether he or she has an impairment that has a substantial adverse effect on his or her ability to perform day-to-day activities. Indeed an employee alleging discrimination will often wish to assert that he or she could do his or her job. In *Law Hospitals NHS Trust v Rush*,[34] Mrs Rush asserted that she was discriminated against because of a disability. She was a staff nurse and experienced difficulties in performing her day-to-day activities due to back pain; however she was able to do her job. The tribunal, in applying the DDA and the Guidance, focused on the tests set out in the act and decided that her back pain did have a substantial adverse effect on her ability to carry out day-to-day activities. The NHS Trust appealed on the basis that the fact that she could do her job meant that her back pain could not be affecting her performance of every day activities. The Scottish EAT held that the tribunal had been correct – what it must consider was the test set out in the DDA, not job specific issues.

On occasions a person will have the physical capacity to perform certain activities, but due to a mental impairment, will not be able to bring himself or herself to actually perform the activity either at all or for any length of time. A person with depression may be able to speak, but due to his or her illness the desire to communicate may be inhibited.

In some cases, the effect of an impairment on one type of day-to-day activity will automatically have an effect on another type of activity. For example, a person with a sight impediment would not have to prove that the impediment affected mobility too. It would be taken as being obvious that the two issues would be linked.[35]

However, what constitutes day-to-day activities will not always be clear. The Guidance offers examples to assist in its determination and, whilst it is not exhaustive, it provides the following clarification:

Impairment and how it affects day-to-day activities:

Mobility
This covers moving or changing position, either in terms of significant movement or minor adjustments to the body. It includes whether a person is able to move around unaided or use normal means of transport (public or otherwise), whether a person can walk a short distance, climb stairs, leave home without assistance or get around in an unfamiliar place. It also includes whether a person can sit, stand, bend or reach.

The Guidance states that it would be reasonable to regard as having a substantial adverse effect:

(i)   the inability to travel a short journey as a passenger in a vehicle
(ii)   inability to walk other than at a slow pace or with unsteady or jerky movements
(iii)   difficulty in going up or down steps, stairs or gradients
(iv)   inability to use one or more forms of public transport
(v)   inability to go outside unaccompanied.

It would not be reasonable to regard as having a substantial adverse effect:

(vi)   Difficulty walking unaided a distance of about 1.5 kilometres or a mile without discomfort or having to stop – the distance would obviously vary according to the age of the person and the type of terrain.
(vii)   Inability to travel in a car for a journey lasting more than two hours without discomfort.[36]

Manual dexterity
This relates to the ability of a person to use their hands and fingers with

---

precision. Consideration needs to be given to the ability to manipulate individual fingers as well as the ability to coordinate both hands together. If a person was unable to pick up small objects, operate manual machinery, write or type on standard machines, this may indicate loss of manual dexterity. It is also noted that the loss of use of the dominant hand may have greater effects on a person than the same loss in the non-dominant hand.

The Guidance states that it would be reasonable to regard the following as having a substantial adverse effect:

(i)   loss of function in one or both hands so that a person cannot use the hands

(ii)   inability to use a knife and fork at the same time

(iii)   ability to press the buttons on keyboards or key pads but only much more slowly than is normal for most people.

It would not be reasonable to regard the following as having a substantial adverse effect:

(iv)   inability to undertake activities requiring delicate hand movements, such as threading a small needle

(v)   inability to reach typing speeds standardised for secretarial work

(vi)   inability to pick up a single small item, such as a pin.[37]

Physical coordination

This covers the balanced and effective interaction of body movement, including the ability to perform composite activities such as walking and using hands at the same time.

It would be reasonable to regard the following as having a substantial adverse effect:

(i)   ability to pour liquid into another vessel only with unusual slowness or concentration

(ii)   inability to place food into one's own mouth without unusual concentration or assistance.

It would not be reasonable to regard the following as having a substantial adverse effect:

(iii)   clumsiness

(iv)   inability to catch a tennis ball.[38]

Continence

This covers the ability to control urination and/or defecation, with account being taken of the frequency and extent of the loss of the person's control and their age.

It would be reasonable to regard the following as having a substantial adverse effect:

(i)   infrequent loss of bowel control

(ii)   loss of control of the bladder whilst asleep at least once a month

(iii) frequent minor faecal incontinence or frequent minor leakage from the bladder.

It would not be reasonable to regard the following as having a substantial adverse effect:

(iv) infrequent loss of bladder control whilst asleep

(v)   infrequent minor leakage from the bladder.[39]

Ability to lift, carry or otherwise move everyday objects

When considering whether a person can lift, carry or move everyday objects account needs to be taken of a person's ability to repeat functions or bear weight over a reasonable period of time. Everyday objects might include things such as books, a kettle of water, bags of shopping, a briefcase, an overnight bag, a chair or other piece of furniture. It does not include abnormal lifting, as was seen in *Quinlan v B&Q plc.*[40]

In this case, Mr Quinlan was employed to work in the garden centre department of B&Q. As part of his duties, he was required to lift heavy objects. Due to recent open heart surgery, he was unable to perform such lifting. However, the tribunal determined that he could still lift everyday objects and so there was no substantial adverse effect on his ability to carry out normal day-to-day activities. On appeal, the EAT agreed with the tribunal's interpretation of the legislation.

The Guidance states that it would be reasonable to regard the following as having a substantial adverse effect:

(i)   inability to pick up objects of moderate weight with one hand

(ii) inability to carry a moderately loaded tray steadily.

It would not be reasonable to consider the following as having a substantial adverse effect:

(iii) inability to carry heavy luggage without assistance

(iv) inability to move heavy objects without a mechanical aid.[41]

Speech, hearing or eyesight

This includes the ability to write and hold face-to-face or telephone conversations.

Where speech is concerned, it is pertinent to take into account the effect that an impairment has on a person's ability to communicate in their native tongue, the ability to speak at a normal pace and rhythm and the ability to understand someone speaking to the person in their native tongue.

The Guidance states that it would be reasonable to regard the following as having a substantial adverse effect:

(i)   inability to give clear basic instructions orally to colleagues or providers of a service

(ii)   inability to ask specific questions to clarify instructions

(iii)   taking significantly longer than average to say things.

It would not be reasonable to treat the following as having a substantial adverse effect:

(iv)   inability to articulate fluently due to a minor stutter, lisp or speech impediment

(v)   inability to speak in front of an audience

(vi)   having a strong accent

(vii)   inability to speak in a language other than one which is not the person's native tongue.[42]

Where hearing is concerned, account needs to be taken of the effect of background noise on the person's ability to hear. If a person wears a hearing aid, the impairment needs to be considered as if he or she was not wearing the aid.

The Guidance states that it would be reasonable to regard the following as having a substantial adverse effect:

(viii) inability to hold a conversation with someone talking in a normal voice in a moderately noisy environment

(ix)   inability to hear and understand another person speaking clearly over the telephone.

It would not be reasonable to regard the following as having a substantial adverse effect:

(x)   inability to hold a conversation in a very noisy place, such as a factory floor

(xi)   inability to sing in tune.[43]

In the case of eyesight, there is a difference to the normal rule that the impairment must be considered without the benefit of medical aids. Where a person's eyesight can be corrected by wearing glasses or contact lenses, the effect of the impairment must be judged by considering the level of the impairment after the effect of the correction of glasses or contact lenses has been applied.

The Guidance states that it would be reasonable to regard the following as having a substantial adverse effect:

(xii)   inability to pass the eyesight test for a standard driving test

(xiii) inability to recognise by sight a person across a moderately sized room

(xiv)   total inability to distinguish colours

(xv)   inability to read normal newsprint

(xvi)   inability to walk safely without bumping into objects.

It would not be reasonable to regard the following as having a substantial adverse effect:

(xvii) inability to read very small or indistinct print without the aid of a magnifying glass

(xviii) inability to distinguish a known person across a substantial distance (such as a playing field)

(xix) inability to distinguish between red and green.[44]

Memory or ability to concentrate, learn or understand

This covers impairments that cause a person to have difficulty in remembering, organising thoughts, planning and carrying out a course of action, taking in knowledge or understanding written or verbal instructions. It can also include learning to do things significantly more slowly than most other people and significant difficulty in reading standard English or straightforward numbers.

The Guidance states that it would be reasonable to regard the following as having a substantial adverse effect:

(i) intermittent loss of consciousness and associated confused behaviour

(ii) persistent inability to remember the names of familiar people such as family and friends

(iii) inability to adapt after a reasonable period to minor changes in work routine

(iv) inability to write a cheque without assistance

(v) considerable difficulty in following a short sequence such as a simple recipe or a brief list of technical tasks.

It would not be reasonable to regard the following as having a substantial adverse effect:

(vi) occasionally forgetting the name of a familiar person

(vii) inability to concentrate on a task requiring application over several hours

(viii) inability to fill in a long, detailed, technical document without assistance

(ix) inability to read at faster than normal speed

(x) minor problems with writing and spelling.[45]

Perception of the risk of physical danger

This includes both the underestimation and overestimation of physical danger, including danger to wellbeing. Account should be taken of whether a person is inclined to neglect basic functions such as eating, drinking, sleeping, keeping warm or personal hygiene. Also pertinent will be reckless behaviour that puts the person or others at risk or excessive avoidance behaviour without a good cause.

The Guidance states that it would be reasonable to regard the following as having a substantial adverse effect:

(i) inability to operate safely properly maintained machinery
(ii) persistent inability to cross a road safely
(iii) inability to nourish oneself
(iv) inability to tell by touch that an object is very hot or very cold.

It would not be reasonable to treat the following as having a substantial adverse effect:
(v) fear of significant heights
(vi) underestimating the risk associated with dangerous hobbies
(vii) underestimating risks, other than obvious ones, in unfamiliar places.[46]

Discrimination in employment

What is unlawful?

It is unlawful for an employer to discriminate against a disabled person:

(i) in the arrangements which he or she makes for the purposes of determining to whom he or she should offer employment,
(ii) in the terms on which he or she offers that person employment,
(iii) by refusing to offer, or deliberately not offering, employment.

It is unlawful for an employer to discriminate against a disabled person whom he or she employs:

(i) in the terms of employment which he or she affords him or her,
(ii) in the opportunities he or she affords him or her for promotion, a transfer, training or receiving any other benefit,
(iii) by refusing to afford him or her, or deliberately not afford him or her, any such opportunity,
(iv) by dismissing him or her, or subjecting him or her to any other detriment.

In the case of an act which is victimisation, the above prohibitions also can apply to someone who is not disabled.[47]

An employer discriminates against a person if:

(i) for a reason that relates to the disabled person's disability, he or she treats him or her less favourably than he or she treats or would treat others to whom that reason does not or would not apply
(ii) he cannot show that the treatment is justified.[48]

Discriminatory treatment is only justified if the reason for it is both material to the circumstances of the particular case and substantial. Where there is a duty to make reasonable adjustments (see below) but the employer fails without justification to make such adjustments, the employer's treatment of the disabled person cannot be justified unless it would have been justified even if the adjustment had been made.[49]

An employer also discriminates against a disabled person if:

(i) he fails to comply with the duty to make reasonable adjustments to any arrangements made by or on behalf of the employer or any physical feature of premises occupied by the employer where that arrangement or physical feature places the disabled person at a substantial disadvantage compared to people who are not disabled

(ii) he cannot show that his or her failure to comply with that duty is justified.[50]

The obligation to make reasonable adjustments to any arrangements made by or on behalf of the employer only applies in relation to arrangements for determining to whom employment should be offered; and any term, condition or arrangements on which employment, promotion, a transfer, training or any other benefit is offered or afforded. This will extend to any decision to dismiss an employee.[51]

Again, failure to make a reasonable adjustment is only justified if the reason for it is both material to the circumstances of the particular case and substantial.[52]

What is the most notable feature of the DDA is that it is possible for an employer to escape liability for discriminating against a disabled person by showing that he was justified in its actions, provided that the employer has properly considered his duty to make reasonable adjustments and is justified in not making reasonable adjustments. This differs from the direct discrimination provisions of the Sex Discrimination Act (SDA) and the Race Relations Act (RRA), where there is no defence available to an employer who directly discriminates.

However, the DDA also differs from the SDA and RRA in that there is no concept of indirect discrimination. Indirect discrimination occurs when an employer applies a term or condition to all employees but that term or condition is such that one sex or race finds it more difficult to comply with than the other sex or another race. The employer must then be able to show that the imposition of the term or condition was justified for a reason that does not relate to sex or race (as applicable). Applying the concept of indirect discrimination to disability discrimination may have been problematic. Many terms and conditions of employment will be more difficult for a disabled person to comply with than a person who is not disabled. The DDA has provided that rather than leave employers to argue that the imposition of such terms and conditions is justified, it will require employers to consider whether it can make reasonable adjustments to work environments or terms and conditions. This is a stronger duty in many respects as it requires considerations as to positive action on the part of the employer to avoid committing a discriminatory act. It is notable that the Task Force did not recommend that the DDA should be amended to include a prohibition on indirect disability discrimination.

It should also be noted that constructive dismissal cannot be a discriminatory act under the DDA. In *Commissioner of Police for the Metropolis v Harley*,[53] the EAT held that the phrase in Section 4 (2)(d) of the DDA which refers to an employer discriminating against an employee "by dismissing him" could not, on the ordinary construction of the words, apply to constructive dismissal. Nor can former employees bring DDA claims in respect of matters arising after termination of employment, most commonly failure to provide references or providing discriminatory references.[54]

The employer's knowledge of the disability

Unlike the SDA and the RRA, it is possible that an employer will not know that an employee or job applicant is suffering from a disability. So when can an employer avoid liability for discrimination by asserting that he or she was unaware that a complainant was disabled?

The position has been examined in a number of cases before the EAT. Indeed the first case which came before the EAT, *O'Neill v Symm & Co Limited*,[55] examined the point. In this case, Miss O'Neill had been dismissed from her job as an accounts clerk on 3 December 1996, the day after the DDA came into force. At the time of her recruitment in September 1996, she had informed Symm that she had taken two months off work earlier that year due to pneumonia, but it was believed she was recovered. In October 1996, she took 5 days absence due to a viral illness. In late November she was again unwell and told Symm that she had a viral illness due to her earlier pneumonia. She was dismissed on 3 December due to her absences.

At the tribunal hearing, Miss O'Neill pointed out that she had a number of hospital appointments whilst she was employed by Symm. She also said that she had been diagnosed with ME/Chronic Fatigue Syndrome (CFS) and that Symm should have received a sick note stating this on the day before she was dismissed. Symm denied receiving the sick note before it dismissed Miss O'Neill, but accepted that it knew she had attended some hospital appointments. However, it put those down to her viral illness and not to an underlying condition that was a disability.

The tribunal decided that the

decision to dismiss…was related to the absences, but not the fact that the applicant was absent with a disability because the respondent was unaware of this.[56]

The EAT upheld the tribunal's decision, saying that knowledge of the disability or at least the material features of it, is relevant to whether the reason for the employer's action relates to the disabled person's disability.

However, this was effectively a mandate for employers to ensure that they remained ignorant when making decisions relating to employees who were ill – if they ensured that they didn't know of the disability or its material features, they couldn't be held liable for discrimination. This was an unpalatable conclusion and so when the EAT came to reconsider the same issue in *HJ Heinz Company Limited v Kendrick*[57] it changed its stance.

> In *HJ Heinz Company Limited*, Mr Kendrick went absent from work in June 1996. He did not have a diagnosis of his illness, although, like Miss O'Neill, he suspected that he was suffering from CFS or ME. In order to confirm his suspicions, Mr Kendrick paid to see an immunologist and arranged an appointment for 28 April 1997. However, prior to that appointment and notwithstanding that Mr Kendrick had informed Heinz of his appointment, Mr Kendrick was dismissed on 4 April 1997. Mr Kendrick was later diagnosed with CFS and complained of disability discrimination.
>
> Heinz argued that it could not have been guilty of disability discrimination as Mr Kendrick had not been diagnosed with CFS (and so it had not known the nature of his illness) at the date of the dismissal. The EAT was not impressed by this argument. They made the point that the test to be determined was whether the person was disabled and whether the person was treated less favourably for a reason which related to the disability. If the test was not this objective test, rather than a subjective test of what the employer knew at the time of the discriminatory act, "there will be difficulties with credible and honest, yet ignorant or obtuse employers who fail to recognise or acknowledge the obvious".[58]

In this case, Mr Kendrick was dismissed due to his absence, the absence was in fact related to a disability and so Heinz had discriminated. The EAT went on to point out "it does require employers to pause to consider whether the reason for some dismissal that they may have in mind might relate to disability and, if it might, to reflect on the [DDA] and the Code before dismissing".[59] It should also be borne in mind that the EAT cast doubt on the reliability of *O'Neill v Symm and Co Ltd* in their decision. Given that *O'Neill* was the first time a complex piece of new legislation had come before the EAT, it is perhaps not surprising that the EAT changed its views, and certainly *Heinz* should be treated as the authority in this area now, a point emphasised in *London Borough of Hammersmith & Fulham v Farnsworth*.[60]

> In *London Borough of Hammersmith*, the London Borough withdrew a job offer made to Ms Farnsworth when a pre-employment medical revealed that she had suffered from bouts of illness in the past that had required her to be hospitalised on occasion. Although the doctor acting for the London Borough noted that Ms Farnsworth had not taken any days off work in the last year, the doctor noted that she was concerned that if a recurrence of the illness were to occur, Ms Farnsworth's performance and attendance would be affected.
>
> When Ms Farnsworth brought a claim of disability discrimination, the

London Borough sought to evade liability on the grounds that it did not know she was suffering from a disability. On receiving the doctor's report, it had elected not to make further enquiries about Ms Farnsworth's condition. It simply withdrew the job offer. The tribunal and the EAT both held that this did not assist the London Borough in defending Ms Farnsworth's claim. Firstly, the doctor was on notice of the disability and, as the London Borough's agent, her knowledge was also the knowledge of the London Borough. In any event, the London Borough was put on notice that Ms Farnsworth had suffered from a serious illness by the doctor. At that point, the London Borough should have made further enquiries of the doctor and/or Ms Farnsworth to see if the illness had a real impact on her ability to do the job offered to her and also to explore whether any reasonable adjustments needed to be made. A deliberate policy of remaining ignorant about the true nature or extent of an employee's illness will not excuse an employer from liability if the employer discriminates.

Employers also need to consider whether they can rely on the defence of justification or argue that they considered making reasonable adjustments in circumstances when they did not know of the disability.

This issue has been considered by the EAT in *British Gas Services Limited v McCaull*[61] and *Quinn v Schwarzkopf*,[62] with differing results. In *Quinn*, the EAT suggested that an employer cannot rely on the defence of justification if it is unaware of the fact that the employee in question is disabled. However, in *McCaull*, the EAT indicated that lack of knowledge of a disability did not automatically preclude an employer from relying on the defence of justification. The EAT pulled back from the position in *Quinn*, saying that if *Quinn* had suggested that an employer could never justify its actions when it was ignorant of the existence of a disability, then *Quinn* went too far. It should be noted that Lord Johnson presided over both of these cases.

Less favourable treatment

It is necessary for a disabled person to show that he or she was treated less favourably than an employer treated or would treat someone to whom the disability did not apply. In essence, the disabled person needs to compare himself or herself to a real or notional person who is not suffering from the same disability.

Confusion arises as to who was an appropriate comparator. Was it someone who was not suffering from the impairment affecting the disabled person and was also otherwise totally able? Or was it someone who was not suffering from the impairment but was suffering from another condition or event that led to the same consequences as those experienced by the disabled person? The most frequent occasion where this raised a question was where a disabled person was dismissed for long-term absence. Was it open for the employer to say that it would have dismissed another employee who was absent for a similar length of time but who was not disabled or would the correct comparator be an employee who had not had any time off work?

This was the dilemma raised in *Clark v Novacold Limited*.[63]

Mr Clark was employed in manual and physically demanding jobs from July 1995 until January 1997. He sustained a back injury at work, which caused him to be absent from work. After five months absence, Novacold dismissed Mr Clark on the basis of a specialist's report which could not be specific about when he would be able to return to work.

When Mr Clark complained to the tribunal, Novacold submitted that it would have dismissed anyone who had been absent from work for five months. The fact that Mr Clark had a disability was irrelevant – when compared to someone without a disability who had been absent from work due to illness for five months, Mr Clark had been treated no less favourably. The tribunal accepted this argument and dismissed Mr Clark's complaint. On appeal, the EAT agreed that the correct comparator was someone who had been on long-term sick leave. However, the Court of Appeal took a different view.

The Court of Appeal looked at Mr Clark's situation by considering how other hypothetical situations are considered by the DDA and the Code. They pointed out that if a café refuses entry to dogs, it would mean that a blind man with a guide dog would be denied access to the café. So would able-bodied people with dogs. However, the effect of denying access to people with dogs may be indirectly discriminatory where the blind man is denied access. The comparator in this case would be able-bodied people who could go into the café, electing by choice not to bring their dogs. They also looked at an example given in the Code on Rights of Access. Where a diner is asked to leave a restaurant because she has difficulties in eating due to a disability but other diners without the disability are not asked to leave, the restaurant may commit a discriminatory act.

In both cases, the comparison is with people who are allowed to enter the café or eat in the restaurant, not with people who are not allowed to enter the café or eat in the restaurant for reasons that do not relate to a disability. Accordingly, and using the same analogy, the comparison in Mr Clark's case should have been with people who were working without time off for illness. The correct comparator is not only one to whom the disability does not apply but further, one who is working.

This would not stop a disabled person from choosing a comparator who was absent for a reason not relating to a disability but who was treated differently to him or her. However, the comparator does not need to mimic the same circumstances as those which affect the disabled person. This left the way open for disabled people to look outside their exact circumstances in identifying comparators and so to show discrimination.

In *Kent County Council v Mingo*,[64] Mr Mingo was employed as an assistant cook. He developed a back problem that meant that he could not carry on in his position. His employer looked to redeploy him and, under its redeployment procedures, categorised him as category B in terms of the priority that should be given to him when considering redeployment opportunities. Category B employees were those that were suffering "incapability/ill health". However, those employees facing redundancy were deemed to be category A in terms of redeployment and so received priority over Mr Mingo if redeployment opportunities arose. Mr Mingo applied for several new internal positions. He was unsuccessful on all occasions, once being told that he would have obtained the position if he had been in category A. He tried to apply for other vacancies, to be told it was reserved for category A employees only. Eventually, and not having been redeployed, Mr Mingo was dismissed.

Mr Mingo argued that he was treated less favourably than someone who was going to be made redundant because, as a disabled person, he fell into a secondary category for redeployment. He positively wanted to be treated in the same way as another category of employee. The EAT agreed – the Council's policy did not live up to its statutory obligation to treat no other employee more favourably than it treated a disabled person. It didn't matter that there were non-disabled people who were treated less favourably than Mr Mingo in considerations relating to redeployment. The fact that any employee could be treated more favourably than him was the determinative issue.

In *British Sugar plc v Kirker*,[65] Mr Kirker had been made redundant. He was registered as partially sighted and, even with his glasses, could not see well enough to drive. As part of the redundancy selection procedure, he was given the worst possible score as to his performance, zero out of ten. However, his performance had never previously been criticised. He scored zero out of five for potential, with his managers suggesting that his disability might amount to a health and safety problem. Points were also deducted for absence, even though the absence related to his disability. When he complained to the tribunal, it was on the basis that he had been underscored on the basis of his disability. He did not allege that any of his colleagues who similarly faced redundancy were overscored, nor did he point to any colleague who he believed should have been made redundant in his place. The tribunal and the EAT found that Mr Kirker had received lower scores because of the prejudice of his managers and that the prejudice was based on his disability. It was not necessary for Mr Kirker to point to a specific comparator – he could show less favourable treatment on the grounds of his disability without one.

Hence, a disabled person may choose the comparator they want from amongst the workforce or indeed dispense with the need for a comparator altogether. The only thing for the disabled person to bear in mind is that if the comparator is not one to whom the disabled person can be readily compared, the employer may find it easier to justify the difference in treatment or to argue that the treatment does not relate to the disability in any event.

Justification

As stated above, an employer can only justify discriminating against a disabled person if the reason for it is both material to the circumstances of the particular case and substantial. An employer will also need to consider the duty to make reasonable adjustments.

The Code makes it clear that the reason for the discrimination must relate to the individual circumstance in question and not just be trivial or minor.[66] In effect, the definition of "substantial" mirrors that in the definition of "disability". The Code gives a number of examples of what might be justified treatment and what might not.

For example, if a job applicant who is blind is not given a job involving computers because the employer assumes that blind people cannot use computers without making any further investigations into the individual circumstances of the case, it could not justify the resulting discrimination. The assumption that blind people cannot use computers is general and does not relate to the specific circumstances of the person's application.

Similarly, a person with a learning disability cannot sort papers as quickly as his or her colleagues. However, there is very little difference in overall productivity, and so a decision to dismiss him or her would not be justified as the reason for the dismissal would not be substantial.

However, if an employer declined to employ someone with psoriasis for a job modelling cosmetics on a part of the body that was severely affected, the employer would be likely to be justified if the applicant's appearance was incompatible with the purpose of the work. The employer would have a substantial reason which was related to the individual circumstances of the job.

When considering whether an employer can justify discrimination, it is necessary to consider the circumstances of the employer and the employee.[67] It is not enough for the employer simply to consider its convenience, but nor are the employee's circumstances the sole consideration. Employers can consider matters such as the economic consequences of, for example, retaining the employee in employment. However, it is incumbent on employers to assess the real consequences of the employee's disability in determining whether their actions are justified. Hence, where an employer fails to get a full prognosis regarding the disabled person's condition, it may find itself unable to rely on the justification defence. After all, how could the employer know that it was taking the correct actions if it didn't know the extent to which the employee might be inhibited from performing his duties?[68] However, this is not to say that lack of knowledge of a disability will automatically mean that the justification defence is not available to the employer,[69] but inevitably it will be harder to prove.

When considering the application of the justification defence, the tribunal is under a duty to consider all the factors that went to the employer's decision that it had a material and substantial reason to apply less favourable treatment to its employee. However, the tribunal should not consider all the evidence (including evidence specifically obtained for the purpose of the tribunal hearing) and then reach its own decision on the evidence, in the course of so doing, determining whether the employer was right or wrong in its original assessment. In short, and as with unfair dismissal, the Tribunal is not entitled to substitute its own opinion for that of the employer where the employer has reached a decision based on a proper analysis of the circumstances applicable in the case and available medical evidence.[70]

The duty to make reasonable adjustments

As stated above, in order to prove that a decision to discriminate against a disabled person was justified, an employer is likely to need to consider whether it can make an adjustment to arrangements or features of premises if these arrangements or features place the disabled person at a substantial disadvantage compared to the non-disabled. The adjustment need only be made if it is reasonable to do so. The obligation is on the employer to consider the ability to make an adjustment. It is not sufficient merely to accept medical evidence that no adjustment can be made, even in circumstances where the employee is not putting forward suggestions for particular adjustments.[71] However, where an employee fails to cooperate with an employer's attempts to discuss his or her disability and/or suitable reasonable adjustments, then dismissal may be justified without the employer considering specific possible reasonable adjustments.[72]

Complying with the duty of reasonable adjustment:

The DDA and Code set out examples of steps that may need to be taken in relation to a disabled person in order to comply with the duty of reasonable adjustment:

(i) making adjustments to premises – for example, installing a ramp or altering the height of light switches

(ii) allocating some of the disabled person's duties to another person – for example, if a job requires minor, non-essential driving duties and the disabled person cannot drive for a reason relating to the disability, assigning the driving aspects of the job to another person

(iii) transferring the disabled person to fill another vacancy – for example, where the disability means that the employee can no longer carry on in the current position, it might be reasonable to move the person to another vacancy (providing training where necessary)

(iv)   altering his or her working hours – for example, altering work hours to fit in with a carer or to allow additional breaks

(v)   assigning him or her to a different place of work – for example, transferring a wheel chair user to the ground floor if other floors are inaccessible

(vi)   allowing him or her to be absent during working hours for rehabilitation, assessment or treatment – for example, the disabled employee might be allowed more time off work than non-disabled colleagues would normally be allowed in order to receive treatment

(vii)   giving him or her, or arranging for him or her to be given, training – for example, this might include training on specific machinery which would help alleviate or reduce the effect of the disability or to assist someone with a learning disability to do a particular task

(viii)   acquiring or modifying equipment – for example, the purchase of a modified keyboard for someone with a visual impairment or arthritis

(ix)   modifying instructions or reference manuals – for example, conveying instructions orally if a person has difficulty in reading or understanding written instructions or providing Braille versions of manuals

(x)   modifying procedures for testing or assessment – for example, giving oral tests where a person has difficulty in writing

(xi)   providing a reader or interpreter – for example, a colleague may be able to read out mail or in certain circumstances a signer or interpreter may need to be hired

(xii)   providing supervision – for example, allocation of a colleague to support the worker and provide guidance if the disability leads to uncertainty or lack of confidence.[73]

When deciding whether it is reasonable for an employer to have to make any particular adjustment, due regard must be given to:

(i)   the extent to which taking the step would prevent the effect in question

(ii)   the extent to which it is practicable for the employer to take the step

(iii)   the financial and other costs which would be incurred by the employer in taking the step and the extent to which it would disrupt any of his activities

(iv)   the extent of the employer's financial and other resources

(v)   the availability to the employer of financial or other assistance with respect to taking the step.[74]

The obligation to make reasonable adjustments only arises where the employer knows, or should reasonably know, that the job applicant or employee is disabled and is likely to be affected by the arrangements made by or for the employer or a physical feature of the employer's premises.[75]

In *Ridout v TC Group*,[76] Ms Ridout complained that she had suffered discrimination when she applied for a job. She informed TC Group that she suffered from a rare form of photosensitive epilepsy when she applied for a job. When she attended an interview, she made a comment that the lighting in the room might affect her. However, at the time, she was wearing sunglasses around her neck and the interviewer thought that this was what she was referring to. She did not use the sunglasses during the interview and did not complain about the lighting or about feeling unwell. When she did not get the job, she complained of discrimination. The tribunal held that the interviewer could not have been expected to know of the effects of Ms Ridout's condition and so could not be criticised for failing to make reasonable adjustments to the interview conditions. The EAT upheld that view. The result of this is that applicants applying for jobs should make it absolutely clear to prospective employers that they have a disability and what the effect of that disability may be in order to put the employer on notice that he may need to consider making reasonable adjustments.

It should be noted that where an adjustment to premises is required and the employer requires the landlord's consent to make that adjustment, it will always be reasonable for the employer to ask for that consent and it will never be unreasonable not to make the adjustment before consent is received.[77] Consent should normally be received although it is possible for the landlord to attach conditions to that consent.[78]

The Code gives guidance on the factors to be taken into account in determining whether it is reasonable for an employer to be obliged to make an adjustment.

The effectiveness of the step in preventing the disadvantage

It is unlikely to be reasonable for an employer to have to make an adjustment which would have little benefit for the disabled person.

For example, where a disabled person's pay is affected by productivity, it is not likely that an employer would have to make an adjustment that would only marginally affect the person's productivity, and so his or her pay. However, if the adjustment would make a significant difference to productivity, and pay, it may be reasonable for the employer to make the adjustment.[79]

The point was considered in *Campbell v Department of Social Security*.[80]

Ms Campbell had a number of ailments, including chronic bronchitis, allergic asthma and ME/Chronic Fatigue Syndrome. As a result of her health, she was given medical retirement, but subsequently complained of discrimination, alleging that the DSS had failed to make a reasonable adjustment by transferring her to another job. The tribunal held that since Ms Campbell was unable to work due to her illness, it would have been of little benefit to transfer her to another job.

The practicability of the step
It is likely to be more reasonable for an employer to take a simple step, rather than one which is more difficult.

For example, it might be impractical for an employer who urgently needs an employee to fill a vacancy to have to wait whilst consent is obtained and work is carried out to alter premises. However, if it was possible for the disabled person to work in the interim, albeit less conveniently, then the employer may need to take the steps to enable the disabled person to work pending the alterations being made.[81]

The point was considered in *London Borough of Hillingdon v Morgan*.[82] Ms Morgan was suffering from ME. The Council's occupational health doctor recommended that Ms Morgan should be allowed to return to work gradually. It would have been practical for an employer as large as the Council to facilitate that graded return to work. However, the Council's personnel department failed to make provision for her return to work in that manner; instead it unsuccessfully tried to redeploy her. When she was eventually dismissed, she claimed disability discrimination. The tribunal upheld her complaint and criticised the Council for failing to make a reasonable adjustment that could have obviated the need for Ms Morgan's dismissal.

Similarly, in *Kent County Council v Mingo*, it would have been a simple matter for the Council to redesignate Mr Mingo as a category A employee, which would have lead to his redeployment. The Council's failure to do so meant that it had failed in its duty to make a reasonable adjustment.

The financial and other costs of the adjustment and the extent of any disruption caused
If an adjustment costs little or nothing to make, it would be reasonable to make the adjustment unless some other factor, such as practicability or effectiveness, made it unreasonable. Costs are not only financial, but can also include things such as staffing and other resourcing costs. What an employer would otherwise spend may be a factor which needs to be considered. For example, it would be reasonable to spend the same amount of money retraining or resourcing a disabled employee as the employer would spend in recruiting a replacement.[83]

The value and experience of the employee, as well as how long the job is likely to go on, may also be factors. If an employer has already invested significant sums in training the employee, it may be more reasonable for further investment to be made to enable the employee to continue performing the role. Similarly, if the employee is long-standing, it may be more reasonable for the employer to spend a greater sum in enabling the employee to remain at work. If the employee has a higher level of skill and experience, or close relationships with clients, it may also be indicative that greater efforts should be made to retain the employee. This makes commercial sense in any event. Finally, the level at which the employee is paid may be a factor – if the cost of the adjustment is a small percentage of the salary for the job, it may be more reasonable to make adjustments.[84]

Disruption to other employees is also a relevant factor.[85] If a disabled employee would find it more convenient to work from other premises closer to the disabled employee's home, but this would mean moving a team of employees, it may cause more disruption than is reasonable to the other employees. However, if a disabled employee wanted to move to another building close to the original work place because access was more feasible, the disruption to other members of the team may not outweigh the benefits to the disabled employee.

In *Jewell v Stoke Mandeville Hospital NHS Trust*,[86] Ms Jewell complained of discrimination relating to her epilepsy. She had been epileptic long before being employed by the hospital, which was something of which it was aware. However, her condition worsened and medical advice was received which indicated that she should not work at night or on her own. This meant that she needed to be redeployed. The hospital had a number of available vacancies, but rather than simply redeploy her, it sent her for interviews for each position. The only assistance that she was given was in interview techniques. She did not obtain another position and was eventually dismissed. The tribunal held that the Hospital had failed in its duty to make reasonable adjustments. It had substantial resources, there were vacancies available and it would have been a simple matter for the personnel department to redeploy her without the need for her to submit to competitive interview.

In *Kenny v Hampshire Constabulary*,[87] the practicability, financial and other costs and availability of other assistance were all considered. Mr Kenny applied for a job with the Constabulary as an analyst/programmer. He suffered from cerebral palsy and needed assistance in going to the toilet. He was offered the job, subject to the Constabulary being able to find a way in which to accommodate his need for assistance. It asked its staff if anyone would be willing to assist Mr Kenny, but were unable to find the necessary volunteers. It then considered whether Mr Kenny could work from home, but security issues meant that this was not possible. It then applied for outside assistance under the Access to Work Scheme, but the cost of provision of a carer meant that the decision would need to go to the Scheme's headquarters. This would have caused a delay in finalising the recruitment process. The Constabulary urgently needed to fill the post and so withdrew Mr Kenny's job offer. Mr Kenny brought proceedings against the Constabulary arguing that it had failed to comply with its obligation to make reasonable adjustments and that the discrimination was unjustified. It was held that the Constabulary had tried to find a way to employ Mr Kenny and it was not obliged to employ a person to assist Mr Kenny in going to the toilet. If the legislation had intended to impose such an obligation, the Code would have made that clear.

An issue which frequently concerns employers is whether payment of sick pay is a reasonable adjustment.

> In *London Clubs Management Limited v Hood*,[88] Mr Hood suffered from cluster headaches. In 1998, he had 39.5 days of absence as a result of his illness. His employer was not obliged to pay him sick pay but had a discretion to do so. In 1998, he was paid for all of his absence. In 1999, his employer decided that nobody would receive sick pay due to the general high level of absenteeism. He claimed that the failure to pay him sick pay amounted to discrimination. It was held that the failure to pay sick pay was not direct discrimination as the issue was that the employer generally did not pay anyone sick pay, as was its right. However, the EAT did consider that payment of sick pay can amount to a reasonable adjustment, depending on the circumstances of the particular case.

The extent of the employer's financial and other resources
It is more likely for an employer with substantial financial resources to be obliged to make more expensive adjustments than one with limited resources. The employer's overall financial position will be taken into account – the fact that the employer budgets in such a way as to leave a particular area of the business with limited resources will not be determinative.[89] For example, the profitability of one shop in a larger retail chain would not be determinative as to whether that shop should have to make an adjustment. Equally, where an employer is employing a large number of people, it might be more reasonable for certain of a disabled person's job duties to be reallocated to another employee or employees.

The fact that an employer has significant financial and other resources will not necessarily mean that it is obliged to make an adjustment that would involve significant expense. In *Stangoe v British Steel plc*,[90] Mr Stangoe had been involved in an accident at work which lead to the amputation of his thumb. As a result, he could not continue in his position as a mechanical craftsman. He was transferred to a long-term temporary clerical job, which lasted for five years and, when that came to an end, he worked as a stocktaker. However, he could not cope with the supervisory duties involved in that job. British Steel had looked for other opportunities, but when none arose, he was dismissed. The tribunal held that Mr Stangoe had suffered less favourable treatment, but that the treatment was justified. The only available job that might have been suitable for him was that of an operative in the test house. It was accepted that British Steel could have taken steps to make it physically possible for Mr Stangoe to perform that job, however it was not reasonable to require British Steel to take all those steps, notwithstanding its size.

The availability to the employer of financial or other assistance in making the step
Help may be forthcoming in assisting the employer in making an adjustment,

both from external third parties or from the disabled person himself or herself. Grants may be available to assist with the cost of making adjustments, both from public sources as well as charities. Some charities or public bodies may also be able to make equipment available and indeed, the disabled person may be able to utilise his or her own equipment in assisting himself or herself in the performance of his or her job.

Victimisation

An employer also discriminates against an employee if he or she victimises him or her.[91] Victimisation occurs when the employer treats a person less favourably than he or she treats someone whose circumstances are the same as that person (disregarding any disability suffered by that person), and he or she does so for one or more of the following reasons:

(i) the employee has brought proceedings against the employer or any other person under the DDA

(ii) the employee has given evidence or information in connection with such proceedings brought by any person

(iii) the employee has otherwise done anything under the DDA in relation to the employer or any other person

(iv) the employee has alleged that the employer or any other person has (whether or not the allegation so states) contravened the DDA

(v) the employer believes or suspects that the employee has done or intends to do any of the above things.

Where another employee of the employer victimises the employee, the employer may be liable for the victimisation as if the employer had committed the victimisation.

The employee who is victimised does not have to be disabled. Hence an employee who complains of disability discrimination, but is later held not to be disabled within the meaning of the DDA, can still suffer victimisation. So can an employee who supports or assists a person who alleges that he or she has suffered discrimination. The only limit on an employee's ability to claim victimisation is that the allegation of discrimination made by that employee must have been made in good faith and must not be false.

Bringing a claim

The employment provisions are found in Part II of the DDA.

Who can bring a claim?

Both employees and job applicants who consider that they have suffered discrimination can bring a claim under the DDA. "Employment" is defined to mean employment under a contract of service or apprenticeship or a contract personally to do any work.[92] This means that the self-employed can bring a claim under the DDA provided that their contract is to undertake their work personally. This was reviewed in the case of *Sheehan v Post Office Counters Limited*.[93]

> In *Sheehan*, Mr Sheehan was a sub-postmaster engaged under a contract which provided that Mr Sheehan was an agent of the Post Office, not an employee. He was not obliged to provide his services personally in running the sub-post office but he was responsible for its proper management. He also had to inform the Area Manager if he intended to be away for more than three days. When he commenced his claim under the DDA, the Post Office argued that Mr Sheehan was not in "employment" for the purposes of the DDA. He was not obliged to perform his services personally. The tribunal agreed – the definition of "employment" was clear and without an obligation personally to perform a service, an individual could not rely on the DDA. The EAT upheld this decision.

Unlike the law of unfair dismissal, there is no qualifying period of employment before a claim can be brought. However, certain categories of employee are excluded from the DDA.

Categories of employees excluded from the DDA:

(i)   members of the armed forces
(ii)   prison officers
(iii)   firefighters
(iv)   holders of statutory office (including police officers)
(v)   employees working on board ships, aircraft and hovercrafts
(vi)   employees who work wholly or mainly outside Great Britain.

The DDA also prohibits discrimination against contract workers.[94] This means that where a worker is supplied through an agency to an end user, where the end user discriminates against the worker, that end user will be liable for the act of discrimination. The agency will not have any liability for the discrimination, unless it assisted in the discriminatory act.[95] This principle has now been extended to cover workers who supply their services through service companies. This practice is particularly prevalent in the computing industry, where computer consultants provide their services through companies which they have established and which act purely as a vehicle for the provision of the worker's services. The case which established this principle was *MHC Consulting Services Limited v Tansell & others*.[96]

> In *MHC Consulting Services Limited v Tansell*, Mr Tansell provided his services through a company which he owned. His company signed up with an agency, MHC Consulting, which went on to provide Mr Tansell's

services to Abbey Life Assurance Company Limited. When Abbey Life rejected Mr Tansell due to his disability, Mr Tansell sued both MHC Consulting and Abbey Life. In the Employment Tribunal, it was held that Mr Tansell could sue MHC Consulting, but could not sue Abbey Life as the contractual relationship between Mr Tansell and Abbey Life was too remote. The EAT disagreed. They held that where there is an unbroken contractual chain between the individual and the end user, the end user will still have liability for a discriminatory act, and the agency supplying the individual (in this case through a service company) will only have liability where the agency aided the discrimination. The Court of Appeal later endorsed this view.[97]

It should be noted that a claim on behalf of a deceased person may be pursued by that person's personal representatives. This may be particularly important in disability discrimination cases where the chances of an employee dying either before a claim is commenced or during its continuance are higher than with other discrimination claims.[98]

Small employers

Employers with less than 15 employees are exempt from the employment provisions of the DDA.[99] In determining whether an employer has less than 15 employees, the definition of "employees" will be the same as the one found in the DDA, and so will include self-employed people provided that they are performing personal services.[100]

The employer will be the actual entity employing the disabled person. On this basis, the fact that a subsidiary of a company has less than 15 employees will be the determinative issue and the size of associated or group companies will be irrelevant.[101] On the other hand, the size of particular workplaces will be irrelevant if, when two or more work places are added together, it means that the employer employs 15 or more employees.

It is clear that on the current case law, an employer can evade liability for disability discrimination by arranging its affairs in such a way as to ensure that no company within its group employs 15 or more employees. This manner of evasion was recognised in *Hardie v CD Northern Limited*. However, it was equally recognised that it is unlikely that employers will organise their affairs simply to defeat any claim of disability discrimination. In the event that it became apparent that employers were seeking to evade the legislation in such a manner, it would be for Parliament to either lower the threshold for commencement of claims or to change the definition of "employer" to include group or associated companies.

Vicarious liability for employers

As with the other discrimination acts, an employer can be held liable for the acts of its employees, even if the employer did not know of the acts or approve of them. Again, as with the other discrimination acts, there is a defence open to employers to argue that they took such steps as were reasonably practicable to prevent such actions.[102] However, in order to be able to rely on that defence, it is likely that an employer would need to be able to demonstrate that it had actively promoted an equal opportunities policy, which included prohibition of disability discrimination. Part of that promotion is likely to include training of employees and the periodic undertaking of a disability audit. Another employee can also be personally liable for discrimination if he or she knowingly aids another to commit an unlawful act.

Liability for individual employees

An employee who discriminates against a person for the purposes of the employment provisions of the DDA can be held personally liable for the discrimination, in addition to the disabled person's employer. It is usual for an applicant in a DDA claim to cite the employer and those of his or her colleagues that he or she believed perpetrated the discrimination in the claim made. Where an employer is seeking to rely on the defence in Section 58(5), the other alleged discriminators will need to obtain independent advice on their defences to the claim. They will not be able to rely on any statutory defence – their only defence can be that they were not discriminating within the context of the DDA.

Raising a complaint

Complaints are made to the Employment Tribunal. As with most other employment legislation, the complaint should be made within three months of the alleged act of discrimination. A tribunal may allow a complaint to be brought outside the three month time limit where it is "just and equitable" to do so. Whether it is just and equitable to allow an otherwise out of time complaint to proceed will inevitably turn on the facts of the particular case.

Where the applicant alleges that there has been a series of acts of discrimination, the claim should be brought within three months of the last discriminatory act. However, the employee may be entitled to findings of discrimination in respect of the preceding discriminatory acts in the series of discriminatory acts, even though his or her claim was brought more than three months after those acts.

Questionnaires

A person who believes that he or she may have been the victim of discrimination is entitled to obtain information from the alleged discriminators by the use of the questionnaire procedure outlined in Section 56 of the DDA. The questionnaire can be served at any time within three months of the alleged discriminatory act and within 21 days of the issue of tribunal proceedings. Thereafter an applicant will need permission of the tribunal to serve a questionnaire.

The questionnaire is admissible in evidence in any subsequent tribunal proceedings. If the recipient of a questionnaire deliberately, and without reasonable excuse, does not respond within a reasonable time limit or is evasive or equivocal in his or her answers, the tribunal may draw any adverse inference from that fact that it deems it just and equitable to draw. This includes the inference that the recipient committed the discriminatory act.

Remedies

Where a person successfully proves that he or she has suffered disability discrimination, the tribunal can award one or more of the following remedies:

(i) a declaration as to the rights of the person and the discriminator in relation to the matters to which the complaint relates,

(ii) an order for compensation,

(iii) a recommendation that the discriminator take, within a specified period, action which the Tribunal deems to be reasonable in all the circumstances of the case, for the purpose of reducing or obviating the adverse effect on the disabled person of any matter to which the complaint relates.[103]

Settling claims

As with other statutory employment claims, claims under the DDA can only be settled by way of a compromise agreement[104] or by the Advisory Conciliation and Arbitration Service (ACAS). Any claim settled through ACAS will be recorded on a COT3 and will be legally binding on all the parties.

Notes

[1] *Clark v Novacold* (1999) IRLR 318
[2] Article 119 Treaty of Rome and The Equal Treatment Directive
[3] 86/376/EEC
[4] Article 26
[5] Article 2
[6] 200/78/EC
[7] Labour Force Survey, Spring 1999
[8] SI 1996/1456. There are other Regulations also introduced under the DDA by Statutory Instrument. Importantly, Disability Discrimination (Questions and Replies) Order 1996 (SI 1996/2793) which introduces the questionnaire procedure into the DDA
[9] SI 1996/1396, article 3
[10] SI 1996/1996, article 2
[11] (1999) IRLR 4
[12] *Goodwin v The Patents Office* (1999) IRLR 4

[13] Ibid

[14] (1999) IRLR 680

[15] Schedule 1, paragraph 1(1) DDA

[16] *WHO International Classification Of Impairments, Disabilities and Handicaps: A manual classification relating to the consequences of disease*, WHO (Geneva:1980). For more information see www.who.int

[17] (2001) IRLR 644

[18] (2002) IRLR 185

[19] (2002) IRLR 190

[20] The Guidance, paragraph A1

[21] The Guidance, page 5

[22] (2000) IRLR 14

[23] (1999) ICR 969

[24] *Goodwin v The Patents Office* (1999) IRLR 4 paragraph 41

[25] *Kapadia v London Borough of Lambeth* (2000) IRLR 14 paragraph 30

[26] (1998) EAT 43 BMLR 186

[27] DDA Schedule 1 paragraph 8

[28] (2002) IRLR 235

[29] *Goodwin v The Patents Office* [1999] IRLR 4 paragraph 36

[30] Ibid

[31] Guidance page 9 paragraph C2

[32] DDA Schedule 1 paragraph 4

[33] (1999) Unreported

[34] (2000) Unreported

[35] Guidance page 10 paragraph C5

[36] Guidance pages 11 and 12, paragraph C14

[37] Guidance page 13 paragraph C15

[38] Guidance page 13, paragraph C16

[39] Guidance page 13 paragraph C17

[40] (1998) Unreported

[41] Guidance page 14 paragraph C18

[42] Guidance page 15 paragraph C19

[43] Guidance page 16 paragraph C19

[44] Ibid

[45] Guidance page 17 paragraph C20

[46] Guidance page 19 paragraph C21

[47] DDA Section 4

[48] DDA Section 5(1)

[49] DDA Section 5 (3) and (5)

[50] DDA Section 5 (2)

[51] *Morse v Wiltshire County Council* (1998) IRLR 352

[52] DDA Section 5 (4)

[53] (2001) IRLR 263

[54] (2002) ICR 341

[55] (1998) IRLR 233

[56] *O'Neill v Symm & Co Ltd* (1998) IRLR 233

[57] (2000) EmpLR 315

[58] *HJ Heinz Co Ltd v Kendrick* paragraph 26

[59] Ibid paragraph 27

[60] (2000) IRLR 691

[61] (2001) IRLR 60

[62] (2001) IRLR 67

[63] (1998) IRLR 420 and [1999] IRLR 318 CA

[64] (2000) IRLR 90

[65] (1998) IRLR 624

[66] Code paragraph 4.6

[67] *Baynton v Saurus General Engineers Limited* (1999) IRLR 604 paragraph 38

[68] Ibid paragraph 41

[69] *British Gas Services Limited v McCaull*

[70] (2001) IRLR 384

[71] (2001) IRLR 653

[72] (2001) IRLR 724

[73] DDA Section 6(3) and the Code paragraph 4.20

[74] DDA Section 6(4)

[75] DDA Section 6(6)

[76] (1998) IRLR 628

[77] Disability Discrimination (Employment) Regulations 1996 SI 1996/1456 Regulation 10

[78] DDA Section 16(2)

[79] Code paragraph 4.22

[80] (1999) Unreported

[81] Code paragraph 4.23

[82] (1998) Unreported

[83] Ibid paragraph 4.24

[84] Ibid paragraph 4.25 and 4.26

[85] Code paragraph 4.27

[86] (1999) Unreported

[87] (1999) IRLR 76

[88] (2001) IRLR 719

[89] Ibid paragraph 4.28

[90] (1997) Unreported

[91] Section 55.DDA

[92] Section 68, DDA

[93] (1999) ICR 734

[94] Section 12, DDA

[95] Section 57, DDA

[96] (1999) IRLR 677

[97] *Abbey Life Assurance Company Limited v Tansell* (2000) IRLR 410 CA

[98] *Harris (PR to Andrews) v Lewisham and Guy's Mental Health Trust* (2000) Unreported

[99] Disability Discrimination (Exemption for Small Employers) Order 1998 SI 1998/2618, amending the previous small employers threshold of 20

[100] *Hidle v Hi-Drive Plant Services* (1999) Unreported

[101] *Hardie v CD Northern Limited* (2000) IRLR 87

[102] Section 58(5), DDA

[103] Section 8(2), DDA

[104] Section 9, DDA

5

Data protection

LAWRENCE MILNER

Lawrence Milner is a lawyer at Clifford Chance LLP specialising in data protection, privacy and other e-business issues.

Introduction[1]

Since its implementation in March 2000, the Data Protection Act 1998 (the "Act") has had a far reaching effect on the use that businesses can make of information they hold relating to their employees, customers and other individuals. This chapter seeks to highlight some of the key issues arising under the Act and regulatory guidance on its interpretation. It does not identify all situations in which the Act will be relevant but serves as an introduction to the Act in the employment context. To properly understand the Act, it is necessary to view it in its historical perspective. The Act derives from an underlying European Data Protection Directive[2] which was implemented to assist in the creation of the European single market and to promote fundamental rights recognised in the constitutions and laws of Member States of the European Union. The Act therefore forms part of a wider European initiative to assist in the protection of data across the European Union. Critics have challenged the European approach to data protection on the basis that it is overly bureaucratic and protects individuals' rights at a disproportionate cost to business. Whether or not these criticisms are justified, businesses have little choice but to comply with the legislation when sanctions for failure to comply with the Act (and similar laws in other European jurisdictions) include criminal penalties, fines, possible compensation claims and restrictions on the use that businesses can make of information within their possession.

This chapter also touches briefly on ancillary legislation which may affect the data protection analysis, in particular, rules relating to monitoring of employees and rules relating to use of data for marketing (to the extent that these might affect employees). In addition to legislation in this area, there are a number of codes of practice and other guidance issued by data protection regulators and advisory bodies at both an EU and UK level which influence the interpretation of relevant legislation. In particular, the EU's Article 29 Working Party (an influential advisory group composed of representatives of the data protection authorities of

EU Member States) has published an Opinion[3] on the processing of employee data and a working document on the surveillance of electronic communications in the work place.[4]

Guidance on an EU level has been supplemented by guidance issued by the UK data protection regulator, the Information Commissioner. In particular, the Information Commissioner has been working on a code of practice addressing various employee-related data protection issues, which will be issued in four parts. The Information Commissioner's code is still being finalised with only two parts of the code finalised at the date of writing but drafts of the remaining parts of the code which are available are referred to as appropriate in this chapter.

In summary, data protection compliance in the employment context raises complex issues involving a number of overlapping laws, regulations and guidance. This chapter is primarily focused on the Act itself, but related issues and codes are referred to. A section at the end of this chapter also seeks briefly to outline some compliance steps that businesses should consider taking in relation to data protection compliance obligations. Further useful detailed guidance is available from the Information Commissioner's website at www.dataprotection.gov.uk.

Defined terms

The key to understanding data protection legislation is a clear concept of relevant terminology used in the Act. Terms are defined in Section 1(1) of the Act.

The Data Protection Act regulates:

(i) **processing** – defined as including obtaining, recording, holding, organising, altering, retrieving, disclosure, combination or other use

(ii) **of personal data** – defined as data which relates to a living individual who can be identified from those data or from those data and other information which is in the possession or is likely to come into the possession of a relevant "data controller"

(iii) **relating to a data subject** (a living individual). A data subject for data protection purposes might include, for example, a prospective, actual or former employee or an individual client, prospective client or client contact

(iv) **by a data controller**. The data controller is defined as the person who either alone or jointly with others determines the purposes for which and manner in which personal data are processed. A data controller is to be contrasted under the Act with a data processor who merely processes personal data on behalf of the data controller (for example a service supplier with no separate rights to use relevant data other than provide the agreed services).

On the basis of the above, where for example an employer outsources its payroll data processing to a third party service supplier, the employer is likely to be the "data controller" with the service supplier acting as its "data processor" processing "personal data" (for example bank details) relating to relevant "data subjects" (for example employees).

Applicability of the Act

The Act applies to processing of personal data. The Act will only apply to relevant personal data which can either be processed by means of equipment operating automatically (for example data held on computers) or which is part of a relevant filing system (defined as a set of information structured in such a way that specific information relating to a particular individual is readily accessible, such as HR records). Therefore the Act will not apply:

(i)   to the extent that no individual is identifiable from relevant information (for example, statistical data), as such information does not constitute "personal data"

(ii) to the extent that the relevant data is held on paper-based records which are not a relevant filing system (for example, correspondence files which are not structured so that a particular individual's details are readily accessible).

Even if a data controller is processing personal data, the processing must fall within the jurisdiction of the Act. Under Section 5 of the Act, the Act applies only if:

(i)   the data controller is established in the UK and the relevant personal data are processed in the context of that establishment (for example, a UK employer processing information about its staff)

(ii) the data controller is not established in the UK or the European Economic Area but uses equipment in the UK for processing data (other than purely for the purposes of transit of such data through the UK).

For the purposes of the first point above, the Act will apply where a business established in the UK processes personal data in the context of (for example, for the benefit of) that establishment, even if the actual processing is conducted (for example, by a data processor or other service supplier) in a jurisdiction outside the UK.

Despite the above requirements, it is likely that in most cases where a company is established within the UK it will at least to some extent be caught by the provisions of the Act.

Key obligations under the Act

A data controller (for example, an employer) subject to the Act is required to comply with various data protection "principles" set out in Part I of Schedule 1 of the Act in relation to the information it holds about its staff and third parties. These are the core obligations of the Act.

In order to satisfy the data protection principles, certain specific conditions need to be met. These conditions are set out in Schedules 2, 3 and 4 of the Act, which are discussed further below.

This chapter focuses on the following four principles, which in practice tend to cause the most difficulties from a data protection perspective:

Principle 1 - personal data shall be processed fairly and lawfully, and, in particular, shall not be processed unless:

   (a)   at least one of the conditions in Schedule 2 [of the Act] is met, and
   (b)   in the case of sensitive personal data, at least one of the conditions in
          Schedule 3 [of the Act] is also met;

Principle 6 - personal data shall be processed in accordance with the rights of data subjects under this Act;

Principle 7 - appropriate technical and organisational measures shall be taken against unauthorised or unlawful processing of personal data and against accidental loss or destruction of, or damage to personal data; and

Principle 8 - personal data shall not be transferred to a country or territory outside the European Economic Area, unless that country or territory ensures an adequate level of protection to the rights and freedoms of data subjects in relation to the processing of personal data.

The above principles can be summarised as follows:

   (i)   the need to ensure that use of personal data is "fair and lawful"
   (ii)   the need to take particular care with sensitive personal data
   (iii)   the rights of individuals to have access to, and rectify inaccuracies in,
           their data
   (iv)   the need to process data securely
   (v)   restrictions on international transfer of data.

In addition to the above principles the Act imposes an obligation to register ("notify") processing of data with the UK data protection regulator, the Information Commissioner. There are also other principles which are addressed briefly below.

Processing data "fairly and lawfully"

The obligation to process data "fairly and lawfully" comprises two elements as follows:

1. An obligation to ensure so far as practicable that individual(s) (for example, employees) are properly informed of who is processing their data and why this is taking place (the "Notice Obligation"); and

2. An obligation to ensure that use of relevant information is "fair" (the "Fairness Obligation").

The notice obligation

Informing the data subject:

A data controller (for example an employer) is required to ensure so far as practicable that each data subject (such as an employee or prospective or former employee) on whom it gathers information is informed of:

(i)   the identity of the data controller or its representatives

(ii)   the purposes for which personal data are intended to be processed (for example the administration of an employee's employment, recruitment and selection, disciplinary action, payroll, monitoring of employees, conducting assessments, credit checking, etc.)

(iii) any other information which is necessary to enable the processing to be fair. This might include for example informing employees that their details may be made available to other group companies and/or clients or prospective clients and/or transferred internationally.

An employer should therefore take steps to notify relevant job applicants, employees or former employees of the processing of their data. This can be done, for example, by inserting relevant data protection notices in job application forms, responses to unsolicited applications, contracts of employment, staff handbooks, data protection policies and similar documentation when an employee leaves employment so as to ensure that relevant notice requirements have been met.

The Information Commissioner's "Employment Practices Data Protection Code – Part I: Recruitment and Selection" (the "Recruitment Code") includes guidance on good practice in addressing these obligations when dealing with job applicants. Although neither the Recruitment Code (nor any other part of the Employment Practices Code) has legal effect, it reflects the Information Commissioner's recommendations on how the legal requirements of the Act can be met. The introduction to the Recruitment Code notes that "employers may have alternative ways of meeting these requirements but if they do they risk breaking the law". The Recruitment Code is therefore not "the law", but consists of regulatory guidance on how, in practice, the Act should be complied with.

The Recruitment Code: providing data protection notices

The Recruitment Code contains a number of specific recommendations on providing data protection notices to job applicants as part of the recruitment process, including stating that:

(i) Employers should inform individuals responding to job advertisements of the name of the organisation to which they will be providing their information and how it will be used, unless this is self-evident.

(ii) Recruitment agencies used by a prospective employer must identify themselves as such and explain how personal data they receive will be used and disclosed, unless this is self-evident.

(iii) On receiving details of job applicants from an agency an employer should ensure, as soon as possible, that the applicants are aware that their information is being held.

(iv) Application forms should identify to whom information is being provided and how it will be used if this is not self-evident.

(v) Employers should explain any checks that might be undertaken to verify the information provided in application forms, including the nature of additional sources from which information may be gathered.

(vi) Employers should explain as early as is reasonably practicable in the recruitment process the nature of the verification process and the methods used to carry it out.

(vii) Employers should inform applicants if an automated short-listing system will be used as a sole basis for making a decision as to their future employment.

(viii) It should be made clear early in the recruitment process that vetting of applicants (for example, checking criminal records, etc.) will take place and how this will be conducted.

(ix) Where information is collected about a third party (for example an applicant's partner), employers should ensure so far is practicable that the relevant third party is made aware of this.

(x) Employers should advise unsuccessful applicants if there is an intention to keep their names on file for future vacancies (if appropriate) and give them the opportunity to have their details removed from the file.

The Recruitment Code deals with the processing of personal data in connection with the recruitment and selection of employees. With regard to notices to be given to new and current employees, the Information Commissioner's Code of Practice on Employment Records (referred to as the "Employment Records Code") includes the following additional guidance.

Employers should:

(i)   ensure that newly appointed workers are aware of the nature and source of any information stored about them, how it will be used and to whom it will be disclosed

(ii)   inform new workers and remind existing workers about their rights under the Act, including their right of access to the information kept on them

(iii)   ensure that when a worker joins a health or insurance scheme it is made clear what, if any, information is passed between the scheme controller and the employer and how it will be used

(iv)   inform workers if the employer intends to use their personal information in order to deliver advertising or marketing messages to them and give them an opportunity to "opt-out"

(v)   inform new workers of the use of payroll or other data for fraud/prevention exercises and remind them of this periodically

(vi)   in the context of mergers and acquisitions, advise workers wherever practicable that their employment records are to be disclosed to another organisation before an acquisition or merger takes place. In particular, make sure that they are told of the transfer to a new employer should the merger or acquisition proceed.

In many cases, it will be possible for employers to give notices to relevant individuals as regards the processing of their information when they gather relevant information from them (for example, in relevant enrolment forms). However, in certain circumstances information may be provided indirectly, rather than directly by the individual concerned. For example, information about a spouse may be provided by an employee or information about a prospective employee may be provided by a recruitment agency. In these circumstances it may not always be easy to provide an appropriate notice to the relevant individual.

The Act makes allowance for this by providing that it is not necessary to notify an individual of the processing of their data where the relevant information was not provided directly by the relevant individual and where provision of the relevant information would involve a disproportionate effort in all the circumstances.

Where an employer seeks to rely on this exemption it needs to keep a record of why it believes that provision of relevant notices would constitute a "disproportionate effort". The term "disproportionate effort" is not defined by the Act. In assessing what does or does not amount to a "disproportionate effort", the starting point, according to guidance issued by the Information Commissioner, must be that data controllers are not generally exempt from providing the relevant information because they have not obtained data directly from data subjects. What constitutes a "disproportionate effort" will be a question of fact to be determined in each and every case. In any event a data controller claiming the benefit of the misapplication of the requirement to provide information must still provide this information to an individual who subsequently requests it (subject to various provisions referred to further below).

The fairness obligation

In addition to informing people of the processing of their personal data, in order to show that use of personal data is "fair and lawful" at least one of the conditions set out in the Act needs to be satisfied. In the case of processing of information relating to prospective or actual employees, the conditions that are most likely to apply in many cases are:

(i) that the data subject (the employee) has given his consent to the processing of his data. Further commentary on the requirements for a valid employee consent are set out in the section "Validity of consents"

(ii) that the processing is necessary for performance of a contract with or at the request of the relevant individual

(iii) that the processing is necessary for the purposes of legitimate interests pursued by the employer, or by a third party or parties to whom data are disclosed except where the processing is unwarranted in any particular case by reason of prejudice to the rights and freedoms or legitimate interests of the data subject. This "balance of interests" condition may be particularly useful to rely on where it is not practicable to obtain consents from relevant individuals.

Even if one or more relevant conditions identified above (or elsewhere in Schedule 2) is satisfied, the processing still needs to be "fair" in all the circumstances. Factors which may be taken into account in determining whether processing is "fair", include the circumstances in which the data was obtained and whether the relevant individual was misled as to the purposes for which information would be used.

Fair processing of "sensitive personal data"

The Act imposes specific restrictions on the processing of "sensitive personal data".

"Sensitive personal data" is defined in Section 1(1) of the Act as personal data consisting of information as to:
(i)   the racial or ethnic origin of the data subject
(ii)   his or her political opinions
(iii)   his or her religious beliefs or other beliefs of a similar nature
(iv)   whether the data subject is a member of a trade union
(v)   his or her physical or mental health or condition

(vi)   the data subject's sexual life

(vii) the commission or alleged commission of any offence

(viii) any proceedings for any offence committed or alleged to have been committed by the data subject, the disposal of such proceedings or the sentence of any court in such proceedings.

Sensitive personal data might therefore include information about an employee's race or health (for example, maintained as part of his sickness or life insurance records). Mere information about an employee's nationality (for example, that an individual is Israeli) does not necessarily constitute sensitive personal data as to race.

Employers might in particular hold information about their employees' racial or ethnic origin, trade union membership, health or alleged offences. In order to hold such sensitive personal data, certain conditions specified in Schedule 3 of the Act need to be satisfied. Of these, the most likely conditions to apply in a work context are as follows:

(i)   where the data subject has given explicit consent to the processing of the personal data

(ii)   the processing is necessary for the purposes of exercising or performing any right or obligation which is conferred or imposed by law on the data controller in connection with employment

(iii) the processing is necessary to protect the vital interests of the data subject or another person in the case where consent cannot be given by or on behalf of the data subject, or the data controller cannot reasonably be expected to obtain consent of the data subject, or where such consent is unreasonably withheld

(iv)   the processing is necessary for the purposes of, or in connection with, any legal proceedings (including prospective legal proceedings)

(v)   the processing is necessary for medical purposes and is undertaken by a health professional or someone under equivalent duty of confidentiality.

In addition to the conditions identified in Schedule 3 of the Act, sensitive personal data can also be processed in the circumstances specified in the Data Protection (Processing of Sensitive Personal Data) Order 2000. In particular, this Order permits the processing of sensitive personal data about alleged criminal offences, where the relevant processing is in the substantial public interest, is necessary to prevent or detect any unlawful act and must necessarily be carried out without the specific consent of the data subject so as not to prejudice those purposes.

Because the circumstances in which sensitive personal data may be processed are tightly circumscribed, it is likely that in many cases, in order to process sensitive personal data about its employees, an employer will seek the explicit consent of the relevant individual. However, in this respect, see the section "Validity of Consents" below.

The Information Commissioners' Recruitment Code contains specific guidance on the gathering of sensitive personal data from prospective employees. In connection with the condition that processing is permitted where necessary for the purposes of performing obligations imposed by law in connection with employment, the Recruitment Code notes that this condition can have quite wide application in the context of the recruitment and selection of employees.

> For example this condition might be relied on to justify the holding of sensitive data to satisfy various obligations.
> (i)   ensuring the health, safety and welfare at work for employees
> (ii)   selecting safe and competent employees
> (iii) ensuring a safe working environment
> (iv)   not discriminating on the grounds of race, sex or disability
> (v)   ensuring the reliability of employees with access to personal data
> (vi)   protecting customers' property or funds in the employer's possession
> (vii) checking an individual's immigration status before employment.

The Recruitment Code therefore provides that an employer may be able to collect sensitive information as to a job applicants' criminal record or health if this can be shown to be necessary to enable the employer to meet its obligations in relation to the safety of its workers and others to whom it owes a duty of care. However in all cases the relevant processing must be "necessary" to meet the relevant legal requirement.

The Information Commissioner's Employment Records Code contains similar guidance to the Recruitment Code, but also contains sections dealing specifically with sickness records and equal opportunities monitoring, both of which are likely to involve the processing of sensitive personal data.

> Employers are advised to:
> (i)   keep sickness and accident records separate and not use sickness or accident records when records of absence could be used instead
> (ii)   only disclose information about a worker's sickness or accident where there is a legal obligation to do so or with explicit consent from the relevant individual
> (iii) avoid making sickness, accident or absence records of individual members of staff available to other workers except as reasonably required
> (iv)   as far as possible, keep equal opportunities monitoring of information in anonymised form
> (v)   consider advice from relevant bodies before designing, distributing, collating and evaluating an equal opportunities monitoring initiative and incorporating it into procedures.

In connection with the processing of sensitive health data, the Information Commissioner proposes, as the final part of its guidance to employers, to issue a code of practice for employers concerning the processing of medical information (for example, concerning occupational health information, drug testing, drug and genetic screening information) about their employees.

Subject access rights

In addition to the Notice Obligation (see above), under Section 7(1) of the Act, subject to various restrictions under the Act discussed further below, individuals (for example, employees) are entitled on request to be informed whether data relating to them are being processed by an employer. If it is, they are entitled to be given a description of the relevant data, the purposes of processing and details of the recipients or classes of recipients to whom such data may be disclosed. Individuals also have the right to be provided with the information constituting any personal data and information available as to the source of those data. In addition, to the extent that decisions which significantly affect an individual are made by purely automatic means (for example, where recruitment software is used to automatically analyse CVs and make recruitment decisions), an individual is also entitled to be informed of the basis on which that takes place. In summary, individuals have wide rights of access to information that is held about them.

Rights of access to information under the Act are further supplemented by the Data Protection (Subject Access) (Fees and Miscellaneous Provisions) Regulations 2000 which set out procedural rules relating to the exercise of subject access rights under the Act. Generally speaking, employers receiving requests in writing in the appropriate form accompanied by an appropriate fee (not to exceed £10) are obliged to comply with such requests from employees within 40 days' of receipt of the relevant request.

In an employment context, subject access requests might arise, for example, in connection with a claim by an unsuccessful job applicant wishing to have access to interview documentation or requests by employees or former employees in connection with claims for unfair or constructive dismissal.

It is therefore important that employers are aware that information may need to be disclosed to employees at some point in the future and have in place appropriate procedures for dealing with subject access requests promptly. Having said this, there may be valid reasons why an employer may wish to or be required to withhold certain information from an individual making a subject access request. Under Section 7(4) of the Act, an employer is not obliged to comply with a request where to do so would involve disclosing information relating to another individual (such as another employee or third party) unless the other individual has consented to the disclosure of information or it is nevertheless reasonable in the circumstances to comply with the subject access request without the consent of the other individual.

In assessing whether it is "reasonable" to comply with a request without consent an employer needs to consider the circumstances of the request, in particular having regard to:

(a)   any duty of confidentiality owed by it to another individual

(b)   whether the employer took any steps with a view to seeking the consent of that other individual

(c)   whether the other individual is capable of giving consent

(d)   any express refusal of consent by that other individual.

These considerations might mean that it may in certain circumstances be reasonable for an employer to refuse a request by an employee to have access to disciplinary or other records whether those records contain information about third parties (such as line managers) who do not wish the employer to disclose the relevant information and it is reasonable in all the circumstances to withhold the information.

In addition, the Act (and associated statutory instruments) provide a number of general exemptions from the need to comply with subject access requests.

Exceptions to the DPA include situations where:

(i)   it is necessary to process data in connection with crime prevention or tax collection activities and where to comply with the subject access request would prejudice the relevant crime or tax related activity

(ii)   in the case of health data, where the disclosure of the relevant information would be likely to cause serious harm to the health of the employee or a third person (see the Data Protection (Subject Access Modification) (Health) Order 2000). This exemption (which might apply, for example, where an employee is emotionally or psychiatrically disturbed) can only be relied on following consultation with health professionals

(iii)   likewise there are other general exemptions (for example, data which is subject to legal professional privilege or exemptions in respect of certain corporate finance activities) which may apply in a particular case

(iv)   of particular relevance in the employment context, under paragraph 1 of Schedule 7 of the Act, personal data are exempt from the subject access provisions if they consist of a reference given or to be given in confidence by a data controller (for example, a current or former employer) for the purposes of the employment or prospective employment of a data subject. This exemption would therefore protect an employer from having to disclose references given by it.

However, this would not necessarily extend to subject access requests received by an employer in respect of references received from third parties. This appears to be an anomaly in the legislation. Schedule 7 of the Act also provides that personal data processed for the purposes of management forecasting or management planning to assist an employer in the conduct of its business or other activity are exempt from the subject access rights where these rights would be likely to prejudice the conduct of the employer's business. This might be relevant where, for example, an employee requests access to data which pertains to his or her promotion prospects and where to disclose relevant information might damage the employer's business.

It is therefore clear from the above that employees do not have an absolute right to all data that an employer holds on them.

The Information Commissioner's Employment Records Code contains a section dealing specifically with subject access requests. This section identifies the following suggested compliance steps that an employer might be advised to take in connection with requests from employees.

The employer should:

(i)   establish a system that enables it to locate all the information it holds about an employee in order to be able to respond promptly or in any case within 40 calendar days of receiving a subject access request

(ii) check the identity of anyone making a subject access request to ensure information is only given to the person entitled to it

(iii) provide the employee with a hard copy of the information requested, making clear any codes used and the sources of the information

(iv) make a judgement as to what information it is reasonable to release concerning the identities of third parties contained within the information requested

(v)   inform managers and other relevant people in its organisation of the nature of information that will be released to individuals who will make subject access requests

(vi) ensure that on request, promptly and in any event within 40 calendar days, employees requesting information are provided with a statement of how any automated decision-making process to which they are subject is used and how it works

(vii) when purchasing a computerised system that involves automated decisions about workers, it should ensure that the system supplier provides the information needed to enable it to respond fully to subject access requests.

In addition to the rights to request access to relevant personal data discussed above, the Act also provides that an individual has the right to require incorrect data to be corrected and a right of compensation in the event that he or she incurs loss or damage as a result of inaccurate data being held on him or her. It is therefore important that appropriate steps are taken to ensure that employment records (assessments, disciplinary records, etc.) contain accurate information and that inaccuracies are corrected.

Security obligations

The seventh data protection principle set out in Schedule 1 of the Act requires that data controllers take "appropriate technical and organisational measures" against unauthorised or unlawful processing of personal data and against accidental loss or destruction of, or damage to, personal data.

Paragraph 9 of Part II of Schedule 1 provides some guidance on what constitutes "appropriate" security measures although in practice this concept is not clearly defined.

"Appropriate" measures must ensure a level of security appropriate to the harm that might result from unauthorised or unlawful processing or loss, destruction or damage to data and the nature of the data to be protected. In particular, an employer must take reasonable steps to ensure the reliability of employees who have access to personal data. An employer should therefore, for example, ensure that HR records are accessible by certain employees only (such as appropriate HR staff) and are subject to appropriate additional controls as necessary. As part of ensuring appropriate security measures, employees should be told that they are not entitled to use other employees' (or third parties') data except as authorised in accordance with their employment and relevant security procedures (for example, use of passwords) reflecting their roles and responsibilities. In other words, employees are entitled to expect data relating to them to be held securely, but also owe a duty to their co-workers.

In this context, the Information Commissioners' Recruitment Code includes the following guidance for protecting information relating to prospective employees. Employers should:

(i) provide a secure method for sending (and receiving) applications
(ii) ensure that personal data obtained during the recruitment process are securely stored or are destroyed.

The Employment Records Code also contains a section on "Security" which includes the following practical guidance.

Employers should:

(i) apply security standards that take account of the risks of unauthorised access to, accidental loss of, destruction of, or damage to employment records
(ii) institute a system of secure cabinets, access controls and passwords

that ensures that the access of staff to employment records is only granted where there is legitimate business need to do so

(iii) if possible use IT systems to track who accesses and amends personal data

(iv) take steps to check the reliability of staff who have access to work records, ensuring that they are properly trained and including a confidentiality clause in their contracts of employment

(v) ensure that if employment records are taken off site, (for example, on laptop computers), this is controlled. Employers should make sure only the necessary information is taken and there are security rules for staff to follow

(vi) take account of the risks of transmitting confidential worker information by fax or e-mail. Employers should only transmit information between locations if a secure network or comparable arrangements are in place or if, in the case of e-mail, encryption is used.

Particular security concerns arise where an employer engages a third party to carry out data processing activities on its behalf. The Act sets out specific security obligations[5] where a data processor (for example, a payroll processing company) processes personal data on behalf of the employer.

In these circumstances, the processing must be carried out under a contract in writing:

(i) under which the data processor is to act only on instructions from the employer

(ii) which requires the data processor to comply with security obligations equivalent to those imposed on the employer.

In other words, in such situations, an employer is required to contractually impose appropriate security obligations on third parties processing personal data on its behalf. The European Commission has approved a specific form of contract where transfers are made to data processors outside the European Economic Area.[6] This addresses both the security requirements identified above and issues relating to restrictions on the international transfer of personal data referred to in the following section of this chapter.

The Information Commissioner's Employment Records Code also contains a section on outsourcing of data processing which reflects the legal requirements under the Act identified above and includes the following guidance.

An employer should:

(i)   be satisfied that any data processor it chooses adopts appropriate security measures both in terms of the technology it uses and how it is managed

(ii)   have in place a written contract with the data processor that requires it to process personal information only on the employer's instructions and to maintain appropriate security.

International transfers

Under paragraph 8 of Part I of Schedule 1 of the Act;

> personal data shall not be transferred to a country or territory outside the European Economic Area, unless that country or territory ensures an adequate level of protection for the rights and freedoms of data subjects in relation to the processing of personal data.

The European Economic Area currently consists of the 15 EU countries, plus Iceland, Liechtenstein and Norway. A "transfer" in such circumstances might include making employee contact details available via an Internet or Intranet site or the transfer of employee data via e-mail. This provision is a part of the Act that has tended to cause employers great difficulty in practice and has led to tensions both at a governmental level (notably between the European Union and US authorities) and within organisations because of the extra-territorial effect of the UK (and indeed other EU) legislation. Typically the effect of this principle might involve, for example, a UK subsidiary of a US parent entity being unable to transfer employee records to its US parent because the United States is not recognised as a jurisdiction which offers "adequate" security under the Act.

So how can businesses transfer employee records in such circumstances? The Act states that "adequacy" will be assessed in all circumstances of the case, but having particular regard to the nature of the relevant data transferred (for example, whether it is sensitive or not), the country of origin of the data, the country of destination of the data, the purposes for which and period during which the data are intended to be processed, the law in force in the country to which data is transferred, international obligations of that country, relevant codes of conduct and security measures taken in respect of the data.

It is clearly not practicable to make an assessment of this kind in respect of each and every transfer of employee data where businesses may make huge numbers of transfers on a regular basis. However, Schedule 4 of the Act provides "derogations" where the eighth data protection principle does not apply.

International transfers outside the EEA are permitted by Schedule 4 where:
(i)   the data subject (the employee) has given his consent to the transfer
(ii) the transfer is necessary for performance of a contract with the relevant individual or at his request
(iii) the transfer is necessary in connection with legal proceedings
(iv) the transfer is made on terms which are of a kind approved by the Information Commissioner as ensuring adequate safeguards for the rights and freedoms of data subjects.

Are there any countries outside the EEA which are deemed to offer adequate protection? As well as countries within the EEA, the European Commission has decided (in a Decision binding on the UK Information Commissioner) that Switzerland and Hungary are countries which are deemed to offer adequate safeguards for international transfer. Certain transfers to Canada are permitted under the terms of a separate European Commission Decision. However, that Decision does not cover personal data held by private organisations and used for non-commercial purposes, such as data collected in the context of an employment relationship. For these transfers to recipients in Canada, operators in the UK (and elsewhere in the EU) will have to ensure that adequate safeguards are in place. It is likely that other countries will be "approved" in due course, but this has not taken place at the time of writing.

The United States is not a country which is deemed to offer "adequate safeguards". However, the European Commission (and the UK Authorities) have approved transfers to the United States if the recipient organisation in the United States enters the so-called "safe harbour" arrangement. In order to fall within the scope of the US safe harbour regime, entities receiving personal data in the US must publicly subscribe to certain "safe harbour principles" which relate to the protection of personal data and which are similar to the data protection obligations under the Act, for example obligations to provide notice of processing and rights of subject access. A US organisation entering the US safe harbour regime will be subject to US regulatory control (for example, by the US Federal Trade Commission). Although offering a potential solution for transfers to the US, the US safe harbour has a number of problems associated with it. In particular, it only relates to transfers to the US and therefore does not cover transfers to other non-EEA countries. In addition, as a result of the potential exposure to US regulatory action, the safe harbour regime has had limited popularity to date.

An alternative to the US safe harbour regime as a means of ensuring adequate safeguards are the standard contractual clauses for transfers of personal data to third countries approved by the European Commission. On 15 June 2001, the European Commission made a decision (that the UK is bound by) that organisations using the standard contractual clauses for transfer approved by the

Commission are deemed to have put in place "adequate safeguards" as required by applicable law. On 27 December 2001, the European Commission made a separate Decision approving similar (but less onerous) standard contractual clauses in respect of data transferred by a data controller to a data processor outside the EEA.

The standard contractual clauses have the benefit of ensuring that data can be transferred internationally (not just to the US) outside the EEA in accordance with applicable EU data protection laws. However, difficulties with the standard contractual clauses include the fact that they impose on a "data importer" outside the EEA obligations which might not otherwise have applied to it. The standard clauses also provide that individuals have rights of enforcement under the contract as third party beneficiaries to it and it is unclear to what extent a single contract can cover multiple transfers of data that typically take place on a daily basis. The standard contractual clauses therefore do not provide a simple or risk-free solution to the problem faced by organisations wishing to transfer personal data outside the EEA. Their use will give rise to a number of obligations, each of which need careful consideration before a data exporter decides to make use of them rather than pursuing one of the other available strategies. However, the standard contractual clauses offer some certainty in a situation where other options are not available.

In the employment law context, an employer may therefore wish to seek to rely on another condition (for example consent or contractual necessity (where available)) to justify international transfers of relevant employee data. However it may not always be "necessary" as part of the contractual arrangement to make an international transfer of employee data and the validity of consents in the employment context has recently been questioned by regulatory guidance (see below). In such circumstances a contract based on the standard contractual clauses approved by the European Commission may be the best option available.

Validity of consents

It is clear from the above comments on Schedules 1 and 4 of the Act that certain conditions need to be satisfied to ensure that use of employee data is "fair", that one or more specific additional conditions must be met to justify the use of sensitive data and the international transfer of such data. One way of satisfying all these requirements under the Act is to obtain the consent from the relevant individual employee. However, the Act does not give any clear guidance on what form that consent should take, except to state that a consent for processing of sensitive data needs to be "explicit". If it is not practicable to obtain a valid consent, then a more detailed analysis of applicable law may be required to ensure that the use of information is "fair" and the relevant restrictions on sensitive data and international transfer of data can be met.

Where an employer wishes to rely on consent to meet the relevant requirements under the Act in order for the consent to be valid, it needs to be freely given, specific and informed. Employers cannot simply *require* their employees to give consents as the consent will not be "freely given". This in turn raises a question as to what to do in respect of employees who refuse to give consent. An employer might therefore seek to obtain consents from new employees through appropriate documentation but take the view that it is not practicable to seek consents from existing staff (because of the administrative headaches this may entail if staff refuse to consent or simply fail to respond).

If an employer does seek consent from prospective or current employees to the processing of their data then this will not be an entirely straightforward process as it is necessary to ensure that the consent is valid and enforceable.

In this respect, the European Union Article 29 Working Party (an influential advisory body to the European Commission) issued its Opinion in connection with the issue of employee consent in September 2001. This Opinion notes:

> where consent is required from a worker, and there is a real potential relevant prejudice that arises from not consenting, the consent is not valid in terms of satisfying [relevant requirements for fair processing] as it is not freely given. If it is not possible for the worker to refuse it is not consent. Consent must at all times be freely given. Thus the worker must be able to withdraw all consent without prejudice.

This analysis suggests that it is inherently unfair to ask for consent on the understanding that the employee might suffer some prejudice if he or she refuses or subsequently withdraws that consent. Although this view can be challenged (on the grounds that it does not follow that for consent to be "freely given" it must also be possible for the employee to withdraw the consent without any adverse consequence), this appears to be the view that regulators are taking.

The UK Information Commissioner's Recruitment Code includes guidance which suggests that consent may be appropriate in some circumstances, but which broadly following the Article 29 Working Party view.

In relation to the obtaining of explicit consent to the processing of sensitive data, Section 3 of the Recruitment Code notes that employers seeking to rely on consent must bear in mind that:

1. the consent must be explicit. This means that the job applicant must have been told clearly what personal data are involved and the use that will be made of them. The applicant must have given a positive indication of agreement, for example by a signature.
2. the consent must have been freely given. This means that the applicant must have a real choice whether or not to consent and there must be no significant detriment that arises from not consenting.

The Recruitment Code goes on to state:

> The extent to which consent can be relied upon in the context of employment is limited because of the need for any consent to be freely given. However in relation to the recruitment and selection of workers this is less of a constraint. Individuals in the open job market will usually have a free choice whether or not to apply for a particular job. If consent to some processing of sensitive data is a condition of an application being considered this does not prevent the consent being freely given. It must of course be clear to the applicant exactly what he or she is consenting to. As recruitment proceeds it becomes less likely that the valid consent can be obtained. If, for example, the direct consequence of not consenting results in the withdrawal of a job offer, the consent is unlikely to be freely given.

This suggests that the UK Information Commissioner is following the view held by the Article 29 Committee and that it is difficult for an employee to give a valid consent.

In relation to the question of consent the Employment Records Code specifically addresses this issue and states that consent from employees "is not usually required" and "indeed the Commissioner considers it misleading to seek consent from workers if they have no realistic choice. Employers are more likely to need the consent of workers if they are processing sensitive personal data rather than non-sensitive personal data". The Code fails to mention that another reason for seeking employees' consent is to enable international transfers of their data to take place. This is a key issue in terms of compliance which is only dealt with in very superficial terms in the Code. The Code mentions the US safe harbor and the fact that "there are also other alternatives such as providing adequate protection through the terms of a contract between your company in the UK and its parent in the USA". It refers to general guidance on international transfers of personal data as provided on the Commissioner's website". However, perhaps the most straightforward way to ensure an international transfer can take place is through consent and it is significant that the Commissioner's Code does not appear to advocate this option.

In summary, therefore, the Act permits the processing of personal data with consent. However, regulatory guidance in this area suggests that it may be difficult to obtain an appropriately "freely given" consent from employees, because of the potential duress that they may be under if they refuse or withdraw such consent.

In order to resolve this situation, any drafting of consent wording by employers should be undertaken with extreme care. For example, employees might be asked in contracts of employment and other documentation whereby employee details are gathered to confirm the processing or international transfer of personal data supplied by them is necessary for their contract of employment, or to the extent it is not, that such data are processed with their full and free consent. An employer might also reserve the right to continue processing data if otherwise permitted by applicable law (for example, to exercise legal rights) in the event that an employee refuses or subsequently withdraws his or her consent.

Notification

Under Section 17(1) of the Act, processing of personal data needs, subject to certain exceptions, to be registered or "notified". Notification to the Information Commissioner is made on a standard notification document obtained from the Information Commissioner (or which can be downloaded or completed online and posted to the Information Commissioner's Office) and must include certain "registrable particulars" (identifying, for example, the name and address of the data controller, the relevant data subjects whose details are being processed, categories of data processed and purposes of processing). The notification must also include a general description of the security measures taken in respect of the relevant data processing activity. In particular, the notification needs to specify the extent to which transfers of data are made within the EEA, outside the EEA or worldwide.

Notification currently costs £35 and is a relatively straightforward process. There are various exemptions from the notification requirement available under applicable statutory instruments. In particular, under the Data Protection (Notification and Notification Fees) Regulations 2000, there are exemptions from the need to notify for data processing activities carried out for the purposes of (a) staff administration (b) advertising, marketing and public relations and (c) accounts and record keeping.

Therefore, if an employer only processes personal data relating to its own employees in connection with the administration of their employment, it is likely that such processing will benefit from the exemption from notification provided for by the statutory instrument. However, if and to the extent that any use of employee data goes beyond mere staff administration and record-keeping then it is likely that a notification would be required. In any event, if the employer processes other personal data (for example relating to clients) and thereby needs a data protection registration, it may choose to include in its notification details of processing of personal data relating to its staff. Failure to maintain an appropriate data protection registration and keep it accurate is a criminal offence and for this reason many employers seek to register all their processing of personal data, rather than seeking to rely on applicable exemptions. For those wishing to rely on the exemptions and for other guidance on notification, the Information Commissioner's Office has published guidance and notification on its website www.dataprotection.gov.uk.

Other issues

In addition to the principles discussed above, Schedule 1 of the Act identifies a number of other principles that need to be met in respect of any processing of personal data.

Personal data should:
(i) only be processed for one or more specified purposes and not be processed in a manner incompatible with the purposes for which it was obtained
(ii) be adequate, relevant and not excessive in relation to relevant purposes
(iii) be accurate and up to date
(iv) not be kept for longer than is necessary.

Part II of Schedule 1 of the Act provides additional guidance on how these broad various principles should be addressed. For example, in relation to the obligation to ensure that personal data are accurate and up to date, paragraph 7 of Part II of Schedule 1 of the Act provides that this obligation is not deemed to be contravened if the data (though inaccurate) accurately record information obtained by the data controller, the data controller has taken reasonable steps to ensure the accuracy of the data and, if the data subject has notified the data controller of an inaccuracy, the data record that fact.

The Information Commissioner's Recruitment Code also includes the following practical guidance in addressing these issues:
(i) in relation to job application forms, only seek personal data that are relevant to the recruitment decision to be made
(ii) only request information about an applicant's criminal convictions if seeking that information can be justified in terms of the role offered
(iii) in terms of verification checks on an individual's background, give the applicant an opportunity to comment should any of the checks produce a discrepancy with the information that the applicant has provided
(iv) ensure that personal data that are recorded and retained following interviews are necessary for the recruitment process or for defending the process against challenge
(v) do not place [undue] reliance on information collected from possibly unreliable sources as part of the pre-employment vetting checks and allow applicants to make representations
(vi) establish and adhere to retention periods for recruitment records that are based on a clear business need
(vii) destroy information obtained in relation to the vetting of applicants as soon as possible, or in any case within six months. A record of the result of any vetting or verification can be retained

(viii) consider carefully which information contained on an application form is to be transferred to the worker's employment records. Delete information irrelevant to the on-going employment relationship.

The Employment Records Code includes the following guidance on retention of records:

(i)   Establish and adhere to standard retention times for the various categories of information to be held on the records of workers and former workers. Base the retention times on business needs, taking into account relevant professional guidelines.

(ii) Anonymise any data concerning workers and former workers where possible.

(iii) If the holding of any information on criminal convictions of workers is justified, ensure that the information is deleted once the conviction is spent under the Rehabilitation Of Offenders Acts.

(iv) Ensure that records which should be disposed of are securely and effectively destroyed.

In practice, in order to ensure that requirements as to accuracy, retention, etc. under the Act are complied with, many employers choose to implement appropriate data protection policies and staff handbooks/guidance. A data protection policy can be a useful means of informing staff of their obligations and restrictions on the use that they should make of personal data to which they have access as part of their contract of employment.

Sanctions

In light of the complexity of the Act (and associated costs of compliance) many employers question why they need to comply with the Act at all. In short, what are the risks if they fail to do so? Failure to comply with the Act may in certain circumstances give rise to criminal offences, in particular, failure to obtain an appropriate data protection notification where this is required (or failure to ensure it is accurate) may give rise to criminal sanctions. Likewise, where an employee of a data controller misuses personal data to which he or she has access this may constitute a criminal offence. The Information Commissioner therefore recommends ensuring that employees are aware of the extent to which they could be criminally liable if they knowingly or recklessly disclose personal data outside the scope of their employer's policies or procedures. The Information Commissioner also suggests that breach of data protection standards should be treated as a disciplinary offence by the employer.

Where offences are committed under the Act, fines can be imposed (normally

£5,000 per offence, but possibly more in the Crown Court). In addition, individuals who have suffered damage or distress as a result of misuse of data are entitled to claim compensation from the data controller.

What may be of more concern for many companies is the possibility of regulatory investigation by the Information Commissioner. The Information Commissioner has power to serve "information notices" requiring information to be provided as to steps taken by a data controller to comply with data protection obligations and to serve "enforcement notices" preventing use of certain databases until satisfactory compliance steps have been taken.

In practice, the Information Commissioner's activities to date have tended to focus on obviously fraudulent or flagrantly dishonest use of personal data as the Information Commissioner does not have the resources to ensure compliance by most businesses with the provisions of the Act. However, to the extent that an individual, for example a disgruntled employee, makes a complaint to the Information Commissioner, the Commissioner is likely to take action and ask questions based on that complaint. In practice, therefore, although the Information Commissioner's enforcement activities tend to be "reactive" rather than "proactive", the risk of failing to take appropriate compliance steps may include significant reputational damage and business disruption resulting from possible regulatory action.

Monitoring

The above comments relate to the core obligations under the Act. However, there are particular data protection issues in connection with the monitoring of employees. This activity gives rise to obligations not just under the Act itself, but also under associated legislation. Employee monitoring may include for example checking the use of communication systems such as e-mail, telephone, Internet and Intranet usage. Information gathered as a result of such monitoring activity will in many cases constitute "personal data" within the scope of the Act. However, other legislation may also be relevant.

Relevant legislation:	
Regulation of Investigatory Powers Act 2000 (RIPA)	restricts the circumstances in which entities can intercept communications
Human Rights Act which came into force on 2 October 2000	provides that individuals are entitled to respect for their private and family life (see below)
	contractual commitments and employment law obligations between employers and employees

The RIPA restricts the circumstances in which communications on public and private telecommunications systems may be intercepted and is therefore of great significance as regards the monitoring of employee communications systems. The RIPA prohibits the unlawful interception of a private telecommunications system by the operator of that system. Accordingly, any interception of communications by an employer carried out without lawful authority will be actionable by parties to a communication which is intercepted. The RIPA does however permit communications to be lawfully intercepted in certain circumstances (for example where an appropriate warrant has been obtained). In addition, Section 4(2) of the RIPA grants power to the government to specify particular circumstances in which the interception of business communications can take place. The Telecommunications (Lawful Business Practice) (Interception of Communication) Regulations 2000 were made under this section and came into force on 24 October 2000.

These regulations provide that interception of communications without the consent of the parties to the communication is permitted where:

(i) the person with the right to control the operational use of the telecommunications system (for example, the employer) has given consent to the interception

(ii) the interception is effected to monitor or record communications relevant to the employer's business

(iii) the system is used wholly or partly in connection with the employer's business

(iv) the employer has made "all reasonable efforts" to inform all persons who use the telecommunications system that interceptions may take place for one of a number of specified legitimate business purposes. These include, for example, the need to monitor communications in order to establish the existence of facts relevant to the business or to ascertain that regulatory or self-regulatory practices or policies or procedures are being complied with or to detect crime or to ensure effective operation of the system.

As the employer must make "all reasonable efforts" to inform users of the telecommunication system that communications are being monitored, this means that an employer should inform its employees of interception of their communications and the resulting use that it will make of their data. Typically employers might do this through the use of an appropriate Internet usage policy or data protection policy. The extent to which employers are required to notify third parties (such as outside callers) of the interception of their communications is less clear-cut and outside the scope of this chapter (regulatory guidance acknowledges the difficulties of doing this in practice), but reasonable efforts should be taken to do this where possible.

Article 29 Working Party Code

The European Union's Article 29 Data Protection Working Party has produced a working document on the surveillance of electronic communications in the work place.[7] This document is intended to complement the Working Party's Opinion on the processing of personal data in the employment context referred to earlier in this chapter. The working document on surveillance of communications is intended to offer guidance on what constitutes legitimate monitoring activities and acceptable limits on worker surveillance by the employer. However, it notes that in some Member States, legislation may establish higher standards (for example, the need to consult work councils before conducting monitoring in some countries).

The working document notes that employees have a legitimate expectation of privacy in the workplace, although their rights should be balanced against the legitimate rights and interests of the employer.

Before implementing monitoring measures, an employer should assess the following key issues:
(i) Is the monitoring activity transparent to the workers?
(ii) Is it necessary? Could the employer obtain the same result with traditional methods of supervision?
(iii) Is the processing of personal data proposed as a result of the monitoring fair to the workers?
(iv) Is it proportionate to the concerns that it tries to allay?

This document specifically refers to Articles 8 and 10 of the European Convention for the Protection of Human Rights and Fundamental Freedoms. In particular, Article 8 of the Convention provides that "everyone has the right to respect for his private and family life, his home and his correspondence". This concept has been implemented in the UK through the Human Rights Act 2000. The Working Party document notes that

> these rights have traditionally been exercised vertically (that is, the individual vis-à-vis the state) and the debate about the extent to which they can be exercised horizontally (that is, as between individuals or an individual and a private company) is ongoing.

However, the Working Party takes the view that it is clear that these rights are, in general, present in the workplace.

The Working Party document sets out the following general principles applying to e-mail and Internet monitoring.

Compliance with all the following principles is likely to be necessary for any monitoring activity be lawful and justified:

(i) *Necessity* - the monitoring must be necessary for a specified purpose.

(ii) *Finality* - data must be collected for specified, explicit and legitimate purposes.

(iii) *Transparency* - the employer must be clear and open about its activities, including providing information to the data subject as regards its policy with regard to e-mail and Internet monitoring. Employees should be provided with the information as to the breadth and scope of such monitoring.

Information to be provided to employees about monitoring should include:

(i) an e-mail/Internet policy describing in detail the extent to which communication facilities owned by the employer may be used for personal/private communications by employees (such as limitations on time and duration of use)

(ii) the reasons and purposes for which surveillance, if any, is being carried out

(iii) the details of surveillance measures taken - who? what? how? when?

(iv) details of any enforcement procedures outlining how and when workers will be notified of breaches of internal policies and be given the opportunity to respond to any such claims against them.

Specifically in relation to e-mail monitoring, the Working Party document suggests that the following points should be addressed:

(i) whether the worker is entitled to have an e-mail account purely for personal use

(ii) the arrangements whereby other workers can access an employee's e-mail (for example, in his or her absence)

(iii) when back-up copies of messages are made and the period for retention of back-up

(iv) information as to when e-mails are deleted from the employer's server

(v) security issues and the involvement of employee representatives in formulating applicable monitoring policies.

In relation to the monitoring of Internet use, the Working Party states it is up to employers to decide whether or not their employees can use the Internet at work for personal reasons. However a blanket ban may be impractical.

Key principles in relation to Internet monitoring include:

(i) Wherever possible the employer should try and prevent misuse rather than expend resources in detecting misuse.

(ii)   Any monitoring must be proportionate to the harm it is seeking to address.

(iii)   Employers should exercise caution in coming to conclusions based on employee Internet usage.

When giving notices to staff:

(i)   The employer should set out clearly the conditions in which private use of the Internet is permitted and the material which cannot be viewed or copied.

(ii)   Employees should be informed of systems implemented to prevent access to certain sites and to detect misuse.

(iii)   Employees should be informed about the involvement of their representatives both in the implementation of the Internet policy and investigation of alleged breaches.

UK Information Commissioner's code on monitoring

The Article 29 working document referred to above specifically cross-refers to the draft code of practice on monitoring currently being prepared by the UK Information Commissioner. This has not been finalised at time of writing. However, a recent draft of the Information Commissioner's code identifies various considerations that companies undertaking monitoring should consider.

General considerations identified in the draft code include the following suggestions that employers should:

(i)   identify within their organisation people who can authorise the monitoring of workers and inform them of their responsibilities under the Act

(ii)   before monitoring, establish the specific business benefits which monitoring might bring. Do not introduce monitoring where the impact is not justified by the benefits

(iii)   in considering monitoring activities, consult trade unions or other workers' representatives, if any, or the workers themselves

(iv)   if monitoring is to be used to enforce an organisation's rules and standards, make sure that the rules and standards are clearly set out in a policy which also refers to any associated monitoring

(v)   tell workers what monitoring is taking place and why, and periodically remind them of this, unless covert monitoring is justified

(vi)   if sensitive data are processed in the course of monitoring, ensure that a sensitive data condition (see above) is satisfied

(vii) keep to a minimum those who have access to personal information obtained through monitoring. Subject them to confidentiality and security requirements and ensure that they are properly trained where the nature of the information requires this

(viii) avoid using personal information collected through monitoring for purposes other than those for which the monitoring was introduced, unless it is clearly in the workers' interests to do so or it reveals criminal activity or gross misconduct

(ix) if information gathered from monitoring might have an adverse impact on workers, present them with the information and allow them to make representations

(x) ensure that the right of access of workers to information about them kept for or obtained through monitoring is not compromised. Monitoring equipment must be capable of meeting this and other data protection requirements

(xi) do not monitor workers simply because a customer for your products or services seeks to impose a condition of business requiring you to do so.

In summary therefore, any monitoring must be targeted, necessary and proportionate in view of the risk it is seeking to address. Further guidance for businesses in this area will be available once the Information Commissioner's code on monitoring has been finalised.

Marketing

Where employee data are used in connection with marketing activities then the general data protection rules under the Act identified above will apply. In particular, employees need to be informed of the use of their details for this purpose and told to whom their data may be disclosed (for example, prospective clients).

Where the employees themselves are the subject of marketing by the employer, then an employer should bear in mind the provisions of Section 11 of the Act whereby an individual is entitled at any time by notice in writing to the data controller to require the data controller to cease use of personal data for direct marketing purposes. Therefore if an employee requests that he or she no longer be the subject of direct marketing, then employers should abide by any such request.

Direct marketing can take a number of forms, including by post, fax, telephone, e-mail or SMS texting. Employers should be aware of the fact that specific restrictions arise in relation to direct marketing through use of electronic communications equipment. The current law in this area is set out in

Telecommunications (Data Protection and Privacy) Regulations 1999 which contain specific provisions in restricting direct marketing by phone and fax and by means of "automatic calling machines". The extent to which these regulations also cover marketing by e-mail or other electronic means (such as SMS text) however has been the subject of much debate. As a result, in order to ensure a harmonised regime for direct marketing through electronic means across Europe, the European Union recently approved a directive concerning the processing of personal data and the protection of privacy in the electronic communications sector. This addresses various issues, including restricting the circumstances in which unsolicited marketing messages can be sent by various electronic means, including e-mail. Although this directive has not yet been implemented in the UK (and must be implemented by October 2003), businesses should bear this in mind if and to the extent they are proposing to conduct marketing of this kind in relation to their staff. In particular, once this directive is implemented, in many cases it will require the prior consent from individuals to receive marketing materials via e-mail.

Compliance steps

Businesses seeking to ensure compliance with the Data Protection Act need to consider a number of possibly overlapping laws and regulations including the Data Protection Act and its associated statutory instruments, employment law obligations, human rights legislation and rules relating to interception of communications and monitoring of employees. In addition, there is important regulatory guidance issued both by the European authorities and by the UK regulator. Similar laws apply in other jurisdictions and any company operating internationally needs to bear in mind similar and often conflicting rules on other jurisdictions.

How, therefore, can a business ensure that it complies with these multiple obligations? Clearly it is outside the scope of this chapter to provide definitive guidance on how specific businesses should address their compliance concerns. However, by way of introductory guidance, the first point for any data protection compliance activity is typically to establish the scope of the compliance project itself. For example, will the project only address the business's data protection obligations as regards its employees, or will it be of wider application? Will it address only standard employee administration-type issues, or wider concerns such as employee monitoring and interception of communications and marketing?

Once the scope of the review has been clarified, then it is necessary to identify the actual data processing activities taking place within the defined project. To assist businesses in this area, the UK Information Commissioner has produced a guide on data protection auditing. The guide itself is very extensive; however, its purpose is to identify various means of ensuring that a systematic review of data processing activities is carried out. In summary, an audit is likely in many cases to involve use of appropriate questionnaires to be completed by key personnel in various business units (for example, HR, marketing and sales, IT, etc.) which will be familiar with relevant data processing activity. It will then be possible to build up a picture of data processing activities.

Once the data processing activities have been identified, then compliance obligations and associated compliance steps need to be identified and implemented to reflect the relevant legal obligations. These might include, for example, implementing notices and/or consents in employee job application forms, agreements with recruitment agencies, contracts of employment, data protection and Internet usage policies, handbooks, guidelines and other documentation used in relation to prospective, existing and former employees. In particular, the employer will need to consider to what extent it wishes to implement a data protection policy and the scope of that policy (that is, whether it is intended for internal usage only or whether it is also to be made more widely available).

In addition to addressing the core obligations under the Act, the employer may also consider ancillary areas where data protection issues might arise, for example, in relation to the monitoring of employees, use of CCTV (in relation to which the Information Commissioner has issued a code of practice) and use of employee data for marketing. In respect of all of these issues, useful guidance can be obtained by consulting the Information Commissioner's website at www.dataprotection.gov.uk.

Once the employer has addressed obligations under the UK Act, it may also wish to then consider whether and to what extent it wishes to undertake equivalent compliance activities in other jurisdictions.

Notes

1   The author would like to thank colleagues Carmelina Modica, Sandra Percival and Wee-Lin Chua for their invaluable assistance in preparing this contribution to this book
2   Directive 95/46/EC of the European Parliament and of the Council of 24 October 1995 on the protection of individuals with regard to the processing of personal data and on the free movement of such data
3   Opinion 8/2001 on the processing of personal data in the employment context, adopted on 13 September 2001
4   Working document on the surveillance of electronic communications in the workplace adopted on 29 May 2002
5   Paragraph 12 of Part II of Schedule 1 of the Act
6   Commission decision 2002/16/EC of 27 December 2001 on standard contractual clauses for the transfer of personal data to processors established in third countries under Directive 95/46/EC
7   Document 5401/01/EN/Final WP 55, adopted on 29 May 2002

6

The national minimum wage

BOB SIMPSON

Bob Simpson is a Reader in Law at the London School of Economics specialising in labour law.

Introduction

The right of workers to a legally enforceable minimum wage under the National Minimum Wage Act 1998 (NMWA) came into force in April 1999. This followed many years of campaigning by a range of different interest groups. Indeed pressure for some form of legally backed minimum wage, usually confined to a particular industry or sector, has been a recurrent theme in the history of labour relations in Britain at least since it became an industrialised market economy.

While a near-universal legal right to a minimum wage may be new, it is important to be aware that some form of minimum wage regulation has been in existence for over a hundred years. The two most prominent manifestations of this strand of public policy were the Fair Wages Resolutions of the House of Commons which, in general terms, from 1891 to 1983 required government contractors to provide "fair wages" in the sense of the going rate for their labour force, and the Trade Boards or Wages Councils legislation which from 1909 to 1993 provided for minimum wage fixing by tripartite wages councils in selected industries or sectors. Wages Councils established legally enforceable minimum pay rates for workers falling within their scope. Since 1924, separate legislation has provided similar machinery for agricultural workers in the form of Agricultural Wages Boards which set minimum pay rates for agricultural workers. This legislation remains in force and necessitated some special provisions in the NMWA to integrate this sector-specific legal regime with the new national minimum wage entitlement.

Legally enforceable minimum pay rates are not, therefore, new. Nor are many of the economic and social policy issues that dominated the debate over whether a national minimum wage should become a legal entitlement. These issues are likely to remain at the core of deliberations over the level at which the national minimum wage (NMW) should be set, the fixing of different rates for particular workgroups and at least some of the exclusions from entitlement to the NMW. This chapter does not attempt to engage in the debate over these issues. It is, however, important to be aware of the concerns which they address, in particular the impact of the NMW on employment, especially the employment of younger workers, and the role of the NMW as part of government policies to alleviate poverty and ensure that moving from unemployment into employment is a positive move, *inter alia*, in the sense that it does not produce only marginal financial gains for the workers concerned. These issues have clearly been central to the thinking behind the Low Pay Commission's (LPC) recommendations to the government on NMW issues (see below). In evaluating the merits of decisions made on key legal issues, this crucially important wider context needs to be borne in mind.

It is equally important to keep in mind the pre-existing body of law on pay into which the NMW legislation is integrated. The common law context is relatively straightforward. For the overwhelming majority of the labour force, pay is what they are entitled to under their employment contracts in return for work. It is the 'consideration' for the work they do and the right to be paid, or damages for the breach of contract which occurs where the employer fails to pay, can be enforced in the courts. Employees may be able to treat a failure by their employer to pay them as required under the terms of their contracts as a "constructive dismissal" for the purposes of a claim for unfair dismissal. Since 1975 workers have had the right to claim "equal pay" with a fellow worker of the opposite sex who is in the same employment in accordance with the criteria laid down in Section 1 of the Equal Pay Act 1970. Statutory regulation of deductions from pay has a much longer history. This body of law was radically changed in 1986 and is now in Part II of the Employment Rights Act 1996 (ERA 1996). As is explained below, enforcement of the right to the NMW has been linked up to this body of law by the NMWA. The legal right to the NMW was not, therefore, enacted in a vacuum, but had to be integrated with an extensive body of pre-existing law. As experience of enforcing the NMW increases it may well become necessary for adjustments to this wider legal framework for the regulation of pay to be considered.

The Low Pay Commission

The LPC was established in 1997 as a non-statutory body to make recommendations to the government on a range of issues relating to the introduction of the NMW. The most important of these were the rate at which the NMW should be introduced and whether any workers under 26 should either have a lower minimum wage entitlement or be exempted from the new legal right. The Commission's first report in 1998 also contained crucial recommendations on which payments should count as part of a worker's wage for NMW purposes and the periods of "working time" for which the NMW would be payable. While this could have been a one-off exercise seen to be a necessary accompaniment to the passage of the NMW Bill through Parliament, it was widely expected that the LPC would be established on a permanent basis with a continuing advisory role.

Sections 5–8 of the NMWA made appropriate provision for the government to set up a Low Pay Commission and for the "Non-statutory Low Pay Commission" to be treated for most purposes as if it was this statutory body.

The government had resisted amendments to the NMW Bill which would have required it to set up the LPC on a permanent basis, and it continued to do so until 2001 after it had received the first part of its third report.[1] This was rather odd in view of the central importance of the work of the LPC to the NMW regime established by the NMWA. This was clear from the time when its first report was published in June 1998, before the NMW Bill was passed, and became increasingly evident from its second and third reports on references concerning increases in NMW rates and a range of other issues in 1999 and 2001, and the research which it has commissioned.

In one respect the LPC is a very familiar type of industrial relations institution. This is its tripartite composition with independent academic members as well as representatives of employers' organisations and trade unions. In modern terms, the government endorsed this very traditional format as "the right model to ensure ownership of the policy [to introduce a NMW] by the social partners".[2] The LPC has however discharged its tasks in a new way by carrying out an extensive programme of visits to and consultations with employers, managers, workers and union officials on the ground in those sectors where the NMW has its greatest impact. On the evidence of its first four years' work, the LPC is entitled to claim much of the credit for what is widely accepted to have been the successful introduction of the NMW.

Who is entitled to the national minimum wage?

Many of the statutory employment rights which are now consolidated in the ERA 1996 only benefit "employees", that is those who work under a contract of employment. An extensive body of case law on the issue of who is an employee has shown that this may have the effect of excluding many of the lowest paid and most vulnerable workgroups from the scope of statutory rights such as redundancy pay and the right to complain of unfair dismissal.

Like the law which regulates deductions from pay in Part II of the ERA, the NMWA has a wider coverage as it applies to workers. The definition of 'worker' includes those who work under contracts to do or perform personally any work or services provided for other parties except work or services provided for a client or customer of a profession or business carried on by the individual.[3] While the precise scope of "worker" is as difficult to identify as that of "employee", it almost certainly brings casual workers within the ambit of the NMW legislation. Since many casual workers are in low paid jobs, they ought to be one of the workgroups which benefit from the floor which the NMWA places under their pay.[4] While a survey of employment tribunal (ET) decisions carried out for the LPC found only four cases where the status of the applicants as workers was an issue,[5] Citizens Advice Bureaux (CABx) have reported a significant body of experience of clients who complained that their employer had refused to pay them the NMW either by misrepresenting the law – for example by asserting that the NMW did not apply to part-time work or to small employers – or by claiming that the worker was self-employed in circumstances where it was highly unlikely that the individuals concerned would have fallen outside the definition of "worker".[6] The evidence points to the difficulties in enforcing the law rather than any failing in the legislative provisions on who is entitled to the NMW.

The NMWA, however, goes beyond use of the wider category of "workers" rather than "employees" in three respects, one of which is familiar while the other two were, in 1998, novel. The familiar provisions are those which extend the scope of the legislation to particular workgroups: those in Crown employment (s36), House of Lords and House of Commons staff (ss38 and 39), seafarers (s40) and those in specified types of offshore employment (regulations made under s42).

The first of the novel provisions are those in Sections 34 and 35 which apply to agency workers and outworkers. The Employment Relations Act 1999 (ERA 1999) made some significant amendments (some of which are not yet in force) to the Employment Agencies Act 1973 which, together with the regulations made under it, has provided the starting point for identification of the status of those who are provided with work through employment agencies or employment businesses. As far as the pay of these workers is concerned, the policy of the NWMA is clear: agency workers do qualify for the NMW in the same way as other workers. The effect of Section 34 of the NMWA is that even if they are not, as a matter of law "workers" of either the principal or user for whom they are working, or the agency or business through which they were provided with the work, are deemed to be workers with contracts with whichever of the two, the principal or the agent is responsible for paying them or, if neither is responsible, in fact pays them.[7]

In a similar attempt to anticipate and avoid fine distinctions which might be drawn by the courts, Section 35 of the NMWA provides that outworkers – that is those who contract to do work at any place other than their employer's workplace and not just those home workers who work in their own home – are still workers even where they do not carry out the work they are contracted to do 'personally' but employ others to work for or with them. These provisions are particularly important as some agency workers and many, particularly manufacturing home workers were among the workgroups which the NMW was intended to benefit.[8]

The other novel provision is potentially more far-reaching. Section 41 of the NMWA enables the Secretary of State to designate any individual who would not otherwise fall within the definition of "worker" to be a worker of a prescribed employer for the purposes of the NMWA. Section 23 of the ERA 1999 subsequently made similar provision in relation to other employment rights. As yet it remains to be seen what use will be made of these provisions. The existence of the Section 41 power has the potential to be an important guarantee that any lacuna in the law which takes low paid dependent workgroups outside the entitlement to the NMW will be swiftly remedied.[9]

Excluded groups

As well as those provisions which are designed to ensure that particular workgroups do qualify for the NMW, the NMWA expressly excludes other groups from the right to be paid the NMW. Again, some of these are familiar exclusions from statutory employment rights while others are novel. Share fishermen who are paid by a share in the earnings or profits of the ship are excluded from the NWMA as they are from most rights under the ERA 1996.[10] Prisoners are excluded in respect of work carried out in prison (NMWA s45); so too are members of the Armed Forces by Section 37, although it should be noted that they do have, in effect, a form of minimum pay guaranteed them as their pay is fixed following recommendations of the Armed Forces Pay Review Body. The NMWA also contains provisions excluding voluntary workers (s44) and residential members of certain "intentional" religious communities (s44A). Voluntary workers who might otherwise fall within the definition of worker are not entitled to the NMW if they are "employed" by charities, voluntary organisations, associated fundraising bodies or statutory bodies (all as defined in ss44(4)), but only if the terms of their employment provide no entitlement to payment except for actual, or reasonable estimates of, expenses, and do not provide for any benefits in kind other than reasonable subsistence or accommodation.

Responding to evidence received, the LPC recommended in its second report in 2000 that further guidance should be provided on the scope of this exclusion which has evidently been a matter of concern to some voluntary organisations who may have both "workers" who are entitled to the NMW and "volunteers" who are not so entitled undertaking work on their behalf. It is evident from the second part of the LPC's third report in 2001 that this remains a matter of concern for certain voluntary organisations, some of which would like to be able to make payments to "voluntary workers" but not at a level which would comply with the NWMA. The LPC was firm on the need to avoid creating a loophole that could be exploited to deny other workers the NMW.[11]

The addition of the "intentional religious communities" exclusion in 1999 gave effect to a recommendation made by the LPC in its report on the Accommodation Offset against NMW entitlement which is discussed below. Although the exclusion is general in scope it is directed at particular communities in which members live together for at least part of the time as part of the manifestation of their beliefs. Like voluntary organisations they too may employ others who are workers entitled to the NMW but they were concerned to ensure that no residential member of the community could be deemed to have this right.[12]

There was one group of workers for whom special provision had to be made when the NMW was introduced. This was agricultural workers.

As noted they are entitled to minimum wage rates fixed by Agricultural Wages Boards under separate legislation which long predates the NMWA. Since agricultural workers are also workers entitled to the NMW, they are, in effect, guaranteed whichever is the higher rate, the NMW or the rate fixed for their category of worker under the Agricultural Wages Legislation. Sections 46 and 47 of and Schedule 2 to the NMWA make provision for appropriate amendments to this legislation to apply the more extensive enforcement regime of the NMWA to the payment of Agricultural Wages Board rates while preventing the possibility of two separate sets of sanctions being imposed for underpayments which infringe both pieces of legislation.

It is generally agreed that the introduction of a NMW did not necessarily eliminate the need for separate sectoral regulation of pay, but the simplicity and universality of a single NMW means that the case for any other sector-specific minimum pay laws would have to be compelling before it was acted on.

Exclusions and modifications by regulations

The provisions outlined above on who is entitled to the NMW are all contained in the NMWA.[13] The very broad scope which they give to the coverage of the NMW is, however, subject to a wide, albeit tightly circumscribed power to prescribe further exclusions or provide for entitlement to the NMW at a different rate to that prescribed under Section 1(3), by regulations made under Section 3 of the Act. Moreover, while Section 3(1) limits this power to varying the NMW entitlement of those under the age of 26, Section 4 enables regulations to be made which extend the regulation making power in Section 3 to persons over 26. In effect therefore Sections 3 and 4 of the NMWA give the Secretary of State considerable freedom to exclude or modify the NMW entitlement of all workers.

These powers are, however, subject to important limitations in Sections 3(3) and 4(2); they may not be used to specify different NMW rates for workers in different areas, sectors, sizes of undertaking or occupations, or to provide different NMW rates for age groups over the age of 26. Discussion of the desirability of a legal NMW, including Parliamentary debates on the NMW Bill, almost invariably covered the merits and demerits of different sectoral rates (which was in effect what Wages Councils used to, and the Agricultural Wages Boards still do, set), different regional rates and different – that is lower – rates for small businesses or undertakings. The government was firm in resisting any of these deviations from the norm of a single, national rate. While the use made so far of the regulation making powers in Sections 3 and 4 may have been in some respects controversial except, perhaps, insofar as it has used its powers to prescribe a lower rate for younger workers, it has not caused the government's commitment to this principle to be called into question.

Before the NMWA came into force in April 1999, regulations under Section 4 extended the government's regulation-making power in Section 3 by inserting a new subsection. Under Section 3(1A) regulations may provide different rates for, or exclude from entitlement, workers who are over 26 who fall within one of five categories. Unsurprisingly, the regulations then made under Section 3 to take effect immediately the right to the NMW came into force, made special provision for all of these categories. Some of these provisions were, in turn, modified by further regulations in 2000. The result is that there are currently seven groups whose NMW entitlement is either excluded or modified by regulations made under Section 3. While three of these appear to be relatively uncontroversial, the other four have been the subject of continuing debate.

First, Regulation 12(1) of the NMW Regulations excludes all workers under the age of 18 from any NMW entitlement.

This is in accordance with the recommendation of the LPC in it first report.[14] The total exclusion of 16 and 17 year old workers, as distinct from fixing a lower NMW rate for them, has however been challenged and remains an issue on which opinions differ sharply. In 1998 the LPC estimated that over 70% of this age group were in full-time education or training and observed that the broader state policy of encouraging measures to promote a better educated, more skilled workforce could be seen to discourage 16 and 17 year olds from entering the labour force, or at least from working full-time in jobs which are not accompanied by any training. In its third report in 2001, however, the LPC recorded "considerable strength of feeling" among trade unions, Low Pay Units, youth organisations and others that there should be a NMW rate for this age group. While adhering to its position that 16 and 17 year olds were a distinct group in various respects and should not be considered full-time participants in the labour market, the LPC concluded that their treatment should be kept under review "with a view to assessing the case for extending some kind of protection to this group in the future".[15]

The second group who are totally excluded from any NMW entitlement consists of "apprentices" under the age of 26 who have no NMW entitlement in the first year of their apprenticeship or before they are aged 19.

Evidence recorded in the LPC's first report in 1998 suggested that some apprenticeships did provide pay rates well below the NMW rate during the first year when, it was suggested, the employer received little by way of productive work in return for the training provided.[16] This evidence related to modern apprenticeships which now outnumber traditional apprenticeships and the scope for this exclusion was amended in 2000 to cover all the increasingly extensive current government funded work-based training arrangements of this type.[17]

This exclusion is functionally linked to the fixing of a lower NMW rate for two groups of workers. The first of those is all workers aged 18 to 21 inclusive. The NMW rate for this group was initially fixed at £3 an hour in April 1999, but this was increased to £3.20 in June 2000 and £3.50 in October 2001. Since June 2000 this rate has been the same as the training rate described below and this single lower NMW rate is referred to by the LPC (though not by the NMW legislation) as the "development rate". On this issue the LPC, while of the view that there should be a lower rate for younger workers, has consistently recommended that the full rate should become applicable at age 21.[18]

The government has yet to accept this so that 21 year olds are currently still only entitled to the lower rate for younger workers. It is notable that Section 3 of the NMWA contemplates a sort of surrogate "age of majority" of 26 for NMW purposes, reflecting perhaps reported Treasury concerns about the risks posed by providing entitlement to the full rate at a lower age to the government's wider economic strategy. The LPC has found no evidence to support such concerns and indeed the research evidence to which it has referred indicates that the trend in payment systems generally is overwhelmingly away from age-related pay scales with entitlement to the full adult rate at age 18 becoming the norm.

There seems little doubt that pressures for the NMW to fall into line with the real world on this issue will continue. If and when it does, the focus is likely to turn more sharply on to the currently unprotected 16 and 17 year old members of the workforce.

As a matter of policy the provision of a lower "training rate" for all workers over the age of 22 during the first six months of employment which is accompanied by the provision of at least 26 days "accredited training" attracted a wide body of support as a matter of principle. This is the first of the modifications to the general entitlement to the NMW which reflects the additions to the government's power to provide for different NMW rates under Section 3 of the NMWA, made by the regulations under Section 4 which were referred to above. It was an attempt to harness the NMW to the task of improving the skills of the workforce.

The intention was that employers would be encouraged to enter into agreements for accredited training for new workers by the reduced NMW rate that would apply to the workers concerned. In practice the available evidence suggests that very little use has been made of this reduced rate facility. One reason – and maybe the main reason – lies in the complexity of the conditions laid down in Regulation 13 of the NMW Regulations 1999 which the training has to satisfy.[19] While the existence of the training rate may have the unfortunate effect of allowing some unscrupulous employers to reject claims for the NMW from uninformed workers on the ground that the job includes some training, the low level of take-up suggests that it is not acting as the intended incentive to employers to take steps to improve the skills levels of these lower paid sections of the workforce. This is a matter of some importance in the light of the LPC's acceptance that an age-related lower NMW rate lacks equity and that the "development rate" should be linked solely to the provision of accredited training.[20] A continuing low take up for the training rate will make it less likely that the lower rate for younger workers will be phased out.

There are three other groups of worker who are excluded from any entitlement by Regulation 12 of the NMW Regulations. They all concern very specific situations and again reflect the additions made to the power to modify or exclude entitlement in Section 3 of the NMWA by regulations made under Section 4.

Regulation 12(10)-(12) excludes homeless persons who are participating in certain non-profit making schemes which provide shelter and maybe other benefits in return for work.

Regulations 12(8) and (9) exclude students in higher education while they are on work experience for a period not exceeding a year.

Regulations 12(5)-(7) exclude two groups of workers who are participating in specified schemes designed to provide training, work experience or temporary work or to assist the worker in seeking or obtaining work. These are schemes provided under arrangements made by the government in respect of a trial period of up to three weeks work with a prospective employer, and schemes wholly or partly funded by the European Social Fund. Workers on the latter are excluded unless they are *employees* engaged on a trial period of work with a prospective employer of more than three weeks.

The NMW Regulations also excluded two other groups of worker from the right to the NMW by defining work for the purposes of the regulations so as to exclude work carried out as a member of a family household or for a family business (Regulation 2(2)-(4)). The first exclusion extends to any person who lives in the family home, is treated as a member of the family and does not pay for meals or accommodation. Au pairs are the most obvious group whose work does not qualify for the NMW by virtue of this exclusion if the same work would not be treated as performed under a worker's contract if it was done by a member of the family who lived in the family home and shared in the family's tasks and activities. The second exclusion treats work done for a family business by a member of the employer's family who lives in the employer's family home and participates in the running of the business, as outside the scope of the NMW Regulations. It is far from clear that the NMWA empowers the Secretary of State to effectively exclude workers from the right to the NMW in this roundabout way.[21]

The government's objective in drafting the NMW legislation was said to be the creation of a scheme which combined simplicity with universality. To this end, special pleading by a wide range of interest groups for the exclusion of particular work from the scope of the new right was, and has continued to be, largely rejected.[22] It is however evident from the primary provisions of the NMWA, the extent of the powers to make exceptions by regulations in Sections 3 and 4 of the Act and the way that these powers have been exercised, that while a number of positive steps have been taken to ensure that vulnerable workgroups are covered by the NMW, there is a complex web of exceptions and qualifications to the basic right of workers to be paid at the full NMW rate. While some of these may be uncontroversial, others are the subject of continued debate. The fixing of a lower "development" rate for younger workers and workers who receive accredited training is perhaps the area where modifications to the current provisions are most likely.

Defining "wage" and the working time for which the NMW must be paid

Section 1(3) of the NMWA requires the NMW to be expressed as a single hourly rate.[23] While many payment systems are expressed in terms of an hourly rate of pay, particularly systems which apply to low paid workers whom the NMW is intended to benefit, this is not invariably the case. It was therefore necessary for the law to make provision for calculating a worker's pay over a longer period, identifying the times within that period which count as working time for NMW purposes and which payments count towards meeting the employer's NMW obligations. The relevant provisions on these three issues in the NMW Regulations inevitably involve some complex details. The 1999 Regulations varied from the 1998 consultative draft in order to accommodate particular concerns which had been expressed in the consultation process. Some further amendments were made in 2000 in order either to clarify particular provisions or to achieve a better fit between the law and actual practice. While further fine tuning may prove necessary, the basic structure of the law on these issues appears to have been generally accepted and to have worked satisfactorily so far.

The "pay reference period"

Sections 1(1) and (4) of the NMWA require workers who qualify for the NMW to be paid by their employer not less than the NMW rate in any "pay reference period" (PRP). In accordance with the LPC's 1998 recommendation, Regulation 10 of the NMW Regulations provides that the PRP is one month or, where the worker is paid by reference to a shorter period, that period.[24] For weekly paid workers the PRP will therefore be a week. The decision to align the PRP with the period by reference to which a worker is in fact paid, but with an upper limit of a month, necessitated two further modifications as part of the broad strategy to make the law fit with actual practice.

The first modification is designed to bring into consideration for any particular PRP payments which are "in respect of" that PRP. This is done where either they are made in the immediately following PRP or, if made in a later PRP, they were contingent on the worker completing a record of work done and submitting it to the employer and the worker failed to do this before the fourth working day before the end of the PRP following that to which they relate. The latter category of payments can only count towards an employer's NMW obligations if they are made either in the PRP in which the record is submitted or in the PRP immediately following (Regulation 30(b)(c)). The thinking behind this provision seems to be fairly clear. As a matter of practice some payments for work done are not – and maybe cannot realistically be – made until the following pay period or even later where they depend on information provided by the worker (a time sheet for example) and there is a delay before the worker provides this. Except where the delay is due to some such failure by the worker, it should be emphasised that there is only a short time lag allowed – a month or whatever shorter PRP is applicable – before the payment must be made if it is to count towards meeting the employer's NMW obligations.

Where a worker does fail to submit the necessary record before payment can be made, it might appear that if the pay received for the PRP in question is below the worker's NMW entitlement, the employer would be in breach of the obligation to pay the NMW. In order to avoid this anomaly arising, an amendment was made to the NMW Regulations in 2000 which excludes the hours in respect of which no record has been submitted from the total number of hours which the worker is deemed to have worked in that PRP (Regulation 29A).

The other modification to adapt the law to fit with actual practice was necessary to accommodate workers employed on payment systems which provide for an annual salary to be paid in equal instalments, most commonly 12 monthly payments, although there are marked fluctuations in the amount of time actually worked at different times of the year. While the PRP for these workers remains the standard one month, the provisions on working time include "salaried hours work" as a separate category and deem the worker to have worked a certain portion of their basic hours in each PRP (see further below).

The provisions on the PRP necessarily conflict with the reality of the payment systems of some low paid workers. However the evidence so far is that they do provide an acceptable compromise between the complexity which would result from trying to anticipate and provide for all the many different variants of payments actually in use and the anomalies that would follow a rigid formula such as for example, a PRP of one month which only allowed payments actually made in the PRP to be taken into account. The NMW does not guarantee any minimum pay entitlement for each day worked. Workers are not therefore entitled to any credit under the NMW legislation for greater productivity during some part of the PRP which makes up for slack days when there was less work to do and they therefore earned an amount that may have fallen below the NMW rate at times earlier in the same PRP. Their entitlement is limited to on average at least the NMW for all their working time in the whole PRP; it is not an entitlement to be paid at least the NMW for each hour while they were at work in that PRP. Whether this creates an anomaly given that employees have a statutory right to guarantee pay for totally "workless days" when they do no work at all is an issue which the legislature may have to address in the future.[25]

"Wage"

Section 2 of the NMWA gives the government very wide powers to specify by regulations what counts and what does not count as part of the wage received by a worker for NMW purposes. These powers have been used to create a complex web of provisions in Regulations 30–37, which have to be read together with the relevant interpretation provisions in Regulations 2, 8 and 9 of the NMW Regulations. While the 1999 regulations showed some changes from the 1998 consultative draft, they were not sufficient to qualify the government's stated intention to broadly implement the LPC's recommendations on this issue in its first report.[26] Before providing an analysis of the legal detail, it is therefore helpful to summarise the LPC's views on this central issue.

The LPC considered that only pay for "standard work" should be taken into account. This should be gross pay before income tax and national insurance deductions.

What payments should count for "standard work":
(i)   payments under payment by results systems such as piecework
(ii)   periodic bonuses; and tips, gratuities and the like distributed through the payroll.

And what payments should not:
(iii) premium payments for overtime, different shifts, etc.
(iv) allowances for working in a particular geographical area, such as a London allowance
(v)   allowances for working in inclement weather or dangerous working conditions; and subject to one exception
(vi) all benefits in kind.

The exceptional benefit in kind which could, on the LPC's recommendations, be taken into account in the initial years of the NMW was the provision of accommodation up to a limit of £20 per week.[27] The details of the current regulations can be analysed against the background of these intentions.

Regulation 30 provides that a worker's total remuneration in a PRP is prima facie all money payments paid to him or her by the employer during that period. As already noted, to these may be added first payments in the immediately following PRP which are in respect of the earlier PRP (Regulation 30(b)) and second, payments made after the next PRP where the worker failed to submit the required record of work done before the fourth day before the end of the next PRP. But in order for late payments in this second category to count, they must be made either in the PRP in which the records were submitted or in the one immediately following (Regulation 30(c)).

As defined in Regulation 8 "payments" exclude advances on wages or loans, pensions, allowances or gratuities in connection with retirement or compensation for loss of office, sums awarded by a court or tribunal (or payments made to settle proceedings that were or could have been brought before a court or tribunal) other than payment of an amount due under the worker's contract,[28] redundancy payments, and rewards under suggestion schemes. Further, Regulation 9 provides that, with the exception of the provision of living accommodation, benefits in kind and vouchers and the like which can be exchanged for money, goods or services provided by the employer, do not count as payments. The NMW regulations thereby avoid the right to NMW providing an incentive to low paying employers to revive practices associated with the "tommy shop", one of the abuses to which the Truck Acts 1831-1940 were directed.

When the total "payments" attributable to a PRP have been identified, it may be necessary to make one or more of the "reductions" that are required under Regulations 31-35, and where an employer provides a worker with living accommodation it will be necessary to make an adjustment in accordance with Regulations 36 and 37. Three of the required "reductions" follow specific recommendations made by the LPC in 1998. These exclude overtime premiums (Regulation 31(1)(c)), allowances (Regulation 31(1)(d)) and tips, gratuities and the like which are not distributed through the payroll (Regulation 31(1)(e)).

The last two of these call for some further comment. "Allowance" is defined to include any payment by the employer to a worker in respect of working arrangements or working or personal circumstances that is not consolidated into basic pay.[29] Unsurprisingly there is evidence that some employers have changed their payment systems to consolidate allowances (for example, for unsocial hours or dirty working conditions) and overtime premiums into basic pay in order for them to count towards meeting the obligation to pay the NMW.[30] As a matter of law this can, of course, only occur with the worker's agreement. Moreover, even where this "agreement" was obtained, the circumstances in which the changes were made could well have constituted subjecting the workers to a "detriment" for which they could have sought remedy before an employment tribunal (see below). Other employers have started to distribute tips and gratuities through the payroll where this was not previously the case so that they too now count as part of the wage for NMW purposes. The more fundamental issue here is whether tips or gratuities paid by customers or clients should ever count towards an employer's NMW obligations. In its third report the LPC recorded pressure from some employers' organisations in the hospitality sector for all tips and gratuities to count towards the employer's obligation to pay the NMW. As the LPC commented, that showed a misunderstanding of the objective of the NMW, which is not to provide a minimum income guarantee but to establish a wage floor.[31]

Regulation 31(1)(b) requires the payments made to be reduced to exclude payments in respect of time when the worker was absent from work or engaged in taking industrial action. The latter is directed at time when a worker is taking action short of a strike, such as a go slow or work to rule. Case law has established that a worker is rarely if ever in a position to demand any pay when taking industrial action. The NMW Regulations make clear that this is a matter which is wholly outside the scope of a worker's NMW entitlement.

As regards pay during other absences from work, the effect of this reduction is that sick pay, holiday and statutory guarantee pay do not count towards an employer's NMW obligations, reflecting the exclusion of periods of absence from work from the working time in respect of which the NMW has to be paid (see below). The law does guarantee most workers a minimum level of sick pay, through their social security entitlement to statutory sick pay (SSP), pay for their holiday entitlement under Regulation 13 of the Working Time Regulations 1998, and guarantee pay for a limited number of "workless days" under Sections 28-35 of the ERA 1996. In most cases, while the amount of holiday pay will reflect a worker's NMW entitlement, the amount of SSP and statutory guarantee pay will fall well below this level. The NMW legislation only guarantees workers a minimum level of pay in respect of times when they are actually working.

A complex, interlocking set of provisions excludes expenditure incurred in connection with the employment from being taken into account in calculating the "wage" which a worker has received.

The total "payments" received by the worker are subject to "reductions" to exclude the following:
(i)   payments by the employer to the worker on account of expenditure (Regulation 31(1)(f))
(ii)   expenditure incurred by the worker (Regulations 31(1)(g), 32)
(iii) payments by the worker to the employer on account of expenditure (Regulations 31(1)(h), 34(1)(a))
(iv)   payments by the worker to a third party on account of expenditure to the extent that they are not met, or designed to be met, by the employer (Regulations 31(1)(h), 34(1)(b)).

Subject to four exceptions, payments made by the worker to the employer "for his own use and benefit" are also required "reductions" from the total payments received by the worker whether they are made by way of deductions from pay (Regulations 31(1)(g), 32(1)(b)) or by way of payments by the worker to the employer (Regulation 34(1)(a)):

Exceptions:
(i)   The first exception is deductions or payments on account of the worker's conduct or any other event for which the worker either alone

> or with other workers is contractually liable (Regulations 33(a), 35(a)). The legality of such deductions or payments depends on whether they satisfy the conditions in Part II of the ERA 1996, but it is not clear that an employer would be unable to rely on this exemption if these requirements – basically that the deduction or payment must be authorised by legislation, a term in the worker's written employment contract or a separate, prior written agreement – are not satisfied.
>
> (ii) Second, deductions or payments on account of an advance of wages or a loan are not required reductions (Regulations 33(b), 35(b)).
>
> (iii) Nor are deductions or payments on account of an accidental overpayment of wages (Regulations 33(c), 35(c)).
>
> (iv) The fourth exception is unlikely to be very widespread among low paid workers: deductions or payments in respect of the purchase of shares, other securities or a share in a partnership (Regulations 33(d), 35(d)).

In assessing whether an employer has paid a worker his or her NMW entitlement in a PRP, all the admissible payments made by the employer are taken into account before any of these deductions are made or any of these payments are received by the employer from the worker.

Of course, some workers do buy the goods or services which their employer supplies and the payments which the worker makes for them are not normally relevant for NMW purposes. If they are made by way of deductions from pay, for NMW purposes the worker's pay is the amount received before any such deduction. However, if the purchase of goods or services from the employer is a contractual obligation to which the worker has "agreed" – in historical terms a "tommy shop" arrangement – any such payment made is a required reduction from the total payments received in calculating the "wage" which a worker has been paid for NMW purposes (Regulation 35(e)).

The accommodation offset

The government accepted the LPC's 1998 recommendation that the provision of accommodation by an employer should be the only benefit in kind that was allowed to count towards the employer's obligation to pay the NMW. The LPC recommended then that the maximum amount allowed should be £20 per week[32] and anticipated that this exception to the general principle that benefits in kind should not count towards the NMW would eventually be phased out.[33] In 2001, however, the LPC recommended an increase in the maximum credit which an employer could claim and its recommendations were implemented in October 2001. The effect of Regulations 30(d), 31(1)(i), 36 and 37 is that whether or not an employer is contractually entitled to make a deduction from a worker's pay (or receive a payment from the worker) in respect of accommodation, for NMW purposes, an employer will be credited as having paid a worker the lesser of 57 pence for each hour worked in a PRP, proportionately reduced for the number of days in the PRP for which accommodation was not provided, or £3.25 for each day in the PRP for which accommodation was provided. The maximum credit which an employer can be given is therefore £22.75 per week. It seems likely that the provision of accommodation will remain the one benefit in kind that can count towards the NMW for the foreseeable future.

Working time

The most difficult issue involved in translating the goal of a NMW into an enforceable legal right is providing a workable definition of the working time for which the NMW must be paid. Payment systems vary considerably and some make no reference to the time worked in calculating the pay to which a worker is entitled.

While low paid workers do not, in general, have complex payment systems, in order to ensure that their NMW entitlement could be readily calculated it was necessary to provide some detail in the NMW Regulations on translating the pay received by workers into an hourly rate, in order to calculate whether it satisfied their entitlement to the NMW. To this end, the NMW Regulations allocate all work to one of four categories of working time. They then provide for the calculation of the number of hours worked in each PRP in respect of each of the four categories. This includes express directions on how five particular periods of time – "on call" time, "sleepover" time, travelling time, time spent undergoing training, and periods of absence from work – should be taken into account for this purpose.

The following analysis first identifies the four categories of working time. It then examines the treatment of those five particular issues. Finally, it looks at the calculation of the hours worked for NMW purposes in relation to each of the four categories of working time.

The NMW Regulations assign all work to one of four mutually exclusive categories:

(i)   time work
(ii) salaried hours work
(iii) output work
(iv) unmeasured work.

"Time work" includes not only work paid wholly by reference to a period of time (other than salaried hours work) but also work paid in part by reference to time and in part by reference to output (Regulation 3). It therefore includes, for example, a system of piece work subject to a guaranteed minimum level of pay expressed by reference to a period of time. In effect the NMW legislation requires the hourly equivalent of this guaranteed minimum to be at least equal to the NMW.

"Salaried hours work" is the most complex of the four categories. It is defined as work under a contract in which a worker is entitled to be paid an annual salary for a basic number of hours in a year in equal weekly or monthly instalments (or variable monthly instalments if in each quarter the worker's entitlement is the same) and has no other entitlement except possibly a "performance bonus" (Regulation 4).[34] This is designed to cover payment systems under which workers receive the same pay in each pay period, or over a number of pay periods, even though it is expected that the amount of work will vary as between pay periods. This category was added to the 1998 consultative Draft Regulations in response to pressure from trade unions which had negotiated annual hours contracts for members in particular sectors. In some cases, such as support staff in schools, the actual working time at different times of the year may be fairly predictable. In others, workers may agree to be available for longer hours in accordance with the employer's business needs. For these workers, while the "seasons" when working time may be relatively longer and shorter are likely to be predictable, actual working time may well not be.

"Output work" is work paid wholly by reference to some measure of output, such as the number of pieces made or processed, number of sales made or number of transactions completed (Regulation 5). Manufacturing homeworkers' working time might, perhaps, be the archetype of this category of working time. All other work falls into the fourth category of "unmeasured work" (Regulation 6).

Particular issues

The NMW Regulations make express provision on two issues that have been the cause of some controversy.

Time spent on call
The first is time spent "on call". This counts as either time work or salaried hours work unless the worker is entitled to spend the time at home and his or her home is at or near the place of work (Regulations 15(1) and 16(1)). Underlying this provision was a general concern about the emerging practice whereby some employers engaged workers on "zero hours contracts" under which the workers were required to be available for work on site but were only paid while actually working. This has been widely condemned as an abusive practice and these provisions in the NMW Regulations limit the circumstances in which it can be used to deny workers the right to be paid the NMW while they are available for work to those times when they are free to remain at home "at or near the place of work".

In *British Nursing Association* v *Inland Revenue (National Minimum Wage*

Compliance Team)[35] a related issue arose for decision. This was whether the working time of "duty nurses" who responded to calls from nursing homes and other establishments for nursing assistance from the "bank nurses" provided by the British Nursing Association outside normal office hours when calls were diverted to their homes and they then made further calls to find nurses to do the work, included all the time when they had to be available at night to answer calls. The employment tribunal's decision that it did was upheld by both the Employment Appeal Tribunal and Court of Appeal. The EAT rejected the employer's argument that this was inconsistent with the duty nurse's freedom to do other things when not answering the phone calls; their pay was calculated by reference to their shift and "it is not to be expected that employers will pay employees for periods of time when their employees are not working."[36]

"Sleepover time"

A similar protective function can be identified behind the second issue on which there is particular provision which is 'sleepover time' when a worker sleeps at or near the workplace. This may be excluded from time work or salaried hours work, and will not therefore quality for payment at the NMW rate. The regulations were, however, amended in 2000, in response to the LPC's call for clarification in the light of submissions in evidence to the LPC that as originally drafted the Regulations left some potential for abuse.[37] It is now clear that the exclusion can only apply where a worker is provided with suitable facilities for sleeping at or near the place of work and that times when the worker is awake for the purpose of working do count as time work or salaried hours work which must be paid at the NMW rate (Regulations 15(1A) and 16(1A)).

Time spent on work-related travel

Time spent on work-related travel is normally included within working time. The definition of travelling in Regulation 7 includes times spent waiting at the beginning, during, or at the end of a journey. Time spent travelling for the purposes of time work, salaried hours work, output work or unmeasured work is normally treated as part of the working time spent during that work (Regulations 15–18). In relation to time work and salaried hours work time spent travelling between home and the place of work is excluded. Other travelling time may also be excluded but only if it is incidental to the worker's duties in the sense that those duties are not necessarily carried out in the course of travelling (as they would be, for example, where a worker's job involves driving a vehicle) and it is not for the purpose of carrying out assignments at different places to which the worker is required to travel (Regulations 15(2)-(4), 16(2)-(4)). Travel between home and the premises from which an output worker works or, except in the case of a manufacturing homeworker, to which he or she reports is also excluded (Regulation 17(1)).

Time spent receiving training

In general time during which a worker is receiving training, whether at his or her place of work or elsewhere, and if elsewhere time spent travelling to and from there, is treated as time work (Regulation 19). The exception is training wholly or mainly in connection with salaried hours work, which is treated as salaried hours work but only for the purposes of determining whether the "basic hours" have been exceeded, and then only to the extent that the worker had no entitlement to his or her annual salary or any other payment in respect of those hours (Regulation 16(5)).

Absences from work

Finally, it is possible to identify a general principle running through the NMW Regulations that there is no obligation on an employer to pay workers the NMW for times when they were absent from work. The times when a worker is absent from work are excluded from time work (Regulation 15(5)) and by definition they do not come within the hours spent on output work (Regulation 24(11)) or unmeasured work (Regulation 27). In the case of salaried hours work, where a worker is absent for hours in respect of which his or her annual salary is payable and for that reason receives less than the normal portion of the salary for a PRP, the number of hours deemed to have been worked in that PRP is reduced by the number of hours for which the worker was absent (Regulation 21(3)). The regulations further provide that taking part in industrial action, which is not defined, is treated as absence from work (Regulations 15(6), 17(2), 18(2) and 21(4)). This is consistent with case law which has established that workers who take part in industrial action short of a strike are, in most if not all cases, not entitled to any pay for work actually performed if the employer makes clear that anything less than full performance of normal tasks is unacceptable.[38]

The exclusion of all periods of absence from work from working time which counts for NMW purposes has the effect that workers who enforce their right to a 20-minute break after six hours work under Regulation 12 of the Working Time Regulations 1998 do not have any right to be paid for this period. There is some evidence of employers requiring workers to clock off during breaks in order to underline the point. This may seem rather odd given the health and safety base of the Working Time Directive, which the Working Time Regulations implement, and the desirability of encouraging workers to exercise their "entitlement" to rest breaks. In relation to absence from work on holiday, Regulation 13 of the Working Time Regulations provides for this to be paid at a rate calculated by reference to the provisions on a week's pay in Sections 220-224 of the ERA 1996. Since workers have a contractual right to be paid at least the NMW (see below) this will normally ensure that the statutory minimum holiday entitlement is paid at at least the NMW rate. However, workers whose job involves output work or unmeasured work and who take their holiday after a period in which their working time – and hence their pay – has been limited, may find that their week's pay for each week of holiday taken falls below a week's pay at the NMW rate during a period of normal working.[39]

NMW entitlement for each category of working time

Subject to those points on particular issues, Regulations 20-29 of the NMW Regulations provide for calculating the number of hours in a PRP for which a worker is entitled to be paid the NMW for each of the four categories of working time. For "time work" this is the number of hours actually worked (Regulation 20). In principle, the number of hours actually worked in a PRP is also the number of hours for which a worker is entitled to be paid the NMW for "output work" and "unmeasured work" (Regulations 24(1) and 27). In respect of both these categories, however, it is possible for the actual hours to be displaced by individual agreement between the worker and employer on the number of hours worked.[40] For "unmeasured work" a "daily average agreement" must be in writing, made before the PRP to which it applies, and determine the average number of hours which the worker is likely to work on a day when he or she is available for the full amount of time contemplated by the contract. The "ascertained hours" for the PRP are then calculated on the basis that the worker worked this number of hours on each working day in the PRP, and pro rata for days on which the worker only worked part of the day (Regulation 29).

By way of a safeguard against abuse, the agreement will not be effective to displace actual hours if the employer cannot show that the average number of hours stipulated is "realistic" (Regulation 28).[41]

Fair estimate agreements

In the case of "output work" a "fair estimate agreement" can only displace the actual hours where the worker's employment contract contains no provision on minimum, normal or maximum hours and the hours worked are not in practice determined or controlled by the employer (Regulation 24(2)). Strictly construed, control "in practice" could cover de facto control in circumstances where, for example, a manufacturing pieceworker is supplied with materials on a daily or weekly basis and the output necessary to ensure a continued supply of work would in practice require a minimum number of hours to be worked. However it seems probable that the legislative policy is, nevertheless, to permit if not to encourage "fair estimate agreements" in the circumstances.

Where permitted, it is a necessary precondition of a binding "fair estimate agreement" that the worker is contractually entitled to be paid an agreed rate per piece produced or commission for sale or transaction completed in, or completed as a result of output work done in, the PRP (Regulation 25(1)(b)). The agreement must be made before the PRP to which it relates, be in writing, contain a fair estimate of the number of hours which the worker is likely to spend on output work in the PRP and require the worker to keep a record of the hours of output work done in the PRP and supply a copy of this record to the employer as soon as is reasonably practicable after the end of the PRP. Where a fair estimate agreement applies, the worker is deemed to have worked the number of hours stated to be the "fair estimate" even if in fact longer hours were worked; but if the worker in fact worked for shorter hours than the fair estimate, the NMW entitlement is limited to the actual hours worked (Regulation 26).

"Fair estimate agreements" are clearly open to abuse. There is a vast disparity in bargaining power between low paid manufacturing pieceworkers, who are generally engaged on output work as defined in the NMW Regulations, and their employers. The scope for abuse is limited, in theory at least, by the requirement that to be valid, the estimated number of hours must be at least 80% of the hours which an "average" worker doing the same work in the same working circumstances and producing the same output, would on average spend working in a PRP (Regulation 25(2)). In 1999 the LPC reported that little use had been made of fair estimate agreements. It also noted that there was evidence that where they were used they had been abused.[42]

In its third report in 2001, the LPC again reported the views of the National Group on Homeworking that fair estimate agreements were still the exception and that where used they were effectively imposed on workers and rarely enabled them to regularly earn the NMW. But the LPC also noted a proposal from an unspecified employer's organisation for the NMW Regulations to be amended to allow the NMW to be expressed as a piece rate based on the estimated time for completion of the work. It is not clear whether this proposal was limited to allowing fair estimate agreements to be expressed in this form. The LPC recommended that there should be consultation with representatives of output workers and their employers to examine the case for a change to the law.[43] Any consideration of such a change would need to take into account the uncertain extent to which those engaged on output work whose "output" falls below a level which is acceptable to the employer, and whose piece rate earnings therefore fall below the NMW level, are protected against detriment or dismissal by the employer if they attempt to enforce their right to be paid the NMW. If employment tribunals find that dismissals of such workers are not unfair, then the protective function of the NMW is arguably undermined.[44]

Salaried hours work

The most complex provisions in the NMW Regulations are those which relate to salaried hours work. The basic provision is straightforward. In the normal case it is assumed that the worker works an equal number of hours in each PRP. Thus where the PRP is a month, this will be the "basic" annual hours divided by 12 (Regulation 21).

Where the worker is paid less because of periods of absence from work – which is widely defined (see above) – then the number of hours deemed to have been worked in the PRP is correspondingly reduced. Where a worker actually works more than the "basic" annual hours, then from the time in the year when actual hours exceed those basic hours, he or she becomes entitled to the NMW for the actual hours worked, which include time spent travelling and receiving training in accordance with the provisions described above. Whether and if so when the basic hours have been exceeded is determined by reference to a "calculation year" which begins on 1 April for workers who were employed on salaried hours work when the NMWA came into force in April 1999. Otherwise it begins on the date when they started employment on salaried hours work.

Where a salaried hours worker leaves work which is salaried hours work before the end of a calculation year, his or her working time on salaried hours work for NMW purposes is the pro rata equivalent of the annual hours. Thus a worker who left salaried hours work after nine months of the calculation year would be entitled to be paid at least the NMW, calculated in accordance with the provisions on salaried hours work for three quarters of the annual hours (Regulation 23).

In its third report, the LPC noted and endorsed the GMB's view that the rules on working time, including those on salaried hours work, were working well; annual hours contracts had not had to be "unpicked".[45] However, these provisions may affect workers' other legal entitlements. Unison's evidence to the LPC in 2000 stated that term-time only support workers in education had, apparently, lost the right to claim "job seekers' allowance" in school holidays because they were now deemed to be employed during the holidays as well as the terms. While this would appear to be a consequence of the annual hours agreement[46] rather than the NMW legislation, it serves to underline an important point about the NMW. The complex provisions on pay and working time are intended to guarantee payment at the NMW rate for work done. They do not, and are not intended to, secure a minimum income guarantee for any worker.

Enforcement

Effective enforcement of the NMW legislation requires not only an appropriate body of legal rights and obligations which can be expeditiously enforced. It is also necessary to promote awareness among both low paid workers and their employers of the NMW and the steps that can be taken to enforce it.

Unusually for legislation concerned with employment rights, the NMWA makes express provision for publicity as well as containing a body of more conventional enforcement provisions. These provisions fall into two groups. The first comprises a range of rights for individual workers, some familiar, others less so, though none is totally without precedent. The second group enables designated officers to police employers' compliance with the NMW and take appropriate proceedings to secure payments due to workers and impose penalties on defaulting parties. Early experience has also seen the start of some novel initiatives to promote a culture of compliance within communities where there are groups of workers who are vulnerable to exploitation.

Enforcement rights for workers

The enforcement rights given to individual workers fall into two groups. The first consists of two routes through which the right to the NMW can be directly enforced. Both are reinforced by an important provision which reverses the burden of proof. Under Section 17 of the NMWA, workers who are entitled to the NMW have a contractual right to the difference between the "relevant remuneration received" in a PRP and their NMW entitlement for that PRP where it is greater. Contractual claims for pay can normally only be made in the county court, but this procedure has the advantage that the normal six year limitation period for contract claims applies.[47] This is not unimportant since it is likely that, as happened when the Wages Councils legislation was in force, there will be cases where underpayments are not discovered until months or years after they occurred.

Unless the time limit is an important consideration, the alternative route which the NMWA provides for individual enforcement is likely to be preferred. This is a claim under the provisions of Part II of the ERA 1996 that a shortfall in pay below the worker's NMW entitlement was an unauthorised deduction from pay. Section 18 of the NMWA enables claims to be made under these provisions by those who are "workers" for the purposes of the NMWA even if they are not "workers" within the definition of worker which normally applies for the purposes of Part II of the 1996 Act, and even where there is no contract between the worker and the employer.[48] Thus agency workers, homeworkers and some seafarers who are not otherwise workers within Section 199 of the ERA 1996 – and any other individuals who are deemed to be workers by regulations made under Section 41 of the NMWA – can still use Part II of the 1996 Act to enforce their entitlement. While the limitation period for these claims is three months, this should not prevent recovery of underpayments over a longer period as long as legal proceedings were commenced within three months of a date on which payment below the NMW rate was occurring.[49]

Whichever of the two routes for individual enforcement is chosen, an important procedural modification is made by Section 28 of the NMWA, which reverses the normal burden of proof on two issues: whether the worker qualified for the NMW and whether he or she was paid at a rate below the NMW. The reasoning underlying this provision was that employers possess the relevant information on both the nature of their relationship with their workers and the amount that workers have been paid. Section 28 does not reverse the burden of proof with respect to the amount of any alleged underpayment. In some cases it will be possible for this to be established solely by reference to evidence from the employer of what a worker was paid. But this will not always be the case; the worker may claim, for example, that some of this amount does not count towards the NMW because it represents allowances or reimbursement of expenses which have to be disregarded (see above).

There is little hard evidence of the number of claims made by workers themselves to enforce the right to the NMW.[50] The total number of claims made under Part II of ERA 1996 which were referred to conciliation officers of the Advisory Conciliation and Arbitration Service (ACAS) increased markedly in both 1999-2000 and 2000-2001, but it is not known how many of these concerned the NMW.[51] Both the first two DTI/Inland Revenue Annual Reports on the National Minimum Wage, for 1999-2000 and 2000-2001, stated that most claims were withdrawn either because they were settled privately by the parties or after successful ACAS conciliation. There is clearly a risk that these settlements may have involved workers agreeing to accept less than their full NMW entitlement, even where ACAS has been actively involved. Informal settlement procedures do not contain any clear safeguards to prevent employers from using their superior bargaining power to persuade workers, for example, to accept less than the NMW as a quid pro quo for continued employment.

The second group of enforcement rights for individual workers consists of additions to the body of employment protection rights in the ERA 1996. One of these has yet to be implemented. This is the right of a worker to be given a NMW statement by his or her employer on or before each occasion on which he or she is paid. Section 12 of the NMWA empowers the Secretary of State to give effect to this right by regulations, but the proposals on this issue in the 1998 consultative draft of the NMW Regulations were dropped in response to pressure from employers and employers' organisations that this proposal, together with the original proposals concerning the employer's obligations to keep records, would impose disproportionate costs.[52] The 1998 proposals were arguably over-elaborate, particularly in relation to the details of any individual agreement on working time in relation to output work or unmeasured work. It would, however, be relatively straightforward to amend the existing law on providing employees – but not other workers – with an itemised pay statement to require it to include basic information about the NMW. It seems odd to overlook this obvious source of information for employees about their pay in seeking to maximize awareness among at least some workers of one of their most basic employment rights.[53]

Workers who are not employees do not have the right to an itemised pay statement and the government's failure to exercise its powers under Section 12 of the NMWA unquestionably leaves some of the most vulnerable low paid workgroups with no right to information from their employer about how the amount of pay which they receive has been calculated.

The two employment protection rights which are in force provide some redress for workers who are victimised by their employers for taking action to enforce their NMW rights.

Section 23 of the NMWA creates a right for workers not to be subjected to any detriment by way of acts or omissions by their employer on the ground that the worker had taken action to enforce the right to the NMW, the employer was prosecuted under Section 31 (see below) because of action taken by the worker or that "the worker qualifies or will or might qualify for the NMW". These last words are wide enough to cover action taken against workers who are about to qualify for the NMW or about to qualify for the full rate rather than the lower development rate. Any such detrimental action is likely to be dismissal. For employees who are dismissed a right to redress for unfair dismissal is provided by Section 104A of the ERA 1996, which was inserted in the ERA by Section 25 of the NMWA. It provides parallel redress to that provided by Section 23 of the NMWA in a case of detriment. As with the redress for unfair dismissal for asserting statutory rights provided by Section 104 of the ERA 1996, there is no qualifying period of employment before this right takes effect and no upper age limit for complainants. For workers who are not employees, the detriment covered by Section 23 of the NMWA includes dismissal.[54]

There are now a number of statutory employment rights which are supported by rights to redress for detriment or dismissal which occurs because workers have taken steps to assert their legal entitlements.[55] The provisions in Sections 146 and 152 of the Trade Union and Labour Relations (Consolidation) Act 1992 providing redress for action short of dismissal against, and dismissal of, employees for reasons relating to trade union membership and activities, and those in the anti-discrimination legislation which treat victimisation as discrimination[56] have a similar purpose. None of those different approaches to protecting workers who assert basic social rights has been entirely satisfactory. Reports of early experience of the NMW included evidence that workers were reluctant to take steps to enforce their NMWA rights for fear of incurring some form of detriment or losing their jobs. Some workers who had been penalised in some way by their employer felt frustrated that while the Inland Revenue could take steps to ensure that they were paid the NMW (see below), it could neither follow up complaints of detriment or dismissal – for assistance with which it referred workers to ACAS – nor could it initiate legal proceedings on their behalf in respect of these complaints.[57] While the intentions behind the provisions on detriment and dismissal are clear, it appears that as yet for many workers they provide rights which are largely unenforceable.

Employers' obligation to keep records

The obligation on the employer to keep records, which is imposed by Regulation 38 of the NMW Regulations, made in exercise of the power in Section 9 of the NMWA, and the worker's right of access to these records under Sections 10 and 11 of the NMWA provides a bridge between the individual and administrative enforcement mechanisms provided by the NMW legislation. The 1998 consultative draft regulations included proposals for fairly detailed records to be kept in respect of workers paid less than £1000 a month, but as already noted, these details were dropped in response to employers' concerns over costs. Rather like the old Wages Councils legislation, the Regulations simply require an employer to keep "records sufficient to establish that he is remunerating the worker at a rate at least equal to the national minimum wage" (Regulation 38(1)) together with copies of any relevant agreement with the worker on relevant training (which reduces the worker's NMW entitlement to the development rate) or on hours of work (which provides the basis for calculating the time spent on output work or unmeasured work). Some guidance on what sort of records are sufficient is provided in the DTI Guide to the NMW.[58]

While the worker has both a right of access to these records and the right to be accompanied "by such other person as the worker may think fit" when inspecting them, the circumstances when this can be done are fairly closely circumscribed. The worker must believe on reasonable grounds that he or she is being paid below the NMW for a PRP and can only exercise the right of access to records for the purposes of establishing whether or not this is so.

In order to exercise the right the worker must give the employer a production notice which must state whether the worker will exercise the right to be accompanied. The employer must then respond by giving notice of where and when the records will be produced. This must be within 14 days (or later if agreed) and either at the workplace, or another place where it is reasonable for the worker to attend, or elsewhere by agreement. Where the right is denied, or the worker is not allowed to examine or copy the records or be accompanied, the worker may complain to an employment tribunal. If the complaint is upheld the tribunal must award the worker a sum equivalent to 80 times the then current hourly NMW rate (NMWA s22(1)). While the worker's right of access to the employer's records is novel, many workers are likely to be unaware of it. Those who are may well be as reluctant to exercise it as they are to run any other risk of victimisation for trying to enforce their NMW rights. There is as yet little available evidence on this issue.

Enforcement by Inland Revenue officers

The right of access to the records which employers are required to keep extends to officers appointed or designated for the purposes of the NWMA under Section 13. As expected, the government did not appoint a new group of officers but instead the DTI arranged with the Inland Revenue for some of its officers to exercise the enforcement powers which the Act gives to officers, except in relation to agriculture where the existing agricultural wages inspectorates were given the additional NMWA powers. While not identical to the powers of the former wages inspectorate under the Wages Councils legislation, their nature and scope are broadly similar. The Revenue has, however, adopted a higher profile, more proactive approach to the exercise of its powers and there is evidence of a willingness to work with other interested bodies in attempts to secure compliance with the legislation.

The Revenue officers have power to enter employers' premises and require them to produce the records which they have to keep (see above). They can copy these records and require the employer[59] to explain them or provide further information which might reasonably be needed to establish whether or not the Act is being complied with. Their enforcement powers fall into three groups. First, they have novel powers to issue "enforcement notices" and "penalty notices". Under Section 19 of the NMWA an officer who is of the opinion that workers have not been paid at the NMW rate in any PRP can serve an enforcement notice on the employer. This will require the employer to pay the workers at least the NMW rate in future PRPs and may require payment of arrears due within a specified period. An employer has four weeks to exercise the right of appeal against an enforcement notice to an employment tribunal. The tribunal must rescind the notice where the facts are such that there was no reason to serve it and it must rectify a notice where it covers more than one worker and there was no reason for it in relation to some of those covered or it incorrectly or inaccurately required payment of arrears.

Subject to a successful appeal, where an officer is satisfied that an employer has failed to comply with an enforcement notice, a "penalty notice" may be served on the employer under Section 21 of the NMWA. This requires payment of a penalty, to the state, of twice the current NMW rate per worker to whom the failure relates per day. The employer can appeal against a penalty notice to an employment tribunal and in all cases a penalty notice cannot take effect until any appeal against an enforcement notice has been decided (NMWA s22). Appeals against employment tribunal decisions on enforcement or penalty notices can be made to the EAT on points of law in the usual way (NMWA s29).

Enforcement notices and penalty notices do not of themselves secure the arrears due to workers who have been paid below the NMW entitlement. Revenue officers can also take steps to this end after they have issued an enforcement notice. Section 20 of the NMWA enables them to initiate proceedings on behalf of a worker either in an employment tribunal under Section 23 of the ERA 1996 or in the civil courts for recovery of sums due, under Section 18 of the NMWA (see above). It should be emphasised, however, that, as already noted, what the Revenue cannot do is take any action on behalf of workers who claim to have suffered detriment as a result of seeking to enforce their NMW rights.

As with the Agricultural Wages and former Wages Councils legislation, the obligations imposed on employers are reinforced by a number of criminal offences. The offences in Section 31 of the NMWA cover refusing or wilfully neglecting to pay a worker at the NMW rate for a PRP, failing to keep the required records or keeping false records, providing false information and obstructing officers. In relation to failing to pay the NMW or keep records, proof of exercise of all due diligence and taking all reasonable precautions to secure compliance is a defence. The maximum penalty is a fine at level 5 on the standard scale.[60] There seems little doubt that it was not envisaged that these criminal sanctions would be frequently invoked. Use of similar powers under the Wages Councils legislation was confined to the very worst cases. It is unsurprising, therefore, that no prosecutions were brought during the first two years that the NMWA was in force.[61]

The Revenue did, however, make quite extensive use of its powers to issue enforcement and penalty notices during these two years. A total of 349 enforcement notices and 61 penalty notices were issued up to March 2001. A total of 38 employment tribunal cases were heard; some were appeals against enforcement notices, others were taken by the Revenue on behalf of workers to enforce their right to the NMW, some were both. All resulted in a successful outcome for the workers.[62] While it is difficult to identify criteria against which to evaluate those statistics, they are consistent with the general impression, which is reflected in evidence to the LPC and the LPC's second and third reports, that the Revenue are firm and effective enforcers where they identify cases of underpayment.

Providing information

Under the terms of its agreement with the DTI, the Revenue is to provide information on the NMW. This is done, in the first place, through a telephone helpline which responds to all complaints and inquiries concerning the NMW and provides leaflets and guidance.

The DTI and Inland Revenue have also set up a Customer Responsive Outreach Work team (CROW) to respond to requests from organisations to talk about the NMW; it aims to carry out around 25 visits each year. At a more sophisticated level, since the end of September 2000, interactive guidance has been available via the Internet through the TIGER initiative.[63] Complaints of non-compliance received via the helpline are referred to one of the Revenue's 14 regionally based Compliance Teams by the Central Information Unit (CIU) which works alongside the helpline. All complaints of non-compliance made by the workers concerned are followed up. The CIU has to evaluate information received from third parties in deciding whether it merits further investigation.

The Revenue received some 50,000 inquiries about the NMW in January–March 1999 before the NMWA came into force. In the first year from April 1999–March 2000 a further 120,000 were received. The numbers declined, perhaps unsurprisingly, to 75,000 in the year April 2000–March 2001. The 14 compliance teams (a total of 77 staff in 1999–2000) completed 6041 investigations in 1999–2000 and 7256 in 2000–2001; 2532 of those in 1999–2000 and 2834 in 2000–2001 were proactive initiatives. In 2000 it became possible for Revenue Officers engaged on NMW work to exchange information with colleagues elsewhere in the Revenue. This enabled them to use data on workers in receipt of Working Families Tax Credit to identify possible cases of underpayment and some 1908 inquiries followed receipt of this information in 2000–2001. The total of underpayments identified was just under £1.25 million in 1999–2000 and over £3 million in 2000–2001.

Publicity

Part of the work of the Revenue is also directed to fulfilling the government's duty under Section 50 of the NMWA to arrange for appropriate publication of information about the legislation, including the rates, excluded categories of worker and how the hourly rate which a person is regarded as paid for NMW purposes is calculated. To date, a number of publicity campaigns have been carried out at strategic times: in early 1999 before the NMWA came into force, in autumn 1999 targeted at ethnic minorities, in mid-2000 to coincide with the increase in the rate for workers aged 18-21[64] and in September/October 2000 to coincide with the increase in the main rate when there was a special emphasis on targeting the "women's press" as over two thirds of those who stood to benefit were women. For all campaigns the Revenue has reported market research showing levels of awareness of the existence of the NMW in excess of 90%, but much lower (unspecified) levels of knowledge of the actual NMW rates. While the totality of the Revenue's initiatives may well lead over time to an increase in general knowledge of the NMW including the current rates, there is clearly still some way to go before the level of awareness is such that it can contribute to the LPC's goal of the NMW as a largely self-enforcing right.[65]

The need for novel initiatives in order to promote not only awareness but also a willingness among workers to enforce their right to receive, and an acceptance among employers of the duty to pay the NMW, in a number of areas where cultural constraints of different types have been acknowledged to pose an effective barrier to the law, was accepted in the LPC's second report.[66] By way of response the government agreed to fund a number of pilot projects in areas where workers were most likely to be at risk of non-compliance.[67] The Revenue's Report for 2000-2001 records that a number of those were under way and would be evaluated in 2001-2002. While it is clear that the Revenue can justifiably claim to have made a good start in its role as the primary enforcer of the NMW, there is still some way to go before the NMW can be said to be a right which is effectively enforced in all those low paying areas of the economy where it was intended to make a real difference to the employment rights and quality of life of working people.

Notes

1 The Secretary of State for Trade and Industry announced that the LPC was to be made a permanent body on 5 March 2001. HC Deb vol.364 col.25
2 Lord Falconer, Solicitor General, HL Deb vol.590 col.1275, 11 June 1998
3 NMWA s.54(3) which is identical to the definition of "worker" in ERA 1996 s.230(3)
4 On the exclusion of casual workers from the definition of "employee" see *O'Kelly v Trust House Forte* (1983) ICR 728 CA and *Carmichael v National Power* (1999) ICR 1226 HL.
5 Incomes Data Services *Report to the Low Pay Commission: Tribunal Cases and the National Minimum Wage*, Research Report to the LPC May 2001
6 National Association of Citizens Advice Bureaux, *The impact of the minimum wage on CAB users*. Report to the LPC, April 2000 paragraphs 5.3 and 5.18 and Margaret Boyle *Winners and Losers. The National Minimum Wage in Tyne and Wear; the experience of CAB clients*, Report by NACAB North Region July 2000, paragraphs 2.1 and 2.32
7 This should avoid the lacuna in the law relating to other employment rights and their availability to agency workers which was evident in (for example) *Montgomery v Johnson*

Underwood (2001) ICR 819 CA: cf *McMeechan v Secretary of State for Employment* (1997) ICR 549 CA.

[8] In *Lockett v British Wool Marketing Board* Case No 2900984/99, an employment tribunal rejected an argument that NMWA s35 applied to wool producers who were required to sell all their wool to the respondent. Selling the wool which the applicants "produced" from their sheep, was contrasted with the activities of manufacturing home workers who sell their time to the businesses for whom they work

[9] On the equivalent provision in Section 23 of the ERA 1999 see Simon Deakin "Employment protection and the employment relationship: adapting the traditional model" Chapter 6 in K.D. Ewing (ed) *Employment Rights at Work: reviewing the Employment Relations Act 1999* (London: Institute of Employment Rights, 2001)

[10] NMWA s43: ERA 1996 s199(2)

[11] *The National Minimum Wage: The Story So Far. Second Report of the Low Pay Commission* Cm 4571 2000 paragraphs 5.3–5.7. *The National Minimum Wage. Making a Difference: The Next Step. Third Report (Volume Two) of the Low Pay Commission* Cm 5175 June 2001 paragraphs 5.13–5.18

[12] See *The National Minimum Wage Accommodation Offset. A Review by the Low Pay Commission* Cm 4321 ch4. It may be questioned whether any member of such a community would want to assert the right to receive the NMW in any event. If they did, it might be that their right to membership of the community could be called into question

[13] The provision on offshore employment is contained in regulations made under Section 42 of the NMWA in accordance with normal practice in relation to the statutory employment rights of workers in this sector

[14] *The National Minimum Wage. First Report of the Low Pay Commission* Cm 3976 1998 paragraphs 5.6–5.10

[15] *LPC Third Report (Volume Two)*, note 11 above, paragraphs 2.45–2.52. The LPC's own survey and commissioned research disclosed some evidence of employers substituting 16 and 17 year old for older workers, most notably in hairdressing. The trade union USDAW's evidence to the LPC in 2000 records employers in retail pharmacy and retail footwear sections taking advantage of the absence of any minimum rate for 16 and 17 year olds: *The National Minimum Wage. Written Evidence* (to the LPC) October 2000 pp.1–5

[16] *LPC First Report*, note 14 above, paragraph 5.16

[17] National Minimum Wage Regulations 1999, SI 1999 No 584 Regulation 12(2)–(4) as amended by SI 2000 No 1989 Regulation 4. In England and Wales these are National Traineeships, Modern Apprenticeships, Foundation Modern Apprenticeships and Advanced Modern Apprenticeships. A summary of all the relevant training programmes in the United Kingdom is provided in paragraphs 4–10 of Appendix 7 to the LPC's *Third Report, Volume 2*, note 11 above

[18] LPC *First Report*, note 14 above, paragraph 5.48; *Second Report*, note 11 above, paragraphs 6.10–6.21; *Third Report Volume Two*, note 11 above, paragraphs 2.53–2.73, especially 2.71 and 2.72

[19] In England and Wales the training must be for a qualification which before 1 April 2001 was approved for the purposes of Schedule 2 to the Further and Higher Education Act 1992, or which leads to a qualification approved under Section 98 or 99 of the Learning and Skills Act 2000 for the purposes of Section 97 of that Act

[20] *Third Report Volume Two*, note 11 above, paragraph 2.95

[21] For development of this point see (1999) 28 *Industrial Law Journal* 171, 174

[22] In addition to the issues discussed above, it may be noted that the LPC has recommended government action to clarify the benefits entitlement and legal status of certain disabled persons who undertake work for therapeutic purposes: *Second Report* note 11 above paragraphs 5.10-5.16

[23] As has already been noted regulations made under NMWA s3 may provide for more than one NMW rate in specified circumstances

[24] Where a worker's contract comes to an end, Regulation 10(2) treats payments made in the month after the last day on which the worker worked as if they were made in the worker's final PRP

[25] The GMB drew attention to this issue in its 2000 Evidence to the LPC: *Response to the Low Pay Commission's third review of the National Minimum Wage* November 2000, p.10. The LPC considered that this was not an issue on which it should make recommendations: *Third Report Volume 2*, note 11 above, paragraph 5.51.

[26] See Margaret Beckett, President of the Board of Trade and Secretary of State for Trade and Industry: HC Deb volume 314 cols 507-9, 18 June 1998

[27] *LPC First Report*, n 14 above paragraphs 4.4-6.30

[28] A court order for payment of a sum due under the contract must be distinguished from an award of damages or other compensation for breach of contract; the latter does not count as a "payment" for NMW purposes. On the distinction see *Abrahams v Performing Right Society* (1995) ICR 1028 CA

[29] Reg 2(1). The definition excludes allowances made in order to refund expenses, which are excluded from NMW calculations by other provisions. Allowances in connection with retirement or by way of compensation for loss of office are excluded from the "payments" made by an employer to a worker for NMW purposes by Regulation 8

[30] For the same reason, some employers have replaced benefits such as free tea and coffee with small additions to pay which count for NMW purposes

[31] *LPC Third Report Volume Two*, note 11 above, paragraphs 5.34-5.42, especially 5.37

[32] *LPC First Report*, note 14 above, paragraph 4.30

[33] There is clear evidence that the practice of employers providing accommodation for their workers is in decline. See *Pay Structures and the Minimum Wage* LPC Occasional Paper 3 September 1999 paragraphs 2.11-2.18

[34] Regulation 2(1) defines a performance bonus as a performance bonus or other merit payment attributable to the quality or amount of work done in the course of more than one pay reference period, and not therefore payable directly in respect of work done in specific hours

[35] (2001) IRLR 659, EAT. The Court of Appeal decision is noted in IDS Brief No 000, May 2002

[36] (2001) IRLR 659, 661

[37] *LPC Second Report*, note 11 above paragraphs.5.38-5.41: TUC *evidence to the Low Pay Commission* 1999, 15-16. cf. *Wright v Scottbridge Construction Ltd.* (2001) IRLR 589 where the EAT held that the pre-2000 amendment form of Regulation 15 only excluded hours when the employer told the worker that he was entitled to take time off for sleep

[38] See *Miles* v *Wakefield MDC* (1987) ICR 368 HL; *Wiluzynski v Tower Hamlets LBC* [1989] ICR 493 CA and *British Telecommunications v Ticehurst* (1992) ICR 383 CA

[39] For workers with no normal working hours, a "week's pay" is the average of the last 12 weeks in which the worker did some work: ERA 1996 s224

[40] These agreements do not vary the terms of the worker's employment contract and have

effect solely for the purpose of determining the amount of output work or unmeasured work (as the case may be) which the worker is treated as doing for NMW purposes (Regulations 25(3) and 28(3))

[41] In its third report, note 11 above, paragraph 5.50, the LPC appears to confuse the "daily average" agreement for unmeasured work with the "fair estimate" agreement for output work in its observation that the difficulties experienced by a leisure organisation because of seasonal fluctuations in hours could be overcome "by the use of the 'unmeasured hours' calculation (that is, a fair estimate)". Moreover it is far from clear that the work referred to was either "output work" or "unmeasured work" which could be the subject of an individual agreement on working time

[42] *LPC Second Report*, note 11 above, paragraphs 5.42-5.44

[43] *LPC Third Report (Volume Two)*, note 11 above paragraphs 5.47-5.49

[44] The GMB reported a tribunal decision that the reason for the dismissal of an employee in these circumstances was the failure to maintain the production rate set rather than the employee's right to be paid the NMW: GMB *Response to the Low Pay Commission's third review of the National Minimum Wage*, 2000 p.10

[45] *LPC Third Report (Volume Two)*, note 11 above, paragraph 5.52

[46] These workers might well not qualify for jobseekers allowance anyway in the light of the House of Lords' decision in *Banks v Chief Adjudication Officer* (2001) ICR 877

[47] A claim made after the termination of an employee's employment could be made to an employment tribunal under the Employment Tribunals Extension of Jurisdiction Orders SI 1994 No 1623 (England and Wales) SI No 1624 (Scotland)

[48] Under Section 18(3) of the NMWA civil proceedings under Section 17 can also be brought where there is no contract between worker and employer who has the legal responsibility for paying the worker the NMW. This could be relevant to agency workers who are relying on Section 34 of the NMWA (see above)

[49] See *Reid v Camphill Engineers* (1990) ICR 435 where the EAT allowed recovery of arrears of pay where the applicant had been paid below the relevant wages council rate for a period of over three years

[50] 32 out of the 44 cases in the survey carried out by IDS for the LPC, note 5 above, concerned claims for underpayment, many of these involved disputes over whether particular payments or working time counted for NMW purposes

[51] ACAS received 36837 "protection of wages" claims in 1999-2000 and 39664 in 2000-01: *ACAS Annual Report 2000-2001* Appendix 1 Table 7

[52] *The NMW Regulations Regulatory Impact Assessment* estimated that modifying the proposed record-keeping requirements and eliminating the NMW Statement would reduce the one-off costs of the NMW by £85 million and recurring costs by £51 million per year (DTI, 1999) paragraph 4

[53] Section 12(3) of the NMWA envisaged that for employees, the information required for the NMW statement could be included in the itemised pay statement provided under Section 8 of the ERA 1996

[54] NMWA s23(4). Section 24 applies the provision concerning complaints to employment tribunals of infringements of the right not to suffer detriment in Sections 48 and 49 of the ERA, to complaints of detriment under NMWA Section 23

[55] See Sections 44-49A and 99-105 of ERA 1996

[56] Sex Discrimination Act 1975 Section 4, Race Relations Act 1976 Section 2 and Disability Discrimination Act 1995 Section 55

[57] See the two NACAB reports in 2000, note 6 above

[58] *A detailed guide to the national minimum wage*, DTI, October 2000 edition, paragraphs 205-217

[59] The "relevant persons" on whom officers can make demands under Section 14 extend to those who supply work to anyone who qualifies for the NMW, both the principal and agent where workers are supplied through agencies, any worker, servant or agent of the employer, supplier of work, principal or agent, and anyone who qualifies for the NMW: s14(4)

[60] Section 32 makes provision for extending liability to certain individuals, including managers and directors, where the offences are committed by corporations

[61] See *DTI/Inland Revenue National Minimum Wage Annual Report* 1999-2000 Section 3. The *Report* for 2000-2001 makes no reference to any criminal prosecutions

[62] *Ibid. Annual Report* 1999-2000 Section 3; *Annual Report* 2000-2001 Section 2 from which all the statistics on the enforcement activities of the Revenue are taken

[63] The initiative enables workers and employers to see how the NMW applies to them and to calculate whether or not the NMW is being paid in their circumstances. The website address is www.tiger.gov.uk

[64] For which the publicity included beer mats: *DTI/Inland Revenue Annual Report* 2000-2001 Section 1. Information on publicity is provided in Section 3 of the 1999-2000 Report and Section 1 of the 2000-2001 Report

[65] *LPC First Report*, note 14 above, paragraph 8.11

[66] *LPC Second Report*, note 11 above, paragraph 7.39

[67] *The Government's Evidence to the Low Pay Commission*, December 2000, 13-15

7

Whistleblowing

DAVID LEWIS

David Lewis is Professor of Employment Law at Middlesex University.

Whistleblowing and the public interest

Introduction

There is no universally accepted concept of whistleblowing. Some commentators define it narrowly as the reporting of illegal activities. Others prefer a more expansive definition which includes a broad range of wrongdoing. For example, in 1972 Ralph Nader defined whistleblowing as

> an act of a man or a woman who believing in the public interest overrides the interest of the organisation he serves, and publicly blows the whistle if the organisation is involved in corrupt, illegal, fraudulent or harmful activity.[1]

More than 20 years later the Australian Senate Select Committee on Public Interest Whistleblowing adopted a more extensive definition:

> the whistleblower is a concerned citizen, totally or predominantly motivated by notions of public interest ,who initiates of his or her own free will, an open disclosure about significant wrongdoing directly perceived in a particular occupational role, to a person or agency capable of investigating the complaint and facilitating the correction of wrongdoing.[2]

Nevertheless, this Select Committee came to the commonsense conclusion that in the final analysis " what is important is not the definition of the term, but the definition of the circumstances and conditions under which employees who disclose wrongdoing should be entitled to protection from retaliation".[3] This is also the approach adopted in the United Kingdom by the Public Interest Disclosure Act 1998 (henceforward PIDA 1998). As we will see below, this legislation sets out the types of disclosure which can give rise to protection ("qualifying disclosures"), the circumstances in which "qualifying disclosures" will be protected ("protected disclosures") and the categories of worker to whom the protection applies.

Although in some situations it may be difficult to decide whether a particular incident amounts to internal or external whistleblowing, there are good reasons for drawing a distinction. [4] Internal reporting offers advantages to both employer and worker. The employer is given the opportunity to deal with a problem without external pressures or publicity. From the worker's point of view, once a matter has been raised externally, he or she may be seen as an adversary and be more likely to suffer retaliation.[5] Thus workers who believe some wrongdoing is having an adverse effect on their terms and conditions of employment may choose to raise a grievance. Similarly, other internal channels may be available for specific matters, for example, equal opportunities and health and safety procedures. However, if the subject of the concern does not fit within existing procedures and the matter is thought to be sufficiently serious, a worker may feel inclined to raise the matter externally.

It should also be noted that the law provides support for internal rather than external disclosures in two ways. First, while internal reporting to higher management might be perceived by supervisors as disloyal, it cannot be treated as a breach of the employee's common law duty of confidence or fidelity. Second, in determining whether there is a "protected disclosure" within the meaning of PIDA 1998, regard will be had to whether or not the worker complied with a procedure authorised by the employer (see below).

Is whistleblowing in the public interest?

A conventional but simplistic view of whistleblowers is that they are troublemakers who deserve to be punished for disloyalty.[6] An alternative approach is to treat them as dedicated individuals who provide a valuable safety net when other forms of regulation fail. Such an approach recognises that workers are often in the best position to know whether there is malpractice within an organisation. More positively, there is the "enlightened self-interest approach" which sees whistleblowers as benefiting their employers by offering solutions to work problems. Those who first contact their managers about malpractice give them the chance to correct it before the matter escalates. It is not simply a question of internal communication being preferable to external whistleblowing; there is also the desirability of avoiding work stoppages over employee concerns. Thus whistleblowing can also be viewed as part of a strategy to maintain and improve quality. No doubt some employers would baulk at the idea of providing rewards for ethical behaviour. However, viewed from this "quality" perspective, it may well be appropriate to offer financial incentives to those who disclose malpractice. Arguably, those who report concerns about malpractice are in an analogous position to those who propose improvements in organisational efficiency through a suggestion scheme. Indeed, both the USA and the UK governments provide financial inducements to "blow the whistle" in certain circumstances.[7]

As regards the argument that whistleblowing poses a challenge to an organisation"s authority structure, this may not be the case where disclosures are positively encouraged and a channel for reporting is available (see below for a discussion of the possible contents of whistleblowing procedures). If a mechanism for employees to raise their concerns is not provided, then either the problem will not be dealt with or the employee will feel obliged to air the matter externally.[8] As Lord Borrie put it: "The result can be that conscientious and loyal employees become aggrieved or disillusioned".[9]

Apart from helping to expose financial scandals, like those which occurred at BCCI, Barlow Clowes and with the Maxwell pensions, in some situations whistleblowing may be vital to preserve the health and safety of both the workforce and the general public. For example, the investigation into the *Herald of Free Enterprise* disaster in 1987 found that employees had aired their concerns on five previous occasions about the ship sailing with its bow doors open. A member of staff had even suggested fitting lights to the bridge to indicate whether the doors were closed. The inquiry concluded: "If this sensible suggestion ... had received the serious consideration it deserved this disaster might well have been prevented." [10] The enquiry into the 1988 Piper Alpha oil platform disaster found that: "workers did not want to put their continued employment in jeopardy through raising a safety issue that might embarrass management".[11]

Thus, at one level, it can be argued that the disclosure of serious wrongdoing must always be in the public interest. However, it is important to acknowledge that there are circumstances in which this could be open to debate. For example, if the disclosure leads to a factory shutdown and mass redundancies which decimate the local community. Equally, it should not be assumed that all whistleblowers are motivated by altruism. It is an unfortunate fact that concerns are sometimes raised out of malice. But does it necessarily follow that a malicious disclosure, perhaps of a serious crime, should not be regarded as being in the public interest? We will show below that current legislation is reluctant to accept that a person who makes a truthful disclosure in bad faith should be treated as acting in the public interest.

Types of whistleblower

Dr Lucy Vickers draws a distinction between "watchdog" and "protest" whistleblowers.[12] The former discover and then expose wrongdoing in order to avoid safety or financial disasters. The latter raise more general concerns about the effects of their employer's activities. Both "watchdog" and "protest" whistleblowers would view themselves as good citizens, but there may be suspicions that protest whistleblowing involves a political dimension. For this reason society may be more willing to encourage and protect those who speak out as "watchdogs". Put simply, it is more difficult to justify breaking a duty of confidence (see below) purely on the grounds of freedom of speech than where safety is compromised or fraud is suspected.

Although there may be certain characteristics which predispose a worker to report wrongdoing, existing research does not allow us to explain why one individual is prepared to "blow the whistle" while others choose to turn a blind eye. A stereotypical approach is to regard whistleblowers as "heroes" – loyal employees who report their concerns simply to ensure that institutional faults are rectified. Another view is that whistleblowers are "idealists" who speak out because of the mismatch between their expectations and organisational realities. A third category is the "defensive" whistleblower – the calculating employee who, in anticipation of disciplinary proceedings for poor performance, reports a concern with a view to establishing that the true reason for disciplinary action was victimisation for speaking out. Finally, there is the "vengeful" whistleblower – a former employee who reveals an employer's wrongdoing as a form of retribution for perceived mistreatment.[13]

How do we fit whistleblowers into these categories and is it necessary to do so? In practice, it may be virtually impossible to distinguish "heroic" whistleblowers from those who have more selfish motives. Indeed, the decision to report a concern is likely to involve a complex mixture of factors which cannot be readily identified by either the whistleblower or an outsider. Perhaps for this reason the UK Parliament has chosen not to focus attention on motive other than to make employment protection rights dependent on workers demonstrating that they acted in good faith and not for personal gain (see below).

Constraints and encouragement to disclose

Constraints on disclosure

Workers have never had a general right to disclose information about their employment. Even the revelation of non-confidential material could be regarded as undermining the implied duty of trust and confidence and give rise to an action for breach of contract. Indeed, prior to the implementation of the PIDA 1998, express terms were extensively used to prevent any external discussion of an employer's activities (so-called "gagging clauses" are discussed below).

In relation to confidential information obtained in the course of employment, the common law again provides protection against disclosure through both express and implied terms. The duty of fidelity can be used to prevent disclosures while the employment subsists and express terms (restrictive covenants) can be used to inhibit the activities of former employees after the relationship has ceased. However, post-employment restraints will only be enforceable if they can be shown to protect legitimate business interests and are reasonable in all the circumstances. Where employees have allegedly disclosed confidential information in breach of an express or implied term they may seek to invoke a public interest defence to a legal action. Although the common law allows the public interest to be used as a shield against an injunction or damages, we will see that it is a weapon of uncertain strength.

Since the case of *Initial Services v Putterill*,[14] the Court of Appeal has allowed an exception to the principle of non-disclosure of confidential information where there is "any misconduct of such a nature that it ought in the public interest to be disclosed to others".

In *Initial Services v Putterill* a sales manager was sued for breach of confidence to stop him passing documents relating to unlawful price-fixing to a national newspaper. However, the disclosure must be to someone who has an interest in receiving it and, in this case, Lord Denning was of the opinion that the media had a sufficient interest for these purposes.

In *Lion Laboratories v Evans*,[15] two employees gave a national newspaper copies of internal documents doubting the reliability of the breathalysers manufactured by their employer. The company sought an injunction to prevent publication of the information on the grounds of breach of confidence. The action failed because the employees were found to have "just cause or excuse" for disclosure. However, the Court of Appeal indicated that the press might not always be the appropriate medium for disclosure.

Subsequently, in *Re a Company's Application*,[16] the High Court refused to grant an injunction preventing an employee in the financial services sector from disclosing confidential information about his company to a regulatory body, notwithstanding that the disclosure might be motivated by malice. Although Mr Justice Scott continued an injunction against general disclosure, he held that an employee's duty of confidence did not prevent them disclosing to regulatory authorities matters which it was within the province of those authorities to investigate. (Such regulatory authorities are likely to be "prescribed persons" for the purposes of PIDA 1998: see below).

A particular inhibiting factor was the widespread insertion of so-called "gagging clauses" into work contracts. Such clauses expressly prohibited the disclosure of information acquired during employment and caused particular confusion when placed alongside codes of conduct which encouraged the internal reporting of malpractices. However, Section 43J of the Employment Rights Act 1996 (ERA) now renders void any provision in an agreement which "purports to preclude the worker from making a protected disclosure". This section impacts on both work contracts and agreements to settle legal proceedings but will not apply to matters which fall outside the definition of a "qualifying disclosure".[17]

According to Section 43B(1) ERA, a "qualifying disclosure" is one which a worker reasonably believes tends to show one or more of the following:
(i)   a criminal offence
(ii)   a failure to comply with any legal obligation
(iii)   a miscarriage of justice
(iv)   danger to the health and safety of any individual
(v)   damage to the environment
(vi)   the deliberate concealment of information tending to show any of the matters listed above.

Thus a clause which prevented the disclosure of information about a type of wrongdoing which is not listed in Section 43B(1) ERA would still be enforceable. For example, an express term could restrain disclosures about mismanagement (so long as it did not amount to a criminal or civil law wrong) but not unlawful maladministration. Nevertheless Section 43J ERA may make it easier for those who are bound by professional codes of practice (for example, public service accountants, health visitors, nurses and midwives) to reconcile their contractual and professional obligations.

Another potential constraint has been the imposition of short and fixed-term employment contracts.[18] For example, in the offshore oil and gas industries many workers have been employed on two-week contracts. Given management's almost unfettered discretion whether or not to renew a contract, no doubt many workers felt inhibited about making unauthorised disclosures of information. However, Section 103A ERA, which applies irrespective of a complainant's age or length of service, now makes it automatically unfair to dismiss employees on the grounds that they have made a protected disclosure. (For these purposes, the expiry of a fixed term contract "without being renewed under the same contract" amounts to a dismissal).

Alternatively, workers who cannot claim unfair dismissal because they do not have a contract of employment can complain under Section 47B ERA that they have been subjected to a detriment for making a protected disclosure. In these circumstances Section 48(2) ERA obliges the employer to show the grounds for non-renewal. Of course, determined employers may try to invent potentially fair reasons for ending the relationship (for example, relating to conduct, capability, redundancy, etc.) and much will depend on the vigilance of employment tribunals. However, it will no longer be enough simply to assert that those who have raised concerns are unsuitable for further employment.

Thus, apart from the situation where an employee reports a breach of statutory duty to a relevant regulatory body, the common law has not provided reliable guidelines about what could be disclosed and to whom.[19] Certainly it affords little protection for those who are penalised by their employer for disclosing in the public interest. Pressure exerted on a whistleblower may be regarded as breaching the employer's duty to maintain trust and confidence. However, since the employer can also argue that the disclosure itself destroyed trust and confidence, it is highly unlikely that a court would order specific performance of the contract. As regards damages, an employee could expect to be compensated for pecuniary losses arising from a breach of contract, for example, if there was a wrongful dismissal. Nevertheless, employees are unlikely to be successful claiming for non-pecuniary losses suffered as a result of making a disclosure in the public interest, for example, if the employer fails to show respect for the employee.

Finally, the potential role of the law of defamation should not be underestimated. Assuming there has been sufficient publication, a whistleblower may be sued on the basis that his or her allegations were defamatory. If defamation proceedings are commenced, it is insufficient that the whistleblower had an honest belief on reasonable grounds[20] unless they can also rely on the defence of qualified privilege, that is, they had a legal, moral or social duty to communicate their concern and did so to a person who had an interest in receiving it. Since legal aid is not available in such proceedings, individuals may well feel inhibited if an organisation threatens to seek an injunction.

Encouragement to disclose

Whether employees have a general obligation to report the misdemeanours of fellow workers to their employer depends on the individual contract and the circumstances.[21] Thus, in *Swain v West Ltd*[22] there was an express term in a manager's contract that he would do "all in his power to promote, extend and develop the interests of the company". The Court of Appeal ruled that this imposed an obligation to disclose the wrongdoing of a managing director. Similarly, in *Sybron Corporation v Rochem Ltd*,[23] the Court of Appeal held that a senior executive in a multinational financial corporation had an implied duty to disclose to his employer the involvement of colleagues in a serious fraud, even if that required him to disclose his own misdeeds. Since workers are less likely to report concerns if they fear retaliation, we will now examine the circumstances in which the law provides specific protection against victimisation.

Regulation 14 of the Management of the Health and Safety at Work Regulations 1999 requires employees to inform employers of any work situation which could be reasonably considered to represent a serious and immediate danger to health and safety, and of any shortcomings in the employer's protection arrangements which have not previously been reported. This duty is supported by Sections 44(1)(c) and 100(1)(c) of ERA 1996, which provide that, where there is no safety representative or it is not reasonably practicable to raise the matter through such a representative or a safety committee, it is unlawful to dismiss or to impose a detriment on an employee who has

> brought to his employer's attention, by reasonable means, circumstances connected with his work which he reasonably believed were harmful or potentially harmful to health and safety.

Whereas Sections 44 & 100 ERA 1996 require employees to report their concerns internally in the first instance, Sections 104 & 104A ERA 1996 are relevant to external whistleblowing. These offer some protection to those who assert that their employer has infringed certain statutory rights.

> A dismissal is to be regarded as unfair if the reason or principal reason for it was that the employee
> (i)   brought proceedings against the employer to enforce a relevant statutory right
> (ii) alleged that the employer had infringed a relevant statutory right.[24]

However, it should be noted that both the claim to the right and that it has been infringed must be made in good faith.

Similarly, Section 4(1) of the Sex Discrimination Act 1975 and Section 2(1) of the Race Relations Act 1976 allow a complaint to be brought where the discrimination takes place by reason that the person victimised has "given evidence or information in connection with proceedings brought by any person against the discriminator or any other person" under the Act, or "has alleged that the discriminator or any other person has committed an act which ... would amount to a contravention of" the Act. This protection is unavailable if the allegation made by the victim is false and not made in good faith. Thus it would seem that the section applies if the allegation was either true but made out of malice, or false but made in good faith.[25] As we will see below, such an approach is less restrictive than the requirements for making a protected disclosure under PIDA 1998.

Prior to the implementation of the PIDA 1998, the general law of unfair dismissal provided scant protection for those making disclosures in the public interest.[26] Apart from the problem of exclusions and qualifications, a dismissal could be justified under Section 98(1) & (2) ERA 1996 either on the grounds of misconduct or "some other substantial reason". Assuming that a potentially fair reason could be established, Section 98(4) ERA 1996 requires a consideration of whether it was reasonable to dismiss in all the circumstances. At this stage the employment tribunal might consider a range of factors, including the employee's motive in making the disclosure and whether steps were taken to resolve the matter internally before going outside the organisation. Also relevant are the general issues of warnings, consultation, consistency of treatment and the availability of alternative employment. Even if there was a finding of unfairness, an employee's desire for reinstatement or re-engagement could be frustrated easily[27] and compensation capped.

Mention should also be made of the Human Rights Act 1998 (HRA 1998), which incorporates the European Convention on Human Rights into UK law. Article 10 of the European Convention states that: "Everyone has the right to freedom of expression. This right shall include freedom to hold opinions and to receive and impart information and ideas without interference by public authority and regardless of frontiers". However, Article 10(2) refers to the necessity for restrictions on this freedom in order to prevent the disclosure of confidential information.

The potential value of Article 10 was highlighted in the case of journalist William Goodwin.[28] When Goodwin's magazine proposed to publish information supplied by an informant about Tetra Ltd, the company obtained an injunction. The High Court ordered Goodwin to reveal his source so that the company could take proceedings against the informant. He refused to do so and was fined £5000 for contempt. The European Court of Human Rights (ECHR) ruled that, since the company was adequately protected by the injunction, the UK courts' treatment of Goodwin constituted an interference with his freedom of expression. The ECHR was of the opinion that this particular freedom constituted one of the essential foundations of a democratic society and the safeguards to be offered to the press were of particular importance. It almost goes without saying that protection for journalists indirectly benefits whistleblowers who offer themselves as sources of information.

The Public Interest Disclosure Act 1998

The purpose of this Act, which was introduced as a Private Member's Bill by the Conservative MP Richard Shepherd, is to protect individuals who make certain disclosures of information in the public interest. It does so, primarily, by inserting a new Part IVA into the ERA and by making other amendments. Part IVA ERA sets out the types of disclosure which can give rise to protection (a "qualifying disclosure"); the circumstances in which a "qualifying disclosure" will be protected (a "protected disclosure"); and the workers to whom the protection applies. Thus, in a sense, the approach of the common law to disclosures in the public interest has been maintained, i.e. for protection to be afforded the information must be of a particular kind and revealed to an appropriate person. What is different is that the factors to be taken into account are known in advance. Nevertheless, because there is considerable imprecision in the legislation, much will depend on the interpretation given by employment tribunals.

We have seen above that Section 43B(1) ERA defines a "qualifying disclosure" very broadly. The six categories are not restricted to confidential information and there is no requirement for any link between what is revealed and the worker's employment. Indeed, the matter disclosed may have occurred in the past, be currently occurring or likely to occur, and relate to events outside the UK. The main restriction is that a disclosure will not qualify if the worker "commits an offence by making it". Clearly, while the Official Secrets Act 1989 remains on the statute book breaches will not be treated as being in the public interest.[29]

We now turn to the potential recipients of information and the requirements that must be fulfilled for a "qualifying disclosure" to become a "protected disclosure". Section 43C(1) ERA 1996 protects workers who make qualifying disclosures in good faith to their employer or to another person who is responsible for the matter disclosed. On the assumption that internal disclosures are preferable, Part IVA of ERA provides incentives for employers to introduce procedures for reporting concerns but does not oblige them to do so. In the light of recent health and safety disasters and financial scandals, it has been argued that whistleblowing procedures should be mandatory.[30]

Good faith

The requirement of "good faith" will oblige workers to show that they acted honestly. Two main questions arise from making employment protection dependent on the worker's motive (the issue of personal gain is dealt with below). First, is it not foreseeable that the possibility of motive being examined will deter some important disclosures, for example, in relation to serious crime? Second, if motive is relevant, isn't the effect of the right to freedom of expression (see above) to place the burden on the employer to prove that the worker acted in bad faith?

It could also be argued that if a worker reasonably believes that the information is true, the motive for reporting should be disregarded. This would not necessarily expose employers to great harm. Malicious allegations could be deterred by making it a serious disciplinary offence to report a concern where there were no reasonable grounds for believing that the information supplied was accurate (see below on the possible contents of a whistleblowing procedure).

Section 43D ERA encourages workers who have a concern to seek assistance by providing that a disclosure will be protected if it is made in the course of obtaining legal advice. Solicitor-client relationships are also reinforced by Section 43B(4) ERA 1996. This provides that where information has been given to a person in the course of obtaining legal advice, and the information would be subject to professional privilege in legal proceedings, disclosure by that person will not be protected.

Section 43E ERA protects workers in government-appointed organisations (such as non-departmental public bodies) if they make a disclosure in good faith to the sponsor department rather than their legal employer. It is worth noting that the minister, like other designated recipients under the PIDA 1998, has no duty to take any action in relation to matters which may be disclosed. Nevertheless, those who have knowledge of potential wrongdoing may be held liable for culpable inaction under both the civil and criminal law, for example, in relation to health and safety matters.

Section 43F(1) ERA protects workers who make disclosures in good faith to a person (or class of persons) prescribed for the purpose by the Secretary of State.[31] However, the worker must reasonably believe that:

(i)   the matter falls within the remit of the prescribed person
(ii) the information and any allegation contained in it are substantially true.

As regards the second point, it might be argued that the public interest may not be served if workers are deterred by the requirement to demonstrate their reasonable belief in the "substantial truth" of information and allegations. In addition, workers cannot report what they have been told by another person unless they themselves reasonably believe that there is a qualifying disclosure. This is designed to ensure that the prescribed persons are not overwhelmed by hearsay and anecdotal evidence.

Section 43G ERA enables workers to make a protected disclosure to outsiders in other limited circumstances. Parliament's preference for disclosures to be made to employers or prescribed persons is highlighted by the number and nature of the hurdles that must be overcome for protection to be afforded by this section.

For protection to be afforded, workers must:

(i)   act in good faith

(ii)   reasonably believe that the information and any allegation contained in it are substantially true

(iii) not act for personal gain

(iv)   have already disclosed substantially the same information to the employer or to a person prescribed under Section 43F ERA, unless they reasonably believe that they would be subject to a detriment for doing so, or that the employer would conceal or destroy the evidence if alerted

(v)   act reasonably. In assessing reasonableness, regard shall be had, in particular, to
   • the identity of the person to whom the disclosure is made
   • the seriousness of the matter
   • whether there is a continuing failure or one likely to recur
   • whether the disclosure is made in breach of a duty of confidentiality owed by the employer to another person
   • any action the employer (or prescribed person) has taken or might have been expected to take in relation to a previous disclosure
   • whether the worker has complied with any procedure authorised by the employer for making a disclosure.

The issue of disclosing for personal gain is problematic. Since there is a separate requirement to demonstrate good faith, it is clear that this is not being used as a test of the worker's motive. The possibility that personal and public interests might coincide is recognised, to some extent, by Section 43L(2) ERA. This states that for these purposes a reward payable under any enactment will be disregarded.[32] Cheque book journalism may not be desirable but, if a financial incentive enables one disaster to be avoided, isn't disclosure in the public interest? It could be argued that, if all the other requirements of Section 43G ERA are satisfied, it may not be appropriate to oblige workers to prove that their purpose was not personal gain.

Section 43H ERA deals with disclosures about exceptionally serious failures. In order to be protected workers must fulfil the first three requirements of Section 43G ERA (above). In addition, the relevant failure must be of an exceptionally serious nature and it must be reasonable in all the circumstances to make the disclosure. Again Parliament's concern that disclosures should be no wider than necessary is emphasised by reference, in particular, to the identity of the recipient in determining reasonableness. It would defeat the object of this catch-all section if failures of an exceptionally serious nature were defined by statute. However, the effect is that these will be determined by employment tribunals and the courts on a case-by-case basis. Thus, as with the common law, workers will learn only after the event whether their disclosures were protected.

Section 43K(1) ERA is designed to enable everyone who works to benefit from Part IVA ERA. Thus the definition of "worker" in Section 230 ERA is extended for these purposes to include certain agency workers, certain workers who would not otherwise be covered because they are not obliged to carry out all of their duties personally, NHS practitioners such as GPs, certain dentists, pharmacists and opticians and certain trainees. Section 43K(2) ERA extends the definition of employer accordingly. In the author's opinion, granting employment protection rights to the widest range of people is desirable as a matter of principle.[33]

Detriment and dismissal

Section 47B(1) ERA provides the right not to be subjected to any detriment on the ground that the worker has made a protected disclosure. A major issue here is whether tribunals will use the Human Rights Act 1998 to interpret this section purposively by applying it to those who have been penalised for "attempting to make" a protected disclosure. If they do not, the consequences could be grave – employers will have an incentive to victimise those who are in the process of exposing misdeeds but have not completed the procedure.[34] Although Section 47B(1) ERA does not deal with a detriment imposed by someone who has no direct relationship with the worker, workers may complain that their employer has subjected them to a detriment by failing to protect them from the actions of third parties (for example, another employer).

Section 103A ERA makes it automatically unfair to dismiss employees on the grounds that they have made a protected disclosure. Similarly, Section 105(6A) ERA 1996 makes it unfair to select employees for redundancy if the reason for doing so is that they have made a protected disclosure. In both situations the normal qualifying period of service and the upper age limit do not apply. In addition, Section 237(1A) TULRCA 1992 is amended so that an employee who is taking part in an unofficial strike or other unofficial industrial action who is dismissed for making a protected disclosure can complain of unfair dismissal. Interim relief is provided for and Section 124(1A) ERA 1996 allows unlimited compensation to be awarded for dismissal contrary to Section 103A or 105(6A) ERA 1996.

In relation to general exclusions and qualifications, it should be noted that Part IVA ERA 1996 applies to Crown employees who are not subject to a certificate exempting them on grounds of national security. However, it does not currently apply to the security services or those who have a contract of employment in the police service.

Employment tribunal cases

Finally, it might be worth referring to some of the early cases under the legislation.

In *Miklaszewicz v Stolt Offshore Ltd*[35] the Scottish Court of Session had to decide whether or not an employment tribunal had jurisdiction to consider a complaint under Section 103A ERA 1996. The protected disclosure was originally made to the Inland Revenue when the applicant was dismissed in 1993. However, he continued to work in the oil industry and was hired again by Stolt Ltd in 1999. When he was informed in September 2000 that his employment was terminated on the grounds of redundancy, the applicant alleged that the real reason for the dismissal was the disclosure he made in 1993. In remitting the case back to the employment tribunal for a full hearing, the court held that it is the dismissal that triggers the employee's entitlement to invoke the statutory remedies. The making of the disclosure requires to be considered at that time and it is then that the criteria for treating it as a protected disclosure are applicable. It is immaterial whether the disclosure was made before or after the Public Interest Disclosure Act 1998 came into force (2 July 1999).

In *Parkins v Sodexho Ltd*,[36] Parkins alleged that he was dismissed after complaining about lack of adequate on-site supervision. He maintained that this gave rise to a breach of contract and therefore constituted a protected disclosure. In allowing his appeal from the decision of the Employment Tribunal, the EAT accepted that a legal obligation which arises from a contract of employment falls within Section 43B(1)(b) ERA 1996 (see above).

In *Stephens v Englishcombe House Residential Home*[37] a night supervisor complained to management that medical treatment had not been properly administered. The tribunal held that this was a health and safety issue and amounted to a qualifying disclosure within Section 43B ERA 1996.

In *Chattenton v City of Sunderland City Council*,[38] Chattenton reported finding pornographic images on a personal computer in his office. The tribunal accepted that there was a qualifying disclosure because Chattenton reasonably believed that a criminal offence had been committed.

In *Boughton v National Tyre Ltd*[39] the tribunal found that Boughton had made a protected disclosure because he reasonably and genuinely believed that a criminal offence had occurred and reported this to a senior manager. The senior manager failed both to investigate the information and to show support for Boughton. The tribunal held that he had been entitled to consider himself constructively dismissed and that this was automatically unfair under Section 103A ERA.

By way of contrast:

> In *Yates v Endoline Machinery Ltd*,[40] it was held that there had been no qualifying disclosure. According to the tribunal, when Yates said "I believe that there have been various kinds of wrongdoing", this was simply an allegation rather than a disclosure of information. The tribunal also doubted whether Yates had a reasonable belief that the allegations were well-founded and held that they had not been made in good faith.

> In *Bladon v ALM Medical Services Ltd*[41] the tribunal decided that Bladon's first disclosure about the standard of patient care, to the managing director's personal assistant, was a protected disclosure to the employer under Section 43C ERA. The tribunal also found that Bladon's second disclosure, to the Social Services Inspectorate, was protected under Section 43G ERA for the following reasons. Bladon reasonably believed that his allegations were substantially true; he had previously made them to his employer and his disclosure was reasonable in the circumstances. The information was of a serious nature, the Social Services Inspectorate was an appropriate investigatory body and his employer did not have a whistleblowing procedure. After finding Bladon's dismissal automatically unfair, the tribunal awarded £13,000 compensation for past and future loss. It awarded a further £10,000 under Section 49(2) ERA for the detrimental treatment he had suffered. This took account of injury to Bladon's feelings and contained a substantial element of aggravated damages.

The highest compensation for unfair dismissal to date is the £293,441 awarded to Antonio Fernandes.[42] Mr Fernandes, a chief financial officer, had suspicions about expenses claims and was dismissed after sending a letter and supporting documents to members of the management board. Fernandes obtained interim relief and an order for continuation of his contract pending a tribunal hearing. The tribunal found him to have been unfairly dismissed for making a protected disclosure and were of the view that the 58-year old would not secure similar work in the future. He was therefore entitled to be compensated for losses up to retirement age.

Conclusion

If the public interest in protecting whistleblowers was never clearly articulated prior to the PIDA 1998, this legislation attempts to do so, albeit in a restrictive fashion.[43] We have noted that PIDA 1998 offers nothing to citizens who wish to report employer wrongdoing but do not have the status of being a "worker". For less obvious reasons, the legislation fails to deal with discrimination at the hiring stage against those who have made a protected disclosure. Although cynics will argue that victimisation in the recruitment process can easily be concealed,

Parliament has marked its disapproval in relation to discrimination on the grounds of sex, race, disability and trade union membership. In the author's opinion, workers should have the right to complain about any situation in which they believe they have been victimised for making (or attempting to make) a protected disclosure.

Although Lord Nolan commended the PIDA 1998 for so skillfully achieving the essential but delicate balance . . . between the public interest and the interests of employers, it could be argued that in reality employers' interests have been given priority. Of course, it remains to be seen how the PIDA 1988 will operate in practice and whether it will be bolstered by the implementation of the Human Rights Act 1998 and the Freedom of Information Act 2000. Section 3(1) of the HRA 1998 requires employment tribunals to give effect to primary and subordinate legislation in a way which is compatible with the European Convention on Human Rights "so far as it is possible to do so". In addition, it will make it "unlawful for a public authorities to act in a way that is incompatible with a Convention right" (see above on freedom of expression). One possibility is that workers employed by public authorities will be able to use both the PIDA 1988 and the HRA 1988 to justify their disclosures.

The management of whistleblowing

Why have a whistleblowing code?

In the USA, the Organizational Sentencing Guidelines have focused attention on the extent to which employers have developed self-governance systems that address whistleblowers' concerns. To take advantage of these Guidelines employers must adopt mechanisms to promote internal reporting and to facilitate remedial action in the event that concerns prove well founded. We have seen that the Public Interest Disclosure Act 1998 does not oblige UK employers to have whistleblowing codes or procedures but provides obvious benefits to those who have them. According to Public Concern at Work (PCAW),"unless there are effective procedures in place which demonstrate your organisation's willingness to listen and address concerns, employees are more likely to take their concerns outside – and to be protected by the Act in doing so. Employers with good whistleblowing policies and procedures are less likely to be exposed to claims under the Act. Additionally, it is less likely that any wider public disclosure will be protected under the Act".[44]

The responsibility for creating an open and communicative culture rests with top management. In practice many organisations will give the personnel or human resources department the task of devising a whistleblowing procedure and ensuring that it fits in with other procedures. Indeed, unless careful consideration is given to the potential impact of whistleblowing on discipline (see below) there may be a suspicion that a new procedure could be used to monitor performance and investigate staff without their knowledge. If everyone in the organisation is to understand why a whistleblowing procedure is being introduced and what it is trying to achieve, it is vital to get the commitment of both senior management and worker representatives.[45] Ideally there should be agreement as to the contents of a whistleblowing code which contains both a policy statement and a procedure.

The following arguments might be used in order to persuade top management of the desirability of formulating such a code:

(i)   By deterring malpractice and avoiding crisis management it can contribute to the efficient running of the organisation.

(ii) By providing accountability it can help to maintain the organization's reputation.

(iii) It can help to ensure compliance with the law and minimise external disclosures.

(iv) It is a good practice which does not cost much to implement.

A survey of 57 private and 57 public sector organisations conducted by Industrial Relations Services Employment Trends and Public Concern at Work in May 1999 (henceforward the IRS/PCAW survey) found that 46 organisations had, and 44 intended to introduce shortly, a whistleblowing policy.[46] Public sector employers were more likely than those in the private sector to have a policy or have plans – 95% compared with 63% in the private sector. Respondents were asked to indicate from a given list what provided the impetus to introduce a whistleblowing policy. Several employers offered more than one reason but the motives behind the introduction of such policies were the same within both the public and private sector. The reasons identified were: good practice (60 employers); to comply with the law (38 employers); because management saw it as an issue (20 employers); requested by a union (six employers) and because an incident highlighted the need for a policy (two employers)

A survey of 600 colleges and universities conducted by researchers at Middlesex University in 2000 (henceforward the education survey), revealed that 91% of respondents had a whistleblowing procedure;[47] 43% of these procedures had been in operation for more than twelve months. When asked why their procedure had been introduced, 260 institutions indicated that it was a result of good practice, 193 suggested compliance with the law, 114 stated that it was a management initiative, six said that it was prompted by an incident and two mentioned that it was introduced as a result of a trade union initiative.

In 2001 the same researchers at Middlesex University carried out a survey of the 414 English and Welsh local authorities on behalf of the Employers Organisation for Local Government (the local authority survey).[48] 93% of respondents stated that they had a whistleblowing procedure and 86% of procedures had been in existence for more than a year.[49] The most frequently cited reasons for introducing a procedure were good practice (89%), compliance with the law (44%) and management initiative (43%).

Formulating a whistleblowing policy

Before discussing the issues involved in devising an appropriate whistleblowing *procedure*, the possible contents of a whistleblowing *policy* will be considered.

In order to reflect the Nolan Committee's views on best practice in this area, it is suggested that such a policy might contain the following:

(i)   a clear statement that malpractice is taken seriously in the organisation and an indication of the sorts of matters regarded as malpractice

(ii) respect for the confidentiality of staff raising concerns if they wish, and the opportunity to raise concerns outside the line management structure

(iii) penalties for making false and malicious allegations

(iv) an indication of the proper way in which concerns may be raised outside the organisation if necessary.[50]

According to the Institute of Management Foundation's "Action checklist":

To be effective there should be a sense of organizational ownership of a whistleblowing policy. Discuss the issues at the beginning, explaining the reasons behind the policy and dealing with objections and worries. Circulate the draft policy to employees or make it available for comments and suggestions.[51]

In the author's opinion, a policy statement is likely to be more influential if it has been agreed with or discussed by relevant trade unions (or other workers' representatives) and has their support. Trade unions have always had an important role as a watchdog and have supported members who "speak up". They are likely to be keen to be involved, particularly if they can negotiate over both the contents of the procedure and how problems which it highlights can be resolved. Indeed, some unions have firm ideas about how they would like such procedures to operate.[52] Reflecting the fact that trade unions are more likely to be recognised by public sector than private sector employers, 34 public sector employers in the IRS/PCAW survey involved a trade union representative in formulating a whistleblowing policy compared with eight private sector organisations. Indeed, three public sector respondents negotiated the introduction of their policies. In the education survey, 78% of respondents indicated that a trade union was consulted about the introduction of a whistleblowing procedure. 97% of local authorities which had a procedure stated that a trade union was consulted about its introduction.

Who and what should be covered by a procedure?

Perhaps the first matter to be addressed in relation to a whistleblowing procedure is its scope - to whom does it apply and what issues does it cover? Given the broad definition of a worker contained in Section 43K (1) of the Employment Rights Act 1996 (see above), a procedure should apply not only to employees but should also extend to contractors and other suppliers of services.

The respondents to the education survey indicated that their whistleblowing procedures were open to a wide range of people: 319 institutions made their procedure available to employees, 130 to students, 81 to contractors, 67 to self-employed people, 66 to members of the public, 57 to sub-contractors and 52 to suppliers. In the local authority survey, 100% of respondents stated that employees could use the procedure, 48% indicated that the procedure was open to contractors, 42% to councillors, 34% to sub-contractors, 30% to suppliers, 27% to the self-employed and 26% to members of the public. Thus both of these surveys demonstrate that a significant number of respondents have opened their procedures to people who do not work for them.

As regards coverage of issues, a whistleblowing procedure does not replace existing procedures, for example, those for handling grievances or equal opportunity matters.[53] Thus it should be made clear that the whistleblowing procedure is intended to be used only where a concern falls outside the scope of other procedures. According to the Chartered Institute of Personnel and Development, "It is preferable to deal with whistleblowing separately, rather than as an extension to or part of an existing procedure, while cross referencing procedures on discipline and grievances. This is mainly because the scale of risk to the organisation and to the employee will generally be significantly greater in whistleblowing cases than with other matters. In addition, the whistleblower may have no grievance in relation to terms and conditions, or indeed in relation to the employer (his or her concern may for example relate to the conduct of a contractor)".[54]

A procedure should obviously allow concerns to be raised about the following matters because they are treated by Section 43B(1) Employment Rights Act 1996 as "qualifying disclosures":
(i)   a criminal offence
(ii)   a failure to comply with any legal obligation
(iii) danger to the health and safety of any individual
(iv)   damage to the environment
(v)   the deliberate concealment of information tending to show any of the matters listed above.

However, the organisation may wish to go further by inviting people to report concerns about other unethical conduct.[55] If that is the case, it is obviously imperative to ensure that the contents of any code of conduct or ethics are also well understood.

In the education survey, 89% of respondents who had a procedure indicated that it had never been used and the remainder stated that it had been invoked on less than five occasions. The following types of issue had been reported: 33 mentioned malpractice, 21 stated fraud, 12 indicated health and safety concerns, 11 pointed to harassment and six to discrimination. By way of contrast, 57% of respondents in the local authority survey had some experience of their procedure being invoked. However, the main types of issue reported were similar: fraud, malpractice and harassment.

Confidentiality and anonymity

The next issue to be considered is that of safeguards. A whistleblowing procedure should assure potential users that, whenever possible, the organisation will protect the identity of those who raise a concern and do not want their name disclosed. However, it must also be pointed out that the investigation of a concern may occasionally reveal the source of information. In addition, the organisation may require a statement by the person reporting the concern as part of the process of collecting evidence.

Employers tend to discourage anonymous reporting on the grounds that it is often not very helpful and might suggest that the discloser is doing something morally wrong. Nevertheless, an organisation might wish to reserve the right to consider concerns which are raised anonymously. In exercising any discretion the factors to be taken into account might include the seriousness of the issues raised and the likelihood of obtaining information from attributable sources.

Two-thirds of employers in the IRS/PCAW survey indicated that their whistleblowing policy offered confidentiality to users. Information supplied anonymously was recorded by 62% of respondents. In the education survey, 95% indicated that confidentiality was maintained but only 54% of respondents permitted anonymous reporting. In the local authority survey, 94% had procedures which specified that confidentiality would be maintained and 89% of respondents allowed concerns to be reported anonymously. Thus, not surprisingly, the research shows that confidentiality is consistently seen as a greater priority that anonymity.

Dealing with reprisals and malicious allegations

Perhaps the best way of acknowledging the perceived vulnerability of whistleblowers would be to give undertakings about possible reprisals. The Public Interest Disclosure Act 1998 provides legal remedies both to those who are dismissed and to those who are subjected to a detriment for making a protected disclosure (see above). A whistleblowing procedure should therefore include an unequivocal statement to the effect that the employer will not tolerate any harassment or victimisation (including informal pressures) and will take appropriate action in order to protect a person who has reasonable grounds for raising a concern. Thus disciplinary rules should state that victimisation or deterring employees from raising legitimate concerns will constitute serious misconduct.

Additional steps may have to be taken to ensure that non–employees are protected from reprisals. Less than a half of respondents (44) in the IRS/PCAW survey reported that victimisation of a whistleblower would lead to disciplinary action. However, 63% of respondents indicated that it was a disciplinary offence to destroy or conceal evidence of malpractice. In the education survey, 72% of respondents indicated that their procedure provided for disciplinary action to be taken against those who victimise anyone reporting a concern. The equivalent figure in the local authority survey was 85% of respondents.

Employers should also make it clear that they will protect themselves and their staff from false and malicious expressions of concern by taking disciplinary action where appropriate. It is interesting that in both the education and local authority surveys, 90% of respondents stated that their procedure provided for disciplinary action to be taken against those who maliciously reported a concern. Of course, concerns which are genuinely believed may prove to be unfounded on investigation. Thus organisations should also undertake to ensure that the negative impact of either a malicious or unfounded allegation about any person is minimized. One way of protecting managers from disgruntled poor performers is by ensuring that performance reviews are properly documented.

Obtaining advice and assistance

It follows from what has been said already that a whistleblowing procedure should specifically encourage workers to seek advice at an early stage. It should indicate where advice can be obtained internally, for example, from designated persons (see below). However, in recognition of the fact that some workers might insist on a more objective or independent opinion, it might also be sensible to inform staff about external sources, for example, Public Concern at Work's confidential helpline or persons prescribed by the Public Interest Disclosure (Prescribed Persons) Order 1999.

In addition, workers should be informed that they have the right to be represented by their trade union, staff association or a friend when invoking the procedure.[56] Two-thirds of respondents in the IRS/PCAW survey stated that employees could bring a union representative or colleague with them to a meeting dealing with a concern. Just over a third of respondents (largely in the public sector) said that independent advice was available to whistleblowers. In the education survey, 83% of respondents stated that people could bring a representative to a meeting to discuss a concern and 51% indicated that independent advice was available; 97% of respondents in the local authority survey indicated that a person reporting a concern could bring a representative of their choice along to a meeting and 62% stated that independent advice was available.

With whom should a concern be raised?

Concerns should normally be raised initially with an appropriate level of line management, that is the immediate supervisor or his/her manager. However, the most appropriate person to contact will depend upon the seriousness and sensitivity of the issues involved and who is suspected of malpractice. Thus it is recommended that included in or attached to the procedure should be the names and work addresses of "designated persons". Such people will be those who have agreed to be a point of contact for workers wishing to report a concern but do not want to approach their line manager initially. For example, departmental heads, the chief accountant or head of human resources might be appropriate to serve as "designated persons". Under such a scheme line managers would report that a concern had been received by them via a "designated person".

In some organisations "hotlines" have been introduced as an alternative channel of communication.[57] In the IRS/PCAW survey, 23% of respondents provided a telephone "hotline" to enable employees to raise a concern. In the education survey only 2% of respondents operated such a "hotline" but 33% of respondents in the local authority survey stated that they did so. Whether a "hotline" operates internally or via an external provider, information about a concern should eventually reach a "designated person" or the person in the organisation who is ultimately responsible for ensuring concerns are investigated.

Almost two-thirds of respondents in the IRS/PCAW survey had policies which indicated that an employee could raise a concern with someone other than their immediate line manager. In the education survey, 93 institutions stated that concerns should be reported to a line manager, 70 to the principal/vice-chancellor, 57 (colleges) to the clerk/secretary to the corporation, 48 to the head of human resources, 40 (colleges) to the clerk to the governors/the governors themselves, 32 to designated officers/advisors/assessors, 28 to the director of finance and 25 to the head of department. As alternative recipients of concerns, 127 indicated the clerk to the governors/the governors themselves, 99 respondents mentioned the principal/vice-chancellor, 46 suggested the head of human resources. 65% of respondents in the local authority survey said that concerns should normally be reported to the line manager. However, various people were regarded as alternative recipients of a concern.

How should a concern be raised?

A whistleblowing procedure should give people the choice of raising their concerns verbally or in writing. Those wishing to make a written report could be encouraged to use a particular format. For example, to give relevant times and dates in describing the background to the concern and to state why the worker is particularly worried about the situation. It should be made clear that, although whistleblowers are not expected to prove the truth of an allegation, it will be necessary to demonstrate to the person contacted that there are sufficient grounds for concern. It might also be pointed out that the earlier a concern is expressed the easier it might be to take remedial action.

How should a concern be handled?

To avoid doubt, it might be useful if the procedure states that the action to be taken by the organisation will depend on the nature of the concern. An initial confidential interview should be conducted by the "designated person" who should send an agreed summary or report of it to the person with overall responsibility for the whistleblowing procedure. This "responsible person", who should be the chief executive or other senior person in the organisation, should maintain a record of concerns raised and their outcomes for monitoring purposes (see below).

In the IRS/PCAW survey 44% of respondents stated that the director or chief executive had overall responsibility for the whistleblowing policy. In the education survey, 58% of colleges indicated that the governing body had overall responsibility for the whistleblowing procedure, 21% pointed to the principal and 10% to the human resources department. In universities, 45% stated that the governing body had overall responsibility, 40% mentioned the vice-chancellor and 11% pointed to the human resources department. In local authorities, the monitoring officer (39%) and the chief executive (34%) were most likely to have overall responsibility for the procedure. The head of human resources was mentioned by only 8% of respondents.

On the basis of the "designated person's" summary or report, the "responsible person" should decide whether or not an investigation is required and, if so, what form it should take. Where a concern is about the "responsible person", the "designated person" should refer the matter to the chairperson of the organisation (or equivalent) who will decide how to proceed and whether an external investigation is appropriate. Concerns or allegations which fall within the scope of other procedures, for example discrimination issues, should normally be referred for consideration under those procedures.

In the IRS/PCAW survey, 44 respondents followed a set procedure for investigating an allegation. 25 respondents indicated that the line manager was responsible for investigating concerns and 23 stated that the personnel function leads the investigation. The education survey reveals that the person most likely to be responsible for investigating concerns at colleges was the clerk/secretary to the corporation. At universities, auditors were most likely to have this responsibility. In the local authority survey, respondents indicated that the following investigated concerns: internal audit (64%); monitoring officer (51%); line manager (41%); Head of Department (37%); chief executive (30%) and Head of Human Resources (29%).

The whistleblowing procedure should point out that some concerns may be dealt with by agreed action without the need for investigation. Equally, sometimes, urgent action may be required before any investigation is conducted. In order to protect the confidentiality both of the person reporting and the subject of the concern, it should be provided that the person being investigated will not be informed until (or if) it becomes necessary to do so. It must also be pointed out that where there are serious allegations of misconduct a person under investigation may have to be suspended.[58] If as a result of an investigation a prima facie case of misconduct is established, the organisation's disciplinary rules and procedure will have to be invoked.

As with other employment procedures, it is good practice for a whistleblowing procedure to contain time limits for action to be taken.

Within a stipulated period after a concern has been raised, for example 10 working days, the "designated person" should:
(i)   send the whistleblower a copy of the initial interview summary which was sent to the "responsible person"
(ii)   state how the organisation proposes to deal with the matter and whether preliminary enquiries have been conducted
(iii) indicate whether further investigations will take place and, if not, why not
(iv)   give an estimate as to how long it will take to provide a final response
(v)   supply information about staff support mechanisms, for example advice and counselling.

The amount of contact between the whistleblower and those investigating the concern will depend on the nature of the concern, the potential difficulties involved and the clarity of the information that has been provided. The procedure should point out that, where necessary, further information may be sought from the whistleblower. Indeed, where very serious allegations are made it may be appropriate to hold a formal enquiry and/or refer the matter to the police. Whistleblowers should also be reminded that they have the right to be represented by trade union, staff association or friend at any stage.

In order to demonstrate the efficacy of the procedure (and avoid legitimate external disclosures) whistleblowers need to be assured that their concerns have been properly addressed. Thus the procedure should specify that the "responsible person" will inform the "designated person" as to the outcome of any investigation. In turn, the "designated person" should arrange a meeting with the whistleblower in order to provide as much information as possible about the outcome of any investigation. Again, this feedback should be provided within agreed time limits. More than two-thirds of respondents in the IRS/PCAW survey aimed to inform the whistleblower about the outcome of the investigation.

In the education survey, 90% of respondents stated that people were kept informed about the progress of an investigation. The equivalent figure in the local authority survey was 91%.

Taking the matter further

The whistleblowing procedure is intended to provide workers with an avenue to raise concerns within the organisation. However, a person who is dissatisfied with the organisation's response may wish to take the matter outside.

Since workers have legal protection if they make external disclosures in certain circumstances, it is in an employer's interest to specify whom they regard as appropriate recipients. It is obviously desirable that any external scrutiny is conducted by a reputable body rather than the general media. Thus employers are advised to draw attention to the list of persons prescribed by regulations, relevant professional bodies or agencies with specialist expertise, for example, Public Concern at Work. Although employers would prefer workers who take their concern outside the organisation not to divulge confidential information, it should be noted that Section 43J ERA 1996 renders "gagging clauses" ineffective in so far as they purport to inhibit a person from making a protected disclosure. In the IRS/PCAW survey 58 respondents (51%) stated that if the whistleblower is dissatisfied with how their concern has been handled they can take it further. In the education survey, 88% of respondents had a procedure which specified another person who could be approached if the whistleblower was dissatisfied in the outcome of an investigation. The equivalent figure in the local authority survey was 79%.

Communicating and monitoring the procedure

Workers can be made aware of the contents of a whistleblowing procedure by a variety of mechanisms, for example, staff handbooks, induction training, printed policy statements, intranet web pages, posters, contracts of employment, newsletters, e-mail and payslips. All three surveys referred to in this chapter show that the method most commonly used was the staff handbook. The other methods most frequently used in the education and local authority surveys were the induction programme, printed policy statements and web pages. Ideally a flowchart or diagram should be supplied with the procedure which shows precisely how the organisation will process a concern.

According to the IRS/PCAW survey, training for managers about how the whistleblowing policy works was not common – only 18 respondents (16%) had instigated this and 12 (11%) were planning to do so. However, 24 respondents (21%) trained managers on what they should do if a concern was raised and a further 11 (10%) planned to offer such training. Issuing written guidance was the most common form of training. In the Middlesex education survey, 14% of respondents indicated that training in the whistleblowing procedure was provided. By and large this was designed for people who might have to handle concerns rather than those who might wish to raise them. In the local authority 33% of respondents survey indicated that training was provided for managers in how to handle concerns. Coincidentally, the same percentage stated that training was provided for employees in how to use the procedure. In both cases, the induction process and written instructions were the forms of training most frequently mentioned.

As with other procedures, it would be sensible for employers to commit themselves to monitor and review the operation of the whistleblowing procedure on a regular basis. In the IRS/PCAW survey 60% of respondents indicated that they maintained records of how a concern was dealt with under their policy. Details were kept about how a concern was raised, how it was handled and the outcome. Over half of the respondents stated that they reviewed the policy and 61% did so on an annual basis. Many organisations used a combination of personnel specialists, senior management and a working group to review the policy. In the education survey, 77% of institutions claimed that their whistleblowing procedure was monitored and, of these, 77% stated that this occurred annually, 55% of respondents in the local authority survey stated that the effectiveness of their procedure was monitored and, of these, 73% stated that this occurred annually or more frequently.

Individuals who invoked the procedure might be asked if they were satisfied with the way their concerns were dealt with and if they suffered any reprisals. More generally, an attitude survey might be conducted to discover whether staff think that the organisational culture supports the raising of concerns. Monitoring and review are particularly important in the light of the Public Interest Disclosure Act 1998. Put simply, if an internal procedure is defective it may be easier to demonstrate that an external disclosure was reasonable under Sections 43G and 43H ERA 1996.

Summary and conclusion

Employees are often the first to realise that there may be something seriously wrong within an organisation. However, they may not express their concerns because they feel that "speaking up" would be disloyal to their colleagues or to their employer. They may also fear harassment or victimisation. In these circumstances it may be easier to turn a blind eye rather than report what may just be a suspicion of malpractice. Thus in order to prevent problems being overlooked and to avoid legal pitfalls, personnel practitioners should endeavour to devise policies and procedures which both encourage and enable staff to report their concerns.

Such a procedure should aim to:

(i)   define the types of concern that it covers. This definition may well be broader than the matters regarded as "qualifying disclosures" by Section 43B ERA 1996

(ii)   explain its relationship to other procedures. For example, that it does not replace harassment or grievance procedures but is intended to cover circumstances which fall outside their remit. It should also be made clear that the disciplinary procedure may be invoked if there are no reasonable grounds for making an allegation

(iii)   indicate how and with whom concerns should be raised and the advice and support that is available (both internally and externally)

(iv)   allow staff to be accompanied by a representive of their choice at any meetings or interviews connected with the concerns raised

(v)   outline a target timetable for the employer's response and provide feedback on the outcome of any investigation and any action taken

(vi)   indicate how staff can take the matter further if they are dissatisfied with the employer's response

(vii)   reassure staff that they will be protected from possible reprisals or victimisation.

Despite all that has been said above, it could be argued that it is not the precise arrangements established by an organisation that are significant. What is essential, however, is that employers demonstrate commitment to ethical behaviour at the highest level, that procedures for handling concerns are agreed with employee representatives and communicated to the workforce and that staff is positively encouraged to use them when appropriate. Certainly those who have introduced whistleblowing procedures see them as contributing to their image as an ethical and efficient organisation. They may also be less likely to fall foul of the law.

Notes

[1]   Nader, Ralph, Petkas, Peter and Blackwell, Kate (eds). *Whistleblowing: The Report of the Conference on Professional Responsibility*, Bantam (New York: 1972)

[2]   Senate Select Committee on Public Interest Whistleblowing, "In the Public Interest", AGPS, Canberra, 1994, paragraph 2.2. For other definitions see Jubb, Peter. "Whistleblowing: A Restrictive Definition and Interpretation" in *Journal of Business Ethics*, 1999, pp 77-94

[3]   Senate Select Committee on Public Interest Whistleblowing, "In the Public Interest", AGPS, Canberra, 1994, paragraph 2.12

[4]   It should be acknowledged that some writers do not accept that internal disclosures amount to whistleblowing: see Jubb, Peter. "Whistleblowing: A Restrictive Definition and Interpretation" in *Journal of Business Ethics*, 1999, pp 77-94

5   Micelli, M and Near J. *Blowing the whistle*, Lexington Books (New York:1992)

6   On the compatibility of whistleblowing with notions of employee loyalty: see Larmer, Robert "Whistleblowing and Employee Loyalty" in *Journal of Business Ethics*, 1992, pp 125-8

7   See: the False Claims Act 1986 (USA) and the rewards offered by the Inland Revenue and Customs and Excise in the UK

8   See: Sims, Randi and Keenan, John. "Predictors of External Whistleblowing: Organisational and Intrapersonal Variables" in *Journal of Business Ethics*, 1998, pp 411-21

9   See: *The Police*, Public Concern at Work (London: 1993)

10 Department of Transport, "Court of Enquiry No. 8074", HMSO, London, 1987

11 "Public inquiry into the Piper Alpha Disaster", CM 1310, London, 1990

12 Vickers, Lucy, "Protecting whistleblowers at work", Institute of Employment Rights, London, 1995

13 For a useful discussion of the social/psychological dimensions of whistleblowing see: Gobert, James and Punch, Maurice. "Whistleblowers" the Public Interest, and the Public Interest Disclosure Act 1998" in *Modern Law Review*, 2000, pp 25-54

14 (1968) 1 QB 396

15 (1985) QB 526

16 (1989) IRLR 477

17 On the enforceability of secrecy agreements in the USA see: Dworkin, Terry and Callahan, Elletta. "Buying silence" in *American Business Law Journal*, 1998, pp 1594

18 The Fixed Term Employees (Prevention of Less Favourable Treatment) Regulations 2002 came into force on 10th July 2002. These Regulations aim to prevent abuses arising from successive contracts

19 It should be noted that if the police acquire confidential information, which in their reasonable view, in the interests of public health and safety, should be considered by a professional or regulatory body, then they are entitled to give that information to such a body whether or not it was requested: see *Woolgar v Chief Constable of Sussex (1999) 3 AER 604*

20 A claim for malicious falsehood cannot succeed if a whistleblower had an honest belief that an allegation was true

21 It should also be noted that Section 93A of the Criminal Justice Act 1993 imposes a duty on "all persons" to report money laundering

22 (1936) Ch 261

23 (1983) IRLR 253

24 The relevant statutory rights include those conferred by the ERA 1996 which can be exercised at an employment tribunal; some sections of the Trade Union and Labour Relations (Consolidation) Act 1992 and rights conferred by the Working Time Regulations 1998

25 See also Section 55 of the Disability Discrimination Act 1975 which contains analogous provisions

26 The general law of unfair dismissal still applies if a person is sacked for making a disclosure which is not "protected" within the meaning of the PIDA 1998

27 Not only must employment tribunals be persuaded that it would be practicable to order re-employment but the employer could simply choose to pay additional compensation rather than comply with any order: see Sections 116 & 117 ERA 1996

28 See *Goodwin v United Kingdom (1996) 22 EHRR 123*

[29] See *R v David Shayler (2002) AER 477*

[30] See: Lewis, David "Whistleblowers and Job Security" in *Modern Law Review*, 1995, pp 208-21

[31] The Schedule to the Public Interest Disclosure (Prescribed Persons) Order 1999 S.I.1549 specifies the persons prescribed and the description of matters in respect of which they are prescribed

[32] Recent US Federal Statutes and some State laws which provide protection for whistleblowers encourage reports of wrongdoing by offering rewards: see Dworkin, T and Callahan, E. "The state of state whistleblower protection" in *American Business Law Journal*, 2000, Vol.38, pp 99-175

[33] Section 23 of the Employment Relations Act 1999 gives the Secretary of State the power to confer rights on individuals

[34] It is worth noting that several US State statutes protect so-called "embryonic whistleblowers"

[35] (2002) IRLR 344

[36] (2002) IRLR 109

[37] Case 5301067/00

[38] Case 6402938/99

[39] Case 1500080/00

[40] Case 1202582/99

[41] Case 2405845/99

[42] *Fernandes v Netcom Consultants Ltd Case 2200060/00*

[43] For general assessments of PIDA 1998 see: Bowers, John, Mitchell, Jack and Lewis, Jeremy. *Whistleblowing: The New Law*, (London: 1999); Hobby, Catherine. *Whistleblowing and the Public Interest Disclosure Act 1998*, (London: 2001); Lewis, David. "The Public Interest Disclosure Act 1998" in *Industrial Law Journal*, 1998, pp 325-30 and Gobert, James and Punch, Maurice. "Whistleblowers, the Public Interest, and the Public Interest Disclosure Act 1998" in *Modern Law Review*, 2000, pp 25-54

[44] See: PCAW "Policy Pack", London, 1998

[45] It has been suggested that an organization's structure may perform a significant role in deciding whether or not to report wrongdoing. See: King, Granville "The Implications of an Organization's Structure on Whistleblowing" in *Journal of Business Ethics*, 1999, pp 315-26

[46] *Industrial Relations Services Employment Review* No. 685, August 1999

[47] There were 349 respondents, giving a response rate of 58%

[48] There were 281 respondents, giving a response rate of 68%

[49] 53% of procedures had existed for more than 2 years

[50] See: *Second Report of the Committee on Standards in Public Life*, (London: 1996) Volume 1

[51] Institute of Management Foundation "Introducing a Whistleblowing Policy", Checklist 072, 1999

[52] For example, see Frieze, Jennifer and Jennings, Karen. "A trade union perspective on whistleblowing" in *Whistleblowing at Work*, (edited by Lewis, David) Athlone Press (London, 2001)

[53] See paragraph 47 of the ACAS Code of Practice on Disciplinary and Grievance Procedure. 2000

[54] Chartered Institute of Personnel and Development "Whistleblowing", Information Note 32, London, 2000

[55] For example, see the Local Government Management Board's (now Employer's Organisation) "Confidential Reporting Code", London, 1998

[56] Section 10 of the Employment Relations Act 1999 gives workers the right to be accompanied when they attend disciplinary or grievance hearings

[57] See: Lewis, David and Ellis, Catherine. *Confidential Reporting at Work: a survey of employer "hotlines"*, Centre for Research in Industrial and Commercial Law (Middlesex University: 1999)

[58] On the matters that need to be considered before suspending an employee see the Court of Appeal's decision in *Gogay v Hertfordshire County Council (2001) IRLR 703*

8

Transfers of undertakings

STEPHEN CAVALIER

Stephen Cavalier is Head of the Employment Rights Unit at Thompsons Solicitors and Chair of the Industrial Law Society.

Introduction

Few pieces of legislation have provoked as much controversy, confusion and litigation as the Acquired Rights Directive (ARD) and the Transfer of Undertakings (Protection of Employment) Regulations (TUPE).

It is a risky venture to attempt to unravel the convoluted strands of the TUPE story and even riskier to state with certainty the correct interpretation of key provisions or to predict subsequent case law developments. But it is a task that lawyers, and more importantly workers, trade unions, employers, public authorities, courts and governments, must attempt.

The ARD first saw the light of day in 1977 as Council Directive 77/187/EEC. It was amended in 1998 by Council Directive 98/50/EC. The Directive as amended has now been consolidated into Council Directive 2001/23/EC.

The initial UK implementing legislation was the Transfer of Undertakings (Protection of Employment) Regulations 1981. The 1981 Regulations were amended by the Trade Union Reform and Employment Rights Act 1993, the Collective Redundancies and Transfer of Undertakings (Protection of Employment) (Amendment) 1995 and Collective Redundancies and Transfers of Undertakings (Protection of Employment) (Amendment) Regulations 1999.

Details of these provisions and the amendments are discussed later in this chapter. The amendments made to the The ARD by the 1998 Directive have not yet been transposed into UK law and the necessary draft regulations to amend the TUPE have not yet been published.

As the TUPE is intended to implement the ARD, it must be interpreted consistently with the ARD so far as is possible. As with interpretation of all European directives, courts must adopt a "purposive approach", that is, attempting to interpret legislation in a manner consistent with the purpose of the Directive. The preamble to the Directive describes its purpose as:

> to provide for the protection of employees in the event of a change of employer, in particular, to ensure that their rights are safeguarded.[1]

This purpose has played an important part in the interpretation of the ARD and the TUPE by the European Court of Justice (ECJ) and the UK courts and tribunals.

References in this Chapter to Articles are to Articles of the ARD and to Regulations are to Regulations of the TUPE.

Scope

The legislation applies where there is a "relevant transfer". This is a transfer of an undertaking or part of an undertaking from one legal person to another.[2]

There are two questions to be addressed in each case: is there an undertaking and has it been transferred? The two questions sometimes overlap, but they are nonetheless separate issues and both must be satisfied for the legislation to apply.

What is an undertaking?

The ARD now defines an undertaking as

> an organised grouping of resources which has the objective of pursuing an economic activity, whether or not that activity is central or ancillary.[3]

This opaque definition is an attempt by the European legislature to encapsulate the case law of the ECJ on this issue.

The Conservative government which introduced the TUPE in 1981 was hostile to the legislation.[4] The original regulations were limited in coverage to those undertakings in the nature of a commercial venture. This was taken in the UK to exclude from coverage many transfers in the public sector, particularly the contracting out of public services. This narrow interpretation of the ARD on which this exclusion was based was blown away by a series of ECJ decisions in the 1990s. In the case of *Dr Sophie Redmond Stichting v Bartol*,[5] the ECJ decided that the ARD applied to the operation of a non-profit making charity: the ARD applied when there was a transfer of an economic entity and this was not limited to organisations seeking to make a profit. The European Commission had already commenced infringement proceedings against the UK government on this issue in the ECJ. The judgment in 1994 rejected the government's argument and confirmed that the ARD covered all organisations engaged in economic activities.[6]

The TUPE was amended to reflect this in 1993.[7] The amendment was not retrospective. Prior to the amendment, workers transferred within the public sector could rely on the direct effect of the Directive.[8] Workers in the private sector and those transferred from the public to private sector could not rely on this approach. A number of them, backed by their unions GMB, TGWU and UNISON took claims against the UK government based upon the principle in *Francovich v Italian Republic*.[9] In 1997, the then new Labour government rightly conceded that the UK's failure properly to implement the TUPE in this respect was a sufficiently serious breach to give rise to the possibility of compensation from the government under the *Francovich* principle.[10]

The other significant development in relation to the applicability of the ARD and the TUPE to contracting out, was the decision in *Rask and Christensen v ISS Kantineservice A/S*[11] that the ARD applied to the contracting out of a staff canteen. The ARD can apply even where the service concerned is ancillary to the main business and where the facility was only open to staff at the factory at prices fixed by the company which owned the factory and which had contracted out the canteen. This led to subsequent UK decisions confirming the applicability of the ARD to public services such as refuse collection, street cleansing, housing maintenance and hospital cleaning.[12]

The ECJ took a similar view in *Schmidt v Spar und Leihkasse*, a case involving the contract cleaning of a bank – even though only one cleaner was involved[13] reasserting that the ARD applied even where the part of the undertaking carried out an ancillary activity not connected with the objects of the overall undertaking. The *Schmidt* decision prompted a political backlash and also a more restrictive interpretation of the ARD by the ECJ.

In *Rygaard v Stro Molle Akustik*,[14] the ECJ said that the ARD did not apply to an agreement to take over the obligation to perform the remainder of a fixed term building contract for a specific project, because there was not a stable economic entity. However, in a subsequent case the change of a car dealership was held to be covered by the ARD.[15]

The case which has had the most profound impact on subsequent interpretation, and on the revision to the ARD, is *Süzen v Zehnacker Gebaudereinigung GmbH Krankenhausservice*.[16] The ECJ took the view that an undertaking, or an economic entity, could not be interpreted as meaning simply the activity which was being carried out (in this case cleaning). It held that

> the term entity thus refers to an organised grouping of persons and assets facilitating the exercise of an economic activity which pursues an economic objective.[17]

As can be seen earlier, the revised the ARD adopts similar (although not identical) wording. In *Süzen* the ECJ recognised that

> in certain labour-intensive sectors a group of workers engaged in a joint activity on a permanent basis may constitute an economic entity.[18]

The issue was considered again in subsequent ECJ cases concerning contracting out[19] which recognised that whilst such an undertaking must be sufficiently structured and autonomous, it will not necessarily have significant assets and, in certain circumstances these assets are often reduced to their most basic and the activity is essentially based on manpower.[20]

The amendment to the ARD is intended to codify these decisions and should not of itself lead to a change of interpretation.

Transfers within the public sector

As mentioned above, the ARD applies to transfers in the public or private sector. This is confirmed by the amendment to Article 1.1(c) which provides that

> this Directive shall apply to public and private undertakings engaged in economic activities whether or not they are operating for gain.

This codifies the ECJ decisions,[21] but there are limits on the applicability of the ARD in the public sector. In *Henke v Gemeinde Scheirke & Verwaltungsgemeinschaft Brocken*[22] the ECJ decided that the ARD did not apply to the amalgamation of a number of smaller local authorities in Germany to form one larger authority. This decision is reflected in the amended wording now in Article 1.1(c) that the ARD does not apply to

> an administrative reorganisation of public administrative authorities, or the transfer of functions between public authorities.

This restriction should be given a narrow interpretation. This was the view of the ECJ in *Sanchez Hidalgo v Asociación de Servicios Aser*[23] where it stated:

> the fact that the service or contract in question has been contracted out or awarded by a public body cannot exclude application of [ARD] if neither the activity of providing a home-help service to persons in need nor the activity of providing surveillance involves the exercise of public authority.

The UK courts have taken a similarly limited view of *Henke* when deciding that the TUPE applied to various local authority services[24] and this has been reaffirmed by the ECJ. In *Collino v Telecom Italia*[25] the court concluded that the fact that the service transferred was a telecommunications services operation managed by a public body could not exclude the ARD when the service was transferred to a private company. Similarly in *Mayeur v Association Promotion de l'Information Messine*,[26] where the activities of a non-profit making association promoting opportunities offered by a French city were taken over by the local authority. The Directive applied regardless of the legal status of the entity or the manner in which it is funded. A similar view was taken with the re-tendering of bus services, where the ECJ also concluded that the EU Public Procurement Directives do not exempt public authorities and service providers from compliance with the ARD.[27] Most recently the EFTA court, covered by the ARD for these purposes, concluded that the conversion of a state entity into a limited liability company was covered by the Directive.[28]

The UK government currently takes a similar view on the scope of *Henke*. This is reflected in its Cabinet Office guidance "Staff Transfers in the Public Sector"[29] where there is a general assumption that the ARD will apply to public sector transfers and a policy statement that public authorities should behave as though it does, even where there is a doubt.

The government has also taken the power in Section 38 of the Employment Relations Act 1999 to order that particular transfers of functions between state authorities should be treated as though the TUPE applied. This power has already been exercised in relation to the transfer of Rent Officer functions.[30]

Is there a transfer?

Once it is established that there was an undertaking in existence before the change of employer, the next (and crucial) question is whether there has been a transfer of that undertaking.

The identification of the undertaking is important in this context as the question of whether it has transferred will depend upon which of its characteristics are retained by the new operation after the change of employer.

Article 1.1(a) of the ARD says that the Directive applies to a transfer as a result of a legal transfer or merger. The case law makes clear that this is to be interpreted broadly. There is no need for there to be a contract between the old employer and the new employer.[31] The ECJ has applied the ARD to the removal of a grant from one charitable organisation and giving it to another with similar aims[32] and the change of a car dealership from one dealer to another,[33] in each case without a direct contractual relationship between old and new employer. Similarly, there may be a transfer where a public authority which has contracted out a particular service decides to change the contractor providing the service.[34]

The ARD also refers to mergers. However, in the UK, the TUPE does not apply to mergers or takeovers effected by share transfer.[35] Although the TUPE covers a situation where the transfer is effected by sale or by some other disposition or by operation of law,[36] it only applies where there is a transfer from one person to another.[37] Where a company or individual buys the shares of another company and obtains a controlling interest, the legal identity of the company remains the same. If the employees continued to be employed by the company, that is by the same person (so far as the law is concerned) and there is therefore no transfer. However, where there is a transfer between two separate companies, the ARD applies even where the two companies are in the same corporate group with the same ownership, management and premises.[38]

The amended Article 1.1(b) says there is a transfer where there is a transfer of an economic entity which retains its identity.

The starting point is the ECJ's judgment in *Spijkers v Gebroders Benedik Abattoir*,[39] which is relied upon without fail in every subsequent ECJ decision on the issue. The ECJ stressed that the decision is one of fact and that a transfer does not occur merely because a business disposes of its assets to someone else. The court must consider

> whether the business was disposed of as a going concern, as would be indicated, inter alia, by the fact that its operation was actually continued or resumed by the new employer with the same or similar activities.

But this is not enough in itself. The ECJ in *Süzen* emphasised that a continuation of activities is not sufficient. The ECJ in *Spijkers* (reinforced in subsequent cases) said that courts must consider all the facts characterising the transaction in question. These factors included the following:

(i)   whether or not the tangible assets of the business such as buildings and movable property are transferred
(ii) the value of its intangible assets at the time of the transfer
(iii) whether or not the majority of employees are taken over
(iv) whether or not its customers are transferred
(v)   the degree of similarity of activities carried on before or after
(vi) the period, if any, for which the activities were suspended.

This should not be used as a tick list. As we shall see from the cases following *Spijkers*, the court must consider the type of undertaking to assess the factors to be considered and the weight to be given to those factors. The presence, or absence, of one particular factor is not determinative of the issue.

> This approach led the ECJ to conclude that the ARD was capable of applying to a wide range of situations.
>
> (i)   The removal by a local authority of a grant to a charity operating a drug rehabilitation centre and the award of the grant to another operation with similar aims. The functions continued and there was some co-operation on the transfer of responsibilities. No property or assets were sold on.[40]
> (ii) Where Philips contracted out its canteen services at a factory to a catering company which took on full operational responsibility and the existing staff, enjoying use (but not ownership) of the kitchens, storerooms and utensils; in return for a fixed fee from Philips.[41]
> (iii) The contracting out of the cleaning of a bank, even though it was only carried out by one employee who refused to transfer because worse terms were offered. The ECJ said that the similarity in operations before and after transfer was typical of a situation falling within the ARD.[42]
> (iv) Ford changing its Brussels car dealership from one dealer to another, although there was no transfer of assets and different premises were used. Customers were recommended to use the new dealership. There was a transfer even though only a minority of staff transferred.[43]

The ECJ had cautioned that the ARD did not apply to the transfer of a one-off works contract,[44] but the trend had favoured a liberal, inclusive interpretation of the scope of the ARD until the *Süzen* decision.

The ECJ in *Süzen* reached a decision which is difficult to reconcile with earlier cases, yet the ECJ refused to acknowledge it was departing from its previous approach. The ECJ decided that the ARD did not apply to a change from one cleaning contractor to another, despite the fact that the operation continued in a similar way. The ECJ took the view that the similarity between the old operation and the new was not enough. It was not enough that the activity continued as an entity cannot be reduced to the activity entrusted to it.

The *Süzen* decision emphasised the importance of applying the *Spijkers* approach, but drew a distinction between labour-intensive activities and those which require the use of significant assets, so that the degree of importance to be attached to each criterion "will necessarily vary according to the activity carried on, or indeed the production or operating methods employed in the relevant undertaking, business or part of a business".[45]

In a key passage the ECJ concluded

> since in certain labour-intensive sectors a group of workers engaged in a joint activity on a permanent basis may constitute an economic entity, it must be recognised that such an entity is capable of maintaining its identity after it has been transferred where the new employer does not merely pursue the activity in question, but also takes over a major part, in numbers and skills, of the employees specially assigned by his predecessor to that task.[46]

The rationale for this approach was that in those circumstances the new employer takes over a body of assets enabling him to carry on the activities or certain activities of the transferor undertaking on a regular basis.

A similar approach is evident in the subsequent cases of *Sanchez Hidalgo*[47] and *Hernandez Vidal v Gomez Sanchez*,[48] which in dealing with the identity of the undertaking, state that it

> cannot be reduced to the activity entrusted to it. Its identity also emerges from other factors, such as its workforce, its management staff, the way the work is organised, its operating methods or, indeed, where appropriate, the operational resources available to it.

It follows that a comparison must be made between these components before and after the transfer.

Even by the standards of *Suzen*, the ECJ's decision in a case concerning bus services in Helsinki was astounding.[49] The council re-tendered the operation of seven bus routes and the existing contractor was unsuccessful. Out of the 45 drivers, 33 secured jobs with the new contractor, but different buses were used. Astonishingly, the ECJ concluded that as bus transport cannot be regarded as an activity based essentially on manpower, as it requires substantial plant and equipment there was no transfer in the absence of a transfer to a significant extent of the assets necessary for the proper functioning, that is, the buses. This completely overlooks the transfer of the most valuable asset: the exclusive right to operate buses on those routes. It is a poorly reasoned decision, inconsistent with previous cases.

Fortunately, the UK courts, and in particular the Court of Appeal, have not taken such a restrictive approach and have limited the negative impact of the *Süzen* decision. In *ECM (Vehicle Delivery) Services Ltd v Cox*,[50] the appeal court found there was a transfer where a vehicle delivery contract changed hands. The work was to be carried out from a different site, with different arrangements for delivery and administration. The new contractor refused to offer employment to any of the 24 employees.

In *ADI (UK) Limited v Firm Security Group Limited*[51] the court was considering the contracting out of security services at a shopping centre. The staff were not taken on and very little in the way of assets transferred. In *RCO Support Services v UNISON*[52] there were changes in the arrangements for care between hospitals with new contractors winning the contracts for catering and cleaning. There was no transfer of significant assets and none of the employees were taken on by the new contractors. In all the cases, the appeal court decided that the operation effectively continued in different hands and that the TUPE applied.

The Court of Appeal decisions attempt to place *Süzen* in context by emphasising the importance of the earlier ECJ decisions and the need to make a factual appraisal of all the facts characterising the transaction. The court regarded the importance of *Süzen* as overstated, although it did represent a change in emphasis, reinforced by the decision in *Oy Liikenne*, and did set limits on the application of the ARD (and consequently the TUPE). However, this did not mean that there could never be a transfer in a labour-intensive case without a transfer of staff or assets. This is because the court must still consider all the factors identified in *Spijkers*. It would be wrong to regard one factor (the fact that the workforce did not transfer) as determinative of the issue in every case.

This is an enlightened and welcome approach, in contrast to the restrictive (and often contradictory) recent decisions of the ECJ.

There was one further issue which troubled the Court of Appeal in all three cases. In each case, the workforce was not taken on. In *ECM* and *ADI*, there was a finding that this was because of the contractors concerns about the impact of the TUPE. In *RCO*, the workforce were offered jobs if they first resigned from their jobs with the previous contractor and accepted jobs with the new contractor on worse terms and conditions.

The appeal court decided in all three cases that it was entitled to take account of the reason that the employees were not taken on. In the *ECM* and *ADI* cases this was on the basis that the employer was trying to avoid the TUPE. This approach was refined in *RCO* to a consideration, not of the employer's motive, but whether the circumstances of the decision not to take on the workforce pointed towards the application of the TUPE. The willingness to take on the workforce (but for TUPE considerations) was a factor supporting the service retaining its identity and therefore supporting the application of the TUPE.

The effect of a transfer

Automatic transfer

When there is a "relevant transfer" covered by ARD/TUPE, this operates as an automatic transfer of workers, their rights and liabilities. This is the fundamental principle, but it needs to be explored in more detail as there are qualifications and refinements.

All those employed in the part of the undertaking transferred are themselves transferred to the new employer.[53] Their contracts of employment are transferred without being terminated and without a break in service. They retain continuity of employment. They remain entitled to all terms and conditions of employment (except pensions,[54] on which more later).

This is an important protection for employees. It is also an important benefit for employers. It enables an employer selling a business or losing a contract to pass on the workforce to the new employer, without the need to dismiss and without incurring the cost of redundancy payments. The new employer acquires the workforce, whether the workers like it or not and is thus able to continue the operation. Were it not for the TUPE in the UK this would not be the case; the change of employer would bring the employment to an end entitling the employee to redundancy and a notice payment and requiring the new employer to persuade the workforce to accept offers of employment. The ARD should also be seen in this light: as facilitating re-structuring and the transfer of businesses.

As stated, the transfer is automatic. No action is required by employee or employer. Even if the employers attempt to object to the transfer of staff, or postpone it, this will not prevent the transfer. The contracts of employment transfer on the day of the transfer of undertaking and this cannot be avoided or postponed.[55] The transfer takes place automatically even if the employee does not know about it.[56] Some employers seek to get round this by dismissing the employees before the transfer or by refusing to accept them into employment. This may prevent the workers from becoming employees of the transferee, but it will not prevent the transferee from acquiring legal liabilities to those employees.[57]

The employees automatically transferred are those employed in the part transferred immediately before the transfer.[58] Employers tried to get round automatic transfer by dismissing workers before the transfer took place, leaving a gap before the transfer and then re-employing them after the transfer with no continuity of employment and on worse terms and conditions. The practice was particularly common amongst liquidators, receivers and other insolvency practitioners keen to sell insolvent businesses to new owners without any accumulated liabilities to the workforce.

The House of Lords stepped in with a decision which emphasised that the purpose of the ARD (and therefore the TUPE) was to safeguard the rights of employees.[59] They decided that the TUPE operates so that someone who is unfairly dismissed before the transfer for a reason connected with the transfer must be regarded as employed immediately before the transfer and thus entitled to automatic transfer. This meant that employees dismissed in those circumstances could pursue claims against the new employer, not just against the old employer (who in that particular case was insolvent).

This does not conclude the question of whether a dismissal in those circumstances should be regarded as void and of no effect, or whether the dismissal is valid but liability still transfers. This was discussed in a subsequent House of Lords case and will be dealt with later in this chapter when discussing dismissals and changes to contracts.[60]

Automatic transfer means that all rights and liabilities deriving from the employment relationship transfer to the new employer. The UK has not (as yet) taken up the option in the ARD for joint and several liability,[61] so the transferor ceases to have any liabilities and the transferee acquires all of them.[62]

The automatic transfer of rights and liabilities applies not just to contractual terms. Anything done by the old employer in relation to the employee is treated as done by the new employer.[63] This means the new employer becomes liable not just for previous breaches of contract, but other unlawful acts such as sex discrimination,[64] breaches of the equal pay legislation[65] and industrial action (in relation to which the new employer acquires the benefit of the old employer's insurance indemnity in relation to the particular accident).[66]

Continuity of service is preserved, so the employee can count her/his period of employment with the transferor and transferee combined for the purposes of qualifying for statutory rights such as unfair dismissal protection, redundancy and maternity rights, as well as contractual benefits dependent on length of service.

Those employed in the part transferred

Automatic transfer only applies to those employed in the undertaking or part transferred.[67] This is simple to apply when the whole business is transferred; less so when part of an undertaking is transferred.

The test is whether the employee is assigned to the part transferred.[68] This may either be expressly in the contract or job description of the employee or it may be evident from the duties actually carried out. The ECJ in that case said that a person would not be assigned to the part transferred if they merely carried out administrative or other duties for the part concerned if they were not employed in it or assigned to it.

In a case in the UK, a student nurse undergoing training was found not to be part of the hospital in which he was training at the time the hospital transferred, as he was not assigned to that particular hospital;[69] but other decisions show a more pragmatic approach based upon the practical realities. Security guards who had worked for many years at a particular location, but whose contracts contained a mobility clause which could require them to work elsewhere, were held as employed at the location where they were working.[70] An employee was protected when one company in a group transferred even though his contract required him to work for other parts of the business.[71] An employee who worked for both the sales and servicing sides of a business was employed in the part transferred, even though only one side transferred.[72]

The courts have generally taken a flexible approach and looked at factors such as how much time was spent on different parts of the business, how much value was given to each part, what the contract said about the employee's duties, how the cost of the employee was shared between the parts of the business and whether the employee was retained to work in the part transferred pre- or post-transfer. The employee need not work in the part transferred to the exclusion of all others.

A right to object?

The ARD does provide workers with a right to object to the automatic transfer of their contracts of employment, but in the UK it is a right without any accompanying protection. The right derives from an ECJ decision.[73] The ECJ said that, whilst the principle of employee protection and automatic transfer applied regardless of the wishes of the employer and any agreement to the contrary, this was subject to the fundamental principle that individuals should not be required to work for a particular employer against their will. Consequently, an employee has the right to object to a transfer to a particular employer. The employee would not then be compelled to work for that employer.

This is all very well, but where does it leave the employee? The ECJ said that this is a matter for domestic legislation.

Changes to the TUPE were introduced in 1993 to implement this decision.[74] Regulations 5(4A) and (4B) provide that an automatic transfer of the contract does not take place where the employee informs the employer that he objects to becoming employed by the new employer. The notification can be to the old or new employer. The effect of this is that the employee's contract of employment is automatically terminated when the transfer takes place, but this is not treated as a dismissal by the old employer (or indeed by the new employer). This means that the employee who objects has no job with the new or old employer and cannot claim unfair dismissal or redundancy.

The consequences are therefore drastic for the employee, yet there is authority that an employee who merely "withheld his consent" to the transfer could be treated as objecting and therefore lose his rights.[75] This does seem unduly harsh. It would seem fairer, and clearer, if only an employee who expressly objects to transferring is treated as having his or her contract terminated automatically. A more enlightened approach was taken by the EAT in another case where employees signed an agreement to "opt out" of a transfer, received a redundancy payment and accepted employment with the transferee. The EAT said that this could not amount to an objection to transferring to the transferee as the employees had accepted jobs with the transferee.[76]

As mentioned above, a transfer takes place automatically even if the employee is unaware of it.[77] This would appear to have the effect of depriving employees of a right to object in those circumstances. The EAT appears to suggest that an objection after the transfer may be valid, but this has not been subsequently tested.[78]

Right to object and constructive dismissal

The right to object, and indeed the automatic transfer of the contract of employment, are without prejudice to the right to resign and claim constructive dismissal under domestic unfair dismissal legislation.[79]

The precise wording of this provision is important. The provisions on automatic transfer and the right to object are

> without prejudice to any right of an employee arising apart from these Regulations to terminate his contract without notice if a substantial change is made to his working conditions to his detriment.[80]

Where an employee objects to a transfer because it would involve a substantial change to working conditions or cause him or her detriment, the employee can treat his contract as terminated by the employer and claim unfair dismissal.[81] This right is not overridden by Regulations 5(4A) and (4B). It applies whether the employee leaves before or after the transfer. In this case, the employee left before the transfer and his claim was against the transferor: liability did not transfer to the transferee.

The ECJ appears to suggest that "working conditions" is not confined to terms and conditions of the contract. It covered a situation where remuneration was reduced because of a lower amount earned in commission even where there was no change in the contractual terms.[82] This led the EAT to conclude that the right to resign and claim constructive dismissal on a TUPE transfer is broader than the right under unfair dismissal law in the Employment Rights Act 1996 – it does not require there to be a fundamental breach of a contractual term, merely a substantial adverse change in working conditions.[83] The Court of Appeal disagreed, thinking that this interpretation of the ECJ decision went too far and overturned the EAT decision.[84]

The Court of Appeal emphasised the ECJ decisions which said that the new employer could still change terms and conditions in the same way as the old employer, so far as permitted by national law.[85] The ARD only prevented the transfer from being used as the reason for the change. It did not give an additional right going beyond domestic unfair dismissal law. A fundamental breach of contract was still necessary to justify the right to resign and claim constructive dismissal[86] which then triggered Regulation 5(5) when that breach resulted from the transfer. This suggests that the right only arises where the substantial adverse change involves the breach of a specific contractual term, although this would include a fundamental breach of the implied term of mutual trust and confidence.

The final phrase of Regulation 5(5) states that no right to resign and claim constructive dismissal arises

> by reason only that ... the identity of his employer changes unless the employee shows that, in all the circumstances, the change is a significant change and is to his detriment.

In the light of the Court of Appeal decision requiring a fundamental breach to justify a resignation, it is difficult to envisage circumstances where a change of employer would justify resigning and claiming constructive dismissal. There is a theoretical possibility that it may apply if the new employer's reputation is so bad as to give rise to potential claims for stigma damages,[87] but it would be a brave employee who resigned in those circumstances.

Terms and conditions

Following a transfer, the contract of employment has effect as if originally made between the new employer and the employee, with all rights, powers, duties and liabilities under the contract preserved.[88] Many employers try to make changes in terms and conditions following a transfer, either by agreement or by dismissal and re-employment. This issue is dealt with later in this chapter.[89]

All contractual terms transfer (with the exception of those relating to pensions). This includes terms relating to pay, hours, place of work, etc. The status of terms is unaffected, so if a term was not contractual before the transfer (for example an entirely discretionary bonus), it will not become contractual by virtue of the transfer. The principle is that the new employer is bound only to the same extent as the old employer.[90] The fact that rights arising from the contract or employment relationship derive from a statutory instrument does not prevent those rights from transferring.[91]

Preservation of terms and conditions may be of limited value to the transferred employee if the new employer chooses to offer pay rises to other workers but deny them to the transferred workforce. This is often a means used by new employers to persuade transferred staff to give up their transferred terms and move to new contracts.

The position is different where the contract itself gives a right to a pay rise. There have been two cases where the EAT has said that the contractual terms transferred incorporated a right to a pay increase negotiated nationally between local government employers and unions.[92] In both cases, this was because individual contracts of employment incorporated national terms and conditions which in turn gave a right to receive the nationally negotiated increase. It did not matter that the new employers did not participate in the national negotiations and had no influence on the outcome: they were still bound by the terms of the contract. It will, however, depend on the terms of the contract and where these suggest that the employer is not bound by the increase, but has a discretion, the employee will have difficulty establishing a contractual entitlement to the increase.[93]

A potentially tricky question is the effect of a transfer on profit-related pay or bonuses, restrictive covenants or mobility clauses. Profit-related pay or bonuses may be linked to the employer, but the transfer will change the identity of the employer. Restrictive covenants may restrict activities by reference to clients of the employer, but when the employer changes, a different group of clients may be involved. A mobility clause potentially requiring an employee to work at all locations of an employer may cause very different issues if an employee transfers from a regional business to a national or international one.

Some guidance may be found in the decisions on profit-related pay clauses and restrictive covenants, where employees continued to benefit from a profit-related pay scheme in relation to benefits already accrued and, in another case, were entitled to a scheme of substantial equivalence with the new employer; and the restrictive covenant case where a restriction on dealing with the transferor's customers continued after the transferor (and did not become a restriction on dealing with the transferee's customers.[94]

Another clause potentially affected by the transfer is the "equality clause" implied by virtue of the Equal Pay Act 1970. This issue is before the ECJ. The ECJ is considering the issue of whether employees now employed by a private contractor, including those previously employed by a council, can compare themselves for equal pay purposes with employees of the council. The Advocate General's Opinion has not supported the employee's case. The ECJ decision is awaited and it is not clear what effect any such decision would have on the position following transfer of accrued rights to claim equality with fellow employees who do not themselves transfer.[95] Similar issues will arise in the part-time pensions cases and both types of case also give rise to the issue of whether a TUPE transfer triggers the time limit for Equal Pay claims.

Collective agreements and recognition

Collective agreements are also covered by the principle of automatic transfer.[96] This means that collective agreements between unions and the old employer will apply to the new employer. However, as collective agreements are presumed legally unenforceable unless otherwise stated,[97] this means that neither party can sue the other for breaching or terminating the agreement after the transfer.

This does not mean that collective agreements have no impact when a transfer takes place. As mentioned earlier, where provisions of collective agreements are incorporated into individual employee's contracts, they remain incorporated as contractual terms following the transfer.[98] Employers cannot escape this by terminating the collective agreement or de-recognising the union: the incorporated terms survive as part of individual contracts.[99]

The ARD permits Member States to limit the period for observing terms of collective agreements for a period of one year or more.[100] The TUPE Regulations do not take up this option as the lack of direct enforceability of collective agreements means that employers are not locked into legally binding collective agreements for protracted periods.

The statutory recognition provisions introduced by the Employment Relations Act 1999 provide for legally binding methods of collective bargaining.[101] The legal effect of these will continue following a transfer. The amended TUPE Regulations are likely to make provision for how this will operate in practice.[102] It is also likely that where a transfer takes place and this leads to a change in the bargaining unit, the new employer may seek to re-open the issue of the bargaining unit and recognition under the legislation.[103]

The TUPE provides that recognition (even voluntary recognition) transfers when the undertaking or part of the undertaking transferred maintains an identity distinct from the rest of the transferee's undertaking.[104]

A union which is recognised to bargain for employees of a particular description is deemed as recognised to the same extent by the new employer following the transfer.[105]

Where a union is recognised voluntarily by the old employer and recognition transfers (although the new employer is not legally bound to continue recognition) if the employer terminates recognition for a discrete bargaining unit, the union could apply for statutory recognition under the legislation and would succeed if it could demonstrate majority membership or the necessary majority support in a ballot.

The ARD also provides for the preservation of the status and function of the representatives or the representation of the employees. This affects not just officials and members of recognised trade unions who retain their statutory rights to time off for union duties and activities respectively, but is likely also to affect those elected or appointed with other representative functions, such as safety representatives and representatives under statutory consultation arrangements, such as European Works Councils and the forthcoming provisions on information and consultation directive, subject to provisions providing for changes in representation when there are changes in company structure.

Pensions

Pension rights are excluded from the principle of automatic transfer.[106] This exclusion affects rights to benefits for old age, invalidity and survivors.

This does not include other rights, such as redundancy payments, included in occupational pension schemes provided they do not relate to benefits for old age, invalidity or survivors.[107] The exclusion is to be construed in a narrow way, so that benefits for "old age" means only those which are paid from the time when the employee reaches normal retirement age under the pension scheme, not enhanced benefits on redundancy, even though they were calculated by reference to the rules for the pension scheme.[108]

There have been unsuccessful challenges to the pensions exclusion in the TUPE. The ARD says that the automatic transfer provisions do not apply to pension rights, but that Member States must adopt the measures necessary to protect the interests of employees and former employees who are or will be entitled to pensions. UK legislation freezes the pension already earned in the pension scheme up to transfer and gives a right to a deferred pension on that basis when reaching normal retirement age.[109] This does not provide for any legal entitlement to insist upon equivalent pension contributions or benefits from the new employer. The Court of Appeal rejected a challenge to the exclusion of the transfer of continuing rights and obligations relating to future contributions and benefits.[110]

This leaves a considerable gap in the protection afforded by the ARD and the TUPE.

There has been some suggestion that a failure by a new employer to offer a comparable pension on transfer may amount to substantial detrimental change in working conditions entitling the employee to resign and claim constructive dismissal.[111] Quite apart from the fact that this is an entirely ineffective remedy for an employee whose main concern is to retain pensionable employment, it is also unlikely to be a legally correct analysis following the decision that the right to claim constructive dismissal on a transfer only arises when there has been a fundamental breach.[112] If nothing in the contract of employment relating to pensions transfers, nor do any related rights or liabilities, it is difficult to see how a failure to offer a comparable pension amounts to a fundamental breach. This decision does appear to conflict with the more liberal approach of the ECJ.[113]

A more practical approach is the statement in the Cabinet Office guidance[114] that when public services are contracted out, the public authority must ensure that the contractor provides a broadly comparable pension. This generally involves an assessment by the Government Actuary's Department as to the adequacy of the contractor's scheme.

In local government, the government has gone further, permitting private contractors who meet certain requirements to attain "admitted body status" to the Local Government Pension Scheme (LGPS), thus entitling employees to remain in LGPS when they transfer from local government employment to a private company which is an admitted body.[115]

This still leaves a legal gap, particularly in the private sector. This has been recognised at EU level and the amendments made to the ARD in 1998 now allow Member States the option of making provision for pensions when there is a transfer.[116] The government has not yet decided whether, and to what extent, to implement this in the TUPE.[117] This is discussed later in this chapter in relation to proposed amendments to the TUPE.

Dismissals

A dismissal for a reason connected with the transfer is automatically unfair.[118] This is easier to state as a bald proposition than it is to apply in practice. Automatically unfair dismissal applies whether the dismissal is carried out by the transferor or the transferee and whether it is before or after the transfer.

Protection against dismissal for a reason connected with the transfer is not confined to those employed in the part transferred. It extends to all employees of the transferor or transferee, provided that their dismissal is for a reason connected with the transfer.

The dismissal may take place at the point of transfer or some time before or after. There is no finite period. The further in time from the transfer, the more difficult it may be to establish that the reason for dismissal was connected to the transfer. But it is not impossible. In one case the dismissal was found to be connected to the transfer (and automatically unfair) even though the dismissal took place some two years after the transfer.[119]

There are examples of cases where the EAT has taken a more restrictive view. Dismissals 13 days before a transfer were not connected because they resulted from financial pressure from the bank, not the purchaser of the business.[120] A decision to dismiss employees to make a business more attractive to potential purchasers was not connected as the identity of the eventual transferee was not known at the date of dismissal, so the dismissals, whilst they might be in anticipation of "a" transfer, were not in connection with "the" transfer to the particular eventual transferee. Fortunately, a subsequent EAT decision took a different view: a dismissal is automatically unfair if connected to "a" transfer to a transferee who may appear.[121]

Economic, technical or organisational reasons

The ARD provides that the protection against dismissal

> shall not stand in the way of dismissals that may take place for economic, technical or organisational reasons entailing changes in the workforce.[122]

The TUPE enacts this by providing that it shall not be an automatically unfair dismissal where the economic, technical or organisational reason entailing changes in the workforce is the reason (or principal reason) for dismissal.[123] These reasons have become known in familiar shorthand as "ETO reasons".

Where there is an ETO reason, this does not make the dismissal automatically fair, only potentially fair. The tribunal must still assess whether or not the dismissal is unfair by the normal principles of unfair dismissal under Section 98(4) of the Employment Rights Act 1996. This will involve consideration of whether the employer acted reasonably in treating the reason as sufficient to dismiss. Relevant factors are likely to include, for example, whether the employer followed a fair procedure in selecting particular employees for dismissal, and whether there was proper consultation about the dismissal.

There has been some controversy and confusion about the interrelationship between the concepts of automatically unfair transfer-related dismissals and ETO reasons. One suggested approach was that the two concepts were mutually exclusive. A dismissal was either for a reason connected with the transfer or it was for an ETO reason: it could not be for both. This approach was adopted by the Advocate General to the ECJ, but not picked up by the Court itself.[124]

The EAT would not accept the argument that only those dismissals which would have happened in the absence of the transfer could amount to dismissals for an ETO reason.[125] The Court of Appeal then got hold of the issue. It decided that it was permissible for a tribunal to conclude that a dismissal is for a reason connected with the transfer and then go on to consider whether or not the dismissal is for an ETO reason. The provisions of Regulations 8(1) and 8(2) must be read as a whole and are not mutually exclusive.[126] It followed this with a decision that if there was a dismissal "solely" for a reason connected with the transfer it was unfair, but if, in addition, there is an ETO reason, the court must to go on to consider if it was the principal reason. If so, it effectively supersedes the transfer reason and the court must consider whether the employer acted fairly in relying on the ETO reason to dismiss.[127]

There is a danger that this approach diminishes the protection against dismissal. In the second Court of Appeal cases referred to above, a new firm won the contract to supply prosthetic appliances to a hospital. The contract specified that staffing costs must be reduced by reducing staff from 13 employees to 12. The Court of Appeal said that the transfer was not the reason for the dismissal, but the "occasion" for it, as there would have been cuts even if the contract was not outsourced.[128]

This appears not to take full account of the approach in previous EAT decisions where it was stated that "economic" reasons should be given a narrow interpretation.[129] It was stated

> if the economic reason were no more than the desire to obtain an enhanced price, or no more than the desire to achieve a sale, it would not be a reason which related to the conduct of the business.[130]

Sadly, the recent Court of Appeal decisions do not seem to adopt this analysis. Similarly, in an EAT case concerning the sale of an insolvent business employees were dismissed by a receiver at the request of the purchaser on the same day as the transfer later took place. The EAT upheld a finding that the dismissal was connected with the future conduct of the business as a going concern and therefore for an ETO reason.[131]

The focus must be on the actual reason for dismissal. An employer cannot rely on the fact that there would have been an ETO reason if that was not the actual reason for the dismissal.[132] The dismissing employer cannot rely on another employer's reason. Where the dismissal is carried out by the new employer, he must have his own reason; he cannot rely on the old employer's reason.[133]

An employer cannot only rely on an ETO reason where it entails changes in the workforce. Dismissing the existing workforce and re-employing them all on worse terms and conditions does not entail changes in the workforce and therefore cannot be an ETO reason.[134] Where the total number of workers remains the same, changes in individuals comprising the workforce would not amount to an ETO reason unless there are changes in the jobs involved which could genuinely be described as changes in the workforce.[135] A change in the numbers of the workforce is likely to be regarded as entailing changes in the workforce.

Consultation obligations may arise. Dismissals for an ETO reason are likely to be for a reason not related to the individual concerned and therefore (where there are more than 20 dismissals) it would trigger the obligation to inform and consult with representatives in accordance with the collective redundancy provisions.[136] Many dismissals for ETO reasons may stem from a reduction in the requirement for employees to carry out work of a particular kind in a particular place and may therefore be redundancies, entitling the dismissed employees to a redundancy payment.[137]

Changes to contracts of employment

The extent to which employers can change contractual terms when there is a TUPE transfer is a controversial issue and one which has troubled the courts. As has been said, employees employed in the part transferred automatically transfer with their contractual terms and conditions intact. If the new employer refuses to honour the contracts, the employees may (if it is a fundamental breach of contract) resign and claim constructive dismissal.[138] However, this would be a high risk strategy for an employee to follow.

An alternative would be for the employees to accept the new terms and conditions under protest making it clear in writing that they reserve the right to bring claims for breach of contract and/or for unlawful deduction from wages[139] and/or a declaration as to their employment particulars.[140]

The main issue of controversy is the situation where the employees either agree to the new terms and conditions or continue working without protest. If it were not for the TUPE, this would generally be a valid change to the contract. However, the position is more complex when there is a transfer. The ECJ has said that the old employer should be in the same position as the new employer when it comes to changing contracts. The new employer should be able to change to the same extent as would have been permissible for the old employer.[141] However, this does not justify changes where the reason for the change is the transfer itself.[142] This is the case even where the negotiated changes are more favourable.[143]

The House of Lords considered the issue in two joined cases in 1998.[144] In each case, neither the employer nor the employees had appreciated at the time of the transfer that the TUPE might apply to the transaction. Existing staff were dismissed and re-employed on worse terms. The House of Lords decided that the dismissals were valid and therefore effective to bring to an end the old contract. The ARD did not prevent dismissals taking place. Regulation 8 of the TUPE provides employees with the remedy of an unfair dismissal claim. In a transfer situation, liability for the dismissal becomes the responsibility of the transferee. This led the House of Lords to the conclusion that the old contracts had been terminated and the new contracts were therefore in force. The change to contracts was valid. The employees could not insist on the old contracts. Their remedies were limited to those for unfair dismissal. Although by far the most common remedy for unfair dismissal is compensation, there is at least the theoretical possibility of achieving reinstatement to the old terms and conditions.

This conclusion meant that the House of Lords did not need to consider the question of whether an agreed change (without any dismissal) is effective to change the contracts. Their Lordships said that they would have referred this issue to the ECJ, but they expressed some tentative conclusions. An agreed variation is invalid where the reason for the change is the transfer itself and no other reason. This applies whether the variation takes place before the transfer, at the time of the transfer or later. However, when the reason for the changes is something other than merely the transfer, an agreed change will be effective. It was suggested that where the change was for an economic, technical or organisational reason, the transfer is not the reason for the change and the change may be valid. This appears to bring into changes in terms and conditions the concept of an ETO reason which has no place in this arena: it is confined to the provisions on dismissals.

The ECJ has since re-stated the fact that changes where the transfer is the reason are invalid.[145] Recent cases have shown the difficulty of establishing that changes are due to the transfer.[146]

There is a risk that employers may seek to avoid the TUPE by dismissing and re-employing on worse terms and conditions. This is a dangerous strategy. If there are no changes to the workforce, the dismissals are likely to be automatically unfair. Even if there are changes, an employer is still likely to face unfair dismissal claims.

Information and consultation

A transfer of an undertaking gives rise to rights and obligations in relation to information and consultation.[147]

The obligation is in two parts: to inform and to consult.

The obligation to inform arises whenever a transfer is proposed, regardless of the number of employees affected – even a single employee is sufficient to trigger the obligation.

The obligation to consult arises only where the transferor or transferee envisages "measures" in relation to affected employees.[148] Measures need only be envisaged, not proposed or intended. Measures include any action, step or arrangement.[149]

Measures, therefore, go beyond changes to contracts of employment and may include changes in working conditions such as job location or pension arrangements.

There are separate obligations on transferor and transferee. Each must consult representatives of those of its own employees who may be affected by the transfer or measures taken in connection with the transfer. This covers all employees affected, whether or not they face dismissal and whether or not they are employed in the part to be transferred.[150]

Information

> The employer must provide information on:
> (i)   the fact that there will be a transfer
> (ii)   the reasons for it
> (iii)   when it will take place
> (iv)   the legal, social and economic implications for affected employees
> (v)   any measures envisaged by the transferor
> (vi)   any measures envisaged by the transferee.
> The information must be provided in writing[151] and long enough before the transfer to enable consultation to take place.[152]

Whose obligation?

The obligation to provide information to the employees of the current employer (the transferor) rests with that employer, in respect of all of his/her employees affected including those to be transferred. This is so even in respect of measures proposed by the imminent new employer (the transferee).[153]

The TUPE Regulations purport to impose an obligation on the transferee to give this information to the transferor,[154] but there is no means of direct enforcement of this obligation. The transferee cannot claim against the transferor, nor can the employees or their representatives: the primary obligation rests with the transferor. The only remedy against the transferee is if the employee representatives bring a claim for failure to inform or consult against the transferor, the transferor can join the transferee to the proceedings and seek to pass the blame for the transferee if the transferee's failure to provide information made it not reasonably practicable for the transferor to comply with his/her obligations.[155]

This tends to leave the transferor stuck in the middle. It also means that the employee representatives have no legal means of forcing information from, or consulting with, the potential new employer. This is anomalous as it is the new employer who will have most impact on the employees' working conditions.

There has been one case law development which may affect the position. The EAT has decided that liability for the transferor's failure to inform or consult passes to the transferee.[156] The EAT concluded that the obligation (and liability for a failure) arises in connection with the contract of employment or is something done by the old employer which should be regarded as done by the new employer, thus transferring under TUPE Regulations 5(2)(a) and (b).

This contradicts a previous EAT case[157] and has also been contradicted by a very brief decision of the Scottish EAT.[158] It remains to be seen whether the view that liability transfers will survive.

Responsibility for information and consultation is even more complex where a public authority (or private company) is terminating the contract with an outgoing contractor and awarding the work to an incoming contractor. The obligation to consult rests with the outgoing contractor, yet that organisation may have incomplete information on how the service will be structured by the body awarding the contract and carried out by the incoming contractor. The concerns of the workforce may relate more to matters in the control of the body awarding the contract or the incoming contractor.

The outgoing contractor may seek to argue that special circumstances prevent it from giving information not supplied by the body awarding the contract[159] or seek to pass on liability to the incoming contractor.[160] The problem will not be solved by the provision in the amended the ARD stating that a failure to provide information by an undertaking controlling the transferee does not exonerate the transferor from its failures.[161] Unless, that is, the courts take a radical step and decide that a body awarding a contract is an undertaking controlling the employer in these circumstances.

There is some suggestion that, in a transfer when a the old contractor ceases to provide a service which is then provided by a new contractor, the undertaking transfers via the body awarding the contract, who momentarily becomes the employer of the transferring workforce.[162] If so, the body awarding the contract would be under an obligation to inform and consult.[163]

Consultation

The obligation to consult arises when the transferor or transferee envisages measures affecting some or the entire workforce. The consultation must be with a view to seeking the agreement of the employee representatives to the measures to be taken.[164] Case law suggests this means it must begin at a formative stage before the proposed measures are set in stone at a time when the representatives still have an opportunity to influence the outcome.[165] There must be enough information and enough time to consider it. Both the timing and content must be sufficient to enable the employee representatives to engage in a genuine dialogue with the employer.

In terms of formal requirements, the employer must consider representations made by the employee representatives, reply to those representations and state why any are rejected.[166]

Employee representatives

Employers must consult with representatives of the affected employees.

This has been the subject of legal challenge and legislative change in the UK. Originally, the obligation was to consult with recognised trade unions representing the affected employees. This was fine where there was a recognised trade union, but meant that employers could avoid the obligation where there was no union or the union was not recognised or was derecognised.

The European Commission successfully challenged this in the ECJ proceedings against the UK government.[167] The then Conservative government's response to this legal defeat was to allow employers to bypass trade unions by consulting with ad hoc elected representatives even where a trade union was recognised.[168] This was itself the subject of an unsuccessful challenge in the High Court.[169] Before an appeal against that decision was heard in the Court of Appeal, the new Labour Government passed regulations which restored the primacy of the trade union route where a union is recognised, whilst providing for elected representatives where there is no recognised union.[170]

The consultation must be with the "appropriate representatives".[171] Where the employees are of a description in respect of which an independent trade union is recognised by the employer, the union must be consulted.[172] The employer has no option. This applies to all workers of that description, whether they are union members or not.

Where there are affected employees not of a description covered by recognition, the employer must (in respect of those employees) consult either representatives elected specifically for the purpose of the TUPE consultation or representatives elected for another purpose who have authority from the employees to receive information and be consulted about the transfer on their behalf.[173] The employer can choose which. In deciding whether representatives elected for another purpose are appropriate, regard will be had to the purpose for, and method by which, they were elected. Examples might be a works council or consultative committee where representatives are elected by the workforce.

In a situation where some workers are covered by recognition and others are not, the employer must consult with the union in respect of those covered by recognition and with the elected representatives in relation to the other employees.

The TUPE now sets out requirements for the conduct of the elections.[174] The employer is required to make such arrangements as are reasonably practical to make sure the election is fair. The employer determines the number of representatives, but in doing so must ensure that there are sufficient representatives to represent the interests of all the affected employees, taking into account the number and classes of those employees. The employer is to determine whether the representatives should represent all of the affected employees, or whether there should be separate representatives for different classes of employee. The length of period of office must be long enough for information to be given and consultation to take place.

The election requirements must provide that candidates are "affected employees" at the date of election and that no affected employee is unreasonably excluded from standing for election. All affected employees on the date of the election are entitled to vote for as many candidates as there are representatives to represent them (or to represent their particular class of employees). The election is to be conducted so that voting is in secret and votes are accurately counted.

These requirements are a welcome improvement on the unregulated situation under the previous Conservative Government's legislation. They provide employees with some safeguards and with a means of challenging improperly conducted elections.

The employer is required to give the representatives (whether trade union or elected) access to the affected employees and to give them appropriate accommodation and facilities to carry out their duties.[175]

Where there is no recognised trade union, the employer must invite the employees to elect representatives sufficiently far in advance of the time the employer is required to give the information, to provide time for the elections to take place before the information is provided and the consultation begins.[176] The employer must then comply with the obligation to inform and consult as soon as practicable after the representatives have been elected.[177] If the employees fail to elect representatives within a reasonable time of the invitation, the employer must give the requisite information about the transfer directly to the employees.[178]

Representatives are given protection against dismissal or detriment. It is unlawful to subject an employee to detriment for being an employee representative (or candidate for election) and for performing or proposing to perform functions or activities as a representative or candidate, or to subject an employee to detriment for participating in the election.[179] A dismissal on any of those grounds would be automatically unfair[180] and an employee does not require a qualifying period of service to obtain this protection.[181]

Remedy

The remedy for an employer's failure to inform and consult is for the trade union or elected representatives to apply to the Employment Tribunal within three months of the date of the transfer.[182]

If the complaint succeeds, the Tribunal must make a declaration and may order the employer to pay compensation not exceeding 13 weeks' pay for each affected employee.[183] The amount of compensation is that which the Tribunal considers just and equitable having regard to the seriousness of the employer's failure.[184]

The award is against the employer responsible who had the obligation to consult. So, in respect of the transferor's employees, the award would be against the transferor. However, the EAT has said that this liability transfers to the transferee and so the claim should be against the transferee.[185] A subsequent Scottish EAT took a different view.[186] The safest course at the moment is to bring a claim against both!

There is one specific situation where the transferor can pass on liability to the transferee. This is where the transferor has failed to give information about measures proposed by the transferee because the transferee has failed to provide that information.[187]

It is a defence for the employer to show that there are special circumstances that made it not reasonably practicable to inform or consult and that the employer took all steps as were reasonably practicable.[188] This must be interpreted narrowly and cannot involve the failure by a controlling undertaking to pass on information to the employer.[189]

If there is no recognised trade union and no elected representatives, the claim can be brought by individual affected employees.[190]

If there is a failure to conduct properly the elections for employee representatives, any of the affected employees may bring a claim.[191] The onus is on the employer to show that the requirements have been satisfied.[192] This contrasts with the situation before the 1999 amendments where the employee had no effective means of challenge.[193]

The 13 week limit on compensation paid to affected employees is an improvement on the limit of 4 weeks in the previous version of the Regulations which the ECJ said was unlawful.[194] It is arguable that even this limit may be unlawful and, indeed, that providing only for a financial remedy may be inadequate.[195] Remedies for breaches of directives must be "effective, proportionate and dissuasive".[196] Some commentators argue that this requirement can only be met by providing for the right to an injunction to stop the transfer from proceeding until after the requisite information and consultation.

Proposed changes to the TUPE; implementing the amended Directive

Amended Directive

The original ARD was amended in 1998. The UK government played a key role in the amendment and at the time it was hailed by the minister responsible as a step forward in clarifying and improving the Directive.[197] The amended ARD was to be implemented in to domestic law by July 2001. The government then engaged in discussions with social partners: employers, public authorities and unions. Progress appeared to be made, but the government since appears to have lost enthusiasm for amending the TUPE to reflect the amended ARD (now consolidated in the 2001 Directive). The July 2001 deadline is long past and still there are no draft amending regulations nor a timetable for implementation.

Public consultation

On 10 September 2001 at the TUC Congress, the Secretary of State for Trade and Industry announced the publication of the government's consultation document on proposed revisions to the TUPE.[198] The consultation period ran to 15 December 2001. There has not yet been any government response. The consultation document was not accompanied by draft Regulations. The Government has not yet stated a definite timetable for introducing the changes.

It is not, therefore, possible to comment in detail on the likely changes to the TUPE. However, there are a number of points of interest in the public consultation document which merit discussion.

General objectives and scope of the TUPE

The government recognises the TUPE as based on a positive principle and acknowledges the need to balance flexibility for business with fairness for employees. The government refers to giving assurance to and securing the commitment of employees affected by change.

The government reaffirms its commitment to apply the Cabinet Office Statement of Practice "Staff Transfers in the Public Sector"[199] and, where necessary, to legislate to extend TUPE-style protection to specific transfers within the public sector.

The new Regulations will adopt the changed definition of a transfer of undertaking in the Acquired Rights Directive. The government rightly fears this may not be enough and is contemplating specific regulation to ensure that the TUPE applies whenever there is a "service provision change". This would cover contracting out where the same or essentially the same activities are performed by a contractor in essentially the same manner as they were performed when in-house. It would also cover, on a similar basis, subsequent re-tendering involving a change of contractor or the work coming back in-house.

This approach would involve treating a transfer as covered by the TUPE when before the service provision change there are employees assigned to an organised grouping the principal purpose of which is to perform the service concerned.

This would be a welcome step which would reflect the general practice in UK contracting out and help to insulate the UK from the uncertainty caused by the unpredictable swings of the European Court. It is to be hoped that the Government adopts this approach.

Occupational pensions

The revised Directive gives governments the option of applying the TUPE to pensions.[200]

The Government does not propose to apply the automatic transfer provisions in the Directive to pension rights and obligations. This would be difficult to achieve. But the Government invites views on whether to legislate to provide a degree of protection for occupational pension rights on transfer, for public and private sector employees alike.

There is a need for protection, but the various options in the document fall short of a requirement that the new employer offer a pension which is "broadly comparable". All the options canvassed would mean that employees could be worse off after the transfer than before. It is not yet known what approach the Government will take.

The Government will be legislating to ensure that rights to a redundancy payment under a pension scheme, such as the NHS scheme, are transferred when there is a TUPE transfer, putting the recent ECJ decision on a legislative footing.[201]

Notification of employee liability information

One of the changes introduced by the UK in the amended Directive was the option of requiring the outgoing employer to notify the potential new employer of all rights and obligations relating to the employees who are to be transferred.[202]

The UK is likely to take up this option. This would require written notification in good time before the transfer.

This is sensible, but it is essential that the information is provided at the same time to the workers' representatives. This would enable any errors or omissions to be pointed out before any transfer takes place. Curiously, the Government is equivocal on this.

It is also curious that the Government does not propose that the new employer can sue the old employer for damages if information is inaccurate or incomplete and causes financial loss. Instead the Government floats the idea of liability for any claims by employees being split between the old and new employer. This would cause expense and uncertainty and may mean that employees lose out (through no fault of their own) if one of the employers is insolvent.

Dismissals

The provisions relating to transfer-related dismissals will be changed to make clear that a dismissal for an economic, technical or organisational reason ("ETO reason") is not automatically unfair, even where the ETO reason is connected to the transfer. In other words, a reason which is transfer-related may still be for an ETO reason.

This appears to be correct in the light of recent cases. It would be a cause for concern if it made tribunals more willing to find dismissals fair for an ETO reason.

Changes in terms and conditions

A change in terms and conditions may only lawfully be made by individual or collective agreement. If a change is imposed by an employer it will be a breach of contract (unless the employees acquiesce in the change). If an employer terminates the contract and imposes new terms, it would be a dismissal which may be unfair (and would be if for a reason connected with the transfer unless an ETO reason entailing changes in the workforce).

None of this will be changed by the Government's proposals.

There is one amendment proposed. At the moment, an agreed change in terms and conditions will be unlawful and ineffective where the reason for the change is the transfer itself. The Government proposes that an agreed change in terms and conditions will be valid where the reason for the change is an ETO reason entailing changes in the workforce.

This is the Government's interpretation of the current legal position following the House of Lords decision in the *Wilson* case.[203] This will be a retrograde step if it leads to an increase in changes in terms and conditions which would not have arisen but for the transfer.

Insolvency

The amended version of the ARD has substantial changes in relation to insolvency. The rationale was to increase flexibility when there is the transfer of an insolvent business, the intention being to diminish the liabilities facing potential purchasers. This has led to a number of changes which weaken protection of employees.

Article 5 provides that the ARD need not apply to the transfer of an insolvent business which is subject to winding-up proceedings. The UK has not taken up this option and it is welcome that the Government consultation indicates that the TUPE will still apply to transfers where the business is insolvent.

The Government does, however, intend to take up the options now made available by the new Article 5.2 of the ARD.

The government proposes that where there is a transfer of an insolvent business subject to insolvency proceedings, pre-transfer debts to employees will not transfer to the new employer but will be met out of the state National Insurance Fund. There are limits to the amounts paid out under the Fund. This means that employees will suffer a shortfall.

In addition, it is proposed that the insolvent business will be able to agree transfer-related reductions in terms and conditions with workers' representatives designed to safeguard the survival of the business. No adequate safeguards are proposed. There are as yet no proposals for a requirement that the representatives be independent or accountable to the workers.

These two changes will weaken protection for workers. This is unnecessary as recent cases show it is difficult enough already for workers to succeed in cases involving transfers of insolvent businesses.[204]

Recognition

As indicated earlier, the revised TUPE regulations will provide that statutory recognition is transferred.

Information and consultation of employee representatives

Employers will not be able to hide behind the decision of a controlling undertaking as an excuse for not consulting. This is likely to involve a specific amendment to the "special circumstances" provisions in relation to information and consultation.[205]

Omissions

The main omission is the lack of an anti-avoidance provision. It is too often the case that employers seek to avoid the TUPE by refusing to take on staff, leaving workers with no job and with no redundancy payment from the old employer. The government appears to have ignored the option of allowing employees faced with a loss of employment on a possible TUPE transfer the right to apply to a Tribunal for interim relief to determine urgently whether there is a TUPE transfer and whether the dismissal is unfair.

The document does discuss the possibility of a pre-determination procedure where employers could ask the court whether or not a particular transaction would be covered by the TUPE. The government rightly expresses concern that this may exclude employees from the decision. Employers could collude to "stitch up" employees.

There is also a case that the TUPE should apply to the wider category of "workers" not just to employees, but any development on this is likely to link in with the government's consultation on employee status in relation to statutory employment rights.[206]

Other steps

The Government has been taking steps to address certain issues associated with contracting out in the public sector. This is in response to particular controversy regarding the Private Finance Initiative (PFI) and other schemes concerning the involvement of private companies in public sector provision.

The government has announced that in all future PFI hospital deals staff will remain employed by the National Health Service rather than the private contractors.[207] There are pilot schemes are in place.

In local government, the Secretary of State announced on 26 March 2002 a proposed Code of Practice intended to address the issue of the "two-tier workforce" in public sector transfers. This is the phenomenon that new staff are employed on worse terms and conditions than transferred staff.

The intention is that the Cabinet Office Statement of Practice on Staff Transfers in the Public Sector will become legally binding in transfers in local government and the new Code of Practice will require that any new staff employed by contractors must be on fair and reasonable terms and conditions which are in overall terms broadly comparable to those of the transferred employees. There will also be an obligation to offer membership of a pension scheme which meets certain minimum requirements. The Code will be written into contracts between local authorities and contractors and supported by statutory guidance. The code and guidance will also secure the role of recognised unions in the process.

268 The Law at Work

Notes

1. ARD Recital 3
2. TUPE Regulation 3(1)
3. ARD Article 1.1(b)
4. See comments of the Minister, Mr David Waddington, Hansard, 7 December 1981, column 680
5. [1992] IRLR 366 (ECJ)
6. *Commission v UK* (1994) IRLR 392 (ECJ)
7. Trade Union Reform and Employment Rights Act 1993
8. See, for example, *Kenny v South Manchester College* (1993) IRLR 265 (High Court) and *Porter v Queen's Medical Centre* (1993) IRLR 486 (High Court)
9. (1992) IRLR 84
10. For more details on the principles concerned, see *Francovich* itself (previous note) and the cases of *Dillenkoffer v Germany* (1997) IRLR 60 (ECJ); *R v HM Treasury ex parte British Telecom* (1996) ECR 1–1631 (ECJ) and *Brasserie du Pecheur SA v Germany; R v Secretary of State for Transport ex parte Factortame Limited* (1996) All ER (EC) 301 (ECJ)
11. (1993) IRLR 133 (ECJ)
12. See (respectively) *Wren v Eastbourne Borough Council and UK Waste Control Limited* (1993) IRLR 425 (EAT) and *UK Waste Control v Wren* (19950 ICR 4 (EAT); *Hope and others v Castle Point Borough Council* and *MRS Environmental Services* (Industrial Tribunal, London North, August 1994) appealed on another point as *MRS Environmental Services v Marsh and Harvey* 91997) 1 All ER 92 (Court of Appeal); *BSG Property Services v Tuck* (1996) IRLR 134 (EAT); *Dines v Initial Services Limited* and Pall Mall Services Group Limited (1994) IRLR 336 (Court of Appeal)
13. (1994) IRLR 304 (ECJ)
14. (1996) IRLR 51 (ECJ)
15. *Merckx v Ford Motors Co Belgium SA* (1996) IRLR 467 (ECJ)
16. (1997) IRLR 255 (ECJ)
17. *Süzen*, ECJ judgment at paragraph 16
18. *Süzen*, ECJ judgment at paragraph 16
19. *Sanchez Hidalgo v Asociación de Servicio Aser (*1999) IRLR 136 (ECJ) and *Hernandez Vidal v Gomez Perez* (1999) IRLR 136 (ECJ)
20. See *Hernandez Vidal* at paragraph 19
21. See for example Redmond (note 5) and *Commission v UK* (note 6)
22. (1996) IRLR 701 (ECJ)
23. *Sanchez Hidalgo* (note 19 above) at paragraph 24
24. See *Dundee City Council v Arshad* , EAT, unreported, 14 January 1999 (Scotland)
25. (2000) IRLR 788 (ECJ)
26. (2000) IRLR 783 (ECJ)
27. *Oy Liikenne Ab v Liskojarvi* (2001) IRLR 171 (ECJ)
28. *Viggodsdottir v Islandspostur HF* (2002) IRLR 425 (EFTA court); in this case the worker was not covered as she was a civil servant who fell outside the protection of employment law in Iceland and thus outside the definition of employee
29. Staff Transfers in the Public Sector: Statement of Practice – Cabinet Office January 2000
30. The Transfer of Undertakings (Protection of Employment) (Rent Officer Service) Regulations 1999, SI 1999/2511

[31] See for example *Süzen* at note 16
[32] *Dr Sophie Redmond Stichting v Bartol*, see note 5
[33] *Merckx*, see note 15
[34] See, as one of many examples, *Dines* at note 12
[35] *Brookes v Borough Care Services* (1998) IRLR 636 (EAT)
[36] TUPE Regulation 3(2)
[37] TUPE Regulation 3(1)
[38] *Allen v Amalgamated Construction Company Limited* (2000) IRLR 119 (ECJ)
[39] (1986) ECR 1119 (ECJ)
[40] *Dr Sophie Redmond Stichting v Bartol*, see note 5
[41] *Rask*, see note 11
[42] *Schmidt*, see note 13
[43] *Merckx*, see note 15
[44] *Rygaard*, see note 14; contrast the later decision in *Allen v Amalgamated Construction Company Limited* (2000) IRLR 119 (ECJ) where the ARD applied to the transfer of complete works contracts and a body of assets
[45] *Süzen*, see note 16, at paragraph 18
[46] *Süzen*, see note 16, at paragraph 21
[47] *Sanchez Hidalgo*, see note 19
[48] *Hernandez Vidal*, see note 19
[49] *Oy Liikenne Ab v Liskojarvi* (2001) IRLR 171 (ECJ); contrast the approach taken in the EAT in a case involving a transfer of goodwill and telephone numbers of a taxi company, but no assets – *McLeod and another v Ingram trading as Phoenix Taxis and Rainbow Cars Limited trading as Rainbow Taxis*, IDS Brief 712, July 2002 (EAT)
[50] (1999) IRLR 559 (CA)
[51] (2001) IRLR 542 (CA)
[52] (2002) IRLR 401 (CA)
[53] ARD Article 3, TUPE Regulation 5
[54] ARD Article 3.4; TUPE Regulation 7
[55] *Rotstart de Hertaing v J Benoidt* (1997) IRLR 127(ECJ)
[56] *Secretary of State v Cook* (1997) IRLR 150 (EAT)
[57] *Litster v Forth Dry Dock and Engineering Company Limited* (1989) IRLR 161 (HL) and *Wilson v St Helens Borough Council* (1989) IRLR 161 and *Meade v British Fuels Limited* (1998) IRLR 706 (HL)
[58] TUPE Regulation 5(3)
[59] *Litster*, see note 57 above
[60] *Wilson v St Helens*, see note 57
[61] ARD Article 3.1
[62] *Stirling District Council v Allan* (1995) IRLR 301 (Court of Session) overturning an EAT decision which said that liabilities may remain with the transferor (as well as the transferee)
[63] TUPE Regulation 5(2)(b)
[64] *DJM International Limited v Nicholls* (1996) IRLR 76 (EAT)
[65] *Lawrence v Regent Office Care Limited, Commercial Catering Group and Mitie Secure Services Limited*, Employment Tribunal decision case number 2709/96, sent to parties 16/4/97; currently before ECJ under case number C-320/00, Advocate General's Opinion 14 March 2002, ECJ judgment awaited
[66] *Bernadone v Pall Mall* (2000) IRLR 487 (CA)

[67] TUPE Regulation 5(1); contrast unfair dismissal protection which applies to all employees of transferor or transferee dismissed for a reason connected with the transfer, whether employed in the part transferred or not: TUPE Regulation 8(1)

[68] *Botzen v Rotterdamsche Droogdok Maatschappij BV* (1985) ECR 519 (ECJ)

[69] *Gale v Northern General Hospitals NHS Trust* (1994) IRLR 292 (CA) – the case actually concerned the similar provisions in the National Health Service and Community Care Act 1990

[70] *Securicor Guarding v Fraser Security Services* (1996) IRLR 522 (EAT)

[71] *Duncan Webb Offset v Cooper* (1995) IRLR 633 (EAT)

[72] *Buchanan Smith v Schleicher & Co International Limited* (1996) IRLR 547 (EAT)

[73] *Katsikas v Konstantinides* (1993) IRLR 179 (ECJ)

[74] By the Trade Union Reform and Employment Rights Act 1993

[75] *Hay v George Hanson* (Building Contractors) Limited (1996) IRLR 427 (EAT – Scotland)

[76] *Senior Heat Treatment v Bell* (1997) IRLR 614 (EAT)

[77] *Photostatic Copiers v Okuda* (1995) IRLR 11 (EAT), overturned by *Secretary of State v Cook* (1997) IRLR 150 (EAT)

[78] *Secretary of State v Cook*, see note 77

[79] TUPE Regulation 5(5)

[80] TUPE Regulation 5(5)

[81] *University of Oxford v Humphreys* (2000) IRLR 183 (CA)

[82] *Merckx*, see note 15

[83] *Rossiter v Pendragon plc* (2001) IRLR 256 (EAT)

[84] *Rossiter v Pendragon plc* (2002) IRLR 483 (CA)

[85] *Rask v ISS Kantineservice*, see note 11; and *Collino v Telecom Italia*, see note 25

[86] Section 95(1)(c) Employment Rights Act 1996

[87] See for example *Malik v BCCI SA* (1997) IRLR 467 (House of Lords)

[88] TUPE Regulation 5(1) and 5(2)(a)

[89] See under Changes to Contract of Employment

[90] See *Rask* and *Collino*, note 85 above

[91] *Beckmann v Dynamco Whicheloe Macfarlane Limited*, ECJ C-164/00, 4 June 2002

[92] *Ball v BET plc*, EAT 28 November 1996, unreported and *Whent v T Cartledge Limited* (1997) IRLR 153 (EAT)

[93] *Glendale Grounds Management v Bradley* (unreported) EAT 19/2/98

[94] See *Unicorn Consultancy Services Limited v Westbrook and others* (2000) IRLR 80 (EAT) and *Mitie Managed Services Limited v French and others*, IDS Brief 713, July 2002 (EAT) in relation to interpretation of a profit-related pay clause after transfer and *Morris Angel & Son Limited v Hollande* (1993) IRLR 169 (CA) on restrictive covenant

[95] *Lawrence v Regent and Mitie*, see note 65

[96] TUPE Regulation 6

[97] Section 179 Trade Union and Labour Relations (Consolidation) Act 1992

[98] See *Ball v BET* and *Whent v T Cartledge*, note 92 above

[99] See *Whent v T Cartledge*, note 92 above

[100] ARD Article 3.3

[101] Schedule A1 to the Trade Union and Labour Relations (Consolidation) Act 1992

[102] Transfer of Undertakings (Protection of Employment) Regulations 1981: Government Proposals for Reform and Detailed Background Paper URN01/1158

[103] Schedule A1 at note 101 above, Part III paragraphs 64–95

[104] TUPE Regulation 9(1)

[105] TUPE Regulation 9(2)

[106] ARD Article 3.4; TUPE Regulation 7

[107] TUPE Regulation 7(2)

[108] *Beckmann v Dynamco Whicheloe Macfarlane Limited*, ECJ C-164/00, 4 June 2002

[109] Part IV of the Pensions Schemes Act 1993

[110] *Adams and others v Lancashire County Council and BET Catering Services* (1997) IRLR 436 (CA) ; see also decision of the EFTA Court in *Eidesund v Stavanger Catering A/S* (1996) IRLR 684 (EFTA Court)

[111] See advice of Attorney General, 18 January 1990, to House of Commons Standing Committee D, Hansard column 201

[112] *Rossiter v Pendragon plc*, see note 8

[113] *Merckx*, see note 15

[114] Staff Transfers in the Public Sector, Statement of Practice; Cabinet Office January 2000

[115] Local Government Pension Scheme Regulations 1997, as amended by the Local Government Pension Scheme (Amendment etc) Regulations 1999 and subsequently re-amended a number of times

[116] ARD Article 3.4

[117] See note 102

[118] TUPE Regulation 8(1)

[119] *Taylor v Connex* IDS Brief 670, EAT 5 July 2000

[120] *Longden v Ferrari Limited* (1994) IRLR 157 (EAT), but see different outcome in *Harrison Bowden v Bowden* (1994) ICR 186 (EAT)

[121] *Michael Peters Limited v Farnfield and Michael Peters Group plc* (1995) IRLR 190 (EAT); *Morris v John Grose Group Limited* (1998) IRLR 499 (EAT)

[122] ARD Article 4.1

[123] TUPE Regulation 8(2)

[124] *D'Urso v Ercolle Martell* [1992] IRLR 136 (ECJ)

[125] *Trafford v Sharpe and Fisher* (Building Supplies) Limited (1994) IRLR 325 (EAT)

[126] *Warner v Adnet* (1998) IRLR 394 (CA) and *Kerry Foods Limited v Creber* (2000) IRLR 10 (EAT)

[127] *Whitehouse v Blatchford & Sons* (1999) IRLR 492 (CA)

[128] *Whitehouse*, see note 127

[129] *Wheeler v Patel and J Golding Group of Companies* (1987) IRLR 211 (EAT) and *Ibex Trading Company Limited v Walton* (1994) IRLR 564 (EAT)

[130] *Wheeler v Patel*, see note 126

[131] *Thompson v SCS Consulting Limited and others* [2001] IRLR 801 (EAT)

[132] *BSG Property Services Limited v Tuck*, see note 12

[133] *BSG Property Services Limited v Tuck*, see note 12

[134] *Berriman v Delabole Slate* (1985) IRLR 305 (CA)

[135] *Gorictree Limited v Jenkinson* (1984) IRLR 391 (EAT)

[136] Section 188 and 195 Trade Union and Labour Relations (Consolidation) Act 1992

[137] See, for example, *Gorictree Limited v Jenkinson*, see note 135

[138] TUPE Regulation 5(5) and *Rossiter v Pendragon plc*, see note 84

[139] Section 13 Employment Rights Act 1996

[140] Section 11 Employment Rights Act 1996

[141] See *Rask* and *Collino* cases at note 85 above

[142] *Foreningen af Arbejdsledere I Danmark v Daddy's Dance Hall* (1988) IRLR 315 (ECJ) and *Collino*, note 85

[143] *Credit Suisse First Boston v Padiachy* (1998) IRLR 504 (HC)

[144] *Wilson and others v St Helens Borough Council and British Fuels Limited v Meade and Baxendale* (1998) IRLR 706 (HL)

[145] *Collino*, see note 85

[146] *Lutak v William West and Sons (Ilkeston) Limited* IRLB January 2002 (EAT); *Ralton v Havering FE College* (2001) IRLR 738 (EAT)

[147] ARD Article 7; TUPE Regulation 10

[148] TUPE Regulation 10(5)

[149] TUPE Regulation 10(1)

[150] *Institute of Professional and Civil Servants v Secretary of State for Defence* (1987) IRLR 373 (EAT)

[151] TUPE Regulation 10(4)

[152] TUPE Regulation 10(2)

[153] TUPE Regulation 10(2)(c)

[154] TUPE Regulation 10(3)

[155] TUPE Regulation 11(3)

[156] *Kerry Foods Limited v Creber* (2000) IRLR 10 (EAT)

[157] *Angus Jowett & Co v NUTGW* (1985) IRLR 326 (EAT)

[158] *TGWU v James McKinnon Junior (Haulage) Limited* (2001) IRLR 597 (EAT)

[159] TUPE Regulation 11(2)

[160] TUPE Regulation 11(3)

[161] ARD Article 7.4

[162] See *Dines v Initial and Pall Mall* (1994) IRLR 336 (CA)

[163] As at least one Industrial (as was then) Tribunal has found, see *Leeds School of Music* case, unreported Industrial Tribunal decision 1997

[164] TUPE Regulation 10(5)

[165] *R v British Coal ex parte Vardy* (1993) 104 (per Glidewell LJ) adopted by *King v Eaton* (1998) IRLR 686 (Court of Session). These cases relate to the wording in the Collective Redundancies Directive and s188 et seq of Trade Union and Labour Relations (Consolidation) Act 1992 which requires consultation "with a view to reaching agreement", a slight difference the significance of which has not yet been legally established

[166] TUPE Regulation 10(6)

[167] *Commission v UK* (1994) IRLR 392 (ECJ)

[168] Collective Redundancies and Transfer of Undertakings (Protection of Employment) (Amendment) Regulations 1995

[169] *R v Secretary of State for Trade and Industry ex parte UNISON* (1996) IRLR 438 (Divisional Court)

[170] Collective Redundancies and Transfer of Undertakings (Protection of Employment) (Amendment) Regulations 1999

[171] TUPE Regulation 10(2)

[172] TUPE Regulation 10(2A)(a)

[173] TUPE Regulation 10(2A)(b)

[174] TUPE Regulation 10A

[175] TUPE Regulation 10(6A)

[176] TUPE Regulation 10(8)
[177] TUPE Regulation 10(8)
[178] TUPE Regulation 10(8A)
[179] Employment Rights Act 1996, Section 47
[180] Employment Rights Act 1996, Section 103
[181] Employment Rights Act 1996, Section 108(1) and (3)
[182] TUPE Regulation 11(1) and (8)
[183] TUPE Regulation 11(4) and (11)
[184] TUPE Regulation 11(11)
[185] *Kerry Foods Limited v Creber* (2000) IRLR 10 (EAT)
[186] *TGWU v James McKinnon Junior (Haulage) Limited* (2001) IRLR 597 (EAT)
[187] TUPE Regulation 10(3) and (4)
[188] TUPE Regulations 10(7) and 11(2)
[189] ARD Article 7.4
[190] TUPE Regulation 11(1)(d)
[191] TUPE Regulation 11(1)(a)
[192] TUPE Regulation 11(2B)
[193] *Ashford School and another v Nixon and others* IDS Brief 709 (EAT)
[194] *Commission v UK* [(994) IRLR 392 (ECJ)
[195] See comments in *Commission v UK*, note 194 above
[196] See for example *Von Colson v Land Nordrhein Westfalen* (1994) ECR 1891 (ECJ)
[197] Ian McCartney MP, then Minister of State who said "These amendments will safeguard employees' rights when the ownership of the business in which they work changes, without setting up barriers to block economic progress. Promoting this co-operative partnership approach to business restructuring will help competitiveness and employment flexibility, by helping the labour market to adapt to structural change in the economy without walking over the rights of employees"
[198] Transfer of Undertakings (Protection of Employment) Regulations 1981: Government Proposals for Reform and Detailed Background Paper, URN01/1158
[199] Staff Transfers in the Public Sector: Statement of Practice January 2000, Cabinet Office
[200] ARD Article 3.4(a)
[201] *Beckmann v Dynamco*, see note 91
[202] ARD Article 3.2
[203] *Wilson v St Helens Borough Council and Meade v British Fuels Limited*, see note 57
[204] See for a recent example *Thompson v SCS Consulting Limited* and others (2001) IRLR 801 (EAT)
[205] ARD Article 7.4 and TUPE Regulations 10(7) and 11(2)
[206] Discussion Document July 2002 URN02/1058, DTI
[207] John Hutton, Minster of State for Health, quoted in *Financial Times* 19 March 2002

9

Information and consultation

MALCOLM SARGEANT

Malcolm Sargeant is a Reader in Employment Law at Middlesex University Business School.

Introduction

This chapter is about an employer's obligation to provide information to and consult with employees. These two terms imply a certain number of characteristics.

Firstly, information is material that will help employees' representatives to reach a considered conclusion on an issue. The definitions offered in the legislation considered here provide that this information should be given in such a form as to make it comprehensible and that it should be provided in good time so that the employees' representatives have time to consider it, using such advice as they may have available. Connected to this is the issue of confidentiality. All the definitions provide that certain information must be kept confidential. There is also the opportunity for employers to withhold information that is too sensitive. Importantly, however, there are provisions for an independent view of whether information is confidential or not.

Secondly, consultation is something that follows on from the provision of information. It is aimed at creating a dialogue between employers and employees' representatives. At the very minimum this means the representatives being asked for a view and then the employer responding to that view with considered reasons for accepting it or not. The important issue on consultation is when it takes place in relation to any management decision. An early version of the Workplace Information and Consultation Directive, for example, provided that a management decision taken without prior consultation would not have any legal consequences. This was, not surprisingly, dropped from the final version. It does, however, emphasise the need for consultation to be part of the decision-making process, rather than a management tool which is concerned with selling a decision to employees once it has been taken.

EU source

Most of the current mandatory requirements for employers to consult their employees in the United Kingdom are as a result of European Union measures. The European Union has had a policy of trying to introduce a comprehensive and harmonised approach to consultation for a number of years and there are a number of levels at which this policy works. These are at the EU level itself, at a transnational level amongst employers who operate at this level, and at the national level within Member States of the Community. This has resulted in a number of measures which have required, and will require, employers, who may not previously had one, to set up a formal information and consultation process with their employees. This includes the Social Dialogue process at EU level, European Works Councils at transnational level and the newly adopted Information and Consultation Directive at the national level.

At all these levels, existing systems of industrial relations are to be adapted to include mandatory rules on information and consultation. The future impact on the United Kingdom and Ireland of these measures is likely to be significantly greater than on most other Member States of the European Community. Characteristics of these initiatives are:

(i) At a European level this may involve participation in the development of Community law with regard to social policy. The social partners[1] have reached framework agreements on parental leave,[2] part-time work[3] and fixed-term work,[4] all of which have been turned into EU Directives. Ironically, of course, they failed to reach agreement, amongst other matters, on the subject of the rights of employees to information and consultation at the national level.

(ii) There should be a formal structure for informing and consulting employees at a transnational and national level. Thus the European Works Council Directive[5] and Information and Consultation Directive[6] require the establishment of formal information and consultation procedures. If such procedures previously existed, then these were able to continue, provided that they met the requirements of the new rules.

(iii) This structure should be negotiated between the parties whilst working together "in a spirit of co-operation". This phrase appears in Article 6 of the European Works Council Directive and Article 1 of the Information and Consultation Directive. Despite this, both Directives provide for a minimum default procedure if the parties fail, for whatever reason, to reach an agreement.

(iv) Minimum standards for the agreement, including matters to be consulted on, are included in the rules. These concern the economic situation of the undertaking and, especially, issues related to employment.

(v) There are specific rules governing confidentiality. This has been a concern of employers and an argument against consultation on certain issues. It has two aspects: firstly, those issues which are told to workers' representatives in confidence, secondly, those matters which are not revealed to those representatives at all. Ultimately, it is difficult to see how the issue can be resolved. There will be some issues which are commercially very secret, but are also likely to have an effect upon future employment structures in an undertaking.

(vi) Employee representatives are to be protected from discrimination in carrying out their duties.

(vii) There will be sanctions if the employer refuses to carry out his duties under the Directives.

Reasons for the policy

This process is motivated by a number of factors, but perhaps especially by the view that information and consultation will engender greater levels of trust between the parties in the workplace. These levels of trust will enable the necessary process of change in work practice and organisation to take place more easily than otherwise. There seems to be an assumption that there is a process by which information and consultation will lead to greater trust, which, in itself, will lead to the creation of a consensus for the management of change.

This also leads to problems, because it is not always possible to immediately identify the partners to the dialogue, whether at European level or at the transnational or national level. The result is that sometimes the representative parties have to be created in order for the model to succeed, as in the present United Kingdom rules on consultation in situations of collective redundancies and transfers of undertakings. This lack of representative parties is one of the uncomfortable issues that the United Kingdom will continue to have to face when implementing the new Workplace Directive on Information and Consultation.

There are a number of motivations for this policy. Important ones are

(i)   to aid the management of change in workplaces which results from the establishment of the internal market in the Community. The EU's view, with some justification, is that the development of the single market will lead to large numbers of mergers and acquisitions as industry and commerce become more European-based, rather than nationally-based. This inevitable re-structuring will affect employees and the process will be eased by keeping employees informed and by consulting them on the changes.

(ii) to aid the management of change resulting from the developments of new forms of work. One of the motivations for Community action on protecting part-time workers, temporary workers and those on fixed-term contracts is the belief that the nature of work is changing. Employment practices are changing from the traditional one-job five-day week. Again, the management of this change process is something that will be helped by a practice of information and consultation.

(iii) it is a reflection of the practice in most Member States apart from the United Kingdom. It is important to accept that the European Community does not act in isolation. Many of its policy makers and employees come from Member States where greater information and consultation practices exist when compared to the United Kingdom.

(iv) it must be comprehensive, because to only do it at one level, such as a national or a transnational level, is to leave further room for avoidance by those who wish to do so.

The contrast between the United Kingdom and other Member States

Part of the problem for the United Kingdom in accepting European Commission proposals on matters relating to participation and involvement, is that there is a different approach to the subject in this country and, perhaps, Ireland as compared with most other Member States of the Community. It is too simplistic to state that there is one model for industrial relations in the United Kingdom and Ireland, say, and a different model in all the other Member States. There is a great variety in the approach of each country. There have, however, been attempts to categorise groups of countries into different models of industrial relations. The Council of Ministers at their meeting in Hanover in 1988 requested a study of the different approaches of the Member States.[7] This study concluded that it was possible to identify three different models of regulating relations between the State, the social partners and the community. These were the Romanic-German system, the Anglo–Irish system and the Nordic one.

The Romanic-German system included the legal systems of Belgium, France, Germany (Western), Greece, Italy, Luxembourg, the Netherlands, Portugal and Spain. Essential features of this system were the existence of written constitutions which enshrined certain fundamental rights and freedoms, the role of statute law in regulating individual and collective relations and the use of collective agreements as a source of regulation. In contrast, essential features of the Anglo–Irish system were the absence of fundamental rights enshrined in a constitution, the abstentionist role of the state in regulating collective relations and the decisive role of the courts. The Nordic system was characterised by the importance of collective agreements as a cornerstone of the system of regulation. This combined with high levels of trade union membership meant that these agreements had wide effect.

Specific and relevant features of United Kingdom post-war industrial relations are

(i) the existence of a strong and unified trade union movement, which was, until the last decade, the traditional means by which employers negotiated with their workers. There has been little demand for the establishment of any formal procedures outside this employer/trade union channel.

(ii) the resistance to any extension of collective responsibility by the governments of the 1980s and early 1990s. Indeed the pressure was in favour of individualisation of employment relations in preference to collective relations between employers and employee representatives.

There are, of course, other characteristics which distinguish the United Kingdom from other Member States, for example, the lack of a constitution safeguarding basic rights, but these two may be particularly important. The contrast with the rest of the European Community is striking in that they have continued to develop their traditional collective approach where rights to information, consultation and, often, collective bargaining are enshrined in statute or tradition.

A report by the European Commission in 2000[8] compared, for example, the nature and extent of employee information and consultation procedures. Apart from a limited number of occasions, such procedures are voluntary in nature in the United Kingdom and Ireland, but compulsory on a general basis in all the other Member States.

The same report suggests that there are two models for employee representation in Europe. The first is a single channel system where the trade unions are the only, or main, channel of communication with the employer. This takes place in the United

Kingdom, Ireland, Finland and Sweden. Other countries have a two-tier system where there is an elected body representing all the employees in each organisation, which often exists alongside the trade unions. These works councils/committees vary between different Member States. In Germany, Greece, Spain, the Netherlands, Austria, and Portugal such bodies are made up entirely of employees. In Denmark and Luxembourg they are joint employer/employee bodies and in Belgium and France they are actually chaired by the employer. They also vary in their rights, which may include the right to be informed, the right to be consulted and the right to decide jointly.

The level at which consultation takes place also varies between the establishment level and the undertaking level:

Country	Basic body	Basic level	Threshold (employees)
Belgium	Works council	Establishment	20–100
Denmark	Cooperation Committees	Undertaking	5–35
France	Staff delegates	Establishment	11
	Works council	Undertaking	50
Germany	Works council	Establishment	5
		Undertaking	100
Italy	Trade union representation	Establishment	5–15

Netherlands	Works council	Establishment	10–50
Portugal	Workers commission	Undertaking	–
	Trade union delegates		
Spain	Staff delegates	Establishment	6–50
	Works council	Establishment	50
Sweden	Trade union	Establishment	–
	delegates		

Features of information and consultation procedures in the Member States:

(i) There are permanent bodies in which workers participate either as the sole members or in partnership with their employers.

(ii) These bodies have the right to be informed and consulted.

(iii) The information and consultation includes:

- material about the financial status of the undertaking and predicted future trends

- material about employment trends and various aspects of the undertaking's policies affecting employees. This might include recruitment, training, redundancies and job grading

- information and consultation on any expected or actual changes in policy or circumstances related to the employees

(iv) This information and consultation takes place periodically, often annually, but sometimes more often and more regularly.

In its proposal for a Directive on Information and Consultation, the European Commission published a summary of the objective and manner of information and consultation in Member States.

Austria

Information – works council may request copies of documents.

Consultation – consultation on current matters at least once every three months, or once a month at the works council's request.

Belgium

Information – information prior to decisions; members of works council may ask for additional information, put questions, express criticism and make suggestions and opinions; the head of the undertaking must say how these will be followed up.

Consultation – consultation prior to decisions; in the event of major changes, then proper consultation in advance, especially on the repercussions on employment; specific rules concerning collective redundancies.

Finland
Information – information must be presented in such a way as allows discussion on the subject.
Consultation – before any major decision, the employer must negotiate with the employees concerned, or their representatives, to discuss the reasons for the planned decision, its effects and the possible alternatives. Proposals must be tabled in writing five days before the start of negotiations.

France
Information – regular information on certain occasions; right to carry out studies and research needed for performance of functions; different procedures depending upon subject.
Consultation – works council must, in order to draw up a reasoned opinion, be provided with precise information, in writing, in sufficient time to consider the matter, and the employer's reasoned response to its observations. Consultation must precede the taking and implementing of decisions.

Germany
Information – The works council must be fully informed and in good time by the employer. Documents essential to the performance of its tasks must be placed at its disposal on request at any time.
Consultation – must take place prior to decisions; right to be consulted, usually after a period of thinking time with a view to expressing an opinion; favourable opinion or agreement needed in some cases.

Greece
Information – right to receive regular information before implementation of decisions.
Consultation – deliberation with employer.

Italy
Information and *consultation* will be in accordance with the sectoral collective agreement, although compulsory in the event of transfers or collective redundancies.

Luxembourg
Information – on the running and status of the undertaking; annual general report.
Consultation – regular consultation; reasoned replies to joint committee opinions; consultation prior to decisive decisions.

Netherlands
Information – the head of the undertaking is required, on request, to provide

full information and details which the central works council needs in order to perform its functions.

Consultation - head of undertaking must request an opinion, in time for it to influence the decision to be taken, by providing reasons for decisions and the consequences of the decisions; consultation meeting must take place before the works council expresses its opinion; where an opinion is expressed, the head of the undertaking must notify the works council of its decision and any reasons why it is different to that expressed by the works council.

Portugal
Information - right to receive all information that they need in order to perform their functions.
Consultation - opinion prior to decisions.

Spain
Information - information for employees on subjects likely to have direct or indirect repercussions on industrial relations.
Consultation - prior consultation in the event of changes likely to effect employees.

Sweden
Information - employer must keep trade unions regularly informed of production and financial developments, as well as main points of staff policy; if possible, without excessive cost or inconvenience, employer must provide, at the request of trade unions, copies of documents.
Consultation - before a major change in activity, the employer must, on own initiative, negotiate with the trade union; the employer must suspend the decision during negotiations.

In addition there are a number of countries that have statutory board level representation, in certain circumstances, for employees or their representatives.[9]

There is, therefore, a greater institutionalised involvement of the social partners in many Member States when compared to the United Kingdom. This difference is perhaps further accentuated by the concept of the "social pact". This is a general term relating to the institutionalisation of collective bargaining by allowing the social partners a role in the decision-making process. It is important not to produce a simplistic formula that suggests that all other countries have formal agreements at national level between the social partners and governments, whilst the United Kingdom does not. The arrangements and methods of reaching agreement vary widely between different countries. Nevertheless, with the exception of France and the United Kingdom, all Member States, during the 1990s, achieved a social pact or social agreement (and it can still be said also that the role of the social partners in France is greater than that in the United Kingdom). These pacts or social agreements concerned issues such as competitiveness, combating unemployment, the labour market, vocational training and social protection.[10]

The more significant role for the social partners and collective bargaining/ consultation is reflected in the policies of the European Community. The Commission has a long history of putting forward a variety of proposals on consultation and participation as well as more recent initiatives in the field of social protection and health and safety. The most recent of these is the proposal for establishing a general framework for consultation within Member States. This partnership or involvement of the social partners in social policy and legislation may also be a reason for the apparent difficulty that the United Kingdom has in accepting new initiatives on health and safety or social protection, for example, when the Working Time Directive was adopted, most Member States had legislation on working hours and holidays. For these States the Directive was an issue of harmonisation of existing approaches. For the United Kingdom it was a question of introducing the approach for the first time.

Transnational information and consultation

The measures considered here are those concerned with the establishment of European Works Councils and those dealing with the information and consultation requirements in a European Company, Societas Europea (SE).

The European Works Council Directive

The European Works Council Directive[11] (EWC Directive) was finally adopted after some 14 years of debate. It was originally adopted under the Agreement on Social Policy 1992 and so did not bind the United Kingdom. After the 1997 general election, and a willingness of the United Kingdom to accept the Social Policy Agreement, the Council adopted an extension Directive with a requirement for it to be transposed into UK national law by 15 December 1999.[12] The purpose of the Directive was

> to improve the right to information and to consultation of employees in Community-scale undertakings and Community-scale groups of undertakings.[13]

A Community-scale undertaking is one that has at least 1,000 employees within the Member States and at least 150 employees in each of at least two Member States. A Community-scale group of undertakings is one where a group of undertakings has at least 1000 employees within the Member States with at least two group undertakings in different Member States employing at least 150 employees.[14]

The EWC Directive was transposed into national law by The Transnational Information and Consultation of Employees Regulations 1999 (TICE Regulations), which came into effect on 15 January 2000.[15] By this time many British employees were already represented in EWCs set up by multinational companies, influenced by the law of other Member States which had already transposed the Directive. The Regulations do not have effect if there is already in existence an Article 6 or an Article 13 agreement, unless the parties have decided otherwise.[16] An Article 6 agreement is one that establishes an EWC in accordance with the Directive. An Article 13 agreement is one that established their own information and consultation procedures before the Directive was transposed into national law.

Consultation is defined in the TICE Regulations as meaning the exchange of views and the establishment of a dialogue in the context of an EWC or in the context of an information and consultation procedure.[17] The central management of an undertaking is responsible for creating the conditions and the means necessary for setting up an EWC, where the central management is situated in the United Kingdom, where it is situated outside the country, but has its representative agent based in the United Kingdom, or, if neither of these, has its biggest group of employees in the United Kingdom. The number of UK employees is to be calculated by taking an average over a two year period, with provision for counting some part-timers as a half number. The number of employees in undertakings in other Member States is to be calculated in accordance with whatever formula that state has adopted in its law transposing the EWC Directive. Employee representatives are entitled to information on these calculations so that they can decide whether the employer qualifies. If the information given to them is incomplete or inadequate, they may present a complaint to the Central Arbitration Committee (CAC).

If central management does not act on its own initiative, the whole process of establishing an EWC can be started with a request from 100 employees, or their representatives, in two undertakings in two Member States. If there is a dispute as to whether a valid request has been made, this can be referred to the CAC for a decision.

The first stage is the establishment of a special negotiating body (SNB), whose task is to negotiate, with central management, a written agreement covering "the scope, composition, functions and terms of office" of an EWC or the arrangements for implementing an information and consultation procedure. The SNB must consist of at least one representative from each Member State and there is a weighting formula to increase representation from bigger units in different states. The UK representatives are to be elected by a ballot of UK employees and any complaints about the ballot are to be made to the CAC. Where there is already an elected body in existence with whom consultation takes place, then that body can nominate the representatives from its membership.

The contents of the agreement to be reached between the SNB and central management are set out in Article 6 of the EWC Directive and are reflected in

Part IV of the TICE Regulations. The two parties are to negotiate in "a spirit of cooperation with a view to reaching an agreement". They may negotiate an agreement to set up an EWC or to establish an information and consultation procedure. The EWC agreement must include agreement on

(i)   the undertakings which are covered by the agreement
(ii)   the composition of the EWC
(iii)   the functions and procedures for information and consultation
(iv)   the venue, frequency and duration of meetings
(v)   the financial and material resources to be allocated to the EWC
(vi)   the duration of the agreement and the procedure for re-negotiation.

If the parties decide to establish an information and consultation procedure instead of an EWC, then this agreement must specify a method by which the information and consultation representatives[18] are to enjoy the right to meet and discuss the information conveyed to them.

The information conveyed to the representatives must relate in particular to transnational questions which significantly affect the interests of employees. If negotiations do not start within six months of a valid request by employees or fail to finish within three years from the date of that request, the Regulations provide for a default agreement, which is contained in the Schedule. These provide for an EWC of between three and 30 members, with at least one member from each Member State where there are undertakings. This representation is weighted according to the relative size of the undertakings in different states. The rules cover the election or appointment of UK delegates and provide that the EWC should meet at least once per annum.

Complaints about the failure of the negotiating process, either because of lack of agreement or a failure to start the process, or because of a failure to keep to the agreement, are to be referred directly to the EAT. The EAT may order the defaulter to remedy the failure and impose a fine of up to £75,000. Central management will have a defence if they are able to show that the failure resulted "from a reason beyond the central management's control or that it has some other reasonable excuse for its failure".

One concern related to statutory rights to information is the revealing by management of "confidential" information. Regulation 24 TICE Regulations provides that central management is not required to disclose any information or document which, "according to objective criteria", would seriously prejudice or harm the functioning of the undertaking concerned. It is interesting to speculate as to what this actually means. Would the sale of a subsidiary undertaking in one Member State be such information, if it would prejudice the price received, even though it might have important effects for employees? There is an obligation for a representative, or an adviser to a representative, not to disclose confidential information unless it is a protected disclosure under Section 43A ERA 1996.

The CAC has the responsibility of settling disputes about confidentiality and can order information to be disclosed by management or order a representative not to disclose information.

Information and consultation representatives, members of EWCs, SNBs and candidates for relevant elections have certain rights. These are:
(i) the right to reasonable time off with pay during working hours
(ii) protection against unfair dismissal; dismissal as a result of performing any of the functions or duties related to any of these bodies will make the dismissal automatically unfair in terms of Part X ERA 1996, the exception to this being where the reason or the principal reason for dismissal is a breach of confidentiality contained in Regulation 23(1), unless the employee reasonably believed the disclosure to be a protected disclosure within the meaning of Section 43A ERA 1996
(iii) the right not to be subject to detriment as a result of performing any of the duties or functions related to the bodies.

Complaints about any infringement of these rights are to be made to an employment tribunal.

The Company Statute

On 20 December 2000 the Council of Ministers reached agreement on a proposed Regulation establishing a European Company Statute. The European Parliament agreed its support for the proposal at its meeting on 4 September 2001. This gives companies operating in more than one Member State the option of establishing themselves as "European companies" or Societas Europea (SE) operating under EU rules rather than a variety of national rules as at present. An SE can be established by the merger or formation of companies with a presence in at least two different Member States.

One concern in establishing this procedure was that companies previously based in countries with strong requirements for information and consultation might be able to avoid these requirements by establishing themselves as an SE, especially if they were merging with companies from countries with weak consultation requirements. As part of this agreement, therefore, there is a directive[19] establishing rules for information, consultation and, possibly, participation of workers employed by the SE.

Information is defined as informing the representatives of the employees

in a manner and with a content which allows the employees' representatives to undertake an in-depth assessment of the possible impact and, where appropriate, prepare consultations with the competent organ of the SE.[20]

Consultation is defined as

> The establishment of dialogue and exchange of views between the body
> representative of the employees . . . and the competent organ of the SE, at a
> time, in a manner and with a content which allows the employees'
> representatives, on the basis of information provided, to express an opinion
> on measures envisaged by the competent organ which may be taken into
> account in the decision-making process within the SE.[21]

When the SE is created there will need to be a special negotiating body to discuss
the arrangements for employee involvement. In the absence of any agreement
standard rules will be established by the directive which will need to be followed.
These require information and consultation on matters such as

(i) the structure, economic and financial situation
(ii) the probable development of the business and of production and sales
(iii) the situation and probable trend of employment and investment
(iv) substantial changes concerning organisation, introduction of new
working methods or production processes
(v) transfers of production, mergers, cut-backs or closures of undertakings,
establishments or important parts thereof
(vi) collective redundancies.

There are also provisions for employee participation for those SE's which include
companies from countries where there are such rules. Participation can include
the right to elect or appoint, or oppose the election or appointment, of members
of the supervisory or administrative board.

It remains to be seen how many such organisations will be established.

Successes and failures of the transnational approach

The European Community has long recognised that a problem for workers
employed by multinational organisations is the ability of the employer to move
work between countries. Taking work from one country and relocating it to
another is a way of making workers more compliant. The European Works
Council Directive (EWC) was designed to ensure that such employers consult
their employees on a multinational basis. There have been some well publicised
failures and some of the lessons to be learnt from these failures are discussed
below. It is important, however, not to let these failures disguise the success of
the EWC Directive in establishing a transnational body for consultation in
hundreds of organisations. This has also enabled the work forces from different
Member States to establish closer links with each other.

> On February 28 1997, the French car manufacturer Renault announced the
> closure of its plant in Vilvoorde, Belgium.[22] The move was justified by Renault
> as being part of a re-organisation brought about by a need to make economies.

The closure was predicted to affect 3,100 employees of the firm's Belgian plant and about 1,000 other jobs in the supply industry. Like the Vauxhall workers in Luton, the Belgian workers had negotiated a flexibility and investment package and the plant was regarded as having good levels of productivity and quality. The closure of the plant was announced without any prior consultation with the workforce.

It was suggested that Renault had breached the rules contained in the EWC Directive and the Collective Redundancies Directive. What is clear is that there were and are no adequate sanctions to stop an employer making a decision of this kind, providing that they are willing to bear the cost of any breach of rules. The problem with the EWC Directive is that whilst it ensures the setting up of an information and consultation procedure, it does not make specific provision for dealing with emergency situations. There is no specific safeguard that requires the employer to call emergency meetings of its workforce representatives in the event of a crisis that might lead to closure or significant redundancies. The Renault information and consultation agreement required the company to notify its European committee of major changes within the group, the economic and financial situation, the investment and production situation, changes in work organisation and production processes and training policy. This clearly did not happen. In the event, after much pressure from governments, trade unions and the European Commission, Renault amended its information and consultation agreement to deal with future situations. The amendment read:

In the event of a planned decision which has transnational consequences and is of a nature such as to affect significantly employees interests, the European group committee will meet in extraordinary session. In this situation, the European group committee will be consulted within the meaning of Article 2 of the Directive of 22 September 1994, that is to say the exchange of views at an appropriate time such that the elements of the discussion can still be taken into account in the decision-making process.

On 16 March 2000, the supervisory board of BMW, which owned the Rover group announced that the company was planning to dispose of parts of its Rover subsidiary, including the Longbridge and the Solihull plants. According to Professor Milberg, Chair of BMW, the decision to discontinue took place between 1 and 16 March, although there had been exploratory talks with potential purchasers in late 1999. The story broke in the *Sud Deutsche Zeitung* on 14 March. There had been no prior information for, or consultation with, the workforce. The House of Commons Trade and Industry Committee[23] stated that

BMW's disgraceful failure to consult or even inform the workforce

(i)   may have constituted a breach of the 1975 EU Directive on Consultation on Collective Redundancies…;

(ii)   emphasises the importance of ensuring that the existing structure for multi-national companies, which would seem to have proved wholly ineffective on this occasion, provides real rights for workforce representatives; the trade unions told us that the last meeting of the European Works Council had been in the Autumn of 1999;

(iii) led to suggestions to us by the local trades unions that there might be merit in reconsidering the firm objections raised by Ministers to the proposed EU Directive on establishing a general framework for informing and consulting employees…;

(iv)   led the British trades unions to suggest to us that their position was weakened by not being on the supervisory board.

Trade union evidence to the committee confirmed that there had been no prior discussions with them, although the supervisory board in Germany, including German trades union representatives had been consulted, in accordance with German law. The BMW European Works Council, which had six Rover representatives as against nine BMW ones, was not consulted.

On 12 May 2000, Ford confirmed rumours that mass car production would end at Dagenham. This was despite a 1997 promise that Ford would produce a new model at the plant. The new Fiesta was to be built in its German facory in Cologne. Mr Nick Scheele, chair of Ford of Europe, blamed over-capacity and denied that the company had chosen to end car making at Dagenham because it was easier to dismiss workers in the United Kingdom than the rest of Europe.[24]

On 12 December 2000 the American car company, General Motors, announced the ending of car production at its plant in Luton, with the loss of 2,000 jobs and perhaps another 5,500 amongst suppliers. The company chair, Mr Nick Reilly, stated that the closure decision had been taken at the company's European headquarters in Zurich and was necessary to retain competitive manufacturing in the United Kingdom.[25] The announcement came as a surprise as the company had previously announced heavy investment in the plant. It is said that many workers and their representatives first heard about the closure from the media.

On 1 February 2001, the Anglo-Dutch steel group announced plans to reduce its UK work force by 6000 over two years. This will include reductions at the Llanwern plant and significant redundancies in Teeside. In this case not only did the workers and their representatives not know of the closure, but the British Government was angered by the failure of the company to consult them. Mr Alistair Campbell, a government spokesperson, is quoted as saying: "It is a pretty extraordinary state of affairs where, as the government, if you were to ask us when is this decision going to be announced we would say we don't know."

The House of Commons Trade and Industry Committee[26] noted that car manufacturers had praised the British work force for its flexibility. Indeed Vauxhall had referred to its 1998 pay deal as "revolutionary". At the same time the Committee noted the trades unions complaint that it was easier to dispose of workers in the United Kingdom, rather than elsewhere and that this was the reason for the reduction at Corus, the reason why Dagenham was chosen by Ford, rather than Cologne and a reason why Luton was selected.

The Committee agreed that this was factually correct and cited as examples:

(i) The normal notice required for redundancy is shorter in the United Kingdom than many other European countries, where "there is a long drawn out process of notification and consultation which may well involve more cost to the employer who is continuing to pay wages".

(ii) Legally binding labour agreements may in practice not always make jobs more secure; but the possibility of facing the legal and financial consequences of a breach of contract may cause an employer to pause.

(iii) Statutory minimum redundancy payments are lower in the United Kingdom than in many other EU countries.

(iv) There is no requirement on an employer in the United Kingdom to fund a "social plan" in the event of a major redundancy.

It also stated:

The justifiable criticism over both the Dagenham and Luton closures and the BMW decision on Longbridge was that the workforce were given no opportunity to comment on the proposals being developed and to come up with alternatives before final decisions were made and announced. There is evidence that viable alternative options overlooked or summarily dismissed by management can come out of such consultation. Prior consultation can make good management sense.

A common feature of all the closures mentioned here is the lack of prior consultation and, usually, information, with the affected workers or their representatives. It is not possible to say whether such information and consultation would have made any difference to the final outcome, but it is possible to say that different outcomes may have resulted.

The reason for closures was not a lack of consultation. This had to do with over-capacity in particular industries when looked at on a global scale. Multinational companies made decisions to reduce their capacity. It is arguable, however, that apparent reduced consultation requirements and lower redundancy penalties in the United Kingdom make it more likely to be selected in the event of such decisions to reduce productive capacity. (It is also arguable that this also makes the United Kingdom a more attractive place for inward investment).

The problem with the transnational approach is that it cannot exist in isolation from what goes on in individual Member States. Its failures stem from a lack of adequate sanctions and an ability to fulfil national obligations to inform and consult without taking the transnational obligations as seriously.

Information and consultation requirements in the United Kingdom

Apart from the consultation requirements related to European Works Councils and the European Company there are a number of other areas where mandatory rules on consultation with employees already exist. Those considered here relate to collective redundancies, transfers of undertakings and health and safety.

Collective redundancies

Council Directive 98/59/EC on the approximation of the laws of the Member States relating to collective redundancies is a consolidation directive. It consolidates Directive 75/129/EEC as amended by Directive 92/56/EEC on the same subject. The original Directive was adopted in 1975 and transposed into British law very quickly. It was incorporated into the Employment Protection Act 1975 and has been part of national law, subject to various amendments, ever since. The provisions are now contained in Part IV Chapter II of the Trade Union and Labour Relations (Consolidation) Act 1992, which outlines the procedure for handling collective redundancies.

The duty to consult rests with an employer who is proposing to dismiss 20 or more employees at one establishment within a period of 90 days or less for reasons of redundancy. This consultation shall begin "in good time" and in any event at least 30 days before the first dismissal takes effect, or at least 90 days before the first dismissal takes effect if the employer is proposing to dismiss 100 or more employees at one establishment within a period of 90 days.

Article 2(1) of the Collective Redundancies Directive provides that consultations should commence when the employer is contemplating collective redundancies. This was transposed into UK law as when the employer is proposing to dismiss.

MSF v Refuge Assurance plc[27] concerned the existing mandatory requirement to consult in the event of collective redundancies. The case involved the amalgamation of two insurance companies, Refuge Assurance and United Friendly Assurance. One outcome from the merger was that 1777 employees were dismissed for reasons of redundancy. This included the closure of one of the head offices and the joining together of the two companies' sales forces. One of the issues was at what point in the process did the obligation to consult the representatives of the employees[28] arise. Formal consultations with the trade union did not commence until after the merged board of the two companies had agreed in principle to the plans concerning staff and redundancies.

The Employment Appeal Tribunal concluded that it was not possible to construe the word 'proposing' in s188 TULRCA as meaning "contemplation" as in Article 2(1) of the Directive. It adopted the view stated in *R v British Coal ex parte Vardy*[29] that "contemplation" is at a much earlier stage than "proposes". The latter term suggests that the employer has decided to take some action, rather than merely contemplating the possibility of redundancies.[30]

Scotch Premier Meat Ltd v Burns[31] concerned a business which had lost a major order and, as a result, decided at a board meeting that the two options to be pursued were either to sell the company as a going concern or to sell it as a development site. The latter course would result in 155 employees losing their jobs. The Employment Appeal Tribunal held that the decision to take one of two alternatives was the point at which the employer proposed to dismiss, even though they retained the option to sell the business as a going concern. The court also stated that "contemplate" may involve a great many options, whilst "propose" suggested specific proposals.

One issue is the linking together of the terms information and consultation. If there is to be consultation upon proposals made by an employer, then it is likely that those proposals will be at an advanced stage before the information can be given. If the information can be given during the course of the consultation, then that consultation can take place in the meantime. If the information has to be given at the start of the consultation,[32] then the whole process will be delayed.

The consultation itself is to include consultation about ways of avoiding the dismissals, reducing the number of employees to be dismissed, and mitigating the consequences of the dismissals. There is an obligation for the employer to undertake such consultations with a view to reaching agreement with the appropriate representatives. There is certain information that the employer must disclose in writing to the appropriate representatives. This information consists of the reasons for the proposals, the numbers and descriptions of employees whom it is proposed to dismiss, the total number of employees of any description employed by the employer at the establishment, the proposed method of selecting those to be dismissed and the proposed method of carrying out the dismissals and, finally, the proposed method of calculating payments if different to those required by statute. This information must be delivered to each of the appropriate representatives. Whether sufficient information has been given is one of fact for the employment tribunal to decide, although there is no rule that states that full and specific information under each of these heads should be given before consultation could begin.

Appropriate representatives

The employer must consult with the appropriate representatives of any of the employees who may be affected by the proposed dismissals or by any measures taken in connection with those dismissals. The appropriate representatives are the employees' trade union representatives if an independent trade union is recognised by the employer. If there is no such trade union then they may either consult employee representatives appointed or elected by the affected employees for some other purpose, but who have authority to receive information and be consulted about the proposed dismissals, or they may be employee representatives elected by the employees for the purpose of such consultation.

The choice of which of these two alternatives should be consulted is left to the employer. Prior to 1995 there had only been a requirement to consult trade union representatives if they were recognised by the employer. Where there were no recognised trade unions, there had been no requirement to consult at all. This approach had been challenged by the European Commission in *Commission v United Kingdom*.[33] As a result the Court of Justice held that the United Kingdom had not adequately transposed the Directive. The legislation was then amended in 1995 to allow the employer to choose whether to consult a trade union or other appropriate representatives. This was then amended again in 1999, so that an employer could choose between the alternative appropriate representatives only if there was not a recognised trade union with whom to consult.

Section 188A TULRCA sets out the requirements for the election of employee representatives where this is necessary. The onus is on the employer to make such arrangements as are reasonably practical to ensure fairness. The election is to be conducted, so far as is reasonably practicable, in secret. The employer's duties include deciding on the number of representatives to be elected, what constituencies those representatives should represent and the term of office of those representatives. The term needs to be long enough to enable the information and consultation process to be completed. The candidates for election must be affected employees at the date of the election. All affected employees have the right to vote and no affected employee must be unreasonably excluded from standing for election. Employees must be entitled to vote for as many candidates as there are representatives to be elected. The elected representatives are to be allowed access to the affected employees and given such accommodation and other facilities as are necessary. They are also entitled to reasonable time off during working hours to carry out their functions as a representative or candidate, or in order to undergo training for the performance of these functions. Where, after the election, one of those elected ceases to be a representative, then there may be a need for the election of a replacement.

Special circumstances

There are two "escape" clauses for employers unable to comply with their obligations under Section 188 TULRCA. Firstly, where there are special circumstances which make it not reasonably practicable for an employer to comply with the consultation and information requirements, they are to take all steps towards compliance that are reasonably practicable in the circumstances. Secondly, where they have invited affected employees to elect representatives and the employees have failed to do so within a reasonable time, then the employer must give all the affected employees the information set out above.

In *The Bakers' Union v Clarks of Hove Ltd*[34] the court held that there were three stages to deciding whether there was a defence in any particular case. These were, firstly, were there special circumstances, secondly, did they render compliance with the statute not reasonably practicable and, thirdly, did the employer take all the reasonable steps towards compliance as were reasonably practicable in the circumstances. In this case even an insolvency was not a special enough circumstance in itself to provide a defence against the lack of consultation.

Where an employer has failed to comply with the requirements to consult a complaint may be made to an employment tribunal. If the tribunal finds the complaint well-founded it will make a declaration to that effect and may make a protective award.

A protective award to those who have been dismissed as redundant or whom it is proposed to dismiss and the protected period, up to a maximum of 90 days, begins with the date on which the first dismissals take effect or the date of the award, whichever is earlier. The length is that which the tribunal decides is just and equitable. The object of the award is to compensate the employees for the failure of the employer to consult with their representatives. The employment tribunal needs to consider the loss of days of consultation rather than the loss or potential loss of remuneration by the employee during the protected period.

Transfers of undertakings

The purpose of the Acquired Rights Directive[35] and the Transfer Regulations[36] is contained in Article 3(1) of the amended Directive. Article 3(1) states that the transferor's rights and obligations arising from a contract of employment or from an employment relationship existing on the date of the transfer shall be transferred to the transferee employer. It is as if the contract of employment was originally made between the transferee and the employee (see Chapter 9).

The new employer (the transferee) will assume all debts related to the transferred contracts of employment as if the transferee had incurred them in the first place. This liability is not limited to debts such as pay or accrued holiday pay which arises from the contract of employment. It may also include any obligations in tort. In *DJM International Ltd v Nicholas*[37] the EAT held that liability for an act of alleged sex discrimination transferred to the transferee.

Other examples of matters that transfer are trade union recognition and collective agreements. Regulation 6 provides that collective agreements are transferred and Regulation 9 provides for the transfer of trade union recognition, although if such recognition has been given voluntarily, it is difficult to see how it can be enforced and how it can be used to stop an employer de-recognising a trade union.

Only employees who receive protection under existing national laws will be protected by the Transfer Regulations and if such an employee is dismissed for reasons connected to a relevant transfer, that employee will be treated as unfairly dismissed as in Part X ERA 1996.

Consultation

Regulation 10 of the Transfer Regulations is concerned with the duty to inform and consult employee representatives and Regulation 11 with the consequences of failing to do so. Information should be provided "long enough before a relevant transfer to enable the employer of any affected employees to consult all the persons who are appropriate representatives of any of those affected employees". The High Court, in *Institution of Professional and Civil Servants v Secretary of State for Defence*[38] decided that the words "long enough before" a transfer to enable consultation to take place meant as soon as measures are envisaged and if possible long enough before the transfer. The court held that the words did not mean as soon as measures are envisaged and in any event long enough before the transfer. This case concerned the introduction of private management into the Royal Dockyards at Rosyth and Devonport. A measure which was opposed by the trade unions. Before consultation could take place there needed to be some definite plans or proposals by the employer around which consultation could take place.

The information to be provided should consist of:

(i)   the fact that a relevant transfer is to take place, approximately when it is to take place and the reasons for it
(ii)   the legal, economic and social implications for the affected employees
(iii) the measures which are envisaged to take place in connection with the transfer, in relation to the affected employees or the fact that there are no such measures envisaged.

The rules on who are appropriate representatives and the requirements concerning their election are contained in Regulations 10(2A) and 10A Transfer Regulations. These are identical to those rules concerning the appointment of appropriate representatives for the purposes of consultation in collective redundancies (see above). The representatives are the independent trade union which is recognised by the employer. If there is no such trade union, then there are employee representatives to be elected or appointed by the affected employees, whether for the purpose of these consultations or for some other purpose.

It is, of course, both the transferor and the transferee who need to consult and there is an obligation upon the transferee to provide the transferor with information about his plans, so that the transferor can carry out their duty to consult. Where the employer actually envisages taking measures in relation to any of the affected employees, then the employer must consult the appropriate representatives "with a view to seeking their agreement to the measures to be taken". In the course of these consultations the employer will consider the representations made by the appropriate representatives and, if any of those representations are rejected, the employer must state the reasons for doing so.

There is a special circumstances defence for the employer if it renders it not reasonably practicable to perform the duty to consult and inform. In such a case the employer must take all such steps as are reasonable in the circumstances. There is also a defence for the employer if the employees fail to elect representatives. In such a case the duty to consult is fulfilled if the employer gives each employee the necessary information.

Complaints to an employment tribunal may be made for a breach of the rules concerning consultation. If the complaint is well-founded, the employment tribunal may make an award of up to a maximum of 13 weeks pay.

Health and safety

The European Council Directive on the introduction of measures to encourage improvements in the safety and health of workers[39] has specific requirements both for the provision of information to workers and for consultation and participation of workers. Article 10 ensures that workers receive information from the employer about the safety and health risks of their jobs, or their workplaces, as well as information about what protective and preventive measures are to be taken. Article 11 of the Directive provides that employers shall consult workers and / or their representatives "and allow them to take part in discussions" on all questions relating to safety and health at work. Protection is also offered to the workers or workers' representatives who take part in this process, including the right to time off work with pay for the purpose of carrying out their duties.

Safety Representatives

The Safety Representatives and Safety Committees Regulations 1977[40] (the SRSC Regulations) introduced a requirement for the appointment of safety representatives from amongst the employees by independent and recognised trade unions. These were amended in 1992, by adding Regulation 4A, which provided for the consultation of these representatives in good time on health and safety matters. This meant, of course, that where there was not a recognised trade union, there would not be any safety representatives to be consulted. After the Commission had taken the British Government to the European Court of Justice on the same problem with regard to collective redundancies and transfers of undertakings, the 1977 Regulations were amended by the Health and Safety (Consultation with Employees) Regulations 1996.[41]

The 1996 Regulations were intended to provide for situations where there were no trade union nominated safety representatives. The employer has a general duty to consult with employees, in good time, on a range of safety matters including the introduction of any measure at the workplace which might substantially affect the health and safety of the employees. The consultation must be with the employees directly or their elected representatives, who are called "representatives of employee safety". Similarly, Regulation 5 provides the employer with a duty to provide information necessary for these representatives or the employees directly to participate fully in the process. Representatives of employee safety must also be given information to enable them to carry out their functions.

Union safety representatives may be elected or appointed. If there are employees who are not covered by union safety representatives under the SRSC Regulations, the employers must consult the employees directly or "representatives of employee safety", who have been elected by employees. In either case employers must make available such information within their knowledge as is necessary to enable full and effective participation in the consultation.

Apart from representing all employees in consultation with the employer, safety representatives (or representatives of health and safety) must

(i)   make representations to the employer on potential hazards and dangerous occurrence at the workplace which affect, or could affect, the group of employees represented

(ii)   make representations to the employer on general matters affecting the health and safety at work of the group represented

(iii) represent employees in consultations at the workplace with inspectors appointed under Section 19 of the Health and Safety at Work Act 1974.

Employers who consult representatives of employee safety have a duty to ensure that those representatives are provided with such training in respect of their functions as is reasonable in all the circumstances. The employer must also meet any reasonable costs associated with such training, including travel and subsistence costs.

The Workplace Information and Consultation Directive

Directive 2002/14/EC of the European Parliament and of the Council establishing a general framework for informing and consulting employees in the European Community[42] was finally unanimously adopted by the Council of Ministers in December 2001 after some years of debate. It suffered delays because of opposition from a number of countries including the United Kingdom. The final version is much weaker than the original 1998 proposal, especially in terms of sanctions and in terms of the implementation timetable. Nevertheless it is likely to have an important impact on industrial relations in the United Kingdom.

It is the first EU Directive to introduce a generalised requirement to provide information and to consult with employees or their representatives. All other information and consultation measures have been concerned with specific situations, such as collective redundancies, transfers of undertakings or in situations where companies have a European Works Council. Ms Anna Diamantopolou, European Commissioner for Employment and Social Affairs, stated that

> This Directive provides a "fail-safe" protection for employees and, used intelligently, can be a modern business tool. Enlightened self-interest is already driving companies to anticipate and manage change. Many businesses already involve employees in this. All businesses should provide a baseline level of involvement.[43]

The Directive will eventually apply to all undertakings with 50 or more employees. This represents less than 3% of all EU companies, but about 50% of all employees.

Justification and purpose

In the preamble to the Directive the European Commission provides the justification for the measure. Some of the reasons given are that

(i)   the existence of current legal frameworks at national and Community level concerning the involvement of employees have not always prevented serious decisions, that affect employees, from being taken and made public without adequate consultation[44]

(ii) there is a need to strengthen dialogue in order to promote trust within undertakings. The result of this will be an improvement in risk anticipation, making work organisation more flexible and facilitate employee access to training within the undertaking. It will also make employees more flexible in their approach and involve them in the operation and future of the undertaking as well as increasing its competitiveness[45]

(iii) timely information and consultation is a pre-requisite for successful restructuring and adaptation of undertakings to the needs of the global economy, especially through the new forms of organisation at work[46]

(iv) the existing legal frameworks for employee information and consultation are inadequate, because they "adopt an excessively a posteriori approach to the process of change, neglect the economic aspects of decisions taken and do not contribute either to genuine anticipation of employment developments within the undertaking or to risk prevention".[47]

There are perhaps some, even amongst those who support the proposals in the Directive, who might be a little sceptical about such grand claims about the result of the introduction of employee consultation procedures. Nevertheless these justifications give rise to the purpose of the Directive. This is to establish minimum requirements for information and consultation, whilst not preventing Member States from having or introducing provisions more favourable to employees. The Directive will only apply to undertakings with a minimum size of 50 employees or establishments with at least 20 employees. This is to avoid any action which might hinder the creation and development of small and medium-sized undertakings.[48]

Article 1   Object and principles

The purpose is set out as being to establish a general framework for the right to information and consultation of employees in undertakings or establishments within the European Community.

The practical arrangements for defining and implementing this are to be left to the Member States, who must carry out their obligations in such a way as to ensure their effectiveness. In doing this the employer and the employees' representatives must work "in a spirit of cooperation".

Article 2   Definitions
There are some interesting definitions, particularly with regard to the distinction between undertakings and establishments.

An *undertaking* is a public or private undertaking carrying out an economic activity (whether or not for gain) which is located within the territory of the Member States. An *establishment* is a unit of business where an economic activity is carried out on an ongoing basis with human and material resources. It remains to be seen whether the British Government further defines these definitions when it eventually introduces regulations to transpose this Directive into national law. It might be worth considering this in order to avoid the possibility of further litigation about the precise meaning of these terms.

Information means transmission by the employer to the employees' representatives of data to help them acquaint themselves with the subject matter and to examine it. *Consultation* means the exchange of views and establishment of dialogue between the employer and the employees' representatives.

Article 3   Scope
The importance of the definitions of undertaking and establishment are relevant because the Directive will apply either to undertakings employing at least 50 employees in any one Member State or to establishments employing at least 20 employees in any Member State. The method for calculating the thresholds of employees is left to the Member State.

It will be interesting to see the UK Regulations, because, on the face of it, there will be occasions when undertakings employing less than 50 people will be affected.

It may be possible to make special arrangements for political, religious or charitable bodies; where special rules already exist in the Member State and, as ever, Member States may exclude crews of ships "plying the high seas".

Article 4   Practical arrangements for information and consultation
As mentioned above the practical arrangements are to be left to the individual Member State. There are, however, rules concerning what information and consultation will cover, when it is to take place and what its objectives are. The subject matter is to be

(i)   information on the recent and probable development of the undertaking's or establishment's activities and economic situation
(ii) information and consultation on the situation, structure and probable development of employment and on any anticipatory measures envisaged, especially those that threaten employment
(iii) information and consultation on decisions likely to lead to substantial changes in work organisation or in contractual relations (including those covered in Article 9 below).

Information shall be given at such time, and in such fashion, as to enable employee representatives to conduct an adequate study and, where necessary, prepare for consultation.

Consultation shall take place

(i) while ensuring that timing, method and content are appropriate
(ii) at the relevant level of management, depending upon the subject under discussion
(iii) on the basis of information provided by employer and of the opinion of employee representatives
(iv) in such a way as to enable employee representatives to meet the employer and obtain a response, the reasons for that response, to the employee representative's opinion
(v) with a view to reaching agreement on decisions within the scope of the employers' powers.

Article 5   Information and consultation deriving from an agreement
As with the European Works Council Directive, there is the opportunity for management and labour to negotiate their own information and consultation arrangements, providing that they meet the requirements of the Directive and national legislation. Thus any agreements existing at the transposition date of 23 March 2005 will be able to continue as will any other agreements subsequently negotiated. Presumably the UK regulations will provide a framework for such individually negotiated arrangements.

Article 6   Confidential information
This has always been an important concern of employers and the question of what is confidential and what is not will be part of the interest in watching this Directive put into practice. There are two aspects to confidentiality. One is imposing an obligation upon the parties to maintain a confidence. The second is the decision as to what material is so confidential that it cannot be revealed at all.

In dealing with the first of these, Member States may provide that employee representatives, and any experts who assist them, may not reveal information to employees or third parties if provided in confidence "in the legitimate interest of the undertaking or establishment", unless that other party is bound by a duty of confidentiality. This obligation may continue after the expiry of a term of office.

Member States may also provide that the employer need not provide information or consult when the nature of the information or consultation is such that, "according to objective criteria", it would seriously harm the functioning of the undertaking or establishment or would be prejudicial to it.

Member States shall provide for judicial review of situations where the employer requires confidentiality or does not provide information or consult in accordance the with above. This is the case with the TICE Regulations implementing the European Works Council Directive. The independent body is the Central Arbitration Committee.

This is a difficult area and one that the UK regulations will need to deal with in detail.

Article 7   Protection of employees' representatives
Member States must provide protection for employee representatives and guarantees to enable them to perform the duties which have been assigned to them.

Article 8   Protection of rights
This Article obliges Member States to have suitable judicial processes in place to enable the obligations of employers and employees to be enforced. It also requires adequate sanctions to be available for infringement of the Directive. These sanctions must be "effective, proportionate and dissuasive". This is going to be an interesting provision of any UK regulations. There are potentially large sums of money which may be involved in, for example, a merger or an acquisition. If an employer decided that he or she wished not to consult the employees, is a fine of the sort contained in the TICE Regulations going to be a sufficient deterrent? If it is not, then there might be an issue related to a bigger fine as to whether it would be proportionate.

Article 9   Link with other provisions
The Directive must not lessen existing protection (not an issue in the United Kingdom) and must be without prejudice to other Directives with requirements to consult, namely the Collective Redundancies Directive, The Acquired Rights Directive and the European Works Councils Directive.

Article 10   Transitional provisions
Although Article 11 stipulates 23 March 2005 as the deadline for transposition, there is an extension for Member States who do not have a general, permanent and statutory system of information and consultation (such as the United Kingdom). In such a case the Directive will only apply to undertakings employing at least 150 people or establishments employing 100 people until 23 March 2007 (a two year extension). Thereafter, for one year, it may apply to undertakings employing 100 people or establishments with 50 employees. The full application of the Directive, to undertakings with 50 or more employees and establishments with 20 or more employees, will not therefore take effect until 23 March 2008.

After this date industrial relations practices in the United Kingdom will look very different to those in existence today. They will look far more like those that exist in other Member States of the European Union.

Notes

[1] AT the EU level the social partners, who participate in the social dialogue process, are UNICE (representing private employers' organisations such as the CBI), CEEP (representing public sector employers) and the ETUC (European Employers Federation to which the TUC is affiliated)

[2] Directive 96/34/EC

[3] Directive 97/81/EC

[4] Directive 99/70/EC

[5] Directive 94/45/EC

[6] Directive 02/14/EC

[7] *Comparative Study on Rules Governing Working Conditions in the Member States* SEC(89) 1137

[8] *Industrial Relations in Europe*; Directorate General for Employment and Social Affairs (Luxembourg: 2000)

[9] Denmark, Germany, Greece, Ireland, Luxembourg, the Netherlands and Portugal

[10] *Industrial Relations in Europe*, 2000

[11] Council Directive 94/45/EC on the establishment of a European Works Council or a procedure in Community-scale undertakings and Community-scale groups of undertakings for the purpose of informing and consulting employees OJ L 254/64

[12] Council Directive 97/74/EC OJ L 010/22

[13] Article 1(1) EWC Directive

[14] Article 2(a) and (c) EWC Directive

[15] SI 1999/3323; the Regulations are some 57 pages long, so what follows can only be regarded as a summary of the main points

[16] Regulation 42 TICE Regulations

[17] Regulation 2 TICE Regulations 1999

[18] Defined in Regulation 2 TICE Regulations as a person who represents employees in the context of an information and consultation procedure

[19] Directive 2001/86/EC

[20] Article 2(i)

[21] Article 2(j)

[22] This information has been obtained from the European Foundation for the improvement of living and working conditions

[23] Session 1999-2000, Eighth Report HC 383; the information on Rover contained here comes from this Committee's report

[24] See *Guardian*, 13 May 2000

[25] See *Guardian*, 12 December 2000

[26] Session 2000-2001, Third report

[27] *MSF v (1) Refuge Assurance plc (2) United Friendly Insurance* (2002) IRLR 324

[28] The trade union concerned was MSF, now part of Amicus

[29] (1993) ICR 720

[30] See also *Hough v Leyland DAF* (1991) ICR 696 where there was further support for the distinction between the terms

[31] (2000) IRLR 639

[32] As in *E Green & Sons (Castings) Ltd v ASTMS* (1984) ICR 352

[33] Case 383/92 (1994) IRLR 412 ECJ

[34] (1978) IRLR 366

[35] Now Directive 2001/23/EC

[36] Transfer of Undertakings (Protection of Employment) Regulations 1981

[37] (1996) IRLR 76

[38] (1987) IRLR 373

[39] Directive 89/391/EC

[40] SI 1977/500
OJ L80/29 23.3.02

[41] SI 1996/1513

[42] OJ L80/29 23.3.02

[43] Directorate of Employment and Social Affairs press release 14.03.02

[44] Preamble paragraph (6)

[45] Preamble paragraph (7)

[46] Preamble paragraph (9)

[47] Preamble paragraph (13)

[48] Preamble paragraphs (18) and (19)

Useful websites

www.homeoffice.gov.uk (the Home Office)
www.hmso.gov.uk (for full text of UK legislation)
www.cre.gov.uk (Commission for Racial Equality)
www.eoc.org.uk (Equal Opportunities Commission)
www.who.int (World health Organization)
www.tiger.gov.uk (user-friendly guide to UK employment law)
www.dataprotection.gov.uk (the Information Commissioner)